GOOD NEWS STUDIES

Consulting Editor: Robert J. Karris, O.F.M.

Volume 38

Divorce in the New Testament

Raymond F. Collins

A Michael Glazier Book
THE LITURGICAL PRESS
Collegeville, Minnesota

A Michael Glazier Book published by The Liturgical Press.

Cover design by David Manahan, O.S.B.

Cover etching: "Christ and the Woman of Samaria" by Rembrandt; Rijksmuseum.

1   2   3   4   5   6   7   8   9

Library of Congress Cataloging-in-Publication Data

Collins, Raymond F., 1935–
    Divorce in the New Testament / Raymond F. Collins.
        p.   cm.
    "A Michael Glazier book."
    Includes bibliographical references and indexes.
    ISBN 0-8146-5691-9
    1. Divorce—Biblical teaching. 2. Bible. N.T.—Criticism,
interpretation, etc. I. Title.
BS2545.D58C65   1992
241'.63—dc20   92-18486
                                                CIP

Contents

Abbreviations

Versions of the Bible

*GNT*³	K. Aland, M. Black, C. M. Martini, B. M. Metzger, A. Wikgren, eds., *The Greek New Testament* (3rd ed.)
JB	Jerusalem Bible
N-A²⁶	K. Aland, ed., *Novum Testamentum Graece* (26th ed.)
NAB	New American Bible
NEB	New English Bible
NIV	New International Version
NJB	New Jerusalem Bible
NRSV	New Revised Standard Version
REB	Revised English Bible
RNAB	Revised New Testament of NAB
RSV	Revised Standard Version
The New Translation	*The New Translation of the Epistles by the Society for the New Translation*

Rabbinic and Other Jewish Literature

11QTemple	*Temple Scroll* from Qumran Cave 11
b.	Babylonian Talmud
B.Bat.	*Baba Batra*
Ber.	*Berakot*

CD	Cairo Damascus Document
EH	*Even ha*-Ezer
'Erub.	*'Erubin*
Giṭ.	*Giṭṭin*
Ketub.	*Ketubot*
m.	Mishna
Nid.	*Niddah*
Num Rab	Numbers *Rabbah*
Qidd.	*Qiddušin*
Šabb.	*Šabbat*
Sanh.	*Sanhedrin*
Sipre Deut	*Sipre* Deuteronomy
Tam.	*Tamid*
y.	Jerusalem Talmud
Yebam.	*Yebamot*

Periodicals, Reference Works, and Serials

AB	Anchor Bible
ABRL	Anchor Bible Research Library
AFER	*African Ecclesiastical Review*
AnBib	Analecta biblica
ANET	J. B. Pritchard, ed., *Ancient Near Eastern Texts.*
ANRW	*Aufstieg und Niedergang der römischen Welt*
Anton	*Antonianum*
ASNU	Acta seminarii neotestamentici uppsaliensis
AsSeign	*Assemblées du Seigneur*
ATANT	Abhandlungen zur Theologie des Alten und Neuen Testaments
ATLA	American Theological Library Association
ATR	*Anglican Theological Review*

AusCR	*Australian Catholic Record*
BAGD	W. Bauer, W. F. Arndt, F. W. Gingrich, and F. W. Danker, *Greek-English Lexicon of the NT*
BBB	Bonner biblische Beiträge
BDF	F. Blass, A. Debrunner and R. W. Funk, *A Greek Grammar of the New Testament*
BeO	*Bibbia e oriente*
BETL	Bibliotheca ephemeridum theo-logicarum lovaniensium
BGBE	Beiträge zur Geschichte der biblischen Exegese
BHT	Beiträge zur historischen Theologie
BibOr	Biblica et orientalia
BJRL	*Bulletin of the John Rylands University Library of Manchester*
BJS	Brown Judaic Studies
BLE	*Bulletin de littérature ecclésiastique*
BLit	*Bibel und Liturgie*
BR	*Biblical Research*
BSac	*Bibliotheca Sacra*
BT	*The Bible Translator*
BTB	*Biblical Theology Bulletin*
BZAW	Beihefte zur *ZAW*
BZNW	Beihefte zur *ZNW*
CBQ	*Catholic Biblical Quarterly*
ClR	*Clergy Review*
ColTh	*Collectanea theologica*
CRINT	Compendia rerum iudicarum ad novum testamentum
CTJ	*Calvin Theological Journal*
CTM	*Concordia Theological Monthly*
CurTM	*Currents in Theology and Mission*
DBSup	*Dictionnaire de la Bible, Supplément*
DJD	Discoveries in the Judaean Desert
DR	*Downside Review*
Ebib	Études bibliques

EDNT	H. Balz and G. Schneider, eds., *Exegetical Dictionary of the New Testament*
EglTh	*Eglise et théologie*
EKKNT	Evangelisch-katholischer Kommentar zum Neuen Testament
EncJud	*Encyclopaedia judaica*
EstBib	*Estudios biblicos*
EstEcl	*Estudios eclesiásticos*
EvT	*Evangelische Theologie*
EWNT	H. Balz and G. Schneider, eds., *Exegetisches Wörterbuch zum Neuen Testament*
FRLANT	Forschungen zur Religion und Literatur des Alten und Neuen Testaments
GNS	Good News Studies
Greg	*Gregorianum*
GTA	Göttinger theologische Arbeiten
GTJ	*Grace Theological Journal*
HAT	Handbuch zum Alten Testament
HDR	Harvard Dissertations in Religion
HNT	Handbuch zum Neuen Testament
HTKNT	Herders theologischer Kommentar zum Neuen Testament
IB	*Interpreter's Bible*
IBS	*Irish Biblical Studies*
ICC	International Critical Commentary
Int	*Interpretation*
ITQ	*Irish Theological Quarterly*
JBL	*Journal of Biblical Literature*
JEH	*Journal of Ecclesiastical History*
JES	*Journal of Ecumenical Studies*
JETS	*Journal of the Evangelical Theological Society*
JJS	*Journal of Jewish Studies*
JQR	*Jewish Quarterly Review*
JR	*Journal of Religion*

JSNT	*Journal for the Study of the New Testament*
JSNTSup	Journal for the Study of the New Testament—Supplemental Series
JSOT	*Journal for the Study of the Old Testament*
JSOTSup	Journal for the Study of the Old Testament—Supplemental Series
JTS	*Journal of Theological Studies*
KEK	*Kritisch-exegetischer Kommentar über das Neue Testament*
LD	Lectio divina
LSJ	Liddell-Scott-Jones, *Greek-English Lexicon*
LTPM	Louvain Theological and Pastoral Monographs
MM	J. H. Moulton and G. Milligan, *The Vocabulary of the Greek Testament*
MNTC	Moffatt NT Commentary
MTZ	*Münchener theologische Zeitschrift*
NCB	New Century Bible
Neot	*Neotestamentica*
NICNT	New International Commentary on the New Testament
NICOT	New International Commentary on the Old Testament
NJBC	R. E. Brown, *et al.*, eds., *The New Jerome Biblical Commentary*
NovTSup	*Novum Testamentum,* Supplements
NRT	*La nouvelle revue théologique*
NTAbh	Neutestamentliche Abhandlungen
NTD	Das Neue Testament Deutsch
NTL	New Testament Library
NTS	*New Testament Studies*
NTTS	New Testament Tools and Studies
OrSyr	*L'orient syrien*
OTL	Old Testament Library

PalCler	*Palestra del clero*
PG	J. Migne, *Patrologia graeca*
PL	J. Migne, *Patrologia latina*
PW	Pauly-Wissowa, *Real-Encyclopädie der classischen Altertumwissenschaft*
QD	Quaestiones disputatae
RB	*Revue biblique*
RCB	*Revista de cultura biblica*
RCT	*Revista catalana de teologia*
REB	*Revista eclesiástica brasileira*
ResQ	*Restoration Quarterly*
RevExp	*Review and Expositor*
RevRef	*Revue réformée*
RevistB	*Revista biblica*
RevQ	*Revue de Qumran*
RicBRel	Ricerche bibliche e religiose
RivB	*Rivista biblica*
RNT	Regensburger Neues Testament
RuchBLit	*Ruch Biblijny i Liturgiczny*
RSR	*Recherches de science religieuse*
RTP	*Revue de théologie et philosophie*
SBLDS	SBL Dissertation Series
SBS	Stuttgarter Bibelstudien
ScuolCatt	*Scuola cattolica*
ScEs	*Science et esprit*
ScrTh	*Scripta theologica*
SEA	*Svensk exegetisk årsbok*
Sef	*Sefarad*
SJLA	Studies in Judaism in Late Antiquity
SNTSMS	Society for New Testament Studies Monograph Series
SPB	Studia postbiblica
SR	*Studies in Religion/Sciences religieuses*
Str-B	H. Strack and P. Billerbeck, *Kommentar zum Neuen Testament*
SNTU	Studien zum Neuen Testament und seiner Umwelt

SBibFrLA	*Studii biblici franciscani liber annuus*
StudPat	*Studia Patavina*
SUNT	Studien zur Umwelt des Neuen Testaments
STV	*Studia theologica varsaviensia*
SWJT	*Southwestern Journal of Theology*
TBT	*The Bible Today*
TDNT	G. Kittel and G. Friedrich, eds., *Theological Dictionary of the New Testament*
TGl	*Theologie und Glaube*
ThEd	*Theological Educator*
THKNT	Theologischer Handkommentar zum Neuen Testament
TPINTC	Trinity Press International New Testament Commentary
TQ	*Theologische Quartalschrift*
TRE	*Theologische Realenzyklopädie*
TS	*Theological Studies*
TTZ	*Trierer theologische Zeitschrift*
TU	Texte und Untersuchungen
TvT	*Tijdschrift voor Theologie*
TynBul	*Tyndale Bulletin*
TZ	*Theologische Zeitschrift*
UNT	Untersuchungen zum Neuen Testament
USQR	*Union Seminary Quarterly Review*
VD	*Verbum domini*
WMANT	Wissenschaftliche Monographien zum Alten und Neuen Testament
WUNT	Wissenschaftliche Untersuchungen zum Neuen Testament
ZAW	*Zeitschrift für die alttestamentliche Wissenschaft*
ZBG	M. Zerwick, *Graecitas biblica*
ZNW	*Zeitschrift für die neutestamentliche Wissenschaft*

Introduction

There are few New Testament texts whose meaning has been as vigorously debated as those which contain Jesus' sayings on divorce. As is often the case, the vigor and passion of debate sometimes deprive those involved in the debate of clear vision. Passion has certainly been involved in any past discussion about the meaning of what Jesus had to say about divorce. The New Testament texts themselves reflect the passion which gripped the first generations of Jesus' disciples as they tried to understand the meaning of Jesus' teaching, a teaching that had him at odds with the "Pharisees" (Matt 19:3-9; Mark 10:1-9) and caused confusion among his own disciples (Matt 19:10-12; Mark 10:10-12).

The Fathers of the Church spoke with passion when they directed Christians not to divorce—apart from certain, well-specified cases—and not to remarry, not even in those situations where separation was advisable and perhaps even mandatory. Ecclesiastical passions came into play when the issue of divorce came to be a practical issue in the heated debate between the tradition of the Church of Rome and the movement of the Reform. Erasmus of Rotterdam (ca. 1466–1536), one of the great humanists and no mean biblical critic, found in Matthew's exception clauses (Matt 5:32; 19:9) a scriptural warrant for allowing divorce and remarriage in the case of adultery, but others vigorously disagreed.

As we approach the end of Christianity's second millenium, the topic of the significance of Jesus' teaching on divorce continues to rouse passions within the churches and among believers. Fortunately, the discussion no longer divides the members of the

1

church along confessional lines. Within each of the churches there are those who read Jesus' words as prohibiting all remarriage after divorce and those who hold that his words allow for divorce in certain exceptional cases.

Unfortunately, the passion of discussion is gripping an increasing number of believers who find themselves in a marriage too difficult to bear, and who ask themselves about the cost of discipleship when their marriage is on the rocks and their personal dignity is at stake. Many are now asking whether it is possible to achieve both fidelity in discipleship and authenticity in personal life.

Apart from the truly personal issues involved, there is a major hermeneutical issue to be faced. It is easier to treat the hermeneutical matter in the dispassion of academic discussion than in the passion of personal decision, but this hermeneutical issue is not at all an easy matter to resolve. Only believers, who hold the Scriptures to be more than merely attractive pieces of ancient literature, to be somehow normative for their way of life as believers, raise this kind of hermeneutical issue. The issue is that of the relevance of Jesus' words for the life of the believer today. Are Jesus' words somehow isolable from their historical and scriptural context so that they express a timeless norm for all Christians and a moral challenge for today?

In many respects this hermeneutical question is a theoretical issue. It is the issue of the contemporary relevance and significance of biblical texts in general and, more specifically, the significance and contemporary relevance of New Testament texts in particular. More narrowly focused, the issue is the question of whether Jesus' words somehow express a concrete and immediately engaging norm of morality. Biblical scholars discuss this hermeneutical issue,[1] but it bears upon the lives of individual believers, particularly in the areas of respect for life (Matt 5:21), war and peace (Matt 5:9), and marriage and divorce (Matt 5:32)—the latter being not the least of the burning issues.

It is important that church leaders, biblical scholars, and individual believers—and not only those who have been troubled by a burdensome marriage—come to grips with the hermeneutical issue. I should have liked to do so, and may well do so at some other time, but I thought it better that this book should have a narrower focus. An extended discussion of the hermeneutical issues bearing upon the New Testament tradition of Jesus' sayings on divorce would have made an already long book longer still. Moreover, I considered that it would be quite important to offer an independent and self-contained exegesis of this tradition in the hope that the exegetical discussion would subsequently lead to a more nuanced discussion of the hermeneutical issues as well as to a more nuanced assessment of the contemporary relevance and applicability of Jesus' sayings.

For Roman Catholics there are still other issues to be considered. One can begin with a critical appraisal of the normative value of our tradition in regard to divorce and remarriage. There is also the matter of canon law and its interraction with both theology and personal conscience. For the Roman Catholic who has been divorced and remarried, there is the problem of reconciliation to the church and admission to the sacrament of the Eucharist, the source and summit of the religious life of Roman Catholic believers.

These, too, are important issues—ones that need to be dealt with on all levels. These are issues in which I have been personally involved as a scholar, a pastor, and a friend. These are also issues to which I would like to devote systematic reflection in a pertinent monograph. These, however, are issues which I have carefully tried to avoid in the present study. It is not that they are unimportant, for they are; it is simply that the exegetical issues alone are sufficiently numerous and complex to merit an extended study in their own right.

It is in that study that I have expended a good part of my energies for the past few years. I dare to share the results of that work with the readers of these pages. Those who take the time to read what I have written will realize from the very outset that I have tried to avoid taking Jesus' words out of their context. I have tried to interpret them within their own historical and literary situation.

If I have tried to avoid taking Jesus' words out of context, still more have I tried to avoid taking Matthew's exception clause, "except for unchastity," out of its own proper context. All too often, the scholars' debate and the believers' discussion focus on that exception clause. A great price has been paid for this narrowness of focus. The price is a distortion of the issues. One might almost speak of a kind of tunnel vision which prevents both the scholar and the believer from having a broader view of Jesus' teaching and the role that it had to play in the life of the church.

A discussion which focuses too narrowly on the exception clause smacks of biblical fundamentalism, on the one hand, and a kind of letter-of-the law legalism, on the other. As a biblical scholar, I cannot countenance the former. As for the latter, I suspect that its most vigorous opponent would have been none other than the evangelist Matthew himself, for it is he who has formulated the great antitheses of the Sermon on the Mount—that truly marvelous series of reflections that contrast the letter of the law with the spirit of discipleship (Matt 5:21-48).

Having stated what I have tried not to do, let me say what I have tried to do. I have attempted to offer an interpretation of the sayings of Jesus on divorce in their literary and historical context. The New Testament contains five versions of Jesus' sayings: Matt 5:32, Matt 19:6, 9; Mark 10:9-12; Luke 16:18; and 1 Cor 7:11. Apart from the identity of Matt 19:6b[2] with Mark 10:9, no one of these versions of Jesus' teaching on divorce agrees, in every detail, with another version. Of itself, such diversity is a major concern for biblical scholars.

Typically, those who write about—and certainly those who speak about—Jesus' teaching on divorce begin with a reflection on Jesus' discussion with the Pharisees over the matter of divorce, such as is found in Matt 19:3-9. I did not begin the present study with an analysis of that encounter. There is some advantage, and some insight, to be gained from examining the various versions of Jesus' sayings on divorce in the order in which they were written down in ancient times. So I begin my study with an examination of what Paul has to say about divorce in his First Letter to the Corinthians before I look at the gospels.

Only after I have examined the use which Paul has made of the saying of the Lord do I dare to study the gospels. As I do so, I have chosen to study the gospel according to Mark before I examine the gospels attributed to Matthew and Luke because of my scholarly conviction—shared with most today—that Mark wrote a "gospel" before Matthew and Luke did. Not only that, but Matthew and Luke actually depended upon Mark as they composed their own works. Respecting, therefore, the consensus judgment of most biblical scholars today, I have examined Matthew's gospel after Mark's and Luke's after Matthew's.

It is the extant texts of Paul, Mark, Matthew, and Luke that provide contemporary scholars with our oldest evidence of what Jesus had to say about divorce. Only after I have looked at these very texts have I turned to a study of the tradition that has linked the texts written by these evangelists to the Jesus who confronted his opponents and taught his disciples.

Surely a biblical scholar will recognize that, within these pages, I have tried to make use of more than one methodology of biblical inquiry. I have taken a stand with regard to the Synoptic Problem—the literary relationship among Matthew, Mark, and Luke. Most, but not all scholars, will agree with my position on this matter. Convinced that Matthew's account of the discussion with the Pharisees is dependent upon Mark's, I have had to do some redaction criticism. I have also had to do a bit of textual criticism. We do not have autograph copies of the texts written by Paul, Mark, Matthew, and Luke. The ancient manuscripts of these New Testament texts differ somewhat, one from the other. So I have had to make a decision as to what really are the New Testament texts on divorce, and not all scholars will agree with my decisions—although I think that most will do so.

Differentiating, as I have done, between Paul's letters and the gospels, I have introduced the question of the literary form in which the sayings of Jesus on divorce have been preserved. Form criticism comes into play. Narrative criticism does, too, since the sayings of Jesus on divorce are remembered by most people as part of a short story, namely, Jesus' discussion with the Pharisees, which is part of a still longer narrative, that is, the gospel tale of Mark or Matthew. A synchronic reading of the narratives written by these evangelists provides insight into the way they understood Jesus' teaching and how that functioned in the story about Jesus which they were about to tell.

I am convinced that a storyteller like Mark did not work in a vacuum—certainly Matthew who made use of Mark's gospel did not! Like Matthew, Mark was an author who wrote at a given moment in time and in a certain place. He was heir to important traditions about Jesus and an evangelist for the church who wanted to write good news for the believers among whom he lived.

Accordingly, I could not avoid delving into some elements of narrative criticism as I looked first at Mark's gospel and then at Matthew's.

Many proponents of this approach to the gospels systematically avoid the matter of an author's source material and the shaping of the traditions with which the writer was familiar. Many who read Mark's gospel as a narrative self-consciously choose to avoid reading between (or behind?) the lines of the text. They profess disinterest in any literary sources which the evangelist might have used and they are little inclined to pursue a quest for precise historical information about the events upon which Mark's narrative is based. For them, the Markan story is enough. Other scholars, however, espouse the historical-critical method of biblical interpretation. They choose to read the text in a diachronic fashion. The typical believer is generally uninterested in this type of historical inquiry, but for many a believer what Jesus really had to say about divorce is uniquely important. Because of his or her curiosity, as well as because of my personal commitment to the historical-critical method of biblical scholarship, I have incorporated into the present study some elements of the history of tradition.

As I write about various methodologies and the different opinions of scholars about the usefulness of the various methodologies, the reader of these pages is certainly aware that the study which I have undertaken and whose results I now share has been no easy task. The work had to be many-faceted if it was to do justice to the topic at hand. Not all will agree with everything that I have written because they do not share the same views as to the appropriate methodology or methodologies to be used in biblical scholarship. The work which I have undertaken would have been much simpler had it consisted of a series of journal-length monographs on the topic. I, however, have attempted to provide my readers with a comprehensive overview, challenging them to view the subject from different angles in order to get the whole picture.

In the study of the New Testament, there are more than merely methodological issues which must be considered. Exegesis, the science of the interpretation of texts, is not an exact science, as chemistry and physics may claim to be. Exegesis is a matter of the interpretation of data, a matter of sensitivity and judgment. Even scholars viewing the data from the same angle often come to different conclusions. The use of similar methodology does not always provide the same results. Different scholars have different things to say about the text, but they do have something to say. The names of many of these scholars are cited in the footnotes of this book. The names of others appear in the bibliography. If I have cited so many names, I have done so not only to recognize the fact that so many have been involved in the discussion and to acknowledge my dependence on them, but also because it is important that the readers of these pages realize how and why it is that different things have been said about one and the same series of New Testament texts.

What has been written in the biblical texts has been interpreted for subsequent generations of readers in an almost untold number of translations. Each of these translations offers a slightly different interpretation of the ancient texts, from the perspective of different cultures and different moments in time, let alone a difference in understanding of the ancient texts themselves. Throughout this work I have used the New Revised Standard Version of the New Testament, but I have liberally referred to other translations. I have done so, not only because of the nuances that they provide, but also because I suspect that many, if not most, of my readers are familiar with Jesus' sayings on divorce only from the vantage point of a single translator, editor, or editorial board.

Although the study of Jesus' teaching on divorce is necessarily a complex matter, it is not one that can be avoided. Biblical scholars have no right to avoid the cruces simply because other scholars will disagree, perhaps vehemently. Believers have no right to avoid grappling with the complexities of the matter, because they stand in a long line of people who have tried to understand Jesus' teaching. The line began with those who listened to Jesus for the first time.

I therefore offer these pages to scholar and believer alike—not in the expectation that all will concur with my analysis, but in the hope that my words will contribute to a greater understanding of the words of Jesus. I am grateful for the gospel's witness to the words of Jesus and for the academic challenge which they have posed to me, even as they have posed a personal challenge to others within the church.

In my gratitude, I must express thanks to those who have had to put up with me, especially with the limitations on my time and energy which the writing of this book entailed, as I attempted to meet the thorny challenge of understanding Jesus' words in their context. I owe a special debt of gratitude to my friend and colleague, Jan Lambrecht, S.J., professor emeritus of New Testament exegesis at the Catholic University of Leuven, who was kind enough to read through the manuscript and who offered many suggestions for my consideration, not all of which, I must not fail to add, have entered into my study as it is herewith published. I would also like to express particular thanks to Mary Theresa Burns, C.P., and Niceta Vargas, O.S.A. Willingly, and ever so helpfully, they took on the tedious and time-consuming task of proofreading my various manuscripts.

A special expression of gratitude is directed to Michael Glazier who invited me to take up this challenge. Michael, generously and almost recklessly, took up the challenge of making the Word of God more accessible to the people of God. He challenged me to write about the sayings of Jesus on divorce. I hope that I have adequately satisfied his expectations, for it is to Michael Glazier, who has done so much to advance biblical scholarship in the Anglo-Saxon world and particularly within its Catholic community, that I affectionately dedicate this book.

1

A Problem at Corinth

Barely one generation had passed since the death and resurrection of Jesus of Nazareth when the Apostle Paul arrived in the Achaian metropolis of Corinth to proclaim the good news about the same Jesus Christ. Shortly thereafter, he was joined by his companions, Silas and Timothy. According to the account of the travels of these missionaries provided by Luke in the Acts of the Apostles, it was not unusual that their path should have brought them to Corinth, one of the principal trading centers of the day. What was unusual about their visit was that they stayed. Luke tells his readers that Paul, the hero of the second part of his narrative, stayed among the Corinthians for a year and a half, teaching the Word of God among them (Acts 18:11). The exact chronology of the apostle's travels is difficult to determine, but it is more than likely that this extended stay occurred somewhere between 49 and 51 A.D.

Corinth was a cosmopolitan town, a city situated at a commercial, cultural, philosophical, and religious crossroads. Its population and their interests were characterized by considerable diversity. After Paul's departure from the city, the community of Christian believers which had gathered to hear his preaching of the gospel began to experience a variety of troubles. Internal divisions, theological disputes, and questionable conduct on the part of some of its members caused the "church of God at Corinth" (1 Cor 1:2) no small amount of difficulty.

Some members of the household of a person named Chloe brought reports about these difficulties to Paul (1 Cor 1:11).[1] Another delegation came to Paul in the person of Stephanas, accompanied by Fortunatus and Achaicus (1 Cor 16:17). These men might have been members of the household which Paul commends in 1 Cor 16:15. Stephanas and his companions may have brought with them a letter for Paul which spelled out in some detail the problems besetting the neophyte Christian community. Whether or not it was this group which actually brought the letter, Paul did receive a letter telling him about the problems at Corinth (1 Cor 7:1). The letter was a bill of particulars about the difficult situation of the local Christian community.

In response to the oral reports which he had received from Chloe's people, those which came from Stephanas' people, and the letter which he had received from Corinth, Paul wrote "the first letter to the Corinthians," one of the longest letters in the New Testament—indeed a very long letter by then contemporary standards of letter-writing. In his letter Paul addressed himself in turn to each of the topics of concern which had been mentioned in the letter he had received.[2] Given its nature and its purpose, this First Letter to the Corinthians can be described, in the classic categories of Greek rhetoric, as an epideictic rhetorical letter.[3] It is critical when necessary and praises when possible.

Apparently this was not the first time that Paul had resorted to a letter in an attempt to straighten out the situation at Corinth. He had previously written a letter (1 Cor 5:9)[4] in which he had warned the Corinthians not to associate with immoral people, apparently a suggestion offered as a way of dealing with a problem of sexual immorality. The so-called First Letter to the Corinthians should therefore be considered as part of an ongoing exchange of correspondence. Paul had written an earlier letter in an attempt to help the Corinthians solve some of their problems. The Corinthians answered by sending a letter, and Paul responded to this letter with our extant "first letter to the Corinthians." Sometime later the "second letter to the Corinthians" would have followed. Additional, but no-longer-existing correspondence (see 2 Cor 2:9; 7:12) was written between our present "first letter" and the so-called "second letter" to the Corinthians.

Since Stephanas and his companions apparently stayed with
Paul for some limited time and then returned to their native
Corinth, it is likely that they were the ones who delivered "the
first letter to the Corinthians" to the church at Corinth. This letter was written a few years after Paul's departure from the city,
that is, somewhere between 53 and 57 A.D., probably more towards the beginning than towards the end of this period.[5]

Paul's letter is case specific. A tell-tale "concerning" (*peri*)[6]
introduces his personal reflections on the various problems which
troubled the community. A reading of the letter reveals that the
issues were generally very real and the situations quite problematic.[7] "The way that Paul responds to their topics and slogans,"
writes Antoinette Wire, "shows that he is not answering polite
questions but questioning bold answers."[8] Paul does not write
in generalities nor does he offer doctrinal reflections of a theoretical nature. If he writes about matters with a more general import, it is only because he sees them as pertinent to the issues at
hand.

The discussion begins in 1 Cor 7:1, where the first of Paul's
"*peri*-concerning" phrases appears:

>[1]Now concerning the matters about which you wrote: "It is well
>for a man not to touch a woman." [2]But because of cases of
>sexual immorality, each man should have his own wife and each
>woman her own husband. [3]The husband should give to his wife
>her conjugal rights, and likewise the wife to her husband. [4]For
>the wife does not have authority over her own body, but the
>husband does; likewise the husband does not have authority
>over his own body, but the wife does. [5]Do not deprive one an-
>other except perhaps by agreement for a set time, to devote your-
>selves to prayer, and then come together again, so that Satan
>may not tempt you because of your lack of self-control. [6]This
>I say by way of concession, not of command. [7]I wish that all
>were as I myself am. But each has a particular gift from God,
>one having one kind and another a different kind.
>
>[8]To the unmarried and the widows I say that it is well for
>them to remain unmarried as I am. [9]But if they are not practic-
>ing self-control, they should marry. For it is better to marry
>than to be aflame with passion.

¹⁰To the married I give this command—not I but the Lord—
that the wife should not separate from her husband ¹¹(but if
she does separate, let her remain unmarried or else be reconciled to her husband), and that the husband must not divorce
his wife.

¹²To the rest I say—I and not the Lord—that if any believer
has a wife who is an unbeliever, and she consents to live with
him, he should not divorce her. ¹³And if any woman has a husband who is an unbeliever, and he consents to live with her,
she should not divorce him. ¹⁴For the unbelieving husband is
made holy through his wife, and the unbelieving wife is made
holy through her husband. Otherwise, your children would be
unclean, but as it is, they are holy. ¹⁵But if the unbelieving partner separates, let it be so; in such a case the brother or sister
is not bound. It is to peace that God has called you. ¹⁶Wife,
for all you know, you might save your husband. Husband, for
all you know, you might save your wife.

¹⁷However that may be, let each of you lead the life that the
Lord has assigned, to which God called you. This is my rule
in all the churches. ¹⁸Was anyone at the time of his call already
circumcised? Let him not seek to remove the marks of circumcision. Was anyone at the time of his call uncircumcised? Let
him not seek circumcision. ¹⁹Circumcision is nothing, and un-
circumcision is nothing; but obeying the commandments of God
is everything. ²⁰Let each of you remain in the condition in which
you were called.

²¹Were you a slave when called? Do not be concerned about
it. Even if you can gain your freedom, make use of your present condition now more than ever. ²²For whoever was called
in the Lord as a slave is a free person belonging to the Lord,
just as whoever was free when called is a slave of Christ. ²³You
were bought with a price; do not become slaves of human
masters. ²⁴In whatever condition you were called, brothers and
sisters, there remain with God.

The "*peri*-concerning" formula recurs in verse 25 when Paul
turns to the related issue of "virgins": "Now concerning virgins,
I have no command of the Lord, but . . ." The third occurrence
of the "*peri*-concerning" formula occurs in 1 Cor 8:1, where Paul

takes up the topic of food sacrificed to idols. Thus all of chapter seven deals with the topic of sex and marriage, but Paul separates the discussion into two distinct parts, each beginning with the "*peri*-concerning" formula. Part one (vv. 1-24) deals with those who are already married, part two (vv. 25-40)—at least for the most part[9]—deals with those who are not yet married.

Part one deals with matters about which the Corinthians had written. On first reading, Paul's response to the issue seems essentially to consist of a three-fold movement of thought:

1) The reality of sexual immorality: verses 2-7
2) A three-part address:
   —to the unmarried and widows: verses 8-9
   —to the married: verses 10-11
   —to the rest: verses 12-16
3) A supporting argument: verses 17-24[10]

A Wife's Separation from Her Husband

One of the problems with which Paul was concerned was the case of a woman separated from her husband (1 Cor 7:11a). He addresses himself to the issue within the context of a broad discussion on the avoidance of sex, a reflection that he has introduced under the rubric, "it is well for a man not to touch a woman." This slogan was apparently well-known to the Corinthian Christians.[11] Within some circles, the buzzword had been cited in an attempt to promote celibacy and sexual abstinence within marriage.[12] In typical fashion, Paul makes some concession to the slogan[13]—it may well have developed as a misrepresentation of his own thought—but then takes a critical and practical distance from it. In a series of insightful reflections on the implications of the popular slogan, Paul directs his thoughts to a number of very concrete situations.

His approach is so practical that 1 Corinthians 7 is one of the most "un-theological" chapters in the entire Pauline corpus.[14] Yet because the entire discussion is oriented toward praxis, Paul readily appeals to the formal sources of his authority. It may well have been that Paul's apostolic authority was questioned by some groups within the Corinthian church. Some passages in his letter seem to indicate that some of the Corinthian Christians appealed to Paul's authority, whereas other Corinthian Christians did not accept it (1 Cor 1:12; 3:4, 22). Those Corinthians who did not claim to "belong to Paul"[15] were potentially closed to the advice or instruction that Paul might give. In 1 Corinthians, Paul certainly had occasion to rise to the defense of his own life style, thereby suggesting that some had called into question its apostolic character (1 Cor 9:1-15). Little wonder then that Paul began his letter with the formal declaration that he had been "called to be an apostle of Christ Jesus by the will of God" (1 Cor 1:1) and that he concluded his extensive disquisition on the variety of sexual and marital matters which the Corinthian slogan had set off by claiming that the Spirit of God was with him (1 Cor 7:40).

Paul's need to cite the warrants for what he has written stems not only from the fact that there were those who took issue with his authority, but also from the fact that he was dealing with very practical matters. The matter of divorce to which Paul addresses himself in 1 Cor 7:10-11 seems to have been primarily a woman's issue. The discussion is formulated first and almost entirely in terms of women.[16] Indeed, on first reading, the situation seems to presuppose a Hellenistic legal situation in which a legal initiative towards divorce could be taken by a woman:[17]

> [10]To the married I give this command—not I but the Lord— that the wife should not separate from her husband—[11](but if she does separate, let her remain unmarried or else be reconciled to her husband) and that the husband must not divorce his wife.

Paul's response to the case proposed to him was that "the wife should not separate from her husband, but if she does separate (*ean de kai chôristhê*), let her remain unmarried or else be reconciled to her husband" (1 Cor 7:10c-11). In many of the modern English-language translations of Paul's letter the words "but if she does separate, let her remain unmarried or else be reconciled to her husband" are enclosed within parentheses,[18] as if they were but an aside on the part of Paul. Parentheses were not used in ancient Greek manuscripts, but they have been inserted into modern translations by editors who are trying to capture the rapid movement of Paul's thought[19] as he deals with a variety of issues that relate to sexuality and marriage.[20]

Although not all authors agree,[21] most commentators are of the opinion that Paul[22] had a specific situation in mind as he wrote his parenthetical remark. However, they disagree among themselves as to the precise nature of the situation to which Paul was referring. The modern interpreter would be helped immensely if the text of the Corinthians' letter to Paul were still available or if he or she were able to make use of verbatim reports of the discussions between Paul and his various visitors from Corinth. Unfortunately, the Corinthian letter has been lost and the desired verbatim reports never existed. Thus the interpreter is forced to rely on Paul's words alone as he or she attempts to grasp the specifics of the situation with which Paul was dealing.

Essentially there are four questions to which an answer must be sought if one is to understand the real situation at hand. 1) What is the meaning of "separate" (*chôristênai-chôristhê*) in verses 10c and 11a? 2) Is the situation of 1 Cor 7:11a real or merely hypothetical? 3) If real, has it already happened or is it about to happen? 4) What is the situation?

A Divorce?

The verb which Paul uses when writing about a wife separating from her husband in verses 10 and 11 is *chôrizô*. The primary meaning of *chôrizô* is to "separate" or "divide." The verb can be used of things or of persons. In the passive, it means "to be separated," "to be divided," or, occasionally, "to be different." In 1 Cor 7:10-11, Paul uses *chôrizô* as a deponent verb, that is, the form of the verb is passive,[23] but its meaning is active. As Paul continues with his reflections on the topic of spousal separation in 1 Corinthians and takes up the issue of a man leaving his wife, he changes his vocabulary. He writes about a man "divorcing" his wife: "the husband must not divorce (*aphienai*) his wife" (1 Cor 7:11c).

Is a "Separation" a "Divorce"?

Because Paul has changed his terminology, J. K. Elliott makes a sharp distinction between the two verbs which Paul uses in 1 Cor 7:10-11, namely, *aphiêmi* ("divorce") used in reference to the man in verse 11 and *chôrizô* ("separate") used in reference to the woman in verses 10c and 11a.[24] Differentiating the meaning of the two verbs as he does, Elliott is able to claim that in 1 Cor 7:10 Paul is referring to a case of a wife who has merely separated from her husband without the benefit of a legal divorce. In somewhat similar fashion, E. P. Sanders and Peter J. Tomson have suggested that Paul's terminology reflects his knowledge of Jewish law. Since divorce was a prerogative of the husband under Jewish law,[25] a woman could "separate" from her husband, but she could not "divorce" him.[26] The practical advice offered by Paul in 1 Corinthians reflects, to a very large extent, the kinds of behavior enjoined by rabbinic halakah. Halakah, from the Hebrew verb *halak,* "to walk," was the legal side of Judaism. The various rules of conduct which it embraced were considered to be an authentic interpretation of the Scriptures and the oral tradition. The similarities between some elements of rabbinic halakah and what Paul has to offer by way of practical directives for sexual conduct in 1 Cor 5-7 are particularly striking.[27] Thus the suggestion offered by Sanders and Tomson that Paul's terminology reflects his knowledge of Jewish law must be taken with due seriousness. There are, nonetheless, reasons to doubt that the meaning of "*aphiêmi*-divorce," in Pauline usage, was really so sharply distinguished from that of "*chôrizô*-separate," as these authors seem to claim.

After the two-pronged exhortation in 1 Cor 7:10-11, Paul continues his reflection on spousal separation by citing a specific set of circumstances in which he judged that a husband ought not divorce his wife and a wife ought not divorce her husband. These were situations in which Christians were married to non-Christians. In these circumstances, the situation of a Christian husband was analagous to that of a Christian wife. In Paul's estimation neither a Christian husband nor a Christian wife should divorce an unbelieving spouse so long as the non-believer was willing to remain married to the Christian. Paul says that the Christian husband should not divorce his wife and the Christian wife should not divorce her husband. In his exhortation he uses the verb "*aphiêmi*-divorce" for both husband and wife, that is, the same verb which he had used in verse 11c when he wrote that "the husband must not divorce (*aphienai*) his wife." Apropos of mixed marriage, Paul writes:

> [12]To the rest I say—I and not the Lord—that if any believer has a wife who is an unbeliever, and she consents to live with him, he should not divorce her. [13]And if any woman has a husband who is an unbeliever, and he consents to live with her, she should not divorce him. [14]For the unbelieving husband is made holy through his wife, and the unbelieving wife is made holy through her husband. Otherwise, your children would be unclean, but as it is, they are holy.

In this passage (vv. 12, 13), Paul has used the verb *aphiêmi* with regard to both husband and wife. The primary meaning of the verb is to "send forth" or "let loose."[28] As far as persons were concerned, the term was used with the meaning of "send away," "let go of," "leave." It was used in reference to parents who disowned their children.[29] In the so-called "Erotic Fragment," a second-century (B.C.) papyrus, the verb appears in a plea addressed to her paramour by a woman who had been jilted.[30] As a legal term, *aphiêmi* meant to acquit of a charge or an obligation. In law, "to send someone away" (*aphiêmi tina*) meant that that person was discharged of some legal relationship, for example, an office, marriage, custody, debt, or punishment.[31] Thus, some Greeks used *aphiêmi* with the meaning of "divorce."[32]

Why did Paul use the expression "*aphiêmi*-divorce" of both the husband and the wife in verses 12 and 13 and only of the husband in verse 11? In verses 12-14, Paul addresses himself "to the rest" (*tois loipois*). Tomson has suggested that "the rest" are neither "the unmarried[33] and the widows" (as in v. 8) nor the wives and the husbands of verses 10-11. They constitute a third category of people, those who, in Tomson's estimation, were involved in an informal marriage relationship. Such relationships were permitted under Hellenistic, but not under Jewish, law.[34] For Tomson, Paul's exhortation in verses 12-14 concerns people who are involved in a legitimate informal marriage within a Hellenistic jurisdiction. Under Hellenistic law,[35] women enjoyed the legal right to divorce, but Paul enjoins Christian women from exercising this right, as he similarly exhorts husbands to refrain from exercising the right which they enjoyed.

Rudolf Pesch has taken a rather different approach in trying to discover why Paul changed his vocabulary as he wrote about the possibility of women leaving their husbands, first in verses 10-11 and then in verse 13. In his estimation, the difference between Paul's use of "*chôrizô*-separate" (vv. 10-11) and "*aphiêmi*-divorce" (v. 13) bears upon actuality rather than upon a different legal perspective. According to Pesch, Paul used "*chôrizô*-separate" to refer to marriages that had already broken up and "*aphiêmi*-divorce" when writing about marriages that had not yet broken up.[36] If Paul were to be consistent in his use of vocabulary, and if Pesch's semantic analysis is correct, the situation to which Paul refers in verses 10-11b ("a wife must not separate") is different from that in verse 11c ("the husband must not divorce"). In the first case she had already left, in the second he had not yet sent her away.

For the modern interpreter, Paul himself has complicated matters still further. When he turned his attention from the consideration of a Christian's responsibility in a mixed marriage to a consideration of the conduct of the non-Christian spouse, he changed his vocabulary yet again, this time reverting to the language of "separation" (*chôrizô*):

> [15]But if the unbelieving partner separates, let it be so; in such a case the brother or sister is not bound. It is to peace that God has called you.

The "unbelieving partner" (*apistos*) about whom Paul writes is either a non-Christian wife or a non-Christian husband. Both are assumed under the single word, "*apistos*[37]-the unbelieving partner," a nominal adjective in the *masculine* singular.[38] In the apodosis of this sentence, Paul writes disjunctively of "the brother or sister." Here, as elsewhere in this and other letters, Paul uses kinship language to describe Christians. The language not only evokes the affective bonds that linked Christians with each other;

it also points to the household setting of early Christian gatherings.[39] In 1 Cor 7:15, an "unbelieving partner" (*apistos*) who separates from "a brother" is clearly his wife, while the "unbelieving partner" who separates from "a sister" is her husband. As Paul reflects on a possible course of action taken by the non-Christian partner in a mixed marriage, he uses the expression "*chôrizô*-separate," not once, but twice: "but if the unbelieving partner separates (*chôrizetai*), let it be so (*chôrizesthô*)."[40] In both instances Paul uses the verb, "*chôrizô*-separate," in the passive voice, just as he does in verses 10c-11a. The NRSV and many other modern editions[41] translate the verbs as if they are to be taken in an active sense, and thus to be understood as deponent forms ("the wife should not separate . . . if she does separate . . . if the unbelieving partner separates"), but Joseph Fitzmyer and Jerome Murphy-O'Connor have argued that the use of the passive voice in verses 10c-11a must be taken seriously.[42]

A Wife's Initiative

It is generally recognized that Hellenistic Greek tended to use the passive for the middle voice ("she separates herself").[43] Moreover, in verse 15 the use of the verb in the passive voice obviously describes an *initiative*[44] which might be taken by the non-Christian partner in the mixed marriage. Paul has just finished telling Christian spouses not to take the initiative in bringing about the rupture of a mixed marriage (vv. 12-13). The similarity of expression between the double use of "*chôrizô*-separate" in verses 10c-11a and its repeated occurrence in verse 15 suggests that Paul is using his terminology in the same manner in both instances.

There is, in addition, a parallel between Paul's statement "that the wife should not separate from her husband" (*gunaika apo andros mê chôristhênai*) in verse 10c and his affirmation that "the husband should not divorce his wife" (*andra gunaika mê aphienai*) in verse 11c.[45] Finally, verse 11b, "she must remain single or else be reconciled to him," implies some activity on the part of the wife.[46] In sum, it is more likely that, when Paul writes, "the wife should not separate from her husband, but if she does separate . . .," he has in mind a situation in which a woman has taken the initiative in leaving her husband, rather than one in which a woman has been abandoned or sent away by her husband.[47]

That Paul has in mind a situation in which the wife takes the active role seems also to be suggested by the general tenor of his reflections on sexuality and marriage in 1 Cor 7:1-40. Having cited the Corinthian slogan as a topical introduction for his discussion, Paul addresses his thought to different practical scenarios in the male-female relationship. Mutuality[48] is the characteristic which Paul extols in verses 2-16. Notwithstanding his preferential option for mutuality in the sexual relationship, Paul generally begins his reflections with a reference to the male (vv. 2b, 3a, 8a). This pattern, an exhortation addressed to the male partner in the relationship followed by a similar exhortation to the woman, is abruptly broken off in verse 10. Here Paul begins his reflection by stating "that the wife should not separate from her husband, but if she does . . .," and reserves his comments on the husband until verse 11c. The fact that Paul first, and at length, directs his thoughts to the wife and only later formulates a similar reflection about the husband suggests that he considers her responsible for her own situation. In verses 10c-11b, he was reflecting on what a wife might do.

Paul's words are addressed to the church at Corinth (1 Cor 1:20), that is, to a group of Christians who were fully immersed in the Hellenistic culture of the age, a culture in which, under both Greek and Roman law, women could divorce their husbands.[49] Some moralists, contemporary with Paul, were not happy about the possibility. One of Paul's contemporaries, Seneca, the Roman statesman and Stoic philosopher, bitterly complained about the ease and freedom with which women divorced: "Is there any woman that blushes at divorce now that certain illustrious and noble ladies reckon their years, not by the number of consuls, but by the number of their husbands, and leave home in order to marry, and marry in order to be divorced?"[50] Was, then, Paul thinking about a woman actually divorcing her husband when he wrote that a wife should not separate from her husband?

Her "Divorce"

The social circumstances in Corinth were such that Paul could have had a woman's divorce in mind. That Paul was writing about an initiative which a woman might take is all but certain, but it is not so clear that he was specifically writing about divorce as such, with legal formalities analogous to those which this term implies in our contemporary cultures. Paul writes about a Christian wife "separating from" (vv. 10c-11a) and "divorcing" (v. 13) her husband and mentions the possibility of a non-Christian wife "separating from" her husband (v. 15). His lexis, to use the technical term for his choice of vocabulary, makes use of the verbs *"chôrizô*-separate" and *"aphiêmi*-divorce." In the Hellenistic culture of Paul's times, both of these Greek verbs were widely used in a generic sense. Indeed, Paul himself uses each of these verbs in a more general sense, namely, *aphiêmi* in Rom 1:27; 4:7[51] and *chôrizô* in Rom 8:35, 39 and Phlm 15. Thus it is initially quite conceivable that Paul is writing about marital separation, rather than about divorce in the strict sense.

Both *"chôrizô*-separate" and *"aphiêmi*-divorce" used by Paul in 1 Cor 7:10-16 were, however, commonly used of divorce in the Hellenistic world. Herodotus and other ancient authors had used *aphiêmi* to mean divorce.[52] In classical and Hellenistic Greek, the verb *chôrizô* was also often used of divorce in the strict sense[53]—even in Greek marriage contracts. The use of *"chôrizô*-separate" in this way was so common that, in their lexicon of New Testament vocabulary,[54] Moulton and Milligan state that *chôrizô* "has almost become a technical term in connexion with divorce,"[55] offering papyri dating from 13 B.C.,[56] 66 A.D.,[57] 81 A.D.,[58] and 154 A.D.[59] as their principal references and citing 1 Cor 7:10, 11, 15 as cases in point. In sum, both *"chôrizô*-separate" and *"aphiêmi*-divorce" appear to have functioned as technical terms for divorce in Paul's Hellenistic world.[60]

Thus, the attempt to draw a sharp and fully adequate semantic distinction between *"chôrizô*-separate" and *"aphiêmi*-divorce" is unwarranted. Such a distinction is artificial[61] and not supported by contemporary linguistic usage and is clearly forced insofar as 1 Cor 7:10-16 is concerned.

Mutuality is the hallmark of the entire reflection in which Paul mulls over marital break-up in three different situations: marriage between Christians, marriage between a Christian and a compatible non-Christian, marriage between a Christian and an incompatible spouse. If Paul is writing about divorce in verse 11c, then it is most likely that he is also writing about divorce in verses 10c-11a as well. Paul's reflections on the woman leaving her husband in verses 10c-11a have called forth a parallel comment in verse 11c, namely, that a husband should not "divorce" his wife.

Moreover, Paul's casuistic paraenesis to the effect that a woman who had separated from her husband should "remain unmarried or else be reconciled to him" (v. 11b) seems to imply that she has divorced him. Having separated, she is *"agamos*-unmarried." Were her marriage not terminated, a once-married woman could hardly be called *"agamos*-unmarried."[62] Furthermore, in his subsequent reflection, Paul writes about a woman "divorcing" her husband (v. 13).

For a woman "to separate from her husband" (v. 10c) and for a woman "to divorce her husband" (v. 13) seem to be two ways for Paul to have said the same thing.[63] We can be all the more sure of this because Paul himself has formulated a parallel, from the vantage point of the husband, for each of these statements about women. In both instances Paul's parallel statement is that a husband should not "divorce" his wife (vv. 11c, 12).

Paul does not get into the specifics and legal technicalities involved.[64] It is likely, nonetheless, that Paul had a formal divorce in mind when he wrote "the wife should not separate from her husband," a situation in which the wife might take the initiative.[65] He may have been thinking about a divorce which would become effective by means of an oral declaration, but that is not sure. Paul's words are general enough to cover any legal situation.

A Real or a Hypothetical Situation?

David L. Dungan has stated that in expressing his opinion about a woman's divorcing her husband (v. 11ab), Paul is dealing with an actual situation at Corinth.[66] According to Dungan's analysis, Paul's thoughts have turned from the theoretical considerations suggested by his reference to the teaching of the Lord in verse 10b to the very real situation of a wife who has separated from her husband. Other authors, however, have suggested the possibility that in verse 11a, "if she does separate," Paul is merely offering a somewhat hypothetical illustration[67] of the radical principle which he has enunciated in verses 10c-11c: "the wife should not separate from her husband—and the husband should not divorce his wife."

There are serious reasons which suggest that Paul has a rather specific case in mind as he formulates his remarks in verse 11ab. First of all, the letter as a whole is concerned with very real and very specific problems troubling the young church at Corinth. In 1 Cor 5:1-5, Paul has addressed the specific issue of a man having a sexual relationship with one of his father's wives.[68] That situation is one about which Paul had received an oral report. It is reasonable to think that in 1 Cor 7:11ab, as elsewhere in 1 Corinthians, Paul is dealing with a situation about which he has been apprised by the Corinthians themselves. The situation to which Paul makes reference seems to be one which was at least touched upon in the letter which he had received (1 Cor 7:1).

Secondly, Paul has reversed his normal order in verses 10 and 11. Instead of writing about men and then about women, as he has hitherto done since he began to treat of sexuality and marriage, he now writes about a woman and then about the man.[69]

Thirdly, there is the awkward formulation of verses 10 and 11. Many of the modern English-language translations of the passage deal with the awkwardness of Paul's wording by enclosing one or another phrase between parentheses or dashes. The NJB, the New Translation, and the REB treat "if she does separate, let her remain unmarried or else be reconciled to her husband" as a parenthetical remark;[70] the NIV similarly treats "not I but the Lord" as the parenthesis;[71] while the RNAB and NRSV consider that both clauses constitute a Pauline aside. The interruption of the flow of Paul's thought by the introduction of the awkward conditional clause seems to indicate that some real situation requires the nuancing of the general train of thought. From this point of view there is parity of function between the clauses, "not I but the Lord" and "if she does separate, let her remain unmarried or else be reconciled to her husband," as the RNAB-NRSV's judicious translation suggests.

Fourthly, there is no similar parenthetical remark adduced when Paul urges the Christian husband not to divorce his wife (v. 11c). Somehow, the case of the divorcing woman is different from that of a man who might divorce his spouse. The actuality of the case seems to make the difference.

Fifthly, a specific incident seems to have evoked Paul's reference to the Lord's teaching.[72] Elsewhere, he takes it for granted that marriage is for life (1 Cor 7:39; Rom 7:2). Indeed, Paul rarely makes specific appeal to a command of the Lord. Apart from the saying to which allusion is made in 1 Cor 7:10-11, Frans Neirynck considers 1 Cor 9:14 to be the only explicit reference to a command of the Lord in the Pauline epistles.[73] It was not Paul's custom to cite sayings of the Lord as if they constituted some sort of authoritative corpus which stood in need of halakic exposition. Thus it is hardly likely that Paul entered into this part of his exposition with the intention of explaining a saying of the Lord; rather, as in 1 Thess 4:15, Paul makes reference to a saying of the Lord to clarify his own response to a specific problem at hand.

Finally, were it Paul's intention to have commented upon a saying of the Lord, the order of his exposition is strange indeed. All four gospel citations of the logion of Jesus on divorce (Matt 5:31-32; 19:9; Mark 10:11-12; Luke 16:18) begin with the case of the husband who divorces his wife. None of them begins with the case of the woman who divorces her husband. Indeed, it is only the Markan version of the saying which mentions the case at all (Mark 10:12), and then it is introduced as a parallel statement after the logion of Jesus on the husband who divorces his wife.

In sum, by speaking first about the case of the woman who separates herself from her husband and only then affirming that a husband ought not to divorce his wife, Paul has departed not only from the tradition of Jesus' saying on divorce but also from the balanced pattern which had hitherto characterized the exposition which he has been developing in chapter seven.[74] This departure is best explained if Paul had a very specific case in mind when he began to talk about divorce.

A Fait Accompli?

Most of the recent studies on 1 Cor 7:10-11 suggest that Paul is writing about a situation that has already developed. According to the *opinio communis,* the context requires that the case at hand is one which is already a fait accompli.

A Grammatical Affair

Some grammarians, however, are not happy with the idea that verse 11 expresses a fait accompli.[75] There is, in fact, a grammatical difficulty in taking "if she does separate" (*ean de kai chôristhê*) as if it refers to a separation which has already taken place. The use of a verb in the subjunctive mood with *ean* ("if") suggests a future condition.[76] In Greek, the use of the subjunctive normally implies the existence, at least in principle, of a doubt that the condition will be fulfilled.[77] Even Hans Conzelmann who holds that Paul is referring to an already existing situation mentions "the linguistic difficulty of *ean* with the aorist subjunctive referring to the past."[78]

On the other hand, *ean* ("if"), used with the aorist subjunctive, as it is in 1 Cor 7:11a, refers to a general condition, conceived as having taken place before the time of the action of the main verb.[79] Strictly speaking, the woman's separation from her husband is not necessarily prior to Paul's having written to the Corinthians; rather her separation is prior to her remaining unmarried or being reconciled to her husband (v. 11b). The separation belongs to the relative past, rather than to the absolute past. Not only the use of a concessive *ean* with the subjunctive but also the use of "*kai*-and"[80] constitutes a grammatical argument in favor of the idea that Paul is writing about a real case.

A Single Case?

With attention focused on the grammatical discussion, both Neirynck and Norbert Baumert[81] have suggested that Paul is merely offering a hypothetical illustration in verse 11ab rather than citing an actual situation in the community at Corinth. In contrast, Murphy-O'Connor has opined that "*ean* with the aorist subjunctive can be used in conditions 'referring to something which was impending in past time,' " and that "this meaning is most appropriate here; a divorce was about to take place when Paul's informants left Corinth and it could have been finalized by the time his response reached the city.''[82]

In point of fact, *ean* is used with the subjunctive in verse 11. The construction occurs four other times in 1 Corinthians 7, namely in verses 8, 28, 39, and 40. As a matter of fact, *ean* appears with rather unusual frequency in Paul's First Letter to the Corinthians. It is to be found some thirty-nine times in 1 Corinthians,[83] as compared with a total of just thirty-two times[84] in all the other letters indisputably attributed to Paul.[85] That Paul considers a variety of different possibilities in this fashion somewhat serves to confirm the fact that Paul was truly dealing with real situations when he wrote his "first" letter to the Corinthian Christians.

Paul's grammatical usage does not, however, serve to establish that there already existed at Corinth a de facto situation in which a wife had already divorced her husband—or was about to divorce her husband, according to Murphy-O'Connor's grammar-induced compromise. The principal argument that such a situation did, in fact, exist remains the unusual sequence of Paul's treatment of the issue of divorce—at variance with the pattern of his own presentation as well as with the tradition of the Lord's saying to which he apparently makes reference. While Paul's remark seems to have been prompted by a particular situation, his charge enjoys a general import. This fact alone may have prompted his choice of a grammatical construction which refers to a general condition.

The slogan, "it is well for a man not to touch a woman," shows that there was considerable confusion at Corinth in regard to sexuality. It is hardly likely that there was only one husband or one wife at Corinth whose ascetical zeal led them to want to abandon sexual relationships with their spouses (1 Cor 7:3). It is hardly likely that only one marital relationship was troubled by a spouse who was not Christian (1 Cor 7:12-13). It is hardly likely that there was only one person contemplating marriage (1 Cor 7:28) or only one man who entertained the thought that he might not be behaving properly towards a betrothed woman (1 Cor 7:36).

Paul treats all of these situations as general conditions, but it is unlikely that they were merely hypothetical situations. Rather, he generalizes from the particular. 1 Corinthians 7 does not attempt to pass in review all conceivable marital and pre-marital situations. Paul's knowledge of the real situation at Corinth prompted his various remarks on marriage and sexuality. What Paul has to say about the woman who has left her husband pertains not only to the case which has been reported to him; his remarks are intended to be relevant to all women (and men) who were so disturbed by the confusion about sexuality then reigning in Corinth that they were inclined to leave their spouses.

The Situation

If Paul's remarks on divorce have been prompted by a real-life situation at Corinth, it is important to know precisely what the situation was. One view, called the "usual view" by David Dungan,[86] is that the woman has divorced or is about to divorce her husband because she wants to live in sexual continence.[87] Enticed by the allure of sexual abstinence, whose value was proclaimed by the popular slogan (1 Cor 7:1), a Christian woman at Corinth decided to break off her marriage.

Other Possibilities

Another possibility is that the wife has decided to seek a divorce because of her husband's fascination with the new morality.[88] Even under Jewish law a woman had a right to sexual intercourse with her husband.[89] If a husband sought to forgo conjugal intimacy because of his desire to live in sexual abstinence, it is quite possible that he would face the possibility of divorce by his wife.

A variant on this approach is the view offered by Jerome Murphy-O'Connor.[90] He has suggested that the husband's newly espoused ascetical life is at the root of the marital breakup, but suggests that the divorce has been initiated, not by the wife, but by the husband who is concerned with his own sexual continence. My reading of 1 Cor 7:10-11 suggests that, on the contrary, it is the wife who has taken the initiative in the divorce.

Other authors take a different tack, preferring not to identify religion as the root issue in the separation. Brian Byron writes of "typical marriage difficulties: husband and wife quarreling, wife leaving home, or husband threatening divorce."[91] According to Dungan, it is reasonable to suggest that the woman sought a divorce for what might today seem to be a usual reason, namely that she desires to marry another man.[92] In support of his view, Dungan notes that Paul specifically prohibits a divorced woman from marrying someone else.

Divorce Before Conversion

A specification of this view is proposed by those who suggest that Paul has in mind the case of a woman who, for whatever reason, but most likely in view of a future marriage, divorced her husband before becoming a Christian. Such is the opinion of Rudolf Pesch,[93] whose exegesis of verse 11ab has been followed by many German-language commentators on 1 Corinthians.[94] According to this interpretation, Paul was asked whether a woman who, having been married and divorced prior to her conversion, would have been free to marry "in the Lord" after her entrance into the Church. Paul's response is that even this woman is bound to abstain from a subsequent marriage; even she is obliged to follow the way of life stipulated by Jesus' word.

Paul's language is much too concise for a modern interpreter to judge conclusively just which of these hypothetical situations the apostle had in mind as he wrote about the woman who had separated from her husband. Since Paul specifically charges her to "remain unmarried" (*menetô agamos,* v. 11b), it is hardly likely[95] that he was thinking of a woman who wanted a divorce because she wanted to live in a state of sexual continence. Such a woman would not have needed an exhortation to "remain unmarried." On the other hand, since Paul seems to imply that it was the wife who actively sought the divorce, it is hardly likely that he was thinking of a woman who had been put aside by an ascetical husband.

Thus we are left with three possibilities: a woman who had divorced her husband before becoming a Christian,[96] a Christian woman who has or is contemplating divorce because of her husband's ascetical tendencies, and the woman who divorces for some other reason, presumably because she wants to marry another man. The data provided by Paul are not sufficient to allow for an accurate reconstruction of the situation which he has in mind.[97] To respond to that situation, about which we cannot be more specific, Paul recalls the tradition that the Lord had prohibited divorce.

"Not I, but the Lord"

Prior to addressing himself to the situation of the woman already or about to be divorced in 1 Cor 7:10-11, Paul had already said something about other marital and sexual problems at Corinth—the situation of the man who had had a sexual liaison with his father's wife (1 Cor 5:1-8), men having sex with prostitutes (1 Cor 6:15-20), and the situation of spouses who were imprudently forgoing normal sexual relations (1 Cor 7:2-7). In each of these instances Paul spoke from authority, but was very conscious of the nature and source of the authority with which he spoke (1 Cor 5:3-4; 6:16; 7:6-7).

The Lord

When Paul takes up the matter of divorce in 1 Cor 7:10-16, he continues to remain aware of the limits and source of his authority to speak on the issue.[98] A nuanced expression of his authority to speak on the matter at hand pervades the entire exposition. Paul is well aware that he is not giving a command.[99] His choice of a verb is not *epitassô*, "I command,"[100] but *paraggellô*, "I give this command" (NRSV).[101] This verb is but rarely used by Paul,[102] and seems not to have enjoyed any precise denotation in his usage.[103] *Paraggellô* implies something stronger than a mere "I say,"[104] as if Paul were merely offering advice; yet it is not an "I command," as if Paul were urging some new pattern of conduct on the basis of his own authority. *Paraggellô* implies something more than the evocation of traditional wisdom, yet it is not so impersonal as if to suggest that Paul was about to make a merely administrative decision.[105] In classical and Hellenistic Greek, it was frequently used of giving orders, often with a nuance of passing them along.[106] Paul's use of the word[107] suggests that he is not appealing to his own authority; rather, he seems to be appealing to the authority of another. The implication becomes explicit as Paul interrupts his thought by saying "not I but the Lord" (*ouk egô alla ho kurios*).[108]

"Lord" (*Kurios*) is the most important title which Paul attributes to Jesus. It is the key entry in his Christological lexicon. The title designates Jesus as the risen One. For Paul, Jesus is Lord insofar as he has been raised from the dead by God the Father.[109] The title suggests faith in the resurrection. When Paul alludes to a saying of Jesus which had been transmitted to him by the early church, he inevitably attributes the saying to the Lord.[110] This reveals the transcendent aspect under which Paul regards such sayings[111] and his conviction that it is the power of the risen One which is at work in the tradition of the church. The Lord is the risen Lord present to the community and speaking to it through his authoritative spokespersons.

A Prophetic Saying?

Pace Mary Rose D'Angelo, this does not imply that Paul might have presented the prohibition of divorce in 1 Cor 7:10-11 simply as "a word given through another prophet of this community, or a prophet of another community."[112] D'Angelo has argued that the original source of the sayings on divorce is, most likely, not the Jesus of history. Rather, that source is the "sayings of the risen Lord speaking in the prophets of the Jesus movement and/or the early Christian mission."[113] She draws attention to the fact that the liturgical regulations of 1 Cor 14:26-33 are presented as a "commandment of the Lord" (see v. 37),[114] but that they proceed from Paul, that is, Paul, the prophet.[115] For D'Angelo this establishes a ground for a claim that the saying of the Lord in 1 Cor 7:10-11 is a similar kind of prophetic saying. Since, however, Paul distinguishes his word from that of the Lord in 1 Cor 7:10, the prohibition of divorce must be attributed to a prophet other than the apostle himself.

While the origin of the dominical logion in verses 10-11 is certainly a prophetic word,[116] it is unlikely that Paul would have cited a prophet other than himself in these verses. For Paul to have done so would have been for him to mitigate the force of his paraenetic appeal. In her desire to establish the prophetic character of the logion on divorce,[117] D'Angelo seems to have overlooked the role, admittedly a small one, that the Jesus tradition played in the Pauline correspondence. She has, moreover, suggested a fashion of appealing to authority in 1 Cor 7:10 that is unique in Paul's extant letters and has failed to be properly attentive to the uniqueness of the expression "commandment of the Lord" (1 Cor 14:37), hapax in the Pauline correspondence and formulated in language that is clearly different from the language of 1 Cor 7:10.

The Lord's Authority

More judicious is the comment of Antoinette Wire who remarks, "By identifying the things he has said as the Lord's command, Paul appeals to his own spiritual experience of Christ to challenge them to a like experience in the spirit. The ambiguity rising from the fact that oral tradition about Jesus' words could be spoken of similarly only adds authority to what he says."[118] Indeed, "*Kurios*-Lord" is, in and of itself, a relational and sovereign title, indicating dominion over people or things. To the title of *Kurios*-Lord corresponds the designation *doulos*-servant. As used by Paul, the *Kurios*-Lord title occasionally suggests the risen Jesus' present dominion over human beings.[119] This is particularly the case when Paul uses the *Kurios* title of Jesus in the paraenetic sections of his letters. Christians who proclaim Jesus as Lord acknowledge their fealty to him. When Paul invokes the Lordship of Jesus in his moral exhortation, he is calling for an obedient response on the part of those who acknowledge Jesus as Lord.[120] Indeed, he may be all the more inclined to invoke the authority of the Lord when the thrust of his paraenesis goes contrary to current praxis.[121]

The Saying

It is not uncommon for authors to suggest that, when Paul writes, "the wife should not separate from her husband and the husband should not divorce his wife" (1 Cor 7:10c, 11c), he is really quoting a traditional logion of Jesus.[122] Since the saying appears in four different forms in the Synoptic Gospels (Matt 5:32; 19:9; Mark 10:12; Luke 16:18), many of these same scholars seek to identify the particular form of the saying known to Paul. There are those who opt for his familiarity with a Matthean version of the saying, those who opt for his use of the Markan version, and those who believe that Paul was familiar with a form of the saying akin to that found in the so-called Q-source.[123]

A Synoptic Saying?

The various attempts to identify a relationship between Paul's version of the dominical logion and one to which the Synoptic Gospels bear witness, directly or indirectly, are, to a large extent, dependent upon a given author's view of the Synoptic Problem. Pursuance of this matter[124] would take us too far afield in a book devoted to the issue of Jesus' saying(s) on divorce, but it might be useful to pass in review some of the particular reasons why different scholars argue for a parallelism with—and perhaps even Paul's dependence on—a specific version of Jesus' saying.

Those who argue for Paul's familiarity with a Matthean version of the saying can cite the fact that Matthew is the one Synoptic Gospel which has a close parallel to all three sayings attributed to the Lord in 1 Corinthians.[125] In addition, one might argue that the "exception to the rule" apparently entertained by Paul in 1 Cor 7:15, bears some similarity with Matthew's famous exception clause. Not only is there an exception in both instances,[126] but, as Aidan Mahoney once claimed, the exception in both cases may have had to do with the marriage of a Christian to a non-Christian.[127]

Those who claim that Paul is aware of a version of the saying closer to the Markan form[128] argue that Paul prohibits divorce without exception, that he associates with this prohibition the further prohibition forbidding remarriage, and that in 1 Cor 6:16

Paul cites a modified version of Gen 2:24, the text from the Pentateuch found in the Markan passage on divorce (Mark 10:7-8).[129] To these arguments one might be tempted to add that Paul, like Mark (Mark 10:12), writes about a woman divorcing her husband. However, most exegetes are of the opinion that Mark 10:12 is a redactional addition to the tradition by the evangelist himself,[130] and would therefore have been unknown to Paul.

A third possibility is that Paul knew of the saying of Jesus in a form that was close to that of the Q-tradition, as preserved, for example, in Luke 16:18. Wolfgang Schenk believes that Paul's reference is to an early Q-form of the saying,[131] but Christopher Tuckett, who admits that 1 Cor 7:10-11, along with 1 Cor 9:14 and 11:23-25, serves as an indication that Jesus traditions were used by Paul, doubts that the tradition used by Paul involved the so-called Q-material as such.[132]

Another group of authors, however, is of the opinion that the search for a specific Synoptic parallel with Paul's reference in 1 Cor 7:10-11 is futile.[133] The reason why the search for a specific parallel in the Synoptic Gospels is doomed to failure is that Paul docs not actually cite the traditional logion. He invokes the Lord's authority so as to elicit the appropriate response, but he does not attempt to quote verbatim a word from the past. The authority of the dictum does not come from the fact that it is a traditional saying so much as it comes from the fact that it is construed as the present word of the risen Lord.

Paul's Own Words

The formulation on the teaching on divorce in 1 Cor 7:10-11 is, in fact, Paul's own. That this is indeed the case is clearly established when one looks at these verses in conjunction with those that immediately follow, namely, 1 Cor 7:12-16. Paul prefaces his remarks in this latter section of the letter by stating, "To the rest I say—I and not the Lord." It is clearly Paul's intention to express his own ideas about the relationship between Christians and their non-Christian spouses. He tells Christian husbands and wives not to divorce (*aphiêmi,* vv. 12, 13) their non- Christian spouses, but he counsels them to let go of a non-Christian spouse who is bent on departing (*chôrizô,* v. 15). These are the very words with which Paul spoke about divorce in verses 10 and 11. Since 1 Cor 7:12-16 is an expression of Paul's own thought—and it is surely the case that his thoughts are expressed in his own words[134]—it is likely that what we have in verses 10c and 11c is a paraphrase of the Jesus tradition in Paul's own words.

In 1 Cor 7:10c, 11c, Paul has not only formulated the Jesus tradition in his own words, he has also adapted the Jesus tradition to the Hellenistic setting of the Corinthian community.[135] In the Palestinian setting in which the Jesus tradition originated, it was all but impossible for a wife to divorce her husband.[136] It is quite likely that Jesus spoke only about a man divorcing his wife. Paul's reference to the wife's divorce of her husband seems to represent a Pauline accommodation to the socio-cultural situation in existence at Corinth.

The Authority of the Saying

It is not Paul's intention to give an exact quotation of the Jesus tradition; for him to have done so would have represented a radical departure from his usual practice with regard to the Jesus tradition. What Paul has done is to formulate a rule of conduct, based on the Jesus tradition but expressed in his own words. He has created a kind of halakah based on the tradition. Like rabbis and teachers before him, whose lore he shared,[137] Paul has drawn from the tradition a succinct halakic statement.[138]

The freely formulated dominical logion does not, per se, control Paul's thought.[139] Rather, in an attempt to resolve the problem about which he had been apprised, the apostle has invoked the authority of the risen Lord whose power over the community is inherent in the tradition of the church which has passed along the words of Jesus. Paul does not regard those words as the words of just a deceased rabbi or prophet. He makes no attempt to cite the words of Jesus and comment upon them.[140] It is not the Jesus tradition as such, but the Lord's command, which is authoritative. Paul regards the words which the tradition has passed along as the words of the Lord[141] who is powerfully operative in and has dominion over the church at Corinth. It is the authority of that Lord to which Paul appeals when he gives a command for the woman who has divorced or is about to divorce her husband.

The Lord's authority is the ground of Paul's authoritative command. The appeal to the Lord's authority would be all the more telling if it could be established with certainty that Paul was addressing the situation of a woman who was divorcing her husband because of a religious fervor which led her to seek a life of sexual continence. In that case, Paul's words would have meant something like this: "you may think that it is your religious duty to abandon your husband, but I tell you that that is not the Lord's will in your case." Such a person should have known better than to separate; there is, after all, a word of the Lord that is pertinent to her situation.

Norbert Baumert's suggestion that the woman in question should have known better[142] seems to imply that the tradition of the Lord's saying on divorce was known to the Corinthian community, a point of view espoused by some authors.[143] The tradition was widely known in the early church, and it has been suggested that the saying was used as a rule in Pauline circles.[144] However, most commentators are rather hesitant to affirm that this specific element of the Jesus tradition was already known to the Corinthian community.[145] Paul's tone seems to suggest that the Corinthians had not been aware of the Lord's teaching on divorce.

And What If?

Not only does Paul invoke the Jesus tradition as truly pertinent to the situation at hand, he further confirms it by adding, "if she does separate, let her remain unmarried (*menetō*) or else be reconciled to her husband (*tō andri katallagētō*)" (1 Cor 7:11ab). Dungan claims that the parenthetical remark puts Paul's position in opposition to that of Jesus. Whereas Jesus forbade divorce, Paul allows a woman to continue in her divorced situation, forbidding only her remarriage.[146]

It is, however, highly unlikely that Paul's parenthetical remark is intended to promote a toleration of divorce. Such a toleration would have put Paul in the position of effectively denying the Lordship of Jesus which he has so effectively invoked.[147] Moreover, it would seem to be an exception in what otherwise seems to be an apodictic expression of community rule (vv. 10c, 11c). Finally, such an interpretation seems not to take into account the obvious similarity between the case treated in verses 10-11 and that treated in verses 12-16.

A Choice?

Dungan's interpretation of the parenthesis separates, in fact, the two parts of verse 11b, as if the divorced woman had a pair of options:[148] either she could remain unmarried, or else she could be reconciled to her husband. Paul's words indicate that he has a case in mind in which the woman has not yet remarried.[149] She is *agamos*,[150] "unmarried,"[151] but it should not be presumed that she now has before her a pair of options, either of which she can pursue. It is preferable to consider the entire parenthetical remark as a unit, without any disjunction, rather than as a choice that is available to the woman who divorces her husband.

A unified interpretation of the parenthesis brings it into harmony with the immediate context, which prohibits divorce for women and men alike.[152] If the parenthesis is to be interpreted in unified fashion—and taking account of Paul's paratactic style—her remaining unmarried can be seen as a condition of her reconciliation to her husband.[153] Even under Jewish law a divorced and remarried woman was not allowed to resume a marital relationship with her previous husband.[154] Thus a woman would have to be unmarried in order for it to be possible for her to be reconciled to her husband. If the parenthesis is treated as a whole, rather than as a composite of two component parts, Paul's words serve to reinforce rather than to mollify the tenor of his teaching on divorce.

The major difficulty with a unified interpretation of the parenthetical remark in verse 11ab is Paul's use of the conjunction *ê* ("or"). In classical and Hellenistic Greek, *ê* serves either as a disjunctive or as a comparative. Paul's use of the conjunction is consistent with normal usage. Since the comparative meaning is excluded by Paul's phraseology, it must be acknowledged that *ê* has a disjunctive sense in verse 11b. This, however, should not be taken to mean that the divorced woman has two equally acceptable options to consider. Paul's emphasis lies on reconciliation (*tô andri katallagêtô*), the second of the two "alternatives." Paul desires that the divorced woman be reconciled to her husband.[155]

Reconciliation?

There may, however, be cases where reconciliation is impossible. In a cultural setting where monogamy is the norm, it may be that the former husband has already entered into a second marriage, thereby making it impossible for his former wife to seek a marital reconciliation. If, perchance, the divorce has taken place because of ascetical reasons on the part of either the husband or the wife, reconciliation might prove to be impossible.

If a wife had divorced her husband as an effective way of achieving the sexual continence which she desired, it is hardly likely that he would desire reconciliation with a woman with whom he could not enjoy normal marital relations. The possibility of her achieving a reconciliation might be dependent upon the extent to which she took to heart Paul's teaching in verses 4 and 5. If, however, the wife has divorced her husband because he has refused to have sexual relations with her, it is hardly likely—but not impossible—that he would welcome her into his household. Some would even suggest that reconciliation is dependent upon the husband's conversion.[156]

What About Husbands?

In sum, Paul's teaching on divorce in 1 Cor 7:10-11 seems to be his response to a situation which arose within the Christian community at Corinth. In a rather unusual fashion, he has appealed to the authority of the risen Lord to remind the Corinthians that divorce ought not to take place. Paul has not, however, made any attempt to reproduce verbatim the Jesus tradition on divorce. Rather, he has formulated it in his own words and adapted it to the general socio-cultural conditions and the specific situation at Corinth. Paul is, however, a realist—and he shows that in more than one instance as he writes to the Corinthians. Recognizing that a divorce may have already taken place, Paul commands the divorcée to be reconciled to her husband. Should reconciliation prove to be impossible, Paul, the realist, can only ask that she remain unmarried.[157]

While enjoining a Christian woman from divorcing her husband, Paul also states that "the husband should not divorce his wife" (*kai andra gunaika mê aphienai,* v. 11c). The infinitive clause is complementary to Paul's "I give charge" (*paraggellô,* v. 10a) and falls within the parameters of the Lord's authority, just as did the preceding statement, "the wife should not separate from her husband" (v. 10c).

Verse 10c and verse 11c are parallel infinitive clauses, but the term which Paul uses of the husband divorcing his wife is the verb *aphiêmi,* admittedly a technical term for divorce,[158] but one that is not used in any other of the New Testament's renditions of the saying of Jesus on divorce. Use of this verb is yet another indication that Paul is indeed paraphrasing the Jesuanic tradition on divorce in this letter to the Corinthians. The verb of verse 10c, in reference to a woman's divorce, is in the aorist tense and passive voice, whereas that of verse 11c, in reference to a man's divorce, is in the present tense and active voice. The shift in tense may well reflect a shift in situation. The aorist normally represents punctiliar action, a one-time event, whereas the present normally presents a continuing action. In our case, the shift in tense may be due to the fact that Paul's injunction addressed to the woman is directed to a specific situation whereas the statement about the man represents a matter of principle.

The verve with which Paul presents his thought frequently leads him to plead that he not be mistaken.[159] One might conceivably argue that Paul has complemented the statement about a woman's divorcing her husband with a statement about a man's divorcing his wife in order that one not draw from his words the unwarranted conclusion that, although a wife may not divorce her husband, a husband may divorce his wife.[160] Such a suggestion would not be entirely gratuitous since, under Jewish law, husbands were permitted to divorce their wives, but wives were not permitted to divorce their husbands.

Factors other than the mere desire not to be misunderstood seem, however, to have been operative in Paul's additional reflection in verse 11c that a husband is not to divorce his wife. These are the weight of the tradition of the Jesuanic logion, which speaks always of a husband divorcing his wife, and the gender balance which characterizes this entire section of Paul's letter. What is good for the Christian woman is good for the Christian man. In this instance, Paul has it on the authority of the risen Lord himself. Neither wife nor husband may divorce their spouse. This is the point of the apostle's paraenesis, or moral exhortation, in 1 Cor 7:10-11.

2

A Related Matter

Having treated the issue of a Christian's being involved in a divorce in a rather comprehensive, though non-legalistic fashion in verses 10 and 11, Paul turns his attention to another, yet related issue, in verses 12-16:

> [12]To the rest I say—I and not the Lord—that if any believer has a wife who is an unbeliever, and she consents to live with him, he should not divorce her. [13]And if any woman has a husband who is an unbeliever, and he consents to live with her, she should not divorce him. [14]For the unbelieving husband is made holy through his wife, and the unbelieving wife is made holy through her husband. Otherwise, your children would be unclean, but as it is, they are holy. [15]But if the unbelieving partner separates, let it be so; in such a case the brother or sister is not bound. It is to peace that God has called you. [16]Wife, for all you know, you might save your husband. Husband, for all you know, you might save your wife.

Mixed Marriages

As Paul begins to deal with this new subject, he seems to divide the question.[1] He first considers whether a Christian married to a non-Christian could or should seek a divorce (vv. 12-14). Then he deals with how a Christian married to a non-Christian should react to the latter's seeking a divorce (v. 15). It is not unlikely that both of these issues were raised by the Corinthians themselves.[2] The first issue to be addressed was that of Christians taking the initiative in divorcing their non-Christian spouses. Since endogamy, that is, marriage within one's own group, is undoubtedly a value in many cultures,[3] some people at Corinth might have been of the opinion that Christians should divest themselves of non-Christian spouses, perhaps under the mistaken notion that intimacy and physical union with a non-Christian brought sin too close.[4]

Paul has described the Christians at Corinth as those who are sanctified, those who are saints. In fact, this is the epithet which he uses to describe the Christians at Corinth to whom he writes. The use of this terminology in 1 Cor 1:2,[5] part of the greeting of Paul's letter, is striking. The very word evokes a division between the sacred and the profane. Its function is divisive. Indeed, Paul makes a sharp distinction between those who are saints and those who are not.[6]

In the body of his letter, when Paul addresses himself to the issue of mixed marriage, his principal argument (1 Cor 7:14) focuses on sanctity or holiness. In an earlier section of the letter, Paul had warned the Christians of Corinth not to associate with immoral persons.[7] He had sharp words to address to Christians who had sex with prostitutes. Why? Because their bodies were members of Christ.[8] While one can hardly describe a non-Christian spouse as "immoral" or compare a faithful wife to a prostitute, it is easy to envision how the separatist ideas proposed by Paul, not only in this letter but also in his previous evangelization and correspondence, could lead some Christians to believe that they should radically separate themselves from a non-Christian sexual partner. It is only after this issue has been dealt with that Paul turns his attention to the matter of Christians who have been abandoned by their non-Christian spouses.[9]

In his response to these two concerns, Paul continues to employ the balanced structure which has marked his entire disquisition on sexuality and marriage.[10] He maintains a single point of view throughout the entire exposition, namely, that of the responsibility of the Christian spouse to his or her marital partner. It is from Christians that the queries have come. It is to Christians that Paul responds in the name of his apostolic authority.[11]

Despite the fact that most authors believed that the topic addressed in verses 12-16 is mixed marriages, and that Paul addresses this topic from the angle of two different possibilities, Jeremy Moiser has claimed that Paul is dealing with but one single issue in verses 12-16,[12] namely, the case of the Christian spouse who is abandoned by an unbelieving partner, the topic taken up only in verse 15 according to my reading of Paul's exhortation.

According to Moiser, Paul does not treat the problem of Christian spouses abandoning their non-Christian partners in verses 12-16, because that issue has already been dispatched in verses 10-11 and dispatched on the authority of the Lord himself. It is, however, hardly likely that verses 12-13 speak of the abandonment of a Christian by a non-Christian spouse. In each verse the verb "*aphiêmi*-divorce" is in the active voice and has the Christian as its subject. Moiser's interpretation seems to rely upon an inadequate reading of the text. Verses 12-16 do treat a single topic, namely, mixed marriages, but this topic is treated from two different points of view.

I Say, Not the Lord

Paul's opening gambit, "to the rest I say, not the Lord" (*Tois de loipois legô egô ouch ho kurios;* 1 Cor 7:12a), clearly indicates that he is taking up an issue that he has not previously treated. Paul's words also indicate that he cannot resolve this new issue on the basis of the same authority that he had invoked in dealing with the previous matter. Paul apparently considers that the traditional prohibition of divorce among Christians is not, without further qualification, applicable to mixed marriages.[13] Since there were Christians at Corinth who were involved in mixed marriages, Paul considered himself constrained to address the issue,[14] and to resolve the matter on his own authority. The qualitative difference in the authority supporting the regulation which he is about to formulate is subtly suggested by his choice of the verb "say" (*legô*), which he nonetheless introduces by means of an emphatic "I" (*egô*). While Paul's opinion is a personal one, it is that of one "called by the will of God to be an apostle of Christ Jesus" (1 Cor 1:1), one who has the Spirit of God (1 Cor 7:40).[15]

I Say

Four features of Paul's opening remark (v. 12a) place the new pericope in sharp contrast with his previous exhortation. The words "I say, not the Lord" (*legô egô ouch ho kurios*) call to mind and are almost antithetical to the "not I but the Lord" (*ouk egô alla ho kurios*) of the previous introduction (v. 10). It would have been difficult indeed for Paul to have drawn a sharper contrast than the one that is found in these contradictory remarks. The obvious opposition between the phrases is, nonetheless, accentuated by Paul's use of an emphatic "I" (*egô*)[16] in verse 12a.

This emphatic *egô* serves, in fact, a dual function. The one is negative, contrasting Paul's authority with that of the Lord; the other positive, succinctly highlighting the authority that Paul does enjoy. Paul's authority is apostolic[17] and Spirit-grounded,[18] but it is not the authority of the Lord himself. He writes as a servant of Christ and as one who is a steward of the mysteries of God,[19] but he has no command of the Lord to promulgate anew in the situation at hand.[20] What allows Paul to extend the application of the Jesus tradition to a new, but analogous, situation is what John Howard Schütz calls "the apostolic autobiography, the apostolic *egô*."[21] As an apostle, Paul "is authorized not only to preach the gospel, but also to monitor how men 'stand' within it and advise them of how they should."[22]

A Contrast

Nevertheless Paul has emphasized the contrast to which he gives expression in verse 12 by three additional features of his choice of words, his *lexis,* to use the technical term of Greek rhetoric. First of all, the verb "*legô*-say" of verse 12 is of a different sort from the verb "*paraggellô*-give this command" found in verse 10. The connotation of the latter suggests authority; it is almost equivalent to "I order. . . ." The former merely suggests communication; it is virtually equivalent to "I speak to. . . ."[23]

To express the contrast, Paul uses the conjunctive particle *de,* the second word in the Greek text of verse 12, which, however, has not been specifically translated by the NRSV.[24] *De* has adversative force, but it is not as strong as "*alla*-but." It could possibly be rendered as "on the other hand."

Finally, there is the fact that the instructions of verses 12-16 are directed to "*tois loipois*-the rest." Who are the rest? Paul has already addressed a series of remarks to the once-but-no-longer married (*tois agamois kai tais chêrais*, v. 7) and another series of reflections to those who are married (*gegamêkosin*, v. 10). After this, who can the rest be?[25]

The Rest

Tomson[26] believes that the rest are Gentile Christians who are involved in informal marriages with pagans. David Dungan, on the other hand, holds that the rest are non-believers.[27] He interprets *tois loipois* as "concerning the rest." In his opinion, instead of addressing himself to various groups within the community as he had done in verses 8 and 10, Paul begins, in verse 12, to talk about a group of people with whom some members of the community are related.[28] In my judgment, however, Paul's language makes it rather clear in what follows that he is addressing his remarks to Christians who are married to unbelievers.[29] These are Christians who had been married (to an unbeliever) and who converted to Christianity at a later time.

Marriage with Unbelievers

Who are the unbelievers (*apistoi*)? This kind of vocabulary is Pauline, but it appears only in Paul's correspondence with the Corinthians.[30] Use of this terminology has a social function; it implies the manifest distinction between those who have faith and those who do not. Unbelievers are outsiders (*idiôtai*).[31] Pace Tomson, these terms are presumably applicable not only to pagans, but also to unbelieving Jews.[32] An unbeliever is simply a non-Christian.

Exogamy

The marriage of a Christian with an unbeliever is exogamous. It is a marriage with someone who does not belong to the Christian group.[33] Such a marriage cannot properly be described as a "marriage in the Lord," the kind of marriage which Paul deemed to be preferable for Christians.[34] By introducing his reflections on mixed marriages with, "To the rest I say—I and not the Lord," Paul indicates that the situation is one to which the Jesus tradition—insofar as he knew and understood it—is not immediately pertinent. The apostle apparently considered that the tradition of the Jesus saying—the word of the Lord—was relevant only to those marriages in which both of the partners were Christians.[35] It was not normative for a marriage in which one of the partners did not acknowledge Jesus to be *Kurios*-Lord.[36]

Paul, nonetheless, affirms that, as a matter of principle, Christians ought not to divorce their non-Christian spouses. He affirms this principle on the basis of his own authority: "To the rest I say—I and not the Lord." Since the material content of the norm cited in verses 12-14 does not significantly differ from that of the dominical logion (vv. 10c, 11c), it would seem that the principle which Paul expresses in verses 12-14 is, in some ways, an extension[37] of the basic thrust of the Jesus tradition to a new situation.

What the Lord had Said

The similarity in wording between verses 12-14 and Paul's previous teaching on divorce, suggests that Paul is expanding on the exhortation which he had imparted in verses 10-11. Thus, although the dominical logion is not immediately applicable to the situation of a mixed marriage, Paul is spelling out its implications. His exhortation to Christians involved in mixed marriages is in keeping with the dominical logion which he had received through the early Christian tradition. According to Paul, Christians should not divorce (even) their (non-Christian) spouses. A Christian husband[38] should not dismiss his wife, nor should a Christian wife dismiss her husband. Yet there is a condition, namely, that the unbelieving spouse consents to the continuance of the conjugal union.

If Paul says what he says on the basis of his own authority, in full cognizance of the fact that he has no tradition of the Lord pertinent to the situation at hand, it should be self-evident that the maxim is Paul's own formulation. In this respect it is striking that Paul first treats the matter of a Christian man divorcing his non-Christian wife and then the issue of a Christian woman divorcing her non-Christian husband. His balanced formulation is applicable to the cultural situation of the Christians to whom he is writing, namely, one in which both men and women might legitimately divorce their spouses. In confrontation with this tolerant cultural situation Paul states that neither a Christian husband nor a Christian wife may divorce a non-Christian spouse.

The parallelism between verses 12bd and 13 provides another example of the literary and theological balance that characterizes Paul's exposition. That Paul once again treats first of the responsibility of the Christian husband[39] serves as a confirmatory argument for the suggestion that the situation envisioned in verse 11ab is for real. Paul's words were not intended to suggest a hypothetical instance advanced in the context of a theoretical and systematic exposition on marriage and sexuality.

The counter-cultural stance taken by Paul in verses 12-13 is similar to the position which he had urged in verses 10c-11c for those Christians who were married in the Lord, that is, when both partners were Christian.[40] There, however, Paul could rely on the Lord's authority; here, he cannot. Nonetheless, his teaching is in line with that of the Lord, as it has been encapsulated in the traditional logion. The similarity of the respective maxims indicates that Paul had a rather restrictive view of the applicability of the dominical logion.[41] This should not be seen, however, as some form of ethical minimalism[42] on Paul's part; rather, it is in keeping with his rabbinic background.

According to traditional rabbinic lore, statements of the Scriptures are clearly distinguished from the statements of the rabbis who interpret them.[43] Similarly, the teaching of an esteemed rabbi in the past was clearly distinguished from that of his later pupils.[44] Moreover, Paul's casuistic treatment of the subject at hand—his case-by-case consideration of various related issues—seems likewise to have been influenced by his rabbinic formation. The rabbinic *halakah* were exposited in a similarly casuistic fashion.

A Christian's Response

As he exhorts Christians who are involved in mixed marriages not to abandon their unbelieving and presumably pagan spouses, Paul departs from a principle which has thus far determined his approach to the solution of the sexual and marital problems that were disturbing the Christians at Corinth. Up to this point in his exposition, mutuality in the marital relationship had dominated much of Paul's thought. Now he suggests that a Christian spouse has a specific responsibility vis-a-vis the marital partner,[45] one that need not be exercised by the non- Christian spouse, over whom, in any case, Paul does not enjoy apostolic authority.

Paul's departure from the principle of mutuality is, of course, not based on sexual grounds; it is based on a faith commitment. Those Christians who acknowledge Jesus as Lord and thereby recognize Paul's apostolic *egô* are enjoined from abandoning their non-Christian spouses.

Paul undoubtedly had a preference for marriages in the Lord, and it is more than likely that his preference in this regard was well-known to the Christians at Corinth. Indeed, Wayne Meeks has suggested that this expectation was generally known within the Pauline churches and that this factor may help to explain why the issue of severing mixed marriages arose among the Corinthian Christians.[46] Some may have so misconstrued Paul's teaching as to believe themselves either forced to abandon their pagan spouses or at least justified in doing so.[47] Paul clearly proclaims that marital stability is a value to be maintained by Christian spouses.

Their commitment to their legitimate spouses should take precedence over the value of community endogamy which Paul otherwise espouses. Christian spouses, whether man or wife, cannot justify the abandonment of a spouse who continues to consent to the marital relationship, simply because they are Christian. The Lord's saying, while not strictly applicable to the situation of a mixed marriage, is such that it places a demand upon Christians to live out their married lives in enduring commitment.

A Reasoned Plea

Paul's statement that Christians should remain united to their non-Christian spouses is so radical that it deserves some explanation. This would be in addition to Paul's apostolic extension of the dominical logion to these cases. Accordingly, Paul immediately begins to justify the position that he has taken in his paraenesis. "For the unbelieving husband is made holy through his wife, and the unbelieving wife is made holy through her husband" (1 Cor 7:14ab) is the first thought which he expresses as part of his explanatory exposition. Paul is clearly offering a basis for the thought which he has previously expressed: *"Gar-*for" is an explanatory conjunction. In classic rhetorical terms, Paul is making use of an enthymeme, a form of deductive proof in which a statement is followed by a supportive reason. *"Gar-*for" is a common rhetorical indication of the use of this form.[48]

Holiness

Paul's explanation continues to follow the pattern[49] which he has hitherto used with remarkable consistency: first, he writes about the husband, then, about the wife.[50] Although Paul is clearly offering rational argumentation for the validity of the stated paraenesis of verses 12 and 13—albeit in chiastic fashion— the explanation is not as clear as the statement itself. While the NRSV[51] translates Paul's enigmatic language of 1 Cor 7:14ab as "the unbelieving husband is made holy through his wife,[52] and the unbelieving wife is made holy through her husband,"[53] the REB has "the husband now belongs to God through his Christian wife, and the wife through her Christian husband."[54]

What Is Holiness? Some of the more more popular "translations" of 1 Corinthians attempt to make sense of Paul's enigmatic language by offering what amounts to a paraphrase. For example, the JB reads: "This is because the unbelieving husband is made one with the saints through his wife, and the unbelieving wife is made one with the saints through her husband"[55] and the Living Bible offers: "For perhaps the husband who isn't a Christian may become a Christian with the help of his Christian wife. And the wife who isn't a Christian may become a Christian with the help of her Christian husband."[56]

The variety of these "translations" illustrate the difficulty that we moderns, far removed from Paul's first-century Corinth, have in understanding Paul's "explanation." Jerome Murphy-O'Connor has noted that the modern interpretations of Paul's explanation, namely, the enigmatic reality of holiness, fall into

ten categories.⁵⁷ These explanations respectively take "holiness" to be:
1) a contagious and far-reaching power (F. Hauck, G. Schrenk, J. Weiss); 2) a variant of this, that is, some form of biologically transmitted holiness (J. Weiss, H. Lietzmann); 3) a holiness grounded in the order of creation (B. Weiss, T. Heinrici); 4) a christological-ecclesiological holiness related to "the body of Christ" (O. Cullmann); 5) an appropriation of the salvific influence of the Christian by the non-Christian spouse and a participation in the holiness of the Christian parent by the children (Heinrici, A. Robertson, A. Plummer, H. Windisch);⁵⁸ 6) a certain predisposition towards or call to holiness (P. Bachmann, A. Schlatter); 7) removal of uncleanness; a negative interpretation of holiness insofar as Christian family members are not impure (Windisch); 8) zeal of the Christian with regard to the non-Christian (P. Wilhelm Schmiedel); 9) ritual purity (*kosher*) as distinct from ritual impurity (*mamzer*) (J. M. Ford); and 10) liberation from the control of evil powers (H. Conzelmann, O. Merk, G. Delling⁵⁹).

With regard to this long and varied list of the interpretations of Paul's enigmatic reference to being made holy in 1 Cor 7:13-14, Jerome Murphy-O'Connor has repeated Conzelmann's comment that the "explanations that have so far been suggested are almost without exception unsatisfactory."⁶⁰ Part of the difficulty lies in the assumptions—erroneous assumptions in Murphy-O'Connor's view—that various commentators have brought to the interpretation of this text.

Among the various assumptions that have skewed the interpretation of verses 13 and 14 is the view that the Christians of Corinth feared that a mixed marriage would make Christian spouses and, therefore, their community simply "unclean." Another misleading assumption is that which takes "holy" (*hagios*) and unclean (*akathartos*) in a ritualistic, legal sense,⁶¹ as if Paul, reflecting a Jewish point of view, had taught the Corinthians that unbelievers were unclean and could communicate this uncleanness to Christians. Yet another misleading view—indeed, the most common—is that which considers "holiness" to have been used by Paul in a sense rather different from that of his normal usage, as if sanctity were some sort of an objective reality.[62] Many commentators hold that Paul is speaking of sanctification in a somewhat physical way.

The normal Pauline usage of "holy" and its cognates is one in which holiness is a quality of those who have been baptized into Christ.[63] Its fundamental connotation is that of separation, that is, separation from sin and dedication to the Lord Jesus. Those who are holy are different from others because they belong to the Lord in some unique fashion. Consequent upon this "social" situation is the fact that those who are holy ought to be distinguished by a way of life that is consistent with their baptismal status. Hence, there is an ethical dimension to holiness. Thus, some commentators opt for an ethical interpretation of the (inherently) cultic language of sanctification in verse 14. According to this view, unbelievers can be considered holy since, remaining joined in marriage with their Christian spouses, they have fulfilled the Creator's will.[64]

A Spouse's Holiness. Since it is hardly likely that Paul, who uses the term "holy" so frequently in his letters, has given the familiar term an unfamiliar meaning in 1 Cor 7:14, his words about unbelieving husbands and wives must somehow be consistent with his normal usage. On the other hand, it is clear that these unbelievers are not yet saved (see verse 16). Neither are they called saints. Rather they are "made holy through their respective spouses" (*hêgiastai en tê gunaiki; hêgiastai en tô adelphô*).

Paul's use of the verb "*hagiazô*-make holy" in the perfect tense indicates that he has in mind an event of the past whose effects continue to be realized at the time that he was writing. The use of the preposition "through" (*en*) indicates that this consecration is due to the relationship of the unbeliever with the Christian spouse. It is, however, not necessary to affirm that the Christian spouse is the instrumental cause[65] of the sanctification of the unbelieving spouse. It may well be that Paul's *en* reflects the Hebrew *b*, which simply means "in relationship to."[66]

F. F. Bruce has suggested that Paul's words (v. 14ab) are an "interesting extension of the OT principle of holiness by association."[67] Paul espouses the principle in Rom 11:16: "If the part of the dough offered as first fruits is holy, then the whole batch is holy; and if the root is holy, then the branches also are holy."

In this passage, an extended metaphor is used to speak of the sanctification of Israel. A similar analogy seems to be operative in 1 Cor 7:14ab.[68] Because of the relationship with the Christian spouse, the unbelieving partner in a mixed marriage somehow belongs to God. Through the marital relationship, the unbelieving spouse is brought into the sphere of the Christian community with all that implies.[69] Hence there is no reason why the Christian should abandon the unbelieving spouse; on the contrary, his or her own relationship with the Lord provides a ground for a continuation of the relationship.

Elsewhere in Paul's letters holiness terminology is restricted to Christians. In 1 Cor 7:14 it is clearly extended to non-believers. By stating that non-believing wives and husbands are sanctified because of their relationship with their Christian spouses, Paul has turned the tables on those who have suggested that a mixed marriage somehow taints Christians with sin. Paul states that it is just the reverse which happens; a mixed marriage somehow consecrates non-believers with holiness.

Childrens' Holiness. In verse 14c Paul attempts to clarify his argument. A rhetorical "otherwise" indicates that Paul is continuing to make his point: "Otherwise (*epei ara*)," he writes, "your children would be unclean, but as it is, they are holy." Were the marital unions of Christians with non-believers not sanctifying relationships, the children born of these unions would be unclean (*akatharta*). That, however, is not the case. Paul states that children born of a mixed marriage are indeed holy (*hagia*)[70] and uses this fact to substantiate his claim that their parents' marital union is somehow a holy union. Paul appeals to that holiness in urging Christians to avoid the separation that some have contemplated because of their faith. Paul does not yield to the opinion of those Corinthian Christians who had been disturbed by the "new morality" and sanction the abandonment of non-Christian spouses by their Christian partners.

In the past few decades, a great deal has been written about the holiness of these children, particularly with regard to the baptism of infant children.[71] Among the questions asked has been that of the age of the children: is Paul talking about infant children or those who have reached a level of personal maturity? Is he writing about children who have been baptized or those who have not been baptized? Does he have in mind children born of mixed marriages or children born of Christian marriages? Or both? Is he thinking of children born before the conversion of one or both of their parents or about children who are born at a time when at least one of their parents was a Christian?

The question of infant baptism per se need not detain us at the present time. As a matter of fact, Paul has not written about infants as such. He has spoken of "children" (*tekna*). The term suggests parentage, not age.[72] Any human being, no matter the age, is a child (*teknon*) in relationship to his or her parents.

Since *teknon* is a term which can be appropriately used of adult children, Gerhard Delling has suggested that Paul has in mind adult children who have not become Christian.[73] Christian parents ought not to fear some sort of contamination from their unbaptized children, as if their new faith required that they sever all relationships with the unbaptized,[74] including their spouses and children. Paul, however, has not characterized the children of whom he writes as "unbelievers" (*apista*); rather, he hypothetically describes them as "unclean" (*akatharta*), a term which echoes Jewish ritual language.[75] Should Paul have had the adult, but unbelieving and unbaptized, children of a mixed marriage in mind as he wrote verse 14cd, we would have expected him to describe these children as he has described their unbelieving parent, that is, as "unbelievers" (*apistoi*).

On the other hand, Delling is quite correct in affirming that there is not a complete parallelism between verse 14ab, the cases of the unbelieving husband and the unbelieving wife, and verse 14cd, the instance of children.[76] Paul's categories are different: his first argument focuses on unbelief, his second on uncleanness. Paul's way of arguing is different in the two cases: he grants the lack of belief of the non-Christian partner, but he does not grant the uncleanness of the children. Finally, the tenses of his verbs are different: unbelieving spouses have been made holy (*hēgiastai,* a perfect tense, implying a past action with present consequences[77]), children are holy (*hagia estin,* a present tense).

The distinction between verse 14ab and 14cd is, nonetheless, best maintained when "*tekna*-children" is taken to mean infants and small children[78] living within the parental household. Indeed, the most natural interpretation of verse 14cd is that Paul is referring to children born of a mixed marriage. The use of the verb "*estin*-are," in the present tense, seems to indicate that, in Paul's opinion, these children are simply "holy," that is, that they have been holy throughout their existence. Unlike their non-Christian parent, they have not become holy at some time in the past.

Presumably these children are unbaptized; otherwise, we might have expected Paul to use the verb "to make holy" (*hagiazō*) in the perfect passive, rather than an adjective and a verb (*hagia estin*) in the present. Nonetheless, some commentators suggest that these children have already been baptized and that Paul is arguing that they are not contaminated by the disbelief of their non-Christian parent. According to this line of reasoning,[79] Paul would have argued that just as the baptized offspring of a mixed marriage cannot be contaminated by the lack of Christian faith in one of the parents, so a Christian spouse cannot be contaminated by the lack of faith of a non-Christian partner.[80]

However, verse 14cd must be seen in context. It is closely related to verse 14ab and appears to adduce a reason for Paul's statement that the non-Christian spouses of believers are holy.[81] Were they not holy, says Paul, their children would be unclean. But they are holy and so, too, are the children born of their mixed marriages.[82] They are not separated from God; rather they belong to God because of the holiness of their parents. Paul's argumentation is analogous to the Jewish understanding of the family. In traditional Judaism, the family was subsumed into a covenantal relationship with Yahweh because of the father. By the time that the Mishnah was written (ca. 200 A.D.) it was understood that the children of proselytes were bona fide members of Israel.[83]

Since children of mixed marriages have been drawn into the holiness sphere of their Christian parent, there is no need to assume that these children are called holy because they have adopted a mode of conduct similar to that of their parents.[84] There is certainly an ethical implication in Paul's use of "holy" and its cognates (*hagi-*), but there does not seem to be any reason to assume that in verse 14cd "holy" has a denotation that is principally ethical, whereas, in the first part of the verse (v. 14ab), its principal meaning was "belonging to God."

Peace

The fact that a non-believing spouse is drawn into the sphere of God's people because of his or her marital relationship with a Christian—a reality of which the holiness of their children is a demonstrative sign—is the first and principal reason cited by Paul in support of his statement that a Christian spouse ought not to divorce a non-Christian partner.

David Daube has suggested that, in addition, believers should remain united in marriage to their non-Christian spouses for the sake of peace.[85] According to Daube, the relationship between a husband and wife is no longer a marriage after the conversion of one of them to Christianity. Because of his or her conversion to Christianity, the believer has become a new creation. He or she is no longer the same person as he or she was before the acceptance of the Christian faith. Nonetheless, reasons Daube, the new convert ought to remain with the previous spouse for the sake of peace. "On account of the ways of peace" (*mippene darke shalom*) was a common rabbinic expression, used of the extension of the privileges of the Jews to less-worthy Jews or even Gentiles. The idea of peace with Gentiles was often associated with the idea of winning their admiration. Thus Daube suggests that Paul urges that the Christian remain with the non-Christian in the hope of gaining the admiration of the non-Christian, leading eventually to the latter's conversion (v. 16)[86] and the re-constitution of their marriage as a holy union (vv. 12-13).[87]

Typically, scholars explain that the call to peace (1 Cor 7:15c) is, in the first instance, the principal reason why a Christian spouse can allow him or herself to be divorced by an unbelieving and uncooperative spouse,[88] and Daube himself admits that his understanding of the call to peace (1 Cor 7:15c) deviates from the usual interpretation.[89] While one may express reservations above whether Daube has adequately demonstrated his views on verses 12-16, the call to peace appears to be another reason why Christian husbands and wives should remain united to their non-Christian spouses,[90] provided that the latter are willing to share a common life with them.[91]

Christians are called to peace:[92] "It is to peace[93] that God has called you"[94] (1 Cor 7:15c). "God's call is a call to live in peace."[95]

Later on in this letter, as Paul comes to grip with yet another problematic situation in the Corinthian community, he will remind his correspondents that "God is a God of peace" (*ho theos eirênês*; 1 Cor 14:33). Peace (*eirênê*), corresponding to the biblical *shalôm,* is an expression which designates wholistic well-being, understood as a gift of God.[96] It includes the components of a fulfilled marriage and stability in relationship. Peace is God's will for and gift to his people. To the extent that Christian spouses experience relational stability in their marriages, with the presumption of marital fulfillment, they may not imperil the peace which God has granted to them.

The Call

A third reason for Paul's urging Christian spouses not to abandon their non-Christian partners relates to the nature of the Christian vocation. Christian spouses have been called by God.[97] Paul treats the social implications of the call by God in a pericope (1 Cor 7:17-24) which follows immediately upon his reflections on mixed marriages:

> [17]However that may be, let each of you lead the life that the Lord has assigned, to which God called you. This is my rule in all the churches. [18]Was anyone at the time of his call already circumcised? Let him not seek to remove the marks of circumcision. Was anyone at the time of his call uncircumcised? Let him not seek circumcision. [19]Circumcision is nothing, and uncircumcision is nothing; but obeying the commandments of God is everything. [20]Let each of you remain in the condition in which you were called.
>
> [21]Were you a slave when called? Do not be concerned about it. Even if you can gain your freedom, make use of your present condition now more than ever. [22]For whoever was called in the Lord as a slave is a free person belonging to the Lord, just as whoever was free when called is a slave of Christ. [23]You were bought with a price; do not become slaves of human masters. [24]In whatever condition you were called, brothers and sisters, there remain with God.

This pericope is a distinct topos. Verses 17-24 form a distinct literary unit, demarcated by the literary device called *inclusio* or ring construction.[98] Its content is different from what goes before and what follows, that is, two of the passages in which Paul shares his own views on marriage and sexuality.[99]

The basic thrust of the included verses (vv. 17-24) is that every one should remain in the social situation in which he or she was called. Paul thrice expresses the point of view that Christians are to remain in the life situation in which they came to faith: ". . . let each of you lead the life that the Lord has assigned, to which God called you. . . . Let each of you remain in the condition in which you were called. . . . In whatever condition you were called, brothers and sisters, there remain with God" (1 Cor 7:17, 20, 24).[100]

That each one should remain in the social situation in which he or she was called surely represents Paul's own and fully reflected-upon point of view. Not only has he repeated the exhortation first expressed in verse 17, but he has also explicitly stated that it is his rule (*houtôs . . . diatassomai*) in all the churches.[101] Some authors claim that the first expression of this exhortation to remain "as you were" (v. 17) relates to what Paul has said about marriage.[102] One can indeed argue along these lines, particularly when one realizes that Paul considers the three great social divisions to be sexual, racial, and civic.[103] Paul applies the refrain "as you were" to racial division (Jew-Gentile) in verse 20 and to civic division (slave-free) in verse 24. Thus it is quite likely that the use of this refrain in verse 17 applies to the social situation created by sexual differences.

Urging the Christians of Corinth to remain as they were gives Paul the opportunity to reflect on what it means to be free— from a Christian perspective.[104] He does this in verses 21-24. He reflects that even slaves are freed persons belonging to the Lord. It is the Lord who has freed them. He is their redeemer. Consequently they belong to him.[105] On the other hand, those who enjoy socio-political freedom are slaves of Christ.[106] Those who had been slaves and have the opportunity for socio-political freedom are encouraged to pursue it (v. 21c),[107] but this is presented as an exceptional situation, comparable, one might add, to the exceptional situations cited in verses 11ab and 15a. While pursuing his paraenesis, Paul offers a *digressio*. This procedure is typical of the style adopted by Paul in the entire chapter.[108] His obiter dicta allow him to cover all possibilities. In any case, both "freed" slaves and "enslaved" free persons belong to Christ the Lord. It is to the Lord that they owe their fealty. They are to lead the kind of life which the Lord assigns to them (v. 17).

Social stability is, then, a third reason why Christian spouses should not abandon non-Christian husbands or wives.[109] Added to the holiness of the unbelieving spouse and God's gift of peace, it forms a powerful complement to Paul's argumentation in favor of extending the applicability of the traditional dominical logion on divorce even to the case of Christians who are involved, because of their conversion, in exogamous marriages.

In sum, the exhortation which Paul addresses to Corinthian Christians married to unbelievers in verses 12-14 is not materially different from the charge which he had addressed to Christians married to other Christians in verses 10-11. The paraenesis of verses 12-14 is really an extension of the basic thrust of the Jesus tradition to a new situation. Paul, rabbi that he is, considers the traditional logion on divorce to be, strictly speaking, incumbent only on those marriages in which both partners accept Jesus as Lord. Because the situation of those involved in a mixed marriage is really different from that of Christians married to other Christians, Paul cannot simply cite the Jesus tradition. He must give an instruction which stems from his own authority—apostle that he is—and then argue the validity of his judgment.

That Paul has been able to do so implies that, even if the word of the Lord is not immediately applicable to this new situation, its basic insight must be made relevant to the new situation. In sum, Paul is dealing with the Jesus tradition in much the same way that other rabbis dealt with traditional Jewish Scriptures. By so doing, he is giving the contemporary reader of his letter an example of how the tradition of the church functions.[110] Some years later, the evangelists Matthew, Mark, and Luke will do something similar as they, too, deal with the Jesus tradition on divorce.

A Rejected Spouse

On the basis of his apostolic authority Paul has effectively argued[111] that Christians must not abandon, dismiss, or divorce[112] their non-Christian spouses provided that the latter consent to live in marital harmony with them. What happens, however, when non-Christian spouses do not want to continue a marital relationship with their recently converted Christian spouses? What is the responsibility of a Christian in this situation? In verse 15 Paul gives his response: "But if the unbelieving partner separates, let it be so."[113]

Paul's language is terse:[114] "But if the unbelieving partner separates, let it be so; in such a case the brother or sister is not bound. It is to peace that God has called you." Although dense, Paul's language is reminiscent of the kind of language that he has used throughout his exposition on the question of divorce. The verb used to describe the situation is *"chôrizô*-to separate," twice employed in the passive voice just as it was in verses 10 and 11. Although the verb is in the passive voice, its sense appears to be that of the middle voice ("separates him or herself"). A verb of volition is not used in the Greek text of verse 15a[115], but the contrast between this verse and the condition expressed in verses 12 and 13 ("if . . . she consents to live with him . . . if . . . he consents to live with her") suggests that the non-believer is the responsible agent in the situation to which Paul is alluding.

The reference to the unbelieving spouse (*apistos*)[116] and the brother (*adelphos*) recalls the language of verses 12 and 13. The introduction of *"adelphê*-sister" in verse 15 confirms that the *"gunê*-woman" of verse 13 is to be understood as a Christian woman, that is, in Paul's terms, an *"adelphê*-sister." Paul's reprise of earlier language and the switch of the subject of the principal verb—in verses 12 and 13 it had been "any brother" and "any woman;" now it is "the unbeliever"—indicate that Paul is considering the mixed marriage from another perspective in verse 15.[117] Having addressed himself to the issue of the Christian partner's responsibility, he now considers the matter from the unbeliever's point of view.

Separation

"If the unbelieving partner separates, let it be so." Paul does not have much to say about the action of the unbeliever, over whom he does not have apostolic authority, but neither does he condemn the unbeliever's action. His principal point seems to be to put the conscience of the believer to rest.[118] The exceptional situation[119] of spousal separation or divorce[120] confirms the principle of the permanency of the marital relationship which Paul has thus far promoted. It is a matter of the exception proving the rule.[121]

Not Bound

Yet, just as Paul had offered reasons why a Christian should remain in a marriage with a compatible non-believer, he offers some reflection on the point of view which he has just suggested. In situations[122] in which non-Christian spouses take the initiative in separating from their Christian spouses, "the brother or sister is not bound." Paul's disjunctive language continues to suggest the similarity and mutuality of responsibility with regard to marriage which has characterized his entire reflection. It does not make any difference whether it be a non-believing wife or a non-believing husband who has abandoned a Christian spouse. In either case, the Christian is not bound.

Bound to what? In the passive voice the verb *douloô* literally means "to be enslaved."[123] Elsewhere, when writing about marriage, Paul normally uses the word *deô,* "to be bound" or tied.[124] Most commentators are of the opinion that in verse 15 Paul states that a Christian is not bound or enslaved to an unbelieving and unwilling spouse[125] or to a marriage that a non-Christian partner does not want.[126] Yet there are others who suggest that Paul is indicating that Christians who find themselves in these circumstances are no longer bound by the word of the Lord (v. 10) which enjoins Christians from divorcing their spouses.[127]

Hans Conzelmann, on the other hand, suggests that the Christian spouse is "in principle" not bound.[128] For the Christian the law of freedom prevails. The underlying principle is that God has called Christians in peace.[129] The statement which Paul expresses in verse 15c affects something of a gnomic character, even if it is not a creedal formula or a proverb in the strict sense of those terms.[130] God's peace is an important notion for Paul. He often writes about the God of peace, particularly towards the end of his letters.[131] His classic epistolary greeting indicates that peace is a gift from God.[132] The God of peace calls Christians. The God who calls Christians is a faithful God, "who will do it," to use Paul's own words.[133] From this perspective it would appear that Paul is generally affirming that God calls Christians in peace. His words have a far broader import[134] than the mere suggestion that God does not want disharmony in marriage[135] or that the separation should take place without bitterness and anger.[136]

A Final Reason

What Paul has just said is further explained in verse 16: "Wife, for all you know, you might save your husband. Husband, for all you know, you might save your wife." Paul's words are clearly explanatory; he uses the explanatory particle "*gar*-for." However, Paul's explanation is, once again, not entirely clear to contemporary readers of his letter.

The Optimistic Approach

Basically there are two different approaches to understanding his words. The one is optimistic and the other pessimistic.[137] Joachim Jeremias has formulated the classic exposition of the optimistic approach in a 1954 study.[138] Citing 2 Sam 12:22 and passages in Eusebius as evidence, Jeremias suggested that the meaning of Paul's words is "wife, perhaps you may save your husband; husband, perhaps you may save your wife." It is along these lines that the REB and the NRSV ("for all you know, you might save your husband/wife") translate 1 Cor 7:15. It was along these lines that many ancient Fathers of the Church interpreted the text.[139] This was, in fact, the common interpretation of the passage until the time of Nicholas of Lyra (1270-1340).

According to the optimistic view, Paul would have suggested that a Christian wife might possibly be instrumental in leading an unbelieving husband to the faith—just as the author of the first epistle of Peter suggests[140]—and that similarly a Christian husband might lead an unbelieving wife to the faith. From this perspective, Paul's thought is a continuation of the argument which Paul had been developing in verse 14, and verse 15 is a parenthetical remark similar to the parenthetical remark found in 1 Cor 7:11ab. Christian spouses ought not to opt out of a mixed marriage, a graced situation (cf. v. 14) because there is the possibility of the conversion of the non-Christian. In other words, in verse 15 Paul is offering yet another reason[141] why Christian spouses should maintain their marital relationships with non-Christian spouses.

The Pessimistic Approach

Prior to Jeremias' study, the majority of modern commentators opted for a pessimistic approach. According to this view, Paul's words would have meant something like they appear to mean in the RSV translation: "Wife, how do you know whether you will save your husband? Husband, how do you know whether you will save your wife?"[142] A Christian husband or wife does not know whether his or her non-Christian spouse will ever become a believer. Since the hope for conversion is not necessarily well-founded the mere possibility of the spouse's conversion should not serve to coerce the Christian to remain in a marriage from which the non-Christian wishes to separate. On this approach verse 16 is to be closely linked with the verse which immediately precedes it, namely, verse 15.[143] The pessimistic approach treats 1 Cor 7:12-16 as a unit with two distinct parts, verses 12-14 and verses 15-16; the optimistic approach treats 1 Cor 7:12-16 as a single unit with a casuistic aside (v. 15).

A Mission Statement

Part of the problem faced by the interpreter who must decide between these two approaches is that the conjunction *ei*, normally meaning "if" means "whether" in indirect questions. Then, it is the context which suggests whether the question is to be understood negatively or positively. What then is the proper context for the pair of indirect questions in verse 16?

It is possible to read verse 16 optimistically and then to see it as restrictive of the "concession" expressed in verse 15. Since Christian spouses conceivably have the opportunity of bringing their spouses to the faith, they should not easily allow their Christian spouses to depart. Such an interpretation would, however, seem contrary to the injunction "let it be so" (*chôrizesthô*, v. 15b, literally, "let him/her depart"), in which the verb is imperative. Moreover, it is difficult to imagine just how a coerced marriage could contribute to a religious conversion to the Christian faith.[144]

On the other hand, one could state that verse 16 deals with the possibility of revitalizing the strained marriage relationship rather than with the religious salvation of the non-Christian spouse, as William F. Orr and James Arthur Walther have done in their Anchor Bible commentary on this passage. On their reading of the text, Paul is suggesting that, if the Christian spouse allows a non-believing partner to go in peace, there is a greater likelihood of marital reconciliation than there would have been had the separation taken place with acrimony and bitterness.[145] Not only has such a reading failed to gain the support of the commentators, but it also seems to introduce an extraneous element into the discussion which has thus far focused on divorce and the implications of religious faith for one's marriage.

On balance, it would seem that it is preferable to take verse 16—literally a statement of nescience—as do Jeremias and those who have followed his lead. In this optimistic reading, verse 16 is really a missionary statement. Its argumentation continues along the lines proposed in verse 14. Moreover there is a linguistic connection between these verses. The wife-husband (*gunê-anêr*) vocabulary of verse 16 is a reprise of the husband and wife language of verse 14. There is also a structural parallelism between the two verses insofar as both verse 14a and verse 16a are formulated from the perspective of the sanctifying-salutary influence of the believing wife, whereas verses 14b and 16b consider the matter from the standpoint of a believing husband.

A Brief Aside

Does, then, verse 16 relate to verses 12-14 in such a way that the whole of verse 15 is to be construed as a parenthetical remark?

Or should verse 15c also be considered as a Pauline reflection which refers not so much to verse 15ab as it does to verse 14?[146] There are reasons for suggesting that the latter is indeed the case. The *de* of verse 15c is a loose connective, not explicitly translated in the NRSV.[147] This is the sixth time that this connecting particle has occurred in the present context. Twice it has introduced a new section (vv. 10, 12, where it is similarly left untranslated by the NRSV), once a subsection (v. 15a, "but"), once a parenthetical remark (v. 11, "but"), and once the completion of an argument (v. 14d, "but"). In short, with the possible exception of this last instance (v. 14d), the apostle has used the particle *de* to connect fairly large semantic units with one another. Hence it is quite conceivable that the *de* of verse 15c[148] connects the latter, not with verse 15ab, with whose argumentation it would be closely linked, but with another semantic unit with which it is but loosely linked.

Verse 15c is a pregnant statement with its reference to God (*ho theos*), peace (*eirênê*), and the call of Christians (*keklêken humas*). Two of these elements, God (*ho theos*) and the call (*keklêken*), recur in verse 17a. These seem almost to form an *inclusio* encompassing verse 16.[149] "To call" is in the perfect tense, indicating a past action with implications for the present. It is unlikely that the meaning of the call (*keklêken*) would be substantially different in verse 15c from what it is in verse 17a, where the call, as explained by Paul, clearly has the implication that one remains in the social situation that one had at the time of the call.[150] Verses 15c-17a seem to further develop the exposition of the point of view which Paul had uttered in verses 12-13, with verses 17b-24 contributing a supportive aside.

Free to Marry?

It is really verse 15ab which constitutes the entire gist of Paul's remarks on the marital separation (divorce) of a Christian by a non-believing spouse. May a Christian who has been abandoned or divorced by an unbelieving spouse remarry? Despite the unequivocal statements of some commentators to the effect that Paul considers such Christians free to remarry,[151] the apostle does not explicitly answer our question.[152] As a matter of fact Paul does not even proffer an opinion about the post-separational conduct of the non-Christian. Given the then-current social circumstances, it is quite likely that a non-Christian who would have divorced his or her Christian spouse would have remarried.

As for the divorced Christian spouse, arguments from silence are always weak. The certificate of dismissal or divorce in common use among Jews[153] and Gentiles explicitly stated that the dismissed partner was free to remarry.[154] That was, in fact, the point of the certificate of dismissal, to which Deut 24:1 makes reference. Moreover, Paul does not explicitly forbid remarriage as he did in verse 11ab with regard to the case of the woman with faith who has divorced or separated from her husband.[155]

The divorced Christian becomes an *agamos,*[156] an unmarried person. Paul does not seem overly happy that people who are otherwise *agamoi,* namely, by reason of the death of their spouse, should marry, but he recognizes that they can marry and sometimes should marry (1 Cor 7:8-9, 39).[157] Paul's reluctance in this regard may be due as much to his eschatological perspective as it is due to any negative understanding of human sexuality.[158] Yet he does recognize that these *agamoi* can remarry.

Given this situation it is quite likely that Paul would have expected a Christian who became *agamos* because he or she had been divorced by an unbelieving spouse to remarry. Much to our frustration, however, Paul has not talked about his expectation. He has only expressed his wish, knowing that, in any case, God's disposition is not always according to Paul's own wish.[159]

3

The Debate

One of the most impressive of the New Testament's descriptions of Jesus' teaching on the question of divorce is the gospel narrative about a discussion which Jesus had with the Pharisees on the topic of the relevance of Scripture to Jewish practice in this regard. The discussion is described by Matthew (Matt 19:3-12) and Mark (Mark 10:2-12), but it is not to be found in Luke, nor is it to be found in the Fourth Gospel which is so unlike the Synoptics in this as in so many other regards.

Because the narrative accounts of this discussion found in Matthew and Mark bear traits that are so remarkably similar, yet have particular features that are so different, any interpretation of this discussion must take place within the context of a reflection on the entire Synoptic Problem. In fact, the parallel narratives of Matthew and Mark—along with the fact that a saying of Jesus on divorce also appears in Matt 5:32 and Luke 16:18—make of this single story almost an ideal case study for a consideration of the Synoptic Problem.

That "problem" arises from the fact that the vast majority of material found in the gospel of Mark also appears in both Matthew and Luke, while some smaller portion of it appears in only one of the two longer gospels and virtually none of it[1] is absent from both of the other Synoptic Gospels. Moreover the narrative structure, at least for the "public ministry" of Jesus, beginning with the proclamation of John the baptizer and ending with the discovery of the empty tomb by the Galilean women, is essentially the same in Matthew, Mark, and Luke. Finally there are curious expressions and features of style that are common to all three gospels.

These facts have led most scholars to conclude that there is some literary interdependence among Matthew, Mark, and Luke, and subsequently to ask what is the nature of this literary dependence. To raise that question is to pose the Synoptic Problem.[2] What is the literary relationship among Matthew, Mark, and Luke? What is the "middle term" among them? Which one best explains the origin of the others?

The matter has been debated in scholarly circles since the nineteenth century. Since then, the vast majority of scholars have concluded that Mark is the oldest of the three Synoptic Gospels and that the other two, Matthew and Luke, depend on Mark. Some scholars depart from the general scholarly consensus and continue to maintain the theory of Matthean priority, the traditional position held by Christians since the time of the early Fathers of the Church.

There are weighty reasons for suggesting that it was, in fact, the gospel of Mark which preceded the others and on which the others are dependent. Although the debate as to which of these written gospels came first may seem esoteric at first, the matter is relevant to our understanding of Jesus' teaching on divorce. If there is a literary relationship between the Matthean and Markan accounts of Jesus' discussion with the Pharisees, which came first really does make a difference. The Matthean and Markan narratives do not say exactly the same thing. Thus the question arises: did Matthew change Mark or did Mark change Matthew? And Why?

I would hold that Mark's version of the discussion was written first and that Matthew's is dependent upon it. So it is with Mark's version of the discussion of Jesus with the Pharisees that we must begin:[3]

> [2]Some Pharisees came, and to test him they asked, "is it lawful for a man to divorce his wife?" [3]He answered them, "What did Moses command you?" [4]They said, "Moses allowed a man to write a certificate of dismissal and to divorce her." [5]But Jesus said to them, "Because of your hardness of heart he wrote this

commandment for you. ⁶But from the beginning of creation, 'God made them male and female.' ⁷'For this reason a man shall leave his father and mother and be joined to his wife, ⁸and the two shall become one flesh.' So they are no longer two, but one flesh. ⁹Therefore what God has joined together, let no one separate.''

¹⁰Then in the house the disciples asked him again about this matter. ¹¹He said to them, ''Whoever divorces his wife and marries another commits adultery against her; ¹²and if she divorces her husband and marries another, she commits adultery.'' (Mark 10:2-12, NRSV).

A cursory reading of this text reveals that the Markan narrative describes two interrelated events, a discussion between Jesus and the Pharisees (Mark 10:2-9) and an instruction given by Jesus to his disciples at their prompting (Mark 10:10-12).

The Text

One who reads this narrative readily assumes that the text is simple enough to understand, even though Jesus' statement on divorce might be considered by many people today as one of Jesus' ''hard sayings.''⁴ Yet, when a reader compares this NRSV rendition of the Markan narrative with that found in other popular translations of the New Testament, he or she discovers that the modern English translations do not agree among themselves in every detail.

Gen 2:24

The NRSV's translation of Mark 10:7-8⁵ offers a version of Jesus' scriptural citation that includes the complete text of Gen 2:24. There is, however, a footnote to the effect that the words, ''and be joined to his wife,'' are omitted by other ancient authorities. The text of Genesis reads, ''Therefore a man leaves his father and his mother and cleaves to his wife, and they become one

flesh.'' Some translations of Mark 10:7-8, such as those found
in the NJB⁶ and the NAB,⁷ portray Jesus as having made use of
an elliptical version of Gen 2:24, one which omits "and cleaves
to his wife." According to these translations Jesus is quoted as
saying to the Pharisees: "This is why a man leaves his father and
mother, and the two become one flesh."⁸ Quoted in this fashion, the scriptural text seems to imply that, once their son has
departed from the parental household, a mother and father can
regain the unity which they had enjoyed during the early days of
their marriage. Now it may well be that some parents, once their
children have departed the nest, regain an experience of oneness
which they had previously experienced. Was that, however, the
thrust of Jesus' remark?

   Among the "ancient authorities" which do not contain "and
cleaves to his wife" are two fourth-century Greek-language New
Testament manuscripts, the Sinaiticus and Vaticanus codices.⁹ For
the past hundred years or so,¹⁰ textual critics have generally agreed
that these ancient manuscripts are among the best witnesses to
the text of Mark's gospel. Despite the preferential option which
textual critics generally accord to these major witnesses to the text
of Mark's gospel, the common edition of the Greek text of the
New Testament (*GNT*³-N-A²⁶) now includes the clause "and be
joined to his wife."¹¹ This longer reading is, after all, a complete
version of the Genesis text. Moreover, the longer reading is found
in Matthew's parallel rendition of Jesus' discussion with the
Pharisees.¹² Finally, the longer reading is required for the good
sense of Mark's text. In the shorter reading, the "two in one flesh"
clause grammatically relates to the parents of the husband. In
which case Jesus' quotation of Gen 2:24 would not really be pertinent to his argument.

   Scholars opine that the omission of the disputed clause from
some of the ancient manuscripts may be due to scribal error, the
result of an eye movement.¹³ Because of this possibility and the
serious arguments in favor of the longer reading, the committee
responsible for the edition of the Greek New Testament in common use today has included the disputed phrase within brackets.¹⁴
This use of brackets is reflected in the 1986 revision of the New
American Bible where the words "and be joined to his wife" are
similarly enclosed.¹⁵

Other Textual Variants

A survey of the various Greek manuscripts of Mark 10:2-12 reveals other units of textual variation. For the most part, these units of variation are stylistic. Thus some ancient manuscripts have an alternative phrasing for the introduction of the narrative, "And Pharisees came up" (v. 1). Others begin verse 5 with "and answering Jesus said" or use a qualifying "his" with the "mother" of verse 7.[16] Other alternative readings make Mark's narrative a bit more confrontational. Thus "command"[17] rather than "allowed" appears as the verb in some manuscripts of verse 4 and "God"[18] explicitly appears as the subject of the verb "made" in verse 6.[19] When both of these latter variants are found in the same manuscript,[20] a well-defined confrontation is set up between the command of Moses and the will of God.

With regard to the short instruction given by Jesus to his disciples (Mark 10:10-12), the extant manuscripts do not give as much evidence of textual variation as they do in the case of the discussion with the Pharisees (Mark 10:2-9). Nonetheless, a few manuscripts have the noun *"gunê-wife,"* instead of the pronoun *"autê-she"* as the subject of the verb "divorces" in verse 12 and some manuscripts have an alternate phrasing of "she divorces her husband and marries another," reading "she leaves her husband and marries another."[21] Some few other ancient manuscripts read the clauses of the Jesuanic logion in reverse order, thus, "if a wife divorces her husband and marries another, she commits adultery, and if a husband divorces his wife, he commits adultery."[22]

Some manual editions consider these variants to be so insignificant that they are not even cited in the critical apparatus of the text. Given the relative light weight of the evidence for an alternative reading of the Markan text in Greek and the authority of the various modern editors of that text, we can be reasonably sure of the Greek text of Mark's narrative of both Jesus's discussion with the Pharisees and his instruction of the disciples, except for the citation of Gen 2:24 in verses 7 and 8 where the variant readings remain a moot point among textual critics.

The Form of the Narrative

In assessing the import of the various narratives and sayings of Jesus preserved in the New Testament, it is important to recognize that each unit of gospel material is written according to a distinct literary type and that the literary form of one unit of material is often different from that of the next. Thus it may prove useful to probe a little bit more into the nature of the narrative which I have hitherto called Jesus' discussion with the Pharisees— a neutral description deliberately chosen so as to avoid more precise terminology which might suggest a conclusion prior to any real consideration of the issues involved.

Among the classic form-critics, Martin Dibelius identified our "discussion" as a "conversation."[23] He intimates that the original form of the tradition cannot be reconstructed, but that the present form of the narrative has been so shaped that it serves essentially to teach Christians about an issue of vital importance for the church.

Martin Albertz, on the other hand, identified the discussion as a "controversy dialogue."[24] Albertz' identification of the form of the Markan narrative was seconded by Rudolf Bultmann,[25] who took issue with some details of his predecessor's analysis but nonetheless identified the Markan story as a controversy dialogue. According to Bultmann's analysis, the controversy story is a subcategory of apophthegma, a literary form in which a pregnant saying of Jesus is set in a brief narrative context. In our case, the setting is a controversy and the saying of Jesus would be "therefore what God has joined together, let no one separate." Bultmann's form-critical analysis was essentially supported by the classic British form-critic, Vincent Taylor, who identified the discussion on divorce as a pronouncement story, that is, a short narrative in which everything is subordinated to the desire to highlight a saying of Jesus which was of interest and importance to the earliest Christian communities.[26] Bultmann, however, affirmed that disputes of this kind were typically rabbinic and they reflected discussions which the church had with its opponents or which the members of the church had among themselves on various questions of law.

All four of these classic form-critics claimed that church interests were operative in the narrative formulation of the controversy and that it was Mark who joined an originally independent logion of Jesus on divorce (Mark 10:10-12) to the discussion.[27] The implication is that it might prove quite useful to distinguish between Mark's editorial work on the tradition, his redaction, and the tradition itself. This is a matter which deserves to be pursued.

Mark the Evangelist

Since the time of these classic form-critics, scholars have generally been convinced that Mark was a truly creative author. The form-critics showed that Mark had created a literary framework, whereby he was able to join together various units of tradition which had originally circulated in relative independence of one another. They considered Mark 10:1 to be a transitional verse of Mark's own creation, and thus attributed the narrative setting of the story to the evangelist's literary artistry. Redaction critics have concentrated on the evangelist's style, his theological insights, and the situation of the community from which and for which his work was intended as contributing to the uniqueness of Mark's entire gospel, including his presentation of the issue of divorce. Finally, some more recent scholars have focused their interest on the Markan narrative as a whole, highlighting its artistry and its dramatic quality.[28]

A Writer At Work

Is it possible to discern the writer's hand at work in Mark's narrative account of the discussion and instruction on divorce (Mark 10:2-12)? Are there features of style within the narrative, perhaps even the appearance of Mark's favorite vocabulary, which allows the narrative to be typed as a Markan construction?[29]

One Markan feature of the narrative is its two-part construction: a public discourse followed by an instruction of the disciples. We find such an arrangement in Mark's narrative of the parable of the sower (Mark 4:1-9 + 10-20), the mashal on defilement

(Mark 7:14-15 + 17-23), the healing of the boy with the unclean spirit (Mark 9:14-27 + 28-29), and this narrative of Jesus' teaching about divorce (Mark 10:2-9 + 10-12).

This two-part structure, a discourse followed by an instruction, is similar to other passages in Mark's gospel where the evangelist combines two originally independent units of material. This is most evident in the use of the "sandwich arrangement." Mark combines the narrative of the encounter between Jesus and his family with a controversy on exorcisms (Mark 3:10-21, 31-35 + 22-30), the story of Jairus' daughter with that of the woman who touched his garment (Mark 5:21-24, 35-43 + 25-35), an account of the mission of the Twelve with the death of John the baptizer (Mark 6:7-13, 30 + 14-29), the cursing of the fig tree with the cleansing of the temple (Mark 11:12-14, 20-25 + 15-19), a story about the plot to kill Jesus with the anointing at Bethany (Mark 14:1-2, 10-11 + 3-9), a tale about Peter warming himself with an account of Jesus before the council (Mark 14:53-54, 66-72 + 55-65), and the description of the crucifixion with the mocking of Jesus by the soldiers (Mark 15:6-15, 21-32 + 16-20).

Another Narrative

The way in which Mark links Jesus' instruction of the disciples apropos of divorce (Mark 10:10-12) with Jesus' discussion with the Pharisees on the same topic (Mark 10:2-9) contains specific features which also betray the editor's hand at work. In Mark's gospel, a question or a statement by Jesus' disciples, as a group, frequently provides an occasion for Jesus' further instruction. This technique is employed by Mark in Mark 1:37, 4:10, 5:31, 6:35-36, 7:17, 8:4, 9:28, 10:26, 13:3; 14:12, 19[30] as well as in Mark 10:10.

Specifically we can note that in 10:10 Mark presents the disciples as asking Jesus about this matter (*peri toutou epêrôtôn auton*). "To ask" (*eperôtaô*) is one of Mark's favorite verbs. He uses it twenty-five times,[31] whereas the other New Testament authors combined use it only twenty-eight times,[32] and many of these twenty-eight instances occur in passages where Matthew and Luke have borrowed material from Mark.[33] Mark's predilection for the verb "to ask" is probably due not only to the literary demands of his gospel, with its dramatic character, but also to his characterization of Jesus as a teacher.[34] In our passage (Mark 10:1-12), Jesus' role as teacher is emphasized by the use of one of Mark's favorite adverbs, namely, "*palin*-again" in verses 1 and 10.[35] The repetition of this adverb is a typical Markan device. In verse 1, it underscores the fact that Jesus customarily taught "the crowds." In verse 10, it joins together the public teaching of Jesus with the private instruction of his disciples.[36]

The words, "the disciples asked him" (*hoi mathētai epērōtōn auton*), which belong to Mark's creative setting of the instruction to the disciples, are also found in Mark 7:17 and 9:28.[37] In these passages the clause respectively introduces Jesus' discourses on the meaning of the parable and on the inability of the disciples to perform exorcisms. In these Markan stories, as in Mark 10:10, the disciples' inquiry is situated within the house. Ample reasons exist to suggest that "the house" is also a Markan theme[38] and that it reflects the ecclesial situation of the church(es) for which the gospel according to Mark was originally intended.

Two Stories in One

These considerations make it clear that it was Mark, the creative writer, who appended the instruction of the disciples to the account of the discussion with the Pharisees on the question of divorce.[39] It should also be clear that Mark, the story teller, has created the narrative setting of the whole scene. Mark 10:1 is the work of Mark.[40] The double statement about the place of the discussion, "to the region of Jordan and beyond the Jordan," is typical of the duality recognized as a characteristic feature of Markan style.[41] The verse, moreover, forms an *inclusio* with Mark 9:35. The repetition characteristic of this stylistic device is yet another example of the way in which the Markan text is characterized by duality.[42] "Beyond the Jordan" is a Markan phrase which occurs in the Synoptic Gospels only in Mark[43] and in passages which are dependent on Mark.[44] Furthermore, Mark typically presents Jesus as a teacher and him alone as teaching.[45]

There are substantial reasons to believe that Mark has created the entire scene (Mark 10:1-12) so as to support and elucidate the teaching of Jesus on divorce contained in the saying of Mark 10:11-12. Indeed, traces of the Markan hand are dispersed throughout the entire narrative. If, with Frans Neirynck, one identifies "duality," in its various forms, as a characteristic element of Markan style, one can note "dualistic" features in each of the twelve verses of the narrative. Nine different forms of Markan duality are to be found, namely, the multiplication (in Greek) of cognate verbs (vv. 1-2), the negative and positive (vv. 8, 9), the repetition of an antecedent (v. 11), the double local situation (v. 1),[46] the repetition of the motif (vv. 2, 8, 10), a quotation with comment (vv. 6-8a, 8b-9), correspondence in discourse (vv. 2, 3, 4, 5 and 2, 11, 12), the *inclusio* (v. 1 with Mark 9:35), and parallelism in sayings (vv. 9, 11, 12).[47] Moreover, the phrase "in order to test him" (*peirazontes auton*), intimating the motivation of Jesus' opponents, appears to be quite Markan. It also occurs as an introductory phrase in the setting of a Markan scene in Mark 8:11.

It must also be noted that the entire scene is characterized by thematic unity. The question raised by the Pharisees in Mark 10:2, "is it lawful for a man to divorce his wife (*gunaika apolusai*)," is not, in fact, answered until verse 11: "whoever divorces his wife (*apolusê tên gunaika*) and marries another commits adultery against her." If the entire scene is truly one and if it is characterized by salient features of Markan style as well as by typical elements of Markan vocabulary, it is reasonable to assume that the entire pericope, Mark 10:1-12, as it presently lies before the reader, is Mark's very own composition.

Two further observations confirm that this is indeed the case. First of all, the question posed by the Pharisees, "Is it lawful for a man to divorce his wife?," (Mark 10:2) is one which would hardly come naturally to the lips of a Pharisee versed in the Scriptures—except, of course, if the Pharisees intended a direct confrontation with a teaching of Jesus which they already knew. Deut 24:1 is quite clear on the matter of divorce. This Scripture stipulated the conditions that must be fulfilled in order that a man licitly divorce his wife. The conditions are 1) that he had found some indecency in her, 2) that he write her a certificate of dismissal and put it into her hand, and 3) that he send her out of his house (and that she depart).

Among most Jews the truly moot point was apparently the first condition: the grounds for divorce. The biblical legislation was intended to restrict the arbitrary dismissal of a woman by her husband. To this end, Deut 24:1 required that there be some objective grounds warranting a husband's dismissal of a wife who no longer found favor in his eyes. Before a divorce could legitimately take place there must be "some indecency" in the wife. Scriptural scholars subsequently disputed about the interpretation of the law. What was that indecency which justified a husband's dismissal of his wife?

The last section of the Mishnaic tractate Giṭṭin ("Bills of Divorce") concludes with a classic summary of the rabbinic debate:

> The School of Shammai say: A man may not divorce his wife unless he has found unchastity in her, for it is written, *Because he hath found in her* indecency *in anything.* And the school of Hillel say: (He may divorce her) even if she spoiled a dish for him, for it is written, *Because he hath found in her indecency in* anything.[48]

Hillel the Elder was perhaps the greatest Jewish scholar of the second-temple period. He is credited with the development of the classic hermeneutical principles for the interpretation of the Scriptures. Ancient Jewish sources tell of only three controversies[49] between Hillel and Shammai the Elder, one of the principal leaders of the Sanhedrin at the time, but the sources record several differences of opinion among their disciples and the students belonging to their schools during the latter generations of the second-temple period. Those belonging to the Beth Shammai, the school of Shammai, were generally reputed to offer a more stringent interpretation of *halakah,* while those of the Beth Hillel, Hillel's disciples, proposed a more lenient interpretation. One of the classic disagreements between the adherents of these two schools was on the issue of divorce, centering on the interpretation of Deut 24:1, as is reflected in the Mishnaic summary.

Matthew was apparently aware of the disputes among the rabbis on the issue. His formulation of the test question advanced by the Pharisees is: "Is it lawful for a man to divorce his wife for any cause?" (Matt 19:3) and he offers a direct response to this question in verse 9 of his account of the debate. Mark is apparently unaware of the debate or chooses to ignore it.[50] In any event, Mark's account of Jesus' debate with the Pharisees on the issue of divorce does not seem to reflect the issue which the first-century Palestinian Pharisees debated among themselves.

The Markan narrative of the discussion between Jesus and the Pharisees ends with Jesus' climactic utterance, "Therefore what God has joined together, let no one[51] separate" (Mark 10:9). This saying, cited verbatim in Matt 19:6, does not seem to have a Palestinian provenance. Its original formulation seems to have been Hellenistic rather than Semitic.

The antithetical turn of phrase, joining and separating, upon which the sentence depends for its force, makes use of language commonly used for marriage and divorce in the Hellenistic world. Within Hellenism, words derived from the root *suzeug-* form a technical vocabulary on the subject of marriage. The verb *suzeugnumi* (literally, "to yoke together") means "to marry,"[52] and *suzeugnusthai* "to be married." *Hê suzugê*[53] is "the wife" and *suzeuxis*[54] is the marital union. *Suzugos*[55] and *suzux*[56] are adjectives meaning "wedded" or "married," and an active form of this basic adjective (*suzugios*)[57] was used as a characteristic epithet for Hera, the goddess of marriage. Finally, the verb *diazeugnusthai* means to be divorced.[58] The use of this kind of metaphor for marriage was not often reflected in extant non-Hellenistic Jewish literature,[59] even though vocabulary of this sort was commonly used in the Hellenistic world.

Within Hellenistic literature, "*chôrizô*,"[60] literally, to "divide," "separate," or "distinguish," was commonly employed of the severance of a marital relationship. In fact, *chôrizô* became almost a technical term for divorce in those writings.[61] On the other hand, the verb does not appear as a term for marital separation or divorce in the translation Greek of the Septuagint.[62]

If the *lexis,* or choice of vocabulary, in Mark 10:9 seems to suggest that it is of non-Palestinian origin, so too does its *syntaxis,* or grammatical structure. The use of the accusative relative pronoun "what" (*ho*) to introduce the first antithetical unit, reflects Hellenistic rather than Semitic construction.[63]

In sum, the language, style, and content of Mark 10:2-12 coalesce to suggest that the entire story, that is, the discussion with the Pharisees (vv. 2-9) and the instruction of the disciples (vv. 10-12) is a single unit of material that has been created by the evangelist himself. Has he created the story *ex nihilo*? Apparently not. The divorce terminology of verses 11-12 (*apoluô*) is different from that found in verse 9 (*chôrizô*). Moreover, there is an artificial juncture (v. 10) which links the instruction on divorce with the discussion on the topic. Shifts in vocabulary and artificial seams are among the classic indications that an author has made use of sources.[64] A study of Mark's account of the debate must therefore take into serious account the classic distinction between tradition and redaction.

The Literary Genre

It is, however, not enough merely to talk about tradition. From a form-critical point of view a distinction must be made between the original form of a tradition and the form which that tradition acquired during the period of its (oral) transmission by the early church, that is, prior to its incorporation into one of the written gospels.

A Conflict Story

As a matter of fact, adequate consideration must be given to three somewhat distinct situations in the transmission of any tradition, namely, the life of Jesus, the activity of the early church, and the work of the evangelist. There are three "life situations" to be studied: Jesus', the church's, and the evangelist's.[65] "Life situation"[66] is technical terminology used in respect to a sociological category. It denotes not so much a specific situation, which can be located in a determined geographic space and which took place at one particular time, as it denotes a *kind* of situation which occurs, in the concrete, in various places and at different times.[67]

Since there is a correspondence between the form and function of a text, and since the form corresponds to a specific[68] situation,[69] it may be useful to reflect further on the literary form of Mark 10:2-12. The classic form critics identified the discussion of verses 3-9 as a controversy story, pronouncement story, or rabbinic dialogue. While an analysis of Mark's account of Jesus' discussion with the Pharisees in these terms may prove useful, it may be even more useful to adopt other descriptive terminology in an attempt to obtain a useful entry for understanding the history of the tradition of Jesus' discussion with the Pharisees over the issue of divorce.

Arland J. Hultgren calls this discussion a "conflict story."[70] By doing so, he invites the reader to compare, if only implicitly, the Markan narrative on divorce with other conflict stories in the Synoptic tradition. Typical of the conflict story is its three-part narrative structure: 1) the introductory narrative, 2) the opponent's question or attack, and 3) a dominical saying.

The introductory narrative serves an editorial purpose insofar as it provides a literary link with the preceding narrative, but it also presents a setting which prepares the reader for the inevitable conflict. One of the ways in which the reader is prepared for the inevitable is that stereotypical opponents of Jesus gather to trap or test Jesus, as is the case in Mark 10:2.[71] The introductory scene identifies the nature of the narrative to come and effectively programs the reader who is led to expect a discussion of a controversial issue.

Typically, the conflict stories open with a question or an accusation directed against Jesus. Oftentimes the question is contrived, as would seem to be the case in Mark 10:2. In the narrative formulation, the law of stage duality is operative. The narrative focuses on Jesus and "his opponents" who are considered as a single entity. Jesus is in debate with only one party, never two or three.[72] Thus the narrative suggests that it features not an analysis or an academic study; rather it focuses on a situation which can only be described as confrontational.

The logion of Jesus which brings the conflict story to a close dominates the narrative. Its presence at the close of the dialogue[73] emphasizes its importance. It is, in fact, the "last word." Typically, the final word relates to Jewish law or Jewish doctrine, or it is a defense of Jesus' ministry. The saying in Mark 10:9 obviously deals with an element of Jewish law,[74] specifically, Deut 24:1, to which it is antithetically juxtaposed in the Markan story.

The narrative structure which allows Mark 10:2-9 to be described as a conflict story is a characteristic feature of ten other Markan narratives,[75] namely, the healing of the paralytic (Mark 2:1-12), Jesus' eating with sinners and tax collectors (Mark 2:15-17), the question about fasting (Mark 2:18-22), plucking grain on the Sabbath (Mark 2:23-28), the man with the withered hand (Mark 3:1-5), the Beelzebul controversy (Mark 3:22-30), the tradition of the elders (Mark 7:1-8), the question about authority (Mark 11:27-30), paying tribute to Caesar (Mark 12:13-17), and the question about the resurrection (Mark 12:18-27).[76] Of these eleven conflict stories,[77] four can be identified as unitary conflict stories.[78] The remaining seven are non-unitary conflict stories. The unitary conflict stories are distinguished by the fact that the dominical saying and the opponent's question come from the same stage of tradition.[79] The non-unitary stories are, by definition, narratives in which the adversary's question reflects a secondary construction. The questions have been composed in order to provide a setting for a dominical saying which originally circulated independently.[80]

The analysis given above[81] suggests that, as presently written, Mark 10:1-12 is a Markan creation and that neither Mark 10:9 nor Mark 10:11-12 is a direct response to the question posed in Mark 10:2. Mark 10:11, "Whoever divorces his wife and marries another commits adultery against her," seems to be an adequate response to the Pharisees' question.[82] Their question was: "is it lawful for a man to divorce his wife?" (*ei exestin andri gunaika apolusai*). This question queries about a matter of law (*exestin*) relative to divorce (*gunaika apolusai*), from the perspective of the husband (*andri*). The response given in verse 11 addresses the issue of divorce (*apolusê tên gunaika autou*) from the perspective of the husband (*hos . . . apolusê tên gunaika autou kai gamêsê allên*) and its legal consequences (*moichatai*). According to Mark's narrative, however, this pertinent remark is not addressed to the Pharisees; rather it is directed to the disciples. On the other hand, Mark 10:9, "Therefore what God has joined together, let no one separate," is addressed to the Pharisees, but its language—unlike that of Mark 10:11—is not resumptive[83] of the questioners' language.

If one identifies Mark 10:2-9 to be the basic literary unit under consideration, the climactic logion of Jesus is to be found in verse 9. If verses 2-12 (or better, vv. 1-12, my own preference) constitute the basic literary pericope, the climactic utterance is located in verses 11 and 12. In either case, the final saying of Jesus—the logion highlighted within the literary form—is not dependent on the Pharisees' question. Consequently, Mark 10:1-12 must be considered as a conflict story of the non-unitary type. The entire narrative is a Markan literary creation. Like other conflict stories of the non-unitary type, the narrative has been created out of originally independent sayings, questions, and narrative materials.[84] Can anything, then, be said with regard to its situation in life, that is, in the life of Jesus, the life of the church, and the life of the evangelist?

There can be little doubt that the specific life situation of Mark's own story is that of the community for which his gospel was intended. The narrative was composed by the evangelist as an integral part of the gospel which he was writing. We must then ask about the extent to which the Markan story reflects the life situation of Mark's own faith community, the church for which he was writing. We should also reflect on the situation of the community which might have shaped and handed on a tradition about Jesus' discussion with the Pharisees on the matter of divorce. What was this tradition's life situation in the history of the early church? What was the situation of the tradent community(ies) which shaped and formed the tradition?

First-Century Palestine

Once the form and function of the tradition about divorce in the life situation of an early Christian community have been considered, might we dare to reach beyond the life situation of the church—albeit by means of the written Markan narrative and the life situation of the church which it implies—to a life situation in the historical ministry of Jesus of Nazareth himself? At this point, the resolution of the Synoptic Problem that one adopts as a working hypothesis becomes critical in the discussion. There are authors who take issue with the position that I, along with the majority of New Testament scholars today, hold, namely, that Mark was written before Matthew and that Matthew used Mark in the composition of his own work.[85] If one takes the position that Matthew preceded Mark and that Mark made use of Matthew, then it is obvious that Matthew is the basic document to be used in any attempt to determine what might have been the kind of circumstances in Jesus' life which led Matthew, and later

Mark, to include within their respective gospels a written description of Jesus' conflict with the Pharisees on the matter of divorce.

Those who would seek to re-capture the tradition's situation in the life of Jesus on the basis of Matthew, can take some consolation in the fact that Matthew's formulation of the debate is seemingly more "Jewish" than is Mark's. The situation-setting question of the Pharisees in Matt 19:3, "Is it lawful for a man to divorce his wife for any cause?" for example, seems to represent a question that could plausibly be raised in a Palestinian Jewish milieu, whereas the parallel question in Mark, "Is it lawful for a man to divorce his wife?" would not be likely in the Palestinian setting.

The 1948 discovery of the Dead Sea Scrolls has, however, prompted some nuancing of the common assumption that Matthew's divorce narrative reflects a more Jewish setting than does Mark's. The common assumption was rooted in the idea that first-century Judaism was predominantly Judaism of a Pharisaic sort. First-century Palestinian Judaism was, however, much more diversified than most scholars writing before 1948 had been inclined to think.

With the discovery of the Qumran Temple Scroll (11 Q Temple), we have come to appreciate that even a "Pharisee could well have asked Jesus whether he sided with the majority of Judaism, which apparently allowed divorce, or with the Essenes, who clearly prohibited divorce."[86] The Qumran Temple scroll was composed at some time between the reign of John Hyrcanus and the end of the first century A.D. To a large extent it adopts a polemical point of view, particularly in its halakah, where interpretations of the Law are given that disagree with those given in extant rabbinic literature.

As far as divorce is concerned, the pertinent text is 11 Q Temple 57:17-19: "And he may not take any other woman in addition to her, but she alone shall be with him all the days of his life. And if she dies, he shall take for himself another from his father's house, from his clan."[87] The language of this passage seems to be rather polemical. It deals with a King's second marriage.

The requirement that royal marriages be endogamous is interpreted much more restrictively than it was under rabbinic halakah,[88] which required that the king marry an Israelite woman, but not necessarily one from his own clan. The ban on royal bigamy and divorce is similarly unequivocal and polemical. That the king is prohibited from taking more than one wife is in direct contradiction to rabbinic law, which allowed the king to marry as many as eighteen wives.[89] That the king may not divorce his wife and marry another seems to be based on a "tendentious" interpretation of Lev 18:18. The Essenes took the "sister" of Lev 18:18, "You shall not take a woman as a rival to her sister, uncovering her nakedness while her sister is still alive," to mean an "Israelite woman" rather than "female sibling," as it was commonly understood among the rabbis.[90] Since the king was bound to marry an Israelite, indeed, one from his own kinship, his marrying a second wife while his first was still alive would have been, under this interpretation of Lev 18:18, incestuous and therefore abhorrent to Israel.

Strictly speaking, the ban on divorce in the Temple Scroll is incumbent upon the king,[91] but it is likely that the proscription was recorded so as to exclude both polygamy and divorce from among the adherents to the sect.[92] It was not uncommon in ancient times for royal behavior and life style to serve as a model for commoners.

For some years prior to the discovery of the Temple Scroll, some scholars had suspected that the position of the Essenes was strongly opposed to divorce,[93] but they were not able to convince all the members of the academic guild that their interpretation of the available documentation was correct. In 1910, Solomon Schechter had published the *Fragments of a Zadokite Work.*[94] That text, now commonly known as the *Cairo Damascus Document,*[95] states:

> And during all those years shall Belial be let loose upon Israel as He spoke by the hand of the prophet Isaiah son of Amoz, saying: "Fear, and the pit, and the snare are upon thee, O inhabitant of the land" (Isa 24:17). Its explanation: the three nets of Belial, about which Levi son of Jacob said that he "catches in them the heart [or the house] of Israel: and has made them appear to them as three kinds of righteousness. The first is whoredom, the second is wealth, the third is conveying uncleanness to the sanctuary. He who escapes from the one is caught

in the other, and he who is rescued from the other is caught in the one. "The builders of the wall," "they that have walked after Ẓaw"[96]—the Ẓaw is a preacher, as He has said: "They shall surely preach"—are caught in two respects in whoredom:

(a) by marrying two women "in their lifetime," although the principle of nature is: "a male and a female He created them;" and those that were in the ark, "two and two they went into the ark." And about the prince it is written: "Let him not multiply wives unto himself"; but David had not read in the sealed Book of the Law which was inside the ark of the covenant, because it had not been opened in Israel since the day when Eleazar and Jehoshua [and Joshua] and the Elders died, forasmuch as they "worshipped the Ashtoreth," and it was hidden and was not revealed until the son of Zadok arose. And the deeds of David were reckoned as inadvertent sins, except the blood of Uriah, and God allowed them to him.

Also they convey uncleanness to the sanctuary, inasmuch as they do not keep separate according to the Law, but lie with her that sees "the blood of her flux."

(b) And they marry each man the daughter of his brother and the daughter of his sister, though Moses said: 'Thou shalt not approach to thy mother's sister; she is thy mother's kin,' and the rules of incest are written with reference to males and apply equally to women; hence, if the brother's daughter uncover the nakedness of her father's brother, being his kin . . ." (CD 4:12-5:11).[97]

This passage, a kind of midrash on Isa 24:17, functioned as a criticism of Judaism outside the community.[98] According to Murphy-O'Connor it was a "critique of what was commonly considered safe orthodoxy."[99] It indicates that the community disapproved of a man, even a king, having a second wife and that it had a strong aversion to incest, that is, marriage within the degrees of kinship forbidden by the Mosaic law.

Some authors have taken the Damascus Document's prohibition of a second wife to be merely a condemnation of polygamy,[100] while others considered it to be a condemnation of both polygamy and remarriage after divorce.[101] The crux of the interpreters' problem is the expression "in their lifetime" (CD 4:21). In Hebrew the expression is a single word (*bekhayehem*), with a masculine suffix.[102] Does the expression refer to a husband's lifetime or to the wife's lifetime? The discovery of the Qumran Temple Scroll, with 11 Q Temple 57:17-19, tips the interpretive scales towards the position that the wife's lifetime is meant. A king[103] may not divorce his wife so long as she lives. Hence, the majority of recent scholars believe that the Damascus Document's castigation of a man's marrying two wives reflects the prohibition of both bigamy and divorce with remarriage.[104]

Within the Bible there are no legal texts which can be cited as a warrant for a general condemnation of polygamy and divorce. Both are regulated by biblical norms while the Bible's narrative material offers evidence that both polygamy and divorce did take place within Israel.[105] The Essene community found a warrant for its halakah in a short catena of three biblical passages, Gen 1:27, Gen 7:9, and Deut 17:17. Although the prevalent Jewish ethos found support for polygamy and divorce in the Scriptures, the sectarians found in the Bible's creation story, the story of the flood, and a ban on royal polygamy[106] scriptural warrants for their own more restrictive practice.

In the Bible, the ban on royal polygamy (Deut 17:17) applies to the king (cf. Deut 17:14). In CD 5:2, it is applied to the prince. The prince is "the prince of all the congregation," a model of behavior for the entire community.[107] One should also note that at Qumran, by some sort of metonymy, the "king" is equated with the "congregation."[108] That the king should not divorce his wife or take a second simultaneously with the first had paraenetic value for the Essenes. That this is so is clear on any reading of CD 4:21-5:2. It is part of the real message of 11Q Temple 57:17-19.

By modern standards the appeal to Deut 17:17[109] as providing a scriptural warrant for the exclusion of divorce may appear a bit forced, but it is clear that the Essene community was earnestly engaged in finding appropriate scriptural warrants for its restrictive sexual practices. For example, in 11 Q Temple 66:11-17 a scriptural catena consisting of Lev 20:21, Deut 27:22, Lev 20:17, Lev 18:12-13, and Lev 20:19 is used to expand the biblical ban on incest found in Deut 23:1.[110] CD 5:9 also cites Lev 18:13, "you shall not uncover the nakedness of your mother's sister, for she is your mother's flesh," but broadens its application with the comment that "the rules of incest are written with reference to males and apply equally to women" (CD 5:9-10). The proscription of incest is clearly contrary to traditional Jewish law. The Essene community, however, expanded the traditional ban and provided an extensive scriptural apologetic in order to support the prohibition of incest. The prohibition of divorce and polygamy is, however, not to be found in the Bible. A ban on these practices is another example of the Essene community's more rigorous halakah in sexual matters. By citing the example of the king and appealing to Deut 17:17, the Essene community found both a model and a scriptural warrant for its ban on polygamy and divorce. The ban was applicable to commoners as well as to kings.[111] Deut 17:17 provided the Essenes with one scriptural warrant for their sexual rigor.[112] Gen 1:27 and Gen 7:9 were other texts which could be creatively cited as arguments in support of the community's sexual asceticism.[113]

Essenism seems to have been a sectarian phenomenon in first-century Palestine. Its rigid standards on sexual conduct, to which the Dead Sea Scrolls attest, make it impossible to affirm that the type of question which appears in Mark 10:2 was totally unthinkable in first-century Palestine. As a matter of fact, the Essenes used Gen 1:27, a text which appears in the short scriptural catena used in Mark's narrative account on divorce, as part of their own scriptural apologetic banning divorce.

The Context of the Debate

E. P. Sanders has, in fact, argued that the Synoptics' debate on divorce[114] represents Jesus' original teaching on divorce since, on intrinsic grounds, it is likely that Jesus gave a religious reason for his limitation of the practice of divorce which was both socially and religiously[115] acceptable.[116] Since the Damascus Document used Gen 1:27 as a warrant for its stringent teaching on the issue of divorce, Sanders further argues that it is quite plausible that Jesus used a scriptural argument, notably, Gen 1:27, in the exposition of his own teaching on the matter.[117]

In any study of the history of tradition of a gospel pericope, however, we must begin with the extant documentation and pay due attention to its literary form.[118] Form follows function and both correspond to a given situation in life. Mark 10:2-12 can be identified as a conflict story. What is its situation in life? To what situation in life does the literary genre of the conflict story correspond?

A New Literary Form

No obvious parallel with the Synoptic conflict stories can be found in extant Jewish or other contemporary literature of the period.[119] Accordingly, it may be suggested that their situation in life was a specifically Christian situation. The church's relationship with Judaism was a critical issue during the period when the gospel traditions were being definitively shaped.[120] Hultgren opines that even conflict stories of a unitary type, essentially more primitive than the conflict stories of a non-unitary type, provided the primitive church with a mode of expression for justifying its beliefs and practices in the face of Jewish criticism.[121] The origins of non-unitary conflict stories are to be situated in somewhat different circumstances,[122] but they generally reflect the church's own self-understanding in regard to Judaism.[123]

From Hultgren's vantage point, the conflict story of Mark 10:2-9 represents a response to questions posed by converts concerning a moral matter,[124] just as the discussion about the resurrection in Mark 12:18-27 provided converts with a response to a doctrinal question. There is, in fact, some similarity between the conflict story on divorce and the discussion on the resurrection. Both touch upon the issue of a second marriage (Mark 12:19-23; 10:11-12) and both make use of a scriptural reflection (Exod 3:6, 15-17 in Mark 12:26; Gen 1:27 in Mark 10:6- 8). Hultgren opines that both of these conflict stories originated in Hellenistic churches. Specifically, the tradition of Jesus' discussion with the Pharisees on the matter of divorce would have most likely originated as a response to the questions of Jewish converts to Christianity living in the Diaspora.[125]

Yet another conflict story in the Markan narrative which evinces notable similarities with the Markan tale of the conflict about divorce is his story of the conflict over the tradition of the elders (Mark 7:1-8). The parallels are all the more evident when Mark 7:1-8 is viewed as part of a larger narrative unit dealing with the issue of defilement (Mark 7:1-23). In both accounts, the evidence of Markan redaction is patent. Both narratives have a two-part structure, with the house motif (Mark 10:10; 7:17) serving to provide a setting for the turning point in the narrative. Both narratives highlight a Scripture and a saying of Jesus in part one, and a saying of Jesus himself in part two. In both narratives, this final saying of Jesus includes a word about adultery (Mark 10:11-12; 7:21). An in-depth analysis of Mark's narrative on the topic of defilement leads to the conclusion that the most likely setting for the discussion was that of a Hellenistic Jewish-Christian community and that the "Pharisees" principally serve as a narrative foil.[126]

Sex, Marriage and Divorce

There is indeed a very strong probability that the conflict story of Mark 10:2-9 originated in the Hellenistic church and that its function was essentially didactic.[127] Both its subject matter and its use of Scripture strongly suggest that the narrative was a didactic creation of the Hellenistic church.

First, the subject matter: marriage and divorce. In Jewish literature the claim was frequently made that Jewish morals were superior to those of Gentiles. Specifically it was claimed that Jewish views on marriage and their norms of sexual morality distinguished Jews from Gentiles. The claim is as old as the book of Leviticus which accuses the Gentiles of practicing incest and homosexuality.[128] In the Hellenistic period such a claim appeared frequently, especially in Hellenistic Jewish texts, such as the Letter of Aristeas, the Sibylline Oracles, *Joseph and Asenath,* the *Testament of Job, Pseudo-Phocylides,* and the writings of Philo and Josephus.[129] Gentiles were accused of incest, homosexuality, adultery, and consorting with prostitutes.[130] The rabbis also distinguished between Jews and Gentiles, accusing the latter of sexual immorality.[131] The talmudists prayed that God preserve the Israelites as a rural people, free from the sexual degradation of the city.[132]

Indeed, a negative judgment on the marital practices and sexual conduct of Gentiles seems to have been shared by Paul himself, trained as he was in rabbinic lore. Paul writes disparagingly of the sexual mores of Gentiles in 1 Thess 4:5. There he exhorts the Thessalonian Christians to abstain from unchastity and to live "not with lustful passion, like the Gentiles who do not know God." The lists of vices which Paul cites in Gal 5:19-21 and 1 Cor 5:9, 11; 6:9-11 are of Jewish origin.[133] They put sexual immorality at the top of the list, reflecting the common Jewish attitude towards Gentiles. In Rom 1:19-28 Paul presents sexual immorality as a consequence of idolatry and the rejection of the one God. One of his passing remarks, "immorality . . . of a kind that is not found even among pagans" (1 Cor 5:1), truly betrays Paul's regard for the sexual practices of Gentiles.

Within the early church this presumed superiority of Jewish sexual mores was problematic. To what extent could Jewish Christians expect that Gentile Christians adapt their own traditional sexual norms and practices? If Gentile Christians were to espouse the higher Jewish standards in this regard, what warrants could be cited as support for these higher ethical standards? Questions of this sort provided the context for the major discussions of sexual morality found in the New Testament.

The earliest such discussion is found in Paul's letter to the Thessalonians, 1 Thess 4:3-8.[134] The context is patently Jewish and presents the common Jewish ideal on sexuality.[135] Paul makes a sharp social distinction between insiders and outsiders,[136] that is, between those who know God[137] and those who do not. Those who know the living and true God are exhorted to maintain a standard of sexual behavior that is consistent with their status as God's sanctified people. Those who do not know God are presumed to live lasciviously. Paul's language clearly shows that the basis of his paraenesis is the Jewish ethical tradition. In the light of our present inquiry, what is particularly striking is Paul's reflection that he had already instructed these Gentile Christians in this fashion on the occasion of his missionary activity among them[138] and that the focus of his teaching is the will of God.[139]

The instruction of 1 Thess 4:3-8 is, to a large extent, paralleled in 1 Corinthians 7.[140] This entire chapter is characterized by language which sociologically distinguishes one group from another.[141] The chapter merits a thoroughgoing sociological reading.[142] Paul is obviously giving serious concern to social matters. The chief social issue which the apostle considers is marriage. His extended reflection is a response to questions raised by these neophyte Gentile Christians with regard to marriage and human sexuality.[143] The specific topics under consideration in 1 Corinthians 7 differ from those treated by Paul in his earlier letter to the Thessalonians. Nonetheless, a similarity of perspective characterizes both of these reflections on marriage and human sexuality. Among the salient common features are, in addition to the general subject matter, the authority of the Lord,[144] the manifestly theological perspective,[145] and the notion that there is a close relationship between marriage and sanctification.[146]

A third New Testament text which explicitly treats of marital and sexual matters among Gentiles is Luke's account of the so-called council of Jerusalem (Acts 15:6-29). According to the Lukan report, Gentile Christians were, by and large, exempt from the burden of the Law. They were, nonetheless, expected to observe certain minimal requirements, among which was abstinence from fornication (*porneia*). Exegetes commonly observe that in Acts 15:20 and 29 "*porneia*-fornication" is a reference to the marriages forbidden by the holiness code (Lev 18:6-18).[147] Some interpreters believe that the significance of "*porneia*-fornication" in this pericope provides a valuable clue for understanding the so-called exception clause in Matthew's version of Jesus' teaching on divorce (Matt 5:32; 19:9).[148] Even if this passage in Acts should prove not to be particularly enlightening with regard to the Matthean texts, Luke's account of the council of Jerusalem shows that Gentile Christians—at the very least, Luke himself—were aware that Jewish Christians entertained certain expectations with regard to the marital and sexual standards to be maintained by Gentile Christians and that these Jewish Christians considered that this expectation was grounded in apostolic testimony and therefore quite legitimate on their part.

The Use of Scripture

A second feature of the Markan narrative on Jesus' discussion with the Pharisees and his subsequent instruction of the disciples on the subject of divorce which points to the formation of the tradition within a Hellenistic Christian environment is its use of Scripture. In the Markan narrative, Jesus' discussion with the Pharisees revolves around the interpretation of the Scriptures. In answer to Jesus' question, "What did Moses command you?" the Pharisees respond, with obvious reference to Deut 24:1, "Moses allowed a man to write a certificate of dismissal and to divorce her." This response sets the stage for Jesus' own citation of Scripture, namely, Gen 1:27, "God made them male and female," and 2:24, "For this reason a man shall leave his father and mother and be joined to his wife, and the two shall become one flesh" (Mark 10:7-8), from which the Markan Jesus draws the pointed[149] conclusion, "What God has joined together, let no one separate" (Mark 10:9).

At first blush, the interfacing of these scriptural texts might suggest a rabbinic dialogue and point to a Palestinian provenance of the tradition cited by Mark in 10:2-9. Jesus' use of the two passages from Genesis reminds us of the hermeneutical principle that a scriptural passage never loses its plain meaning (*ein mikra yoze mi-ydei feshuto*).[150] By citing passages from Genesis, Jesus appears to have bested the Pharisees in the "debate" by referring to the order of creation, whose scriptural referents must be interpreted according to their plain meaning, regardless of any interpretation which might be brought to bear upon Deut 24:1.[151]

New Testament authors, however, are wont to adduce scriptural texts "to prove the claims"[152] of the Church. Reflection on the Christian experience in the light of the Scriptures belongs, says Barnabas Lindars, primarily to the apologetic element of early preaching.[153] It has been developed within a context of dialogue with the Jews. Thus it is hardly likely that the scriptural citations attributed to Jesus by the New Testament tradition were actually uttered by him.[154] They do not represent the *ipsissima verba Jesu,* the very words of Jesus. Rather, they express an early Christian reflection on the significance of Jesus, his mission, and his message. A critical reader of the New Testament gets the impression that Jesus did not so much appeal to specific texts of the Torah, as base his teaching upon real life situations.

These general considerations make it rather likely that the scriptural reflection found in Mark's version of Jesus' discussion with the Pharisees emanates from the early church rather than from Jesus himself.[155] Further examination of the Markan narrative provides confirmation that this was the case. The Pentateuchal texts which Mark places on the lips of Jesus are cited as if they were a continuous reading.[156] These texts are cited in Greek, as one would expect them to be in Mark's Greek narrative. The two passages are, moreover, cited exactly[157] as they appear in the Greek Bible, the Septuagint (LXX). In itself that is not surprising. There is, however, a significant difference between the Greek and Hebrew texts of Gen 2:24 and the Hebrew text, the Massoretic text, of Gen 2:24.

The Septuagint has *"hoi duo*-the two" as the subject of the verb *"esontai*-are" in Gen 2:24c, but the Masoretic text does not have an explicit subject for the verb.[158] This difference between the Greek and Hebrew texts is significant because the argumentation of Jesus seems to capitalize upon the fact that the biblical text speaks of *the two*[159] who are made one by God's action. In sum, Mark's Jesus is a Jesus who is conversant with the Greek Bible and who is able to build up a scriptural argumentation on the basis of that Greek Bible.[160] He has the allure of a Hellenistic rabbi, rather than a Palestinian one. This clearly indicates that the scriptural apologetic of Mark 10:2-9 is formulated in a Hellenistic rather than in a Palestinian context.

Mark's Line of Thought

The evangelist has taken over the tradition on divorce from the Hellenistic Christianity to which he is heir and formulated a scenario which is properly his own. He begins with a setting of the scene (Mark 10:1) which locates the "event" in the Jordan valley[161] and situates it within the context of Jesus' journey to Jerusalem which began with his departure from the region of Caesarea Philippi (Mark 8:27). Commentators frequently note that Mark was not particularly knowledgeable about the geography of Palestine. "Beyond the Jordan" is most likely Markan code for a foreign region.[162] Apart from the repeated again (*palin*),[163] there is no temporal indication in the Markan setting. The adverb "immediately" (*euthus*), a salient feature of so many earlier scenes in Mark's gospel, is absent from Mark 10:1.[164] One has the impresssion that the tempo of the narrative has changed. Instead of the urgency which characterized the earlier pericopes, the reader has the impression that Mark wants the reader to let this pericope sink in.

Again and again, Jesus taught the crowds. Significantly, the Markan setting emphasizes Jesus' customary role as a teacher: "and, as was his custom, he again taught them." "He taught them" (*edidasken autous*) comes in the emphatic position, at the end of the scene-setting sentence. In Mark's gospel, there is no other teacher but Jesus.[165] Indeed, the distinctive quality of Jesus' activity is teaching.[166] The role of Jesus as teacher of his disciples is particularly highlighted in Mark 8:27-10:45, the narrative context for our scene. Within this context,[167] Jesus is persistently identified by his role as a teacher, as one who fulfills the teaching function in striking fashion. Jesus is frequently called "teacher" (*didaskalos*)[168] and the verb "teach" (*didaskô*) is used to describe the nature of Jesus' activity.[169] The aura of Jesus the teacher pervades the entire narrative even if Jesus is not explicitly called teacher, either by the Pharisees in Mark 10:2-9 or by his disciples in Mark 10:10-12.

From this perspective Jesus' discussion with the Pharisees on the issue of divorce appears to be an object lesson for his disciples. The lesson begins with the loaded question, apparently formulated in hostile fashion: "Is it lawful for a man to divorce his wife?" (Mark 10:2).[170] Jesus responds with a counter-question, "What did Moses command you?" (Mark 10:3). This rejoinder reminds the discerning reader of the fashion in which Jesus, the complete teacher, orchestrates his instruction throughout the entire unit (Mark 8:27-10:45). Jesus' pointed questions[171] frequently set the stage for profound reflection. In short, the question of the Pharisees is but a foil for the instruction on divorce which Mark's Jesus is about to give.

The Pharisees' response to Jesus' counter-question, "Moses allowed a man to write a certificate of dismissal and to divorce her" (Mark 10:4) provides the setting for a definitive response to the initial question of verse 2, the question about the legitimacy of divorce. Jesus' response consists of 1) a reproach, "Because of your hardness of heart he wrote this commandment for you"

(Mark 10:5), 2) a scriptural proof, "For this reason a man shall leave his father and mother and be joined to his wife, and the two shall become one flesh" (Mark 10:6-8), and 3) a pointed conclusion, "therefore what God has joined together, let no one separate" (Mark 10:9).

Thereupon follows the instruction of the disciples who query Jesus about this matter (*peri toutou*). Unlike earlier sections in Mark's gospel where Jesus' disciples are portrayed as lacking in understanding, their lack of understanding with regard to this specific issue is clearly dispelled by their open question[172] and Jesus' trenchant response. The latter is characterized by its clarity and its legal precision: "Whoever divorces his wife and marries another commits adultery against her; and if she divorces her husband and marries another, she commits adultery" (Mark 10:11-12). There is no room for misunderstanding. Whoever, whether man or woman, divorces the spouse and marries another commits adultery.

A Few Remarks

The narrative has been composed by the evangelist in order to highlight Jesus' clear instruction to his disciples on the question of divorce. Before proceeding to further reflection on the Markan composition, it might prove helpful to note a few things about each of the verses that comprise the Markan text.

Verse 1

Some remarks have already been made apropos of the setting of the Markan narrative. Mark's geographical reference is admittedly vague. Nonetheless some commentators speculate that Mark may have had in mind the route to Jerusalem taken by Galilean pilgrims,[173] who would travel along the Jordan so as to avoid Samaria. In this event, it might be suggested that "the crowds" represented Galilean pilgrims. From the perspective of the entire Markan narrative, the setting of the scene in Mark 10:1 places the event within a context of Jesus' movement towards his passion in Jerusalem, but that kind of contextualization makes full sense only in the light of the entire Markan gospel.

Verse 2

In the question of the Pharisees, the term "divorce" clearly indicates the entire procedure of divorce.[174] At issue is the permissibility[175] of utilizing the procedure. The Pharisees' question[176] is provocative. Nonetheless it seems almost to suggest that they already knew about Jesus' position on divorce. Had it been a question raised during Jesus' historical lifetime, one might ask why the evangelist considers this provocative question to be a test.[177] It has been suggested[178] that the "test" brought Jesus into conflict with the Law or made him suspect in the eyes of Herod Antipas, the client king who had married his brother's wife.[179]

E. P. Sanders contends, however, that in forbidding divorce Jesus did not directly enter into conflict with Mosaic law[180]—the Law of Moses did not require anyone to divorce his wife!—even though the practice which Jesus enjoined was stricter than that permitted under the usual interpretation of the Mosaic law. Given the juridical connotation of Mark's use of "*exestin*-is lawful," it is, nonetheless, more likely that the evangelist is describing a scene in which Jesus' known position is one which apparently sets him opposite the law. His perspective is, however, that of the stance to be taken by Jesus' Hellenistic disciples vis-a-vis the prescriptions of Jewish law on divorce.

Verse 3

Jesus' counter question,[181] "What did Moses command you?" raises the discussion to the level of a consideration of the divine ordinance. Moses was the mediator of the divine Law given to Israel. God's commandments were oriented toward the well-being of his people. In addition to changing the level of discourse, Jesus' counter question suggests that he (and his disciples) had a different attitude towards divorce from that entertained by the Pharisees, the opponents of the early Christians. The introduction of "Moses" allows for a contrast between the traditions derived "from Moses" and the command of God. "*Humin*-to you" suggests a contrast between "you"[182] and "us."[183]

Verse 4

The contrast is continued in the response of the interlocutors. They have moved the discussion from a consideration of what

God has commanded (through Moses) to something that is merely permissible.[184] The contrast between the Christian position and that attributed to Judaism is transparent.[185] Moses' allowance is contrasted with God's command.

What Moses allowed was the writing of a certificate of dismissal and the divorce of the wife (*biblion apostasiou grapsai kai apolusai*). In Mark's Greek text the verbs to write (*grapsai*) and to divorce (*apolusai*)[186] are paired with one another. Both are infinitives in the aorist, signifying a specific event. The "certificate of dismissal" (*biblion apostasiou*) is a term which belongs to the legal register. It is a technical term taken over from Deut 24:1,[187] the scriptural passage to which Mark 10:4 and its parallel in Matthew (Matt 19:7) obviously refer.[188] The Mishnaic tractate *Giṭṭin* is devoted to certificates of dismissal.[189] The Mishnah states that the essential formula in the certificate of dismissal is, "Lo, thou art free to marry any man."[190]

The Deuteronomic text, "Suppose a man enters into marriage with a woman, but she does not please him because he finds something objectionable about her, and so he writes her a certificate of divorce (*biblion apostasiou,* LXX), puts it in her hand, and sends her out of his house," (Deut 24:1) was apparently an old divorce law[191] taken over by the Deuteronomist. In its immediate context within Deuteronomy (Deut 24:1-4) the prescription served as a law of purity, banning the abomination of the remarriage of a divorced and subsequently remarried woman to her first husband.

Within its broader biblical context (Deut 24:1-22) and the jurisprudence cited in the Mishnah,[192] the text served as a social statute to protect a divorced woman.[193] It restricted a husband from arbitrarily dismissing his spouse by requiring grounds for the divorce and by stipulating three formal actions which must be accomplished by the husband who divorces his wife. 1) He must prepare a document citing his wish to divorce. 2) He must personally give it to her. 3) He must formally dismiss her from his home. A man had to think twice about divorcing his wife. Not only was he enjoined from marrying her again (should she become "free" again after a second marriage); but he was also required to follow strict procedure in order to effect his divorce.

Verse 5

Mark narrates the discussion with the Pharisees in such a way as to present the Pharisees' position before Jesus' own position—the way of life to be followed by his disciples—is explained. Presumably Jesus' teaching on the matter is already known both by the Pharisees and by the readers of Mark's gospel. Verse 5 characterizes the contrary position as one which is the result of hardheartedness.

Was the Deuteronomic prescription actually due to hardheartedness or was it intended to put limits upon the actions of hardhearted men? Perhaps the answer is to be found in a Jewish tradition which suggested that the Law had been destroyed after Israel's alliance with the golden calf and that, in its stead, a more permissive version of the Law was promulgated as a concession to the people's hardheartedness.[194] Within this perspective, the "concession" of Deut 24:1-4 would have belonged to the less demanding version of the Law given to Israel.[195]

While such speculation may shed some light on the Jewish (-Christian) background of Mark's tradition, it is clear that the evangelist wishes to present the Jewish practice of resorting to a divorce procedure as the result of human obduracy. To do so, he employs the biblical term[196] *sklêrokardia,* sclerosis of the heart. From a Semitic perspective, the heart is the depth of the human person, the source of strength, intelligence, and perspective. Today we might say that someone who is hardhearted is hardened to the very core of his or her being. To be hardhearted is to have turned away from God with all the moral consequences which that entails.[197] The Markan Jesus minces no words as he passes judgment on the practice endorsed by the Pharisees.

Verses 6-8

The argumentation of these verses provides a scriptural proof for the teaching of Jesus which is about to be proclaimed in succinct fashion (v. 9). Two scriptural passages (Gen 1:17 and 2:24)[198] are cited in continuous fashion as if they formed a single Scripture. In the Markan context they constitute a single scriptural argument, the text of Gen 2:24 (vv. 7-8) being cited as if it flowed directly from Gen 1:27: "for this reason . . ." This combined scriptural argument supports the logion of verse 9, which also has God as its subject.[199]

The perspective is that of late Judaism which grounded various precepts, particularly those pertaining to marriage, in the order of creation.[200] The introductory lemma, "from the beginning of creation," sets the scene. Mark has appropriated from the wisdom tradition a classic formula, "from the beginning," which he then explicates by means of a reference to creation.[201] As used by Mark, the text of Gen 1:27 does not focus upon God's creation of sexual distinction—that is, it does not focus on the point of the scriptural passage in its biblical context—but upon the creation of one man and one woman.[202] "The two" of verse 8, appropriated from Gen 2:24 (LXX), confirms that Mark had in mind a single man and a single woman. The evangelist was not alone in using the biblical text in this fashion. In its scriptural argumentation against polygamy and divorce, the Damascus Document had cited Gen 1:27 in a similar manner: "the true basis of nature being the pairing of one male with one female, even as it is said, 'A male and a female He created them' " (CD 4:21).[203] This Qumran text is particularly significant because, as the Markan narrative does, it grounds an ethical precept in the order of creation and cites Gen 1:27 as the biblical witness to the order of creation.

Because of God's creation,[204] "a man shall leave his father and mother." In the Bible, the introductory phrase, "for this reason,"—which in Mark joins Gen 2:24 to Gen 1:27—links Gen 2:24 to the epithalamium, the bridal song which immediately precedes it: "The man said, 'This at last is bone of my bones and flesh of my flesh; this one shall be called Woman, for out of Man this one was taken.' Therefore a man leaves his father and his mother and clings to his wife, and they become one flesh" (Gen 2:23-24). "One flesh" is not so much a symbol of a new relationship as it is an expression of the physical-sexual union that brings a man and a woman together in marital union, a physical union which encompasses a personal link.[205] In Genesis, the bridal song offers an etiological motivation for sexual attraction, hence the "therefore" of verse 24. Mark, however, does not focus on the sexual distinction per se.[206] Rather, he uses Gen 2:24 to highlight the idea that (only) two have become one according to the divine ordinance.

It has already been noted that Mark's scriptural proof makes use of and is dependent on the Greek version of the biblical text.[207] The generic *anthrôpos* ("man") of the Greek text (Gen 2:24 [LXX] in Mark 10:7) prepares for the use of the same term in verse 9b, "let no one (*anthrôpos*) separate." In verse 9, the generic term presumably encompasses both the male and the female of the human species since Mark goes on to write about a man divorcing his wife and a woman divorcing her husband (vv. 11-12).

Since the Greek text used by Mark in verse 7 has rendered the Hebrew *ish* ("man") by the generic *anthrôpos* rather than by the gender-specific *anêr,* some commentators[208] have capitalized on this idiosyncratic translation to suggest that Mark has effectively defined the male and female (*arsen kai thêlu*) as man-*anthrôpos*[209] and that both husband and wife leave the parental home before being joined in their two-in-oneness. This reflection would possibly be germane if the clause "and be joined to his wife," were not part of the original text. If, however—as is likely on text-critical grounds[210]—the clause was part of the biblical text as cited by Mark, the argument is not apropos.[211]

Verse 9

"Therefore what God has joined together, let no one separate" is the "conclusion" of Jesus' scriptural argumentation. Expressed in Hellenistic idiom and formulated explicitly as a conclusion,[212] it provides the apparent response to the opening question, "is it lawful for a man to divorce his wife?" "What God has joined together" sums up Jesus' scriptural argumentation. Taking his premises from the Scriptures, the Markan Jesus had shown that God had created man and woman so that they be joined together in the unity of one flesh in marriage.

The idea that God brings husband and wife together was not foreign to late Judaism. It appears in the prayer of Tobias, "You made Adam, and for him you made his wife Eve as a helper and support" (Tob 8:6). According to the Testament of Reuben, Jacob had exhorted his son to walk in singleness of heart and expend labor on good works "until the Lord give you a wife (*suzugon*) whom he will" (*T. Reub.* 4:1). From this Jewish perspective, the separation of those who are united in a divinely ordained union would contravene the will of God.[213]

The language of Mark's summation is, however, the language of the Hellenistic world.[214] With it we enter the world of Greek rhetoric. Mark uses the verb "*sunezeuxen*-joined together," a word that belongs to the family of words typically used of marriage in the Hellenistic world and its literature.[215] Rather than using the contradictory verb, *diazeugnusthai,* as the antithesis of *suzeugnumi* in 10:9, Mark employs another technical term for divorce, the verb *chôrizô.* This was also a verb that was commonly used for divorce in the Hellenistic world,[216] including the Christian churches of the Hellenistic world.[217]

Mark uses the verb *chôrizô* in the present tense of the imperative mood: "let no one separate" what God has joined together. The prohibition is one which lasts; no one should attempt to separate[218] what God has joined together. Since God has created the marital union, no human being (*anthrôpos*) may separate (*chôrizetô*) what God has joined together. The separation of those who are united in a divinely ordained union contravenes the will of God.[219]

Whoever separates those joined together in marital union undoes what God has done and stands in opposition to God's action. The antithesis could hardly be more sharply formulated than it is in Mark 10:9. *Suzeugnumi* and *chorizein* are contrary terms. God is the subject of one and the human being (*anthrôpos*) the subject of the other. Whoever accomplishes the action which is contrary to God's own action is a contrary person. He or she (*anthrôpos*) is hard of heart.

Since, however, the language of the apparent response is different (v. 9) from the language of the question (v. 2), it would appear that Jesus' final "response" to the Pharisees (v. 9) is a logion that has been taken over from tradition and supported by a scriptural proof created ad hoc.[220]

Verse 10

The discussion between Jesus and the Pharisees over the issue of divorce is a scene which is complete in itself. In Mark's narrative, however, the account of the discussion is provided with an appendix, in the form of an instruction which Jesus gives to his disciples. The new scene—almost an aside—forms a hiatus in Mark's journey motif.[221] The resumptive "again"[222] links the instruction not only to the discussion with the Pharisees but also with the disciples' previous questions.[223] In contrast to the Pharisees who have posed a hostile question (v. 2), the disciples of Jesus petition their teacher to give them further instruction.[224]

Verses 11-12

In a pair of parallel statements, Jesus declares that whoever— man or woman—divorces the spouse and marries another commits adultery. He declares that divorce and remarriage are in formal violation of the precepts of the Decalogue.[225] Such conduct is an offense against the sixth commandment (Exod 20:14; Deut 5:18).[226] The Decalogue's prohibition of divorce takes precedence over the permission for divorce afforded by Deut 24:1.

The form of the two-part prohibition of divorce in verses 11-12 is different from the form of the saying which concluded the discussion with the Pharisees. That saying (v. 9) had the form of a sapiential warning. The two-part saying of verses 11- 12 has the form of an instruction. It neither legislates nor warns; it merely states. A person who divorces and remarries commits adultery. By putting divorce in the category of a violation of the sixth precept of the Decalogue, the Markan Jesus has effectively responded to the legal question raised in verse 2, albeit in another setting and to another audience.

The perspective of both logia, that is, verse 9 and verses 11-12, is clearly that of Hellenistic monogamy.[227] Within a polygamous culture, the divorce of one spouse is not required in order that a person marry a second wife. What Jesus' instruction of his disciples adds to the warning addressed to the Pharisees is the reflection that the divorce of one's spouse and remarriage is a violation of the commandment.

Since the emphasis of the logion lies on the divorce of one's spouse,[228] Jesus' words must not be so construed as if they commented only on the remarriage and not the divorce which proceeded it.[229] In practice, divorce often takes place precisely because a husband desires to marry another woman.[230]

While Jesus' words place divorce under the rubric of a formal violation of the Decalogue, "commits adultery *against her*" (*moichatai ep' autên*) is not a traditional legal formula. It is found nowhere in the Bible. Nor is it found in secular usage.[231]

Despite the efforts of some commentators to interpret *ep' autên* (the NRSV's "against her") as "with her," that is, the divorced man's second wife, "commits adultery against her," that is, the divorced man's first wife, really is the better interpretation of the Greek phrase.[232] "Commits adultery against her" respects the usual meaning of the preposition *epi* ("against").[233] It is also in keeping with the fact that late Jewish tradition considered the Sixth Commandment to be one which required a husband's fidelity to his wife.[234]

The Jewish interpretive tradition of this commandment, made explicit in the logion of Mark 10:11, goes beyond the purview of the ancient commandment, which had been formulated in a culture which considered adultery to be a crime committed against a husband whose wife was involved in illicit sexual intercourse with another man.[235] Mark's addition of the interpretive *"ep' autên*-against her"[236] hones the traditional logion in such a way as to portray the divorce as not only an offense against the law but also an offense against the rejected wife herself.

Verse 12 appears to be a secondary addition to the traditional logion reflected in verse 11. From a grammatical point of view, it is constructed as a conditional participial clause rather than as a conditional relative clause. Because of this lack of formal parallelism the logion of verse 12 should be considered to be a later addition to an earlier statement.[237] Moroever, from a lexical point of view, this is the only occurrence in the Synoptic tradition in which the verb "to marry" (*gamein*) has a woman for the subject and a man as the object.[238] From the historical point of view, the divorce of a husband by a wife was not generally possible within the Palestinian context in which the narrator has placed his account.[239] From the standpoint of narrative composition, it is only verse 11 which responds to the initial question of verse 3. Any additional material must be considered to be further commentary. Finally, from the Synoptic point of view, the logion is without parallel in the Matthean and Lukan accounts of Jesus' teaching on divorce. All of these factors coalesce to make it indisputable that verse 12 is a later redactional addition to the traditional logion contained in verse 11.

A Reflection

Although a modern feminist author like Elisabeth Schüssler Fiorenza believes that Mark 10:2-9 ought to be separated from Mark 10:10-12,[240] there is ample reason to suggest that Mark 10:1-12 forms a single editorial unit created by Mark.

Mark's composition consists of a narrative introduction (v. 1), a conflict story (vv. 2-9), and an instruction (vv. 10-12). By means of the scene-setter in Mark 10:1 the evangelist has created a narrative setting for his tale. In the conflict story (Mark 10:2-9), Jesus' dialogue with the Pharisees on the issue of divorce, culminates in a logion which contrasts God's ways with the ways of humans (Mark 10:9). It is likely that this incisive logion pre-existed the development of the conflict story which provides it with a narrative setting in Mark's gospel.

The conflict story offers a rationale for Jesus' prophetic warning against divorce by appealing to the will of God as expressed in the creation of man and woman. A proof from Scripture had been developed in a Hellenistic-Jewish environment to demonstrate that divorce was indeed contrary to the order of creation and the will of God. Jesus' teaching on this matter creates a social division between "us," that is, Jesus and his disciples, and "you," that is those who take issue with the Christian position, represented in the Markan narrative by the Pharisees, the traditional opponents of Christians and their way of life.

In a didactic setting, the Markan Jesus is presented as offering an interpretation of his own prophetic utterance (Mark 10:10-12). He teaches his disciples that divorce is a violation of the sixth commandment of the Decalogue. The Jewish flavor of verse 11, as well as the linguistic, syntactic, and narrative tension between it and the related logia of verses 12 and 9, suggest that verse 11 represents the traditional core of material on the basis of which Mark has created his composite narrative.

Mark has added to the traditional Jesuanic logion banning a husband's divorce of his wife an additional saying, which teaches that a woman who abandons her husband and marries another likewise commits adultery. This complementary saying was developed within a Hellenistic-Christian milieu, as was the conflict story itself. The two-part structure of the instruction is a tell-tale sign that the Markan editorial hand is at work. His two-part saying clearly stigmatizes entrance into a second marriage, after divorce, as an adulterous activity.

In sum, Mark gives his reader an expanded version (v. 12) of a traditional dominical logion (v. 11) for which he has provided not only a didactic setting (v. 10) but also an enlightening object lesson (vv. 2-9), for which he has also created an appropriate narrative setting (v. 1).

The conclusion to which our narrative reading of Mark 10:1-12 leads, namely, that Mark 10:11 is the traditional kernel of Mark's narrative, is confirmed by a Synoptic reading of the various New Testament accounts of Jesus' saying on divorce. Mark 10:11 has rather close parallels in Matt 5:32, 19:9; Luke 16:18; and 1 Cor 7:11; passages which are to be found not only in different literary sources but also in contexts which have various literary forms. In all, the Jesus of the New Testament's literary tradition proclaims a counter cultural stance.

4

The Debate Reconsidered

Since source-critical analysis of the Synoptic problem has established that the gospel of Matthew is dependent upon the gospel of Mark, one can consider Matthew's gospel to be a revised edition of the Markan text. The later evangelist, writing at some time during the late 80s,[1] reworked the Markan text for the needs of his own community. He added a prologue, the infancy narratives (Matt 1-2), and an epilogue which consisted of narratives about the appearances of the risen Jesus (Matt 28:9-20).

Matthew's reworking of the Markan text is largely reflected in the addition of a vast quantity of discourse material, the sayings of Jesus, adopted and adapted by Matthew from his Q-source and often arranged in the form of relatively long discourses (Matt 5-7, 10, 13, 18, 24-25). Matthew's editorial work is also to be seen in the use that he has made of scriptural texts, particularly in the form of fulfillment formulae, "this was to fulfill what was spoken through (one of the prophets)," but in other forms as well.

Matthew's revised edition of the Markan gospel also includes modifications of the various stories narrated by the earlier evangelist. As a result, Matthew's version of Jesus' discussion with the Pharisees on the issue of divorce reads as follows:

> [3]Some Pharisees came to him, and to test him they asked, "Is it lawful for a man to divorce his wife for any cause?" [4]He answered, "Have you not read that the one who made them at the begining 'made them male and female,' [5]and said, 'For this

reason a man shall leave his father and mother and be joined to his wife, and the two shall become one flesh'? ⁶So they are no longer two, but one flesh. Therefore what God has joined together, let no one separate." ⁷They said to him, "Why then did Moses command us to give a certificate of dismissal and to divorce her?" ⁸He said to them, "It was because you were so hardhearted that Moses allowed you to divorce your wives, but from the beginning it was not so. ⁹And I say to you, whoever divorces his wife, except for unchastity, and marries another commits adultery." (Matt 19:3-9).

The reader of this text might note that, by and large, this story of Jesus' discussion with the Pharisees is more familiar than the version found in the gospel of Mark and analyzed in the previous chapter. This familiarity is due to the fact that Matthew's gospel, presumed by tradition to have come from one of the "Twelve Disciples,"² has been the gospel most commonly used in Christendom since the end of the second century.³ Roman Catholics are particularly familiar with this gospel since it was from Matthew that, until just a few years ago, most of the gospel passages read during the Sunday Eucharistic liturgy were taken.⁴ Thus church-going believers are generally more conversant with Matthew's version of the gospel and with Matthew's version of Jesus' discussion with the Pharisees on the issue of divorce than they are with Mark's version of the same narrative.

The reader who is familiar with Matthew's gospel is certainly aware that Matthew follows up Jesus' discussion with the Pharisees on the question of divorce with a dialogue between Jesus and his disciples on a related topic. This subsequent discussion is as follows:

¹⁰His disciples said to him, "If such is the case of a man with his wife, it is better not to marry." ¹¹But he said to them, "Not everyone can accept this teaching, but only those to whom it is given. ¹²For there are eunuchs who have been so from birth, and there are eunuchs who have been made eunuchs by others, and there are eunuchs who have made themselves eunuchs for the sake of the kingdom of heaven. Let anyone accept this who can." (Matt 19:10-12).

Since Matthew's gospel is a single consistent narrative,[5] the reader of Matthew's version of Jesus' discussion with the Pharisees on the divorce issue and the follow-up discussion with the disciples in Matthew 19 is certainly aware that the evangelist had previously shown the disciples to have been specifically instructed by Jesus on the matter of divorce. Part of the Sermon on the Mount (Matt 5-7) contained this teaching on divorce:

> [31]"It was also said, 'Whoever divorces his wife, let him give her a certificate of divorce.' [32]But I say to you that anyone who divorces his wife, except on the ground of unchastity, causes her to commit adultery; and whoever marries a divorced woman commits adultery." (Matt 5:31-32).

This text will be treated in detail in a subsequent chapter of the present study, but anyone who reads Matthew's gospel as a continuous narrative is familiar with this passage of the Sermon on the Mount by the time that he or she arrives at the story of Jesus' conflict with the Pharisees in Matthew 19. Ironically, the readers know the answer to the Pharisees' question in verse 3 before any discussion takes place. Presumably Matthew's Sermon on the Mount was written before Matthew rewrote Mark's story of the conversation with the Pharisees, but Matthew was certainly aware of the Markan tale before he compiled the Sermon on the Mount.[6] In any event, the evangelist who put together the entire narrative knew that his presumed readers were already familiar with Jesus' teaching on divorce when they read his version of the discussion with the Pharisees.

Matthew's Text

Reading of the Greek text of Matthew's version of Jesus' conflict with the Pharisees on the issue of divorce (Matt 19:3-9) is somewhat more complex than is the reading of the parallel Markan narrative of the controversy (Mark 10:2-12). The twenty-sixth edition of the *Novum Testamentum Graece* records some thirteen units of variation in these seven verses. Six of these variations have merited comment in Bruce Metzger's *A Textual Commen-*

tary on the Greek New Testament.[7] Two of these six—both affecting verse 9, "whoever divorces his wife, except for unchastity, and marries another, commits adultery"—have earned a footnote in the NRSV.

These units of variation[8] can be passed quickly in review, with some brief commentary being made upon those variants which are more critical for the interpretation of the text as a whole. In Matt 19:3 there are three units of variation. In some manuscripts 1) a definite article appears before "Pharisees" and 2) a "him" after "asked." 3) The Sinaiticus and Vaticanus codices have no indirect object[9] after "lawful," but some manuscripts include "*anthrôpô*-for someone"[10] or "*andri*-for a man" after "*exestin*-is it lawful."

Verse 4

In Matt 19:4, there are two units of variation. 4) Some manuscripts read "them" after "answered" and 5) some read "*poiêsas*-the one who made" rather than "*ktisas*-the one who created."[11] The sentence which begins in verse 4 continues into verse 5 where there is one unit of variation.[12] Some manuscripts[13] have 6) the stronger *proskollêthêsetai*[14] rather than the simpler *kollêthêsetai* as the Greek verb meaning "be joined to."

Verse 6

Verse 6 admits of two units of variation. 7) Some manuscripts invert the order of the two Greek words in the expression "one flesh"[15] and 8) some add an explanatory "into one" after the verb "joined together." For the sake of greater clarity in verse 7, 9) many manuscripts have either "*autên*-her"[16] or "*tên gunaika*-the woman" as the direct object of the verb "divorce," but some manuscripts read the verb without a direct object. 10) Some manuscripts have added a clarifying "Jesus" at the beginning of verse 8 while 11) others have omitted the recitative "*hoti*-that" which serves as an introduction to the direct quotation of verse 9.

Verse 9

The final two units of variation in Matthew's version of Jesus' discussion with the Pharisees on the subject of divorce are also found in verse 9, and each of them relates significantly to the sense of the Jesuanic logion banning divorce. 12) The expression, "whoever divorces his wife, except for unchastity," admits of a variety of readings. Some ancient manuscripts include the expression *"poiei autên moicheuthênai*-causes her to commit adultery" after "unchastity." Others read *"parektos logou porneias*-except on the ground of unchastity" instead of "except for unchastity." A small group of manuscripts includes both of these variants.[17] Each of these variants is clearly the result of an assimilation with the text of Matt 5:32.

It is probable that the influence of Matt 5:32 contributed to that manuscript tradition 13) which reads *"kai ho apolelumenên gamôn moichatai*-and whoever marries a divorced woman commits adultery" as the finale of verse 9.[18] This longer reading is found in a good variety of ancient manuscripts,[19] and its omission from some may be due to the shift of the eye,[20] but the judgment of the committee responsible for the common Greek edition was that it is more probable that the disputed clause was added as an accomodation to Matt 5:32 than that it was dropped as a result of scribal carelessness.[21] The shorter reading, adopted by the editors of N-A[26], is reflected by most of the standard English-language versions of the New Testament, including the NRSV.[22] The longer reading appears, however, in the AV and the NAB.[23] A longer reading is also reflected in some manuscripts of Jerome's Vulgate.[24]

Matthew's Line of Thought

Before comparing Mark's story of Jesus' discussion with the Pharisees on the issue of divorce with Matthew's revision of it, it is important to consider Matthew's story within the context of his own gospel.

The Setting

Matthew has provided a setting for the story of the discussion, but that setting, albeit composed from Markan elements, is clearly his own. In chapter 18, Matthew had offered his readers a long instruction on community life, the fourth of five major discourses which he has compiled.[25] In Matt 19:1, the instruction is brought to a close by a typically Matthean phrase, "when Jesus had finished saying these things," which formally states that the discourse is now complete.[26] This closing formula allows the evangelist to resume his narrative,[27] interrupted, as it had been, by the discursive reflection.

The evangelist then tells us that Jesus "left Galilee and went to the region of Judea beyond the Jordan" (Matt 19:1b). The remark not only suggests a geographical shift in the activity of Jesus; it also brings the Galilean ministry of Jesus to closure. From this moment on, the element of conflict between Jesus and the Jewish religious leaders, which began to appear as a feature of the Jesus story in Matthew 9,[28] will gather intensity as Jesus goes to Jerusalem where he will suffer and meet his death. The shift is symbolized by an editorial use[29] of the verb "*metêren*-left." Jesus left Galilee, then he "went to the region of Judea beyond the Jordan." This last expression is somewhat convoluted and seems to imply that the evangelist intended to locate Jesus' subsequent activity in a part of Judea that lay within Transjordania.[30] In fact the evangelist's infelicitous turn of phrase may be the result of an attempt to portray Jesus as avoiding Samaria as he made his way towards Jerusalem.

Matthew's editorial transition from the discourse of chapter 18 to the discussion in chapter 19 includes a typical summary statement (Matt 19:2). Like other summary statements in Matthew, this one emphasizes Jesus' healing ministry.[31] The Jesus of the first gospel is a Jesus who heals. He does so in the presence of the crowds who follow him.[32] The crowds typically follow Jesus.[33] They are more open than Jesus' antagonists, but they will eventually prove to be persons without real faith. By the time that Matthew's gospel reaches its climax, their good dispositions seem to have been overcome. As the drama of the Passion unfolds, the crowds, seduced by their leaders, can no longer be characterized as curious, well-disposed onlookers. This is, however, not yet their situation as the journey to Jerusalem begins in Matt 19:1-2. According to this summary, the crowds follow after Jesus; and he performs therapeutic miracles for their benefit.

A Confrontation

The Pharisees who meet Jesus after he has entered the Judean region (Matt 19:3) are well-known to the readers of Matthew's gospel.[34] Their root trait is evilness.[35] The inherent malice of the Pharisees is evident in Matthew's description of them in 19:3. The evangelist portrays them as people who put Jesus to the test. In Matt 4:1-11 it was the devil or Satan who was the tester (*ho peirazôn*); now it is the Pharisees who are the testers (*peirazontes*).[36] The Pharisees of Matt 19:3 play the role of Satan. Like Satan they are to be engaged with Jesus in a battle of wits over the interpretation of the Scriptures, the very word of God.

The question which the Pharisees put to Jesus in verse 3 is but an expression of their testing him.[37] This question, "Is it lawful for a man to divorce his wife for any cause?" is hardly innocent. The Pharisees ask whether a man can divorce his wife for whatsoever reason he wishes.[38] Can a man do as he likes insofar as his marriage is concerned?

Some commentators are of the opinion that the question must be interpreted more narrowly, that it really means only: "Is there any reason which legitimizes a man's action in divorcing his wife?" On balance, the broader interpretation of the wily interrogation seems preferable.[39] In his paraphrase of Deut 24:1, Flavius Josephus, the first century Jewish historian and Pharisee, wrote about a man divorcing his wife "for whatsoever cause" (*kath' hasdêpotoun aitias*).[40] According to Matt 19:3, it is the very same text of Deut 24:1 that the Pharisees asked Jesus about. The law presumes that divorce is justifiable. What are the circumstances or reasons which justify divorce? Is it, as Josephus suggests, any and every reason whatsoever?

Jesus' immediate response to the Pharisees' question is a counter question: "Have you not read that the one who made them at the beginning 'made them male and female'?" What was read were the Jewish Scriptures, in which the Pharisees are presumably well-versed. Jesus quotes Gen 1:27c,[41] a citation taken from the biblical narrative about the creation of humankind. Jesus carefully situates creation "at the beginning" (*ap' archês*),[42] a phrase which recalls the language of the Jewish wisdom tradition.[43] In this rhetorical question, Jesus has defined the parameters of the discussion by moving to the interpretation of the Scriptures and offering God's primal creation as a point of reference.

A resumptive "and said" (*kai eipen*) then permits Matthew's Jesus to introduce a commentary on the text which he himself has cited.[44] The commentary consists of another scriptural quotation, namely, Gen 2:24, taken almost word-for-word from the Greek Bible: "For this reason a man shall leave his father and mother and be joined to his wife, and the two shall become one flesh." "And said" formally identifies Gen 2:24 as the word of God, a quality of the text which is not altogether apparent from the Bible itself, where the verse appears as a narrative comment in the book of Genesis.

In their biblical contexts, neither Gen 2:24 nor Gen 1:27c was truly germane to the question raised by the Pharisees. The first belonged to an etiological narrative which placed humanity at the apex of all creation; the second to an etiological narrative which proferred an explanation of the mysterious sexual drive experienced by humans. Nonetheless, the Matthean Jesus drew from these two texts a concluding reflection:[45] "so they are no longer two, but one flesh."

This conclusion serves as a premise for Jesus' halakic consideration: "Therefore what God has joined together,[46] let no one separate." A moral exhortation, a bit of paraenesis on Jesus' part, has been drawn from the scriptural summation.[47] Jesus' punch line is a forceful and challenging utterance. Humans (*anthrôpos*) are exhorted not to undo what God has done. The lines of possible conflict between Jesus and the Pharisees have been drawn with full clarity.

The discussion then moves to a new phase as the Pharisees interject a reference to the command of Moses. They are not at all content with what Jesus has to say. Jesus' prophetic challenge appears to be in opposition with Deut 24:1. So the Pharisees make reference to that Scripture which speaks of the certificate of dismissal which they describe as the commandment of Moses. Deut 24:1 has not been formally quoted, but the mention of the certificate of dismissal (*biblion apostasiou*) makes it clear that it is indeed Deut 24:1 that the Pharisees want to bring into the discussion.

Jesus' response includes both a correction and a judgment. The Pharisees spoke of the "command" of Moses (*Môuses eneteilato*), but Jesus reminds them that Moses' command was but an "allowance" (*Môuses . . . epetrepsen*[48]). Moses did not command anybody to divorce his wife; his law simply stipulated the conditions under which divorce was tolerable. Having thus clarified the terms of the discussion, Jesus qualifies the prescription of Deut 24:1 as a concession to those who are hard-of-heart (*pros tên sklêrokardian*).[49] His language recalls that of the biblical prophets who castigated God's people because of their hardheartedness.[50] There is something very Jewish about Matthew's presentation of the scenario. Not only has the Pharisees' initial question (v. 3) been posed in a manner which recalls the discussion between the schools of Hillel and Shammai about the interpretation of Deut 24:1[51]—the discussion turned on the "cause"[52] for divorce— but the entire scene also seems to affect the manner of a rabbinic disputation. Moreover, the kind of actualizing exegesis that is given in verse 8 is typical of first-century Jewish scriptural interpretation, according to which the relevance of the text to the present was the salient point in its exposition.[53] In this instance, Jesus interprets Deut 24:1 as having been formulated precisely because of his interlocutors' hardness of heart: "because you were so *hardhearted.*" Jesus observation is, moreover, to be considered within a Jewish perspective in which later, concessive precepts were given which departed from those originally handed down.[54] The perspective suggests an implicit critique of the Law.

Despite the judgment which Jesus brings to bear upon the interpretation of Deut 24:1, the evangelist does not present Moses himself as standing in opposition to God. God is the principal focus in Matt 19:4-6ba; Moses is the subject of Matt 19:7-8a. Jesus' judgment on the concession allowed by Moses (Matt 19:8a) identifies Moses as one whose concession is the means by which the Pharisees' hardheartedness is made manifest.[55]

Jesus' concluding remark, "but from the beginning it was not so," forms an *inclusio* with verse 4. The perspective continues to be the meaning of the Scriptures and God's primal will. The ring construction—"*ap' archês*-at/from the beginning" occurs in both verse 4 and verse 8—shapes verses 4-8 as a literary unit. Within this unit there are two dialogical moments, the one focusing on the significance of God's creative activity, the other focusing on the significance of the warrant for a certificate of dismissal provided by Deut 24:1. In both moments of the dialogue, Jesus is presented as an authoritative expositor of the Torah.

Jesus' Response to the Pharisees

The two-part dialogue of verses 4-8 is part of a larger narrative unit in Matthew's gospel, namely, verses 3-9. Verse 9 forms an *inclusio* with verse 3. To the Pharisees' question, "is it lawful for any reason whatsoever," Jesus responds: "No, except for unchastity." Verses 4-8 provide the scriptural background for the answer which Jesus gives to the Pharisees in verse 9, but the language of his answer echoes the language of verse 3. In both verses are to be found the words "divorce one's wife."[56] In both verses the locution about divorce is introduced by the verb *legô*, "to say:" "they asked" (*legontes*)[57] . . . I say (*legô*)."

Jesus' response to the Pharisees' devious question is unequivocal: "And I say to you, whoever divorces his wife, except for[58] unchastity, and marries another commits adultery." Although the exceptive clause may prove to be a bone of contention for later exegesis,[59] a veritable crux, Jesus' response is, in terms of Matthew's narrative, quite clear. Whoever divorces his wife commits adultery, except for one single situation, namely that of unchastity.

Matthew has clearly introduced Jesus' unambiguous reply in antithetical fashion: "And[60] I say to you" (*legô de humin hoti*). This introductory formula, sharply contrasting what Jesus says with what the Pharisees have said, is contrapuntal. It brings the pericope to closure and shapes it into a unity by means of the ring construction. What Jesus has to say recalls and responds to the Pharisees' initial question, introduced by *legontes*-saying ("asked" in the NRSV[61]). To test Jesus they "said" and Jesus responds, "I say to you." "Say-*legô*," however, appears four times in verses 3-9: "they asked . . . they said . . . he said . . . And I say to you." The presence of this kind of language characterizes the narrative passage as a real argument. Even today, " 'he said' . . . 'I said' " is the way that one describes an argument.

Matthew's shift from a third-person narrative to a first-person utterance in verse 9 is striking. The shift identifies verse 9 as both an authoritative utterance of Jesus and as the last word in the argument. The Matthean Jesus responds authoritatively to the Pharisees' question; his authoritative words also stand in tension with what they had to say in verse 7, namely, their appeal to Deut 24:1. His "I say to you" (*legô de humin*) stands over and against their "they said to him" (*legousin autô*). Jesus' authoritative response confounds the Pharisees and confuses the disciples (see vv. 10-12).

The readers of Matthew's gospel, then as now, cannot help but notice the similarity between the latter part of Matthew's description of Jesus' dialogue with the Pharisees (vv. 7-10) and the brief scriptural reflection which they had read in Matt 5:31-32. There, too, was found a contrast between Deut 24:1 and a saying of Jesus. There, too, the contrast was antithetically formulated, by means of an "I say to you." In Matt 19:9 and 5:32, the words of Jesus are virtually the same. Indeed, both passages punctuate Jesus' saying with an exception clause which concerns the matter of unchastity.

Yet the reader of Matthew's gospel will certainly recognize other things as well. An attentive reader will certainly recognize Matthew's characteristic portrayal of Jesus as the authoritative interpreter of the Law, one who gets to the heart of the matter.[62] This characterization of Jesus is clearly presented in the six antitheses (Matt 5:21-48) of Matthew's Sermon on the Mount, whose antithetical style is also reflected in Matt 19:7, 9. An attentive reader will also recognize Matthew's concern to preserve the integrity of the Scripture, yet portray a Jesus whose radical demand spells out the way of life incumbent on those who would enter the kingdom. Matt 5:17-19 proclaims the permanency of the Scriptures.[63] Matt 19:8 allows Deut 24:1 to stand, albeit relegated to the status of a tolerance for those who are hard-of-heart.[64] Finally, the reader of Matt 19:3-9 will note that Matthew's characterization of the Pharisees is consistent with the disparaging portrayal[65] of them which the evangelist has systematically developed since they were first introduced to the readers of the gospel as a brood of vipers in Matt 3:7.[66] Just like John the Baptist, Matthew's Jesus calls the Pharisees a brood of vipers (Matt 12:34; 23:33).[67] In Matt

19:9 he castigates them as being hard-hearted. In the meantime Matthew's readers have come to know the Pharisees as an evil and adulterous generation.[68] Virtually all of the commentators on Matt 19:3-9 note that the question which the Pharisees of Matt 19:3 pose to Jesus is one which was raised in rabbinic circles during the tannaitic period.[69] According to some, Matthew's formulation of Jesus' response (v. 9) to the question presents Jesus as being aligned with the Shammaite position in the great debate between the Hillelites and the Shammaites over the interpretation of Deut 24:1.[70] One must recognize the similarities between Matthew's formulation of the debate and the summary of the debate found in the Mishnah (*m. Giṭ.* 9:10), yet one ought not to be eager to assume that Jesus, during his historical ministry, was put on the spot by a group of Pharisees who tried to get Jesus to adjudicate a rabbinic dispute, thereby alienating the adherents of one or the other position.

Matthew was a creative editor. The text which he edited was the gospel according to Mark. An examination of Matthew's editorial techniques, specifically his redactional use of "the Pharisees" (*Pharisaioi*),[71] leads to the conclusion that "the Pharisees" about whom Matthew is writing really stand for the Jewish leaders with whom Matthew's own community was experiencing so much difficulty as the first century was drawing to its close and the church was experiencing the acrimony of its split from the synagogue. The tannaitic-like formulation of the question in verse 3 is not so much an indication of a question that was actually posed to the historical Jesus, as it is an indication of the type of question that was being raised in Jewish circles at the time of the composition of Matthew's gospel. The question in verse 3 reflects the circumstances in which the gospel was composed more than it serves to indicate the origin of those traditions on the basis of which Matthew composed his story about Jesus.

A Community Instruction

Matthew has appended to his version of the dispute between Jesus and the Pharisees on the matter of divorce (Matt 19:3-9) a community instruction (Matt 19:10-12) formulated for the benefit of a group of Jewish Christians.[72] The two scenes (vv. 3-9 and 10-12) are linked together insofar as both deal with community regulations, community halakah.[73] Married and unmarried members of any community live and work side by side with one another. When, therefore, Matthew turns his attention to a community regulation that deals with the situation of those who are married, it is quite natural for him to reflect as well on the situation of those who are not married.[74] Are those who are not married, people who have never been married?

The short appendage in verses 10-12 is formally presented as an instruction of Jesus' disciples. Matthew has not changed the setting of his story since Matt 19:1,[75] but he does change the characters.[76] In verse 10, Matthew introduces the disciples, the very mention of whom highlights the narrative to follow as an instruction for disciples.[77] The disciples were last mentioned in Matt 18:1, where they were introduced in a way quite similar to the way that the Pharisees were introduced in Matt 19:3.[78] They enter the story again in Matt 19:10, where they pick up on Jesus' discussion with the Pharisees and blurt out, as it were, "well then, it's better not to marry at all."

As Matthew had portrayed the Pharisees of Matt 19:3-9 with typical traits, that is, as wily and obstinate opponents of Jesus, his presentation of the disciples in verse 10 is consistent with his characterization of the disciples throughout the gospel.[79] As did the Pharisees of verse 3, the disciples play a stereotypical role in verse 10. Both groups are stock characters in Matthew's narrative. In literary terms, they are flat rather than round characters.[80] Thus the disciples understand what Jesus has said, but not quite.[81] They draw an unwarranted conclusion from what Jesus has said. As a result, Matthew's Jesus must correct their misunderstanding.[82]

The disciples' outburst is a reaction to the decisive stance taken by Jesus in verse 9. The resumptive "*houtôs*-such" of verse 10 joins the interjection of verse 10 to the prophetic utterance of verse 9 and establishes a formal link between Jesus' argument with the Pharisees (vv. 3-9) and his instruction of the disciples (vv. 10-12). The two pericopes are not juxtaposed to one another; they are joined with one another.

The language of the disciples' outburst recalls the language of the test question which the Pharisees had put to Jesus in verse 3. The key words in the protasis of the disciples' interjection, "*aitia*-case,"[83] "*anthrôpou*-man," and "*gunaikos*-wife" are the words which appear in the Pharisees' question: "*anthrôpô*-man," "*gunaika*-wife," and "*aitian*-cause." Not only does the language of verse 10 recall that of verse 3, but the wording of verse 10 also explicitly recalls verse 9, which in turn evinces verbal links with verse 3.[84] In short, both Jesus' discussion with the Pharisees and his instruction to the disciples focus on the case of the man-wife relationship.

Jesus' response to his disciples' outburst (vv. 11-12) is introduced by an antithetical *lemma*, "but he said to them" (*ho de eipen autois*), just as the climactic utterance of Jesus in verse 9 was introduced by an antithetical *lemma*, "and I say to you" (*legô de humin*).[85] From the standpoint of the narrative structure of Matthew's account, there is a real parallelism between the story of the argument and the account of the instruction. The argumentative Pharisees ask a question (v. 3) to which Jesus responds authoritatively (v. 9). The not-so-bright disciples pursue the discussion, using the same terms, and Jesus again responds authoritatively (vv. 11-12).

Jesus' response begins by speaking about the difficulty of the saying: "Not everyone can accept this teaching, but only those to whom it is given." Matthew has emphasized the difficulty of the saying, not only by stating that not all can accept it, but also by indicating that a gift of God is necessary in order that it be accepted (v. 11). The evangelist has underscored the necessity of God's gift by the use of the stylistic device called *contradictio*, "not this . . . but that." He does not so much stress the exceptional nature of the gift (that is, not given to all), but the fact that it is a gift (that is, given by God). Matthew indicates that the enabling gift is truly a gift of God by using the verb "to give" in the passive voice (*dedotai*). This is an instance of the not-uncommon use of the divine or theological passive[86] in the First Gospel.

Matthew's Jesus then proceeds to explain[87] the gift by means of an enigmatic three-part saying about eunuchs: "For there are eunuchs who have been so from birth, and there are eunuchs who have been made eunuchs by others, and there are eunuchs who have made themselves eunuchs for the sake of the kingdom of heaven'' (v. 12a-c). The topic under discussion is obviously not those who are suffering from a congenital defect which makes them incapable of marriage. Nor is it those who have castrated themselves or who have become courtiers.[88] The subject is those who are unmarried for the sake of the kingdom.[89] Thus, the REB interprets Jesus' graphic metaphor in this way: ''While some are incapable of marriage because they were born so, or were made so by men, there are others who have renounced marriage for the sake of the kingdom of Heaven.''

After this explanation of his teaching, Jesus emphasizes his challenge once again: ''Let anyone accept this who can'' (Matt 19:12d).[90] With this general hortatory remark, the evangelist brings his account to a close. Its thrust was simple enough. The Pharisees open with a question: ''Is it lawful for a man to divorce his wife for any cause?'' Jesus responds: ''I say to you, whoever divorces his wife, except for unchastity, and marries another commits adultery.'' The disciples intervene with a ''yes, but. . .'' Jesus concludes, ''Let anyone accept this who can,'' all the while assuring them that God will give them the necessary gift to do so.

Scholars debate among themselves as to the exact significance of Jesus' instruction of his disciples, with its enigmatic explanation. The crux of the matter is the determination of whether this instruction is an exhortation to celibacy for the sake of the kingdom, the traditional interpretation, or a caveat that the celibate life is to be followed only by those few to whom God has given the gift of celibacy. This is an issue well worth exploring. At the outset it must be recognized that the entire appendage is the work of Matthew's editorial hand.

Instruction of the Disciples

Since the traditional logion on divorce (Matt 19:9 = Mark 10:11) has been utilized by Matthew within his narrative account of the conversation with the Pharisees, Mark's home setting for further instruction of the disciples (Mark 10:10) has been vacated. Matthew fills the vacancy with the instruction on celibacy for the sake of the kingdom, a topos found neither in Mark nor in Luke.

A Matthean Creation

There are many factors which suggest that the entire little scene has been created by Matthew. First of all, the story and its contents are without parallel in the other Synoptic Gospels. Various linguistic and stylistic features of the account betray Matthew's editorial hand at work. Nonetheless, the narrative does evince features which suggest that the evangelist did not create the scene in some sort of tabula rasa fashion.

The basic structure of the addendum harks back to the appendix found in Mark 10:10-12, particularly insofar as Mark focuses on a private conversation between Jesus and his disciples. Their inquisitive comment and Jesus' response have been appended to a unit of material that is more or less complete in itself. Matthew has taken over the schema from Mark, but has provided his own narrative detail. The traditional details which can be found in Matt 19:10-12 have been modified by the evangelist by means of his own editorial techniques and in function of his redactional ideology.[91]

The logion of Jesus in Matt 19:12a-c does not seem to be a Matthean creation. In no other place in his gospel does the evangelist use its characteristic vocabulary, namely, the noun "eunuch" (*eunouchos*)[92] and the verb "to make a eunuch" (*eunouchizō*).[93] Moreover, since eunuchs were held in such opprobrium in Judaism,[94] it is hardly likely that Matthew would have used this kind of language as an apt metaphor for the conduct of Jesus' faithful disciples. We must conclude that Matthew has inserted into the framework of his Markan narrative an otherwise unknown but traditional saying.[95]

It is clear that the disciples' utterance in Matt 19:10 refers back to the discussion between Jesus and the Pharisees. In their astonishment the disciples draw an unwarranted conclusion[96] from what Jesus has said. Jesus' response is to put that very teaching in a new theological perspective. In verse 10, Matthew has created a transitional introduction for this teaching, expressed in rather enigmatic saying, by modifying the setting of the Markan narrative which served as his basic source text (see Mark 10:10). Matthew's editorial introduction to Jesus' explanatory teaching echoes verse 3.[97] Some of the vocabulary of verse 10 is evoked by the context (see v. 3) to which the evangelist has appended the traditional logion, but the presence of other terms in verse 10 reflects Matthew's own characteristic style and vocabulary. *Sympherei,* "it is better," is a Matthean term (Matt 5:29, 30; 18:6; 19:10),[98] one used by neither of the other Synoptists. "The disciples said to him" is likewise a Matthean turn of phrase (see Matt 13:36; 15:12; 17:19; 19:10; 24:3). "Disciples" (*mathētai*) is a word which appears more frequently in Matthew than it does in either Mark or Luke. Similarly "such" (*houtōs*) appears more frequently (33 times) in the first gospel than it does in either the second or the third. Finally, the generic use of *anthrōpos* ("man") is typical of Matthew. Matthew has, in other words, made a self-conscious effort to append the logion of verses 11-12 to the conflict story which he has just narrated. Just what does this logion mean?

The Difficult Saying

Attention must first be directed to verse 11 since Matthew clearly presents verse 12 as an explanation[99] of and therefore subservient to verse 11. The interpretation of verse 11 is, however, a moot question. The discussion turns on two issues, the referent of "this teaching" (*ton logon touton*), on the one hand, and the referent(s) of "not all[100] . . ., but only those" (*ouk pantes . . . all' hois*), on the other. There are essentially three options in the first case, and two in the second. To some extent the option chosen in one case calls for or excludes one or another possibility for the other case.

To what does "this teaching" refer?[101] Is it Jesus' teaching on divorce (v. 9)? Is it the disciples' proclamation that marriage is not useful (v. 10)? Or is it the saying about eunuchs (v. 12), the climax of Jesus' short instruction? Ecclesiastical tradition typically took the phrase as referring to the saying about eunuchs,[102] but the question is one whose answer is a subject of debate among contemporary exegetes.

According to the "traditional" interpretation, Jesus would have basically endorsed the disciples' observation, but corrected it by saying that celibacy cannot be a way of life for all people. Celibacy is only a way of life for those who embrace celibacy for the sake of the kingdom. If the Matthean Jesus were to be exhorting some members of the community to celibacy, his exhortation would be unusual, but not without some background and parallel in Jewish sources.[103] On purely grammatical grounds, however, "this saying"—a phrase which includes the demonstrative adjective *"touton* this"—must refer back to something that has already been stated.[104] Does, then, this saying refer back to the statement of the disciples, that it is better not to marry?[105] Or does it refer back to the discussion with the Pharisees on divorce, and especially to the climactic saying in Matt 19:9?

The second disputed issue concerns the "not everyone . . . but only those." Does this apparently disjunctive expression refer to some of Jesus' disciples, but not all of them, as if there were two classes of disciples, the gifted and those not gifted? Or does it refer to Jesus' disciples and the Pharisees, as if the disciples could receive Jesus' teaching, but the "Pharisees" could not? The first possibility must be excluded since the New Testament does not distinguish two classes of disciples, the ones following a less stringent way of life, the others following a more rigorous way of life for the sake of the kingdom.[106]

On the other hand, Matthew clearly distinguishes between the disciples and "them." The lines are sharply drawn in Matthew's reflective conclusion to the parable of the sower: "To you it has been given to know the secrets of the kingdom of heaven, but to them it has not been given" (Matt 13:11).[107] Thus, the reference to "not everyone" in verse 11 is a reference to Pharisees and outsiders, that is, those who are not members of Matthew's own Christian community.

To return then to our first question, there are several reasons for suggesting that the "teaching" to which Jesus' words in verse 11 refer is the difficult saying of verse 9. Were "this teaching" to refer to the disciples' utterance in verse 10, Matthew would have appended to a story whose point was fidelity in marriage an exhortation not to marry. Such a radical shift in thought between two passages that the evangelist has so carefully brought together seems quite implausible. Having presented Jesus as challenging his interlocutors to live according to the monogamous marriage which was God's purpose in creating man and woman, Matthew would then be presenting Jesus as endorsing the disciples' outburst that it is better not to marry.

In addition,[108] the role of the disciples in Matthew is such that they generally demonstrate some lack of understanding rather than some brilliant new insight into the teaching of Jesus. "The ordinary function of the disciples' speeches in the gospels," writes Quentin Quesnell, "is to ask questions, to misunderstand or object, or simply to advance the action dramatically. They do not enunciate the Christian ideal for life."[109] It would be somewhat inconsistent with the evangelist's typical characterization of the disciples, were he to introduce them in Matt 19:10 as having reached a depth of insight into the teaching of Jesus upon which Jesus has then only to offer some further clarification. The evangelist is too skilled a literary craftsman and far too consistent in his characterizations to allow either of these literary anomalies to slip into his work—especially when he has so carefully joined verses 10-12 to the preceding discussion.

In sum, normal grammatical usage, the unity of the pericope, and Matthew's characterization of the disciples combine to indicate that the difficult saying which Jesus is about to "clarify" by the enigmatic saying of verse 12 is his teaching on divorce. The disciples' lack of understanding serves as a foil for the Matthean Jesus to further elaborate on his teaching.[110] Jesus' words hardly constitute an endorsement of the disciples' all too hasty and all too human conclusion.

A Narrative Parallel

The literary skill with which the First Gospel was so evidently composed offers yet another reason for suggesting that the saying to which reference is made in verse 11 is the logion on divorce (Matt 19:9). From a formal point of view there are some general parallels between Matt 19:3-12 and Matt 19:16-26,[111] a passage which follows almost immediately after Matthew's account of Jesus' discourse on divorce:[112]

Matt 19:3-12

³Some Pharisees came to him, and to test him they asked, "Is it lawful for a man to divorce his wife for any cause?" ⁴He answered, "Have you not read that the one who made them at the beginning 'made them male and female,' ⁵and said, 'For this reason a man shall leave his father and mother and be joined to his wife, and the two shall become one flesh'? ⁶So they are no longer two, but one flesh. Therefore what God has joined together, let no one separate." ⁷They said to him, "Why then did Moses command us to give a certificate of dismissal and to divorce her?" ⁸He said to them, "It was because you were so hard-hearted that Moses allowed you to divorce your wives, but from the beginning it was not so. ⁹And I say to you, whoever divorces his wife, except for unchastity, and marries another commits adultery."

¹⁰His disciples said to him, "If such is the case of a man with his wife, it is better not to marry." ¹¹But he said to them, "Not everyone can accept this teaching, but only those to whom it is given. ¹²For there are eunuchs who have been so from birth, and there are eunuchs who have been made eunuchs by others, and there are eunuchs who have made themselves eunuchs for the sake of the kingdom of heaven. Let anyone accept this who can."

Matt 19:16-26

¹⁶Then someone came to him and said, "Teacher, what good deed must I do to have eternal life?" ¹⁷And he said to him, "Why do you ask me about what is good? There is only one who is good. If you wish to enter into life, keep the commandments." ¹⁸He said to him, "Which ones?" And Jesus said, "You shall not murder; You shall not commit adultery; You shall not steal; You shall not bear false witness; ¹⁹Honor your father and mother; also, You shall love your neighbor as yourself." ²⁰The young man said to him, "I have kept all these; what do I still lack?" ²¹Jesus said to him, "If you wish to be perfect, go, sell your possessions, and give the money to the poor, and you will have treasure in heaven; then come, follow me." ²²When the young man heard this word, he went away grieving, for he had many possessions.

²³Then Jesus said to his disciples, "Truly I tell you, it will be hard for a rich person to enter the kingdom of heaven. ²⁴Again I tell you, it is easier for a camel to go through the eye of a needle than for someone who is rich to enter the kingdom of God." ²⁵When the disciples heard this, they were greatly astounded and said, "Then who can be saved?" ²⁶But Jesus looked at them and said, "For mortals it is impossible, but for God all things are possible."

In one and the other instance an interlocutor poses a question. In each instance, Jesus' response introduces a specifically theological focus, that is, a reference to God without actually citing the divine name. In both, Jesus appeals to the Scriptures. In both, the scriptural argumentation ultimately includes an appeal to the Decalogue. In both, there is an "objection" on the part of the interlocutor (cf. Matt 19:7 and 20). In both, the objection provokes a response by Jesus which not only gets to the heart of the matter but is indeed a hard saying.[113] In both, there is a shift in the setting as the disciples are abruptly introduced (Matt 19:10 and 23), and the previous interlocutor(s) disappear from the scene. In both, the disciples have an objection, a real outburst expressing total futility (Matt 19:10 and 25). In both, there is a reference to a "*logon*-teaching/saying" (Matt 19:10 and 22). In both, Jesus uses the language of the kingdom of heaven (Matt 19:12 and 23). In both, the core of Jesus' particularized instruction is embodied in a challenging similitude (Matt 19:12 and 24). In both, Jesus' response to the disciples' objection distinguishes between humans and God and speaks of divine empowerment.

The many similarities—let alone the proximity of narrative setting—between Matt 19:16-26 and Matt 19:3-12 show that Matthew's Jesus does indeed use enigmatic language to elucidate a solemn teaching and that he speaks about God making possible what is impossible according to the normal course of human events. From this perspective it becomes quite clear that the teaching to which verse 11b refers and which receives a new theological contextualization in verses 11-12 is precisely Jesus' radical teaching on divorce.

Jesus' Explanation

Matthew has enveloped Jesus' elucidation in an *inclusio* featuring the verb "accept" (*chôreô*), a Matthean term. The enveloping framework is certainly of Matthew's own composition.[114] "*Chôreô*-accept," the verb which he highlights, does not so much mean understand with one's mind, as it means to receive into the depths of one's heart.[115] Jesus' reflection contrasts those who cannot accept this teaching, presumably the Pharisees, with those who can, presumably his disciples. In Matthew's gospel, the disciples are those who accept Jesus' teaching and live accordingly.[116] Elsewhere the evangelist contrasts the way of life of Jesus' disciples with the Pharisees.[117] The way of understanding the Scriptures within Matthew's community differs from the way that Jesus and Matthew's antagonists understand the Scriptures.[118]

In Matt 19:11, the rhetorical device of *contradictio,* which articulates a contrast and emphasizes the second member of the clause over and against the first, is used to draw attention to "those to whom it is given" (*hois dedotai*). The clause is formulated with a verb in the theological passive.[119] Not all are open to the radical teaching of Jesus on divorce, but God enables some to be open to it. A similar use of *contradictio,* with emphasis on the enabling gift of God, is found in Matt 19:26: "For mortals it is impossible, but for God all things are possible." In Matt 19:12d we read: "Let anyone accept this who can."[120] The one who can is the one to whom it is given (Matt 19:11c). Jesus' exhortation challenges his disciples to embrace a countercultural stand.

Eunuchs

From the standpoint of Matthean redaction, Matt 19:10-12 is not an independent teaching on celibacy for the sake of the kingdom which the evangelist has loosely appended to the preceding discussion on divorce. Using his literary artistry, the evangelist has quite skillfully appended the instruction for the disciples to his previous narrative precisely in order that they understand how it is possible to live according to the rigorous teaching on divorce proposed in Matt 19:9. Not all can abide that teaching; Pharisees and unbelievers continue to exist. Jesus' teaching finds a place only in the lives of his disciples: to them God gives the power to live according to the teaching of Jesus.

In creating his narrative about Jesus' dispute with the Pharisees (Matt 19:3-9), Matthew has edited a Markan story (Mark 10:1-9[12]) which Mark had created for a didactic purpose, namely, to provide an appealing theological rationale for the teaching of Jesus on divorce (Mark 10:11-12). According to Mark, Jesus' teaching is grounded in the creative will of God and has a scriptural basis.

Jesus' teaching on divorce was the "what" of the tradition. The Markan story created a "why" for that tradition. Matthew's revision of the Markan story expresses that "why" even more clearly, adding, as well, a new element to the "why," namely, the authority of Jesus the teacher.[121] Matthew then adds a "how." How can a disciple of Jesus live according to the demands of his rigorous teaching on divorce? Matthew's answer, given in the instruction to the disciples, is by means of the gift of God himself.[122]

In his important contribution to the understanding of Matt 19:10-12, the Australian exegete, Francis J. Moloney, has expressed the opinion that these verses must be understood not only within their present literary context in Matthew's gospel, but that they must also be seen from the perspective of the real-life situation of Matthew's community. Matthew's addition of the exceptive clause in verse 9 and his appendage of the eunuch saying in verses 11-12 must respond to some situation in Matthew's community. "These insertions," Moloney wrote, "must have been caused by a very *precise* situation in the Matthean Church."[123] Moloney's suggestion is that the problematic situation to which both of the Matthean literary insertions respond is a need for regulating the marital situation of newly arrived Gentile converts.

There is some merit to this suggestion. In the earliest of the New Testament writings, Paul had written to a group of Gentile converts relative to their marital situation. After recalling the previously imparted instructions, Paul concluded his exhortation with a reminder to the Thessalonian Christians that they were continually receiving the enabling gift of the Holy Spirit.[124] Matthew's appended instruction (Matt 19:10-12) makes a similar point in other words.

Thus far our analysis of Jesus' further instruction of his disciples has unabashedly proceeded from a redactional critical analysis of Matthew's gospel. It proceeds from the premise that the evangelist is a skillful editor, adept in the use of his own particular techniques for getting across the message which he wants to convey. It is the careful editor who has deliberately appended the instruction of the disciples (vv. 10-12) to the previous account of Jesus' discussion with the Pharisees on the issue of divorce. These verses should not be considered a loose appendage to the earlier discussion; they constitute a further elaboration of the teaching of verses 3 to 9.[125]

Matthew's line of reasoning is this: Jesus bans divorce: "whoever divorces his wife, except for unchastity, and marries another commits adultery." The disciples overreact: then "it is better not to marry." Jesus explains: "Not everyone can accept this teaching, but only those to whom it is given. Let anyone accept this who can." Those who can are those who are so enabled by God, that is, Jesus' disciples.

The gift may be strange, and Jesus' statement that "not everyone can accept this teaching, but only those to whom it is given" may be enigmatic, but it has earned an explanatory comment which puts everything in the light of the kingdom of heaven: "For[126] there are eunuchs who have been so from birth, and there are eunuchs who have been made eunuchs by others, and there are eunuchs who have made themselves eunuchs for the sake of the kingdom of heaven." As the series of three statements unfolds, the emphasis lies upon the third category of eunuchs, those "who have made themselves eunuchs for the sake of the kingdom of heaven."

Jacques Dupont has identified this logion as a *mashal,* a figurative statement, in which the emphasis lies on the last element in the formulation.[127] The point of the *similitude* is that there are different reasons why people do not get married; one of them has to do with the kingdom of heaven.

The first two categories of eunuchs are well known in Jewish literature. The rabbis distinguished between "the eunuch of the sun" (*seris hammah*), the eunuch by nature, and "the eunuch of man" (*seris 'adam*), the one who has been castrated.[128] For example, Rabbi Akiva said, regarding the ritual drawing off of the shoe when a man refuses to marry the childless widow of his brother, that, "if he was a man-made eunuch he submits to *halitzah*[129] and his brothers submit to *halitzah* from his wife . . .; but if he was a eunuch by nature he does not submit to *halitzah* nor do his brothers submit to *halitzah* from his wife."[130] The two categories of unmarried males known in Jewish lore are those with whom Jesus contrasts people who have made themselves eunuchs for the sake of the kingdom of heaven.[131]

A singularly important factor in the interpretation of Jesus' emphatic "there are eunuchs who have made themselves eunuchs for the sake of the kingdom of heaven" is the meaning of the expression "for the sake of the kingdom of heaven."[132] "The kingdom of heaven" (*hê basileia tôn ouranôn*) is a Matthean expression. It is found regularly and exclusively in the First Gospel, where it replaces the expression "kingdom of God" (*basileia tou theou*) found in Mark.[133] The expression, "kingdom of God" or "kingdom of heaven," generally evokes the notion of God ruling as king.[134] The kingdom of God provided Jesus with a central focus for his proclamation. He proclaimed God's reign about to break into human history in dramatic fashion. The eschatological character of "the kingdom," so central to Jesus' preaching, continues to nuance the notion of God's kingdom in the written gospels, Matthew's as well as Mark's. "Of heaven" (*tôn ouranôn*) is a periphrasis for the divine name, dutifully avoided by various pious Jews out of a sense of respect for the Transcendent One. Matthew's use of the qualifying phrase "of heaven" represents yet another instance of the re-judaizing of his gospel narrative within the context of his own Judeo-Christian community.

When Matthew wrote about the "kingdom of heaven," he was really writing about God's reign. There is, nonetheless, considerable disagreement as to the meaning of the preposition "*dia*-for the sake of" in Matt 19:12. Does this preposition have a final or a causal sense?[135] Does, in other words, the prepositional phrase indicate that some people forgo marriage in order to attain to the kingdom of God (a final sense of *dia*),[136] or does it indicate that God's reign somehow impels them to avoid marriage (a causal sense of *dia*)?

It is preferable to take *dia* in a causal sense. In common parlance, *dia* with the accusative case (Matthew's construction) was a typical way to express causality or motivation. The evangelist himself seems generally to have used *dia* (with the accusative) in a causal sense. Moreover, the parallelism between verse 11c ("those to whom it is given") and verse 12c ("and there are eunuchs who have made themselves eunuchs for the sake of the kingdom of heaven") would seem to suggest that the phrase "for the sake of the kingdom of heaven" should be taken in a causal sense.[137] Living in an unmarried fashion is not something that one does because one wants to enter the kingdom of heaven; rather, the reign of God embraced by the believer impels the one who has been divorced to live as if he had no wife. Indeed, God's gift enables him to do so.

A Matter of Sources

The source critic will undoubtedly comment that Matthew has taken the *mashal* used as an explanation in Jesus' instruction of the disciples from a source other than that used in the discussion with the Pharisees. The unusual vocabulary of verse 12[138] and the structure of the three-part eunuch saying in that verse betray the fact that the material does indeed come from a different source. Accomplished author that he is, the evangelist provides his readers with a clue that he is about to take material from another source by introducing a new set of interlocutors in verse 10. He has already used all the Markan material pertinent to the question of divorce (Mark 10:2-12) in his narrative account of the discussion with the Pharisees. He has taken elements from Mark's domestic instruction of the disciples (Mark 10:10-12) to create a setting for this adventitious material, carefully circumscribed by ring construction.

The intercalated logion is cited in a somewhat different form by Justin the Apologist, "There are eunuchs who were born so; and there are eunuchs who were made so by men; and there are eunuchs who have made themselves so for the kingdom of heaven's sake; not all however can receive this saying."[139] Since there are several discrepancies—ten in all, according to Joseph Blinzler's analysis—between Justin's version of the logion and Matthew's rendition, some scholars have concluded that Justin was not dependent upon Matthew for his version of the saying.[140] Were this to be the case, one could only conclude that the saying enjoyed an existence in early Christian tradition apart from its insertion into the written gospel of Matthew. There are, however, reasons to believe that Justin was at least generally aware of the gospel according to Matthew. He ranks it among the apostolic memoirs.[141] Whether he has taken it from Matthew's Gospel or not, the presence of the eunuch saying in Justin, where it appears as an isolable logion, indicates that the saying enjoyed some currency in the early church.

The spiraling structure of the saying in verse 12 seems to suggest a Semitic origin of the material.[142] It is hardly likely that Matthew would have chosen the crude word "eunuch" as a descriptive epithet for Christians had the *mashal* not been in the tradition known to him. Yet the *mashal* does not seem to have been associated with Jesus' saying on divorce in Matthew's tradition. It is the evangelist himself who has created the (literary) link between the discussion on divorce with the climactic logion of verse 9 and the eunuch saying of verse 12. From where did Matthew get this strange saying?

Its Situation in Life

The Semitic structure of the logion bespeaks its relative age. On the other hand, there seems little reason to suspect that the church would have chosen such a derogatory epithet as "eunuch" to describe some of the "gifted" members of the community. Hence, many scholars are convinced that the eunuch saying originated in the life situation of Jesus himself, the *Sitz-im-Leben Jesu*. To claim, as did Jerome Kodell, that "most scholars consider it original to Jesus because of the original nature of the image, the semitic structure of the declaration, and the novelty of the proposal"[143] may well be an overstatement of the case, but serious biblical scholars do make the claim that the logion originally developed during the lifetime of Jesus himself.[144]

The gospels give evidence of the fact that Jesus and his disciples were frequently subject to derisory abuse. They were accused of violating the Sabbath observance,[145] of not keeping the fast at the appointed times,[146] and of not observing the laws of ritual purity.[147] They were also the victims of blatant name-calling. Jesus himself was called a glutton and a drunkard, a friend of tax collectors and sinners,[148] a Samaritan and a demoniac.[149] It is not unlikely that "eunuch" was also a derogatory epithet hurled at Jesus.[150] The name drew attention to Jesus' unmarried status, a life style held in opprobrium by the Palestinian Jews who were contemporary with Jesus. Judaism normally expected men to marry and have a family.

In response to this kind of derision, Jesus may well have formulated the *mashal* which eventually made its way into a written gospel in Matt 19:12. The gospels give evidence of the fact that Jesus used metaphorical language as an *apologia pro vita sua*. The *mashal* in Matt 11:16-19[151] and several of the parables can be cited as examples of the way in which Jesus used figurative language for this purpose.[152] Moreover, Jesus used the symbol of the reign of God as an evaluative frame of reference for his life and work.[153] Thus it is reasonable to assume—even though the hypothesis cannot be proved beyond any reasonable doubt—that the *mashal* used by Matthew in 19:12 originally derived from Jesus himself. Memory of it may well have been preserved within Matthew's Jewish Christian community as a sort of apologia for Jesus whom the Matthean community was increasingly coming to recognize as its chief rabbi, its principal teacher in the past.

It is not altogether unusual for Matthew to have used material from the Jesus tradition, or his edited version of the Jesus tradition, in his catechetical paraenesis. One can speak of Matthew's subtle use of an *imitatio* motif. For example, a Matthean redactional addition to the tradition of the Beatitudes is Matt 5:5: "Blessed are the meek (*praus*), for they will inherit the earth." Elsewhere in the New Testament "meek-*praus*" appears (apart from 1 Pet 3:4) only in Matt 11:29 and 21:5. In these passages the evangelist uses the adjective to describe Jesus. A Matthean modification of the long beatitude on persecution is the presence of "speak evil" (*pseudomai*) in Matt 5:11.[154] "False witness" borne against Jesus is a notion that Matthew, unlike Luke who does not use the theme, has taken over from Mark 14:56-57, but for which he has used special vocabulary (*pseudomartu-*, see Matt 26:59, 60). As a third example of this phenomenon, one might note that Matt 27:32 takes over from Mark 15:21 the notion that Jesus was "compelled" (*aggareuô*) to carry his cross. In Matt 5:41 the Matthean Jesus exhorts his disciples: "if any one forces (*aggareuô*) you to go one mile, go also the second mile. These are the only three times that "*aggareuô*-compel" is used in the New Testament. Thus it appears that Matthew has subtly presented Jesus with such traits that he functions as a model for his disciples. This is, in fact, explicitly stated in Matt 11:29: "learn from me; for I am gentle and humble in heart."

In Matt 19:10-12, however, Matthew was not so much reflecting on the historical situation of Jesus as he was reflecting on the historical situation of his own community.[155] Within this context he used the traditional *mashal* in an untraditional manner in 19:12.[156] The tradition spoke of Jesus' being unmarried for the sake of the kingdom. Matthew used the tradition to support his contention that those faithful disciples of Jesus who refrain from remarriage after divorce receive divine help to live a celibate life in response to the kingdom of God which they have embraced.[157] It serves as a theological reflection on the disciple's ability to respond to the exhortation of verse 9: Let anyone accept it who is enabled to accept it.[158]

A Synoptic Reading of the Text

Matthew and Mark

Matt 19:3-12

[3]Some Pharisees came to him, and to test him they asked, "Is it lawful for a man to divorce his wife for any cause?" [4]He answered, "Have you not read that the one who made them at the begining 'made them male and female,' [5]and said, 'For this reason a man shall leave his father and mother and be joined to his wife, and the two shall become one flesh'? [6]So they are no longer two, but one flesh. Therefore what God has joined together, let no one separate." [7]They said to him, "Why then did Moses command us to give a certificate of dismissal and to divorce her?" [8]He said to them, "It was because you were so hard-hearted that Moses allowed you to divorce your wives,

Mark 10:2-12

[2]Some Pharisees came, and to test him they asked, "Is it lawful for a man to divorce his wife?" [3]He answered them, "What did Moses command you?" [4]They said, "Moses allowed a man to write a certificate of dismissal and to divorce her." [5]But Jesus said to them, "Because of your hardness of heart he wrote this commandment for you. [6]But from the beginning of creation, 'God made them male and female.' [7]For this reason a man shall leave his father and mother and be joined to his wife, [8]and the two shall become one flesh.' So they are no longer two, but one flesh. [9]Therefore what God has joined together, let no one separate.

but from the beginning it was not so. ⁹And I say to you, whoever divorces his wife, except for unchastity, and marries another commits adultery."

¹⁰His disciples said to him, "If such is the case of a man with his wife, it is better not to marry." ¹¹But he said to them, "Not everyone can accept this teaching, but only those to whom it is given. ¹²For there are eunuchs who have been so from birth, and there are eunuchs who have been made eunuchs by others, and there are eunuchs who have made themselves eunuchs for the sake of the kingdom of heaven. Let anyone accept this who can."

¹⁰Then in the house the disciples asked him again about this matter. ¹¹He said to them, "Whoever divorces his wife and marries another commits adultery against her; ¹²and if she divorces her husband and marries another, she commits adultery."

If one accepts the fact that Matthew was a creative editor as well as the idea that he worked with the gospel according to Mark as his basic document, it becomes readily apparent that Matthew's hand is at work at virtually every turn of this narrative. Each of the seven verses in Matthew's short account of the conflict between Jesus and the Pharisees shows evidence that the evangelist has carefully crafted his story on the basis of his Markan source. Some of his editorial modifications are but stylistic variants; others reflect his theological position or the actualized meaning of the text which he wants to convey to his readers.

Before entering upon a detailed comparative analysis of the two Synoptic versions of the discussion with the Pharisees (Matt 19:3-9; Mark 10:2-12), it is useful to note that Matthew has somewhat altered the format or structure of the text. Whereas Mark presents the disciples of Jesus as querying Jesus about the meaning of his ban on divorce (Mark 10:10-12),¹⁵⁹ Matthew presents the disciples as asking Jesus about another facet of the man-wife relationship (Matt 19:10-12). The result is that one can plausibly argue that Matt 19:3-9 is to be construed as the proper parallel to Mark 10:2-12 and that Matt 19:10-12 is another, but related, unit of material which Matthew has appended to the earlier material.[160]

A Rabbinic Disputation

The literary form of Matt 19:3-9 more closely resembles that of the Jewish disputation[161] than does that of Mark 10:2-12. It does not contain the instruction for the disciples which is part of the Markan narrative.[162] Matthew has highlighted the confrontational aspect of the dispute by means of his initial characterization of the Pharisees: the Pharisees are those who put Jesus to the test (v. 3).[163] The entire scenario is presumably played out before the crowds: all can see that Jesus' instruction will confront Jewish practice.

Besides changing the structure of the text and slightly modifying its setting, Matthew has introduced into his version of the narrative a number of editorial changes. Some of these differences are more apparent when the Greek text of Matthew is compared with the Greek text of Mark. It would be useful—and more accurate—to compare the two accounts according to their Greek text, but as has been the custom in this book, we will attempt to point to these differences by means of a comparison of the two texts according to the English-language version found in the NRSV. Since the present study is not principally concerned with Matthew's Greek style, it will not be necessary to examine each and every difference between Matthew's Greek text and that of Mark. The emphasis of the following Synoptic comparison will fall on those differences between Matthew and Mark that affect and effect the tenor of the Matthean text.

Verse 3 (= Mark 10:2)

Some of the differences between Matt 19:3 and Mark 10:2 are stylistic, but the variation in style betrays the evangelist's redactional interests. Matthew prefers, for example, the verb "to say" (*legō*) in place of Mark's "to ask" (*eperōtaō*), but that is typical of Matthew, editor of the Markan text.[164] On the other hand, Matthew has retained the interrogative particle *ei* even though this is not his normal usage.[165] In Matthew's version of the scene, the Pharisees' question is, in fact, a statement. It is not simply a provocative question as it is in Mark.

Matthew has placed the participle *"peirazontes*-to test" immediately after he has named the Pharisees, rather than leaving this participle until the end of the sentence. In this fashion, Matthew has qualified the Pharisees as "testers" from the very outset of his narrative. Their statement is but an expression of their putting Jesus to the test.[166] Mark highlights the Pharisees' question, whereas Matthew describes the Pharisees coming to Jesus in order to pick a fight.

In place of Mark's gender-specific *"anêr*-man," Matthew has the inclusive *"anthrôpos*-man,"[167] perhaps because of his use of the Greek text of Gen 2:24 in verse 5. The biblical text speaks of an *anthrôpos*-man leaving his father and mother and Matthew, the evangelist, has a tendency to make the language of his narrative conform to the language of the scriptural texts which he cites.[168]

Finally, Matthew has added the phrase "for any cause" (*kata pasan aitian*) to his narrative.[169] Thereby the evangelist retrieves an authentic Jewish question. Should one therefore speak of the rejudaization of this and similar narratives in Matthew's gospel, written for a Jewish Christian milieu? The addition of this phrase, however, does more than merely add an authentically Jewish tone to the narrative which Matthew is about to recount. It also prepares the way for the exception clause which he will introduce in verse 9, an exception clause with which his readers are already familiar since they have already met it in Matt 5:32.

Verse 4 (=Mark 10:3a, 6)

Matthew has transposed the citation of Gen 1:27[170] to the beginning of his account. This reference to the order of creation is unique in the entire New Testament. It defines the scope of the discussion[171] from the Matthean point of view. The "beginning" evokes the entire order of creation.[172] Matthew has taken over "the beginning" from Mark 10:6, but his placement of the term in verse 4 and the repetition of it in verse 8 (it is absent from Matthew's Markan source at this point) gives an emphasis to "the beginning" which it does not enjoy in Mark. The repetition of the term forms an *inclusio* around the entire narrative and provides a perspective for the discussion, that of God's creative will, which it does not have in its Markan version.

Not only has Matthew moved the quotation of Gen 1:27 to the beginning of his narrative, but he has also specifically identified it as a scriptural citation by means of the introductory formula, "have you not read?" (*ouk anegnôte*).[173] Mark had cited the Scripture without any specification of the subject of the verb "*epoiêsen-*made," a lacuna "corrected" within the manuscript tradition by those scribes who inserted "*ho theos*-God" into the text.[174] Matthew, however, has provided the verb with an explicit subject, "*ho ktisas*-the one who made them." More literally, Matthew's text could be rendered as "the creator, from the beginning, 'made them male and female.' " Matthew's expressed subject, an aorist participial form of the verb "*ktizô*-create," is an editorial modification of the Markan "from the beginning of creation (*ktiseôs*)." Placed at the beginning of Matthew's scriptural quotation, "creator" focuses attention on *God's act* of creation and prepares the way for what God the creator has to say about his creation (v. 5).

Matthew has, moreover, deleted from his version of the narrative the "them" (*autois*) of Mark 10:3 and 5. By so doing, the evangelist has directed Jesus' citation of the Scripture not only to the Pharisees, the characters in his narration, but also to the readers of his gospel.[175] They, like the crowds, are to learn from Jesus' scriptural reflection on the order of creation. Matthew's narrative is, at this point, clearly written for the benefit of his readers.

Verse 5 (= Mark 10:7-8a)

As did Mark, Matthew has cited Gen 2:24 according to the Greek Bible (LXX). Matthew has, however, introduced this Scripture by means of the formal introductory lemma, "and said" (*kai eipen*). This separates Gen 1:27 from Gen 2:24 which are presented in run-on fashion in Mark 10:6-8a. The separation might indicate Matthew's greater awareness of the biblical text, where the two scriptural passages belong to two different creation narratives.[176] On any reading, "and said" clearly identifies Gen 2:24 as the word of God and thus strengthens the demonstrative force of the text cited by Jesus. The Creator who created by means of his spoken word[177] has expressed his will in regard to the creation of man and woman. Man and woman have been created in order that they be joined together in one flesh, one being. The God who has created by his word has, by the same word, created the union between man and woman.

Verse 6 (= Mark 10:8b-9)

Matthew has taken over this verse verbatim from his Markan source and has retained its position in the narrative so that it retains its status as Jesus' own reflection on the import of the biblical text. This verse stands out in the Matthean narrative as the only passage in which Matthew is so faithful to his source. His only modification of the Markan text is his reversal of the order of the two words, "one flesh."[178] Matthew's Greek text represents a stylistic improvement over that of Mark insofar as the numerical adjective follows the noun which it modifies.

Verse 7 (= Mark 10:4)

The words, "a certificate of dismissal and to divorce her," with their obvious reference to Deut 24:1 ("certificate of divorce," *biblion apostasiou*) are textually the same in both Matthew and Mark. Mention is made of Moses in both narratives. The placement of the verse, however, as well as the introductory phrasing differs substantially between the Matthean and Markan narratives. On the whole, Matthew's editorial modifications tend to sharpen the confrontational aspect of the conflict story.

In the Markan story, the reference to Deut 24:1 comes from the Pharisees who respond to Jesus' question. Jesus has elicited the reference to the biblical text by asking the Pharisees about Moses' commandment (Mark 10:3). In Matthew's text, however, the Pharisees take the initiative in invoking Deut 24:1. Part of their testing, reminiscent of that of Satan, is that they hurl scriptural passages at Jesus.

Matthew's language is highly charged; it calls for a fight. To classify it according to the categories of the classical critics, one would have to say that the evangelist's language affects a grand style:[179] "they said to him, 'Why then did Moses command . . .' " At least three elements of these introductory words heighten the controversy between the Pharisees and Jesus.

First of all, "they said to him"[180] clearly puts what the Pharisees are about to say in sharp contrast with what Jesus has said. The remark to follow is, moreover, a pointed remark. It is directed to Jesus himself, not to the crowds. The presence of the pronoun "to him" (*autô*) is all the more remarkable in that Jesus' preceding remarks were not directed to any specific narrative audience.[181] Secondly, the "why then?" (*ti oun*) is clearly confrontational. It is the language of argument. The particle *oun*, "therefore," serves to strengthen the words to follow, but it often has the nuance of confirming something in contrast to that which has preceded, deemed to be not quite as well established.[182] The Pharisees' "why then?" is intended to take the wind out of Jesus' sails. Thirdly, the Pharisees contrast what Moses has commanded with what Jesus has said. There is a clear demarcation between what Jesus has taught and what Moses has commanded.

All three verbal elements heightening the tension of the confrontation are the result of Matthean redaction. "To him" (*autô*) is not found in Mark 10:4. Neither is "why then?" (*ti oun*).[183] Finally, Matthew's mention of Moses' command (*Môusês . . . eneteilato*) contrasts sharply with Mark's mention of Moses' allowance (*epistrepsen Môusês*). In fact, there is a significant difference of vocabulary between Matthew and Mark precisely on this point. Mark presents the Pharisees as saying, "Moses allowed (*epetrepsen*) a man to write a certificate of dismissal," whereas the Markan Jesus uses the language of commandment in referring to Deut 24:1: "What did Moses command (*eneteilato*) you? . . . he wrote this commandment (*entolên tautên*) for you." In the Matthean account it is the Pharisees who speak of Moses' command (but only once, in v. 7), and Jesus who speaks of Moses' allowance (but only once, in v. 8).

One should also note that whereas Mark writes of Moses' allowing a man to "write (*grapsai*) a certificate of dismissal," Matthew writes that Moses commanded that a man "give (*dounai*)

a certificate of dismissal.'' In the Matthean text, the authority
of Moses is invoked for that part of the divorce procedure that
focuses more narrowly on the divorce itself. Thus Matthew clearly
establishes that the Pharisees are in a situation of confrontation
with Jesus.

Yet the confrontation is not merely with Jesus himself. By defer-
ring the introduction of Deut 24:1 until after the creative will of
God had been formally presented in the citation of Gen 1:27 and
2:24, Matthew presents the Pharisees as being in opposition to
the spoken will of the Creator himself. Whereas in Mark, the
citation of Deut 24:1 is part of the opening dialogue between Jesus
and the Pharisees and eventually leads to Jesus' exposition of
God's creative will, Matthew exposes the Pharisees as people who
have an objection, not only to Jesus, but also to the expressed
will of the Creator.

Verse 8 (=Mark 10:5)

Matthew's version of the discussion is, at this point, a paraphrase of the elements found in his Markan source. It begins with
a formal introduction, "he said to them,"[184] which provides some
solemnity to the statement which follows. In that statement Deut
24:1 is clearly typed as a concession. Jesus says that "Moses . . .
allowed,"[185] rather than "Moses wrote (*egrapsen;* Mark 10:5)."
In addition, Mark's mention of Deut 24:1 as "this commandment" (*tēn entolēn tautēn*) is replaced by a reference to its contents: "to divorce your wives." This description of the contents
of Deut 24:1, in fact, lacks nuance. The Deuteronomic prescription did not allow—pace the liberal interpretation of the school
of Hillel—all Jewish males to divorce their wives. The generalized "to divorce your wives"[186] essentially brands all Pharisees
as individuals who are callous to the creative will of God.

In Matthew's Greek text, "because you were so hard-hearted"
(*pros tēn sklērokardian humōn*),[187] the reason for the concession
taken over verbatim from Mark 10:5, is inserted between the subject of Jesus' statement in direct address, "Moses," and its verb,
"allowed." In the Markan text this clause is found at the beginning of the logion. The net result is that in Matthew's text, more
clearly than in Mark's, Moses himself appears to have been moti-

vated by consideration of the hardness of heart of those for whom Deut 24:1 was intended. In the actualizing hermeneutic of Jesus and Matthew's era, the Pharisees themselves are the intended recipients of the lenient dispensation. Hence, it is not only Jesus, but also Moses, who qualifies them as hard of heart.

Having corrected the Pharisee's inappropriate qualification of Deut 24:1 and having judged them to be hard of heart, Matthew's Jesus contrasts the concessive legislation with God's creative will: "but from the beginning it was not so." The adversative *de* ("but") and the phrase *ap' archês* ("from the beginning") have been taken over from Mark 10:6a,[188] but are followed by a phrase that is not found in Mark, "it was not so." Matt 19:8c forms an *inclusio* with Matt 19:4. It puts the Deuteronomic legislation within the perspective of God's creative will, now reiterated by Matthew's Jesus. By so doing, Matthew emphasizes the *restitutio principii* principle more clearly than does Mark.[189] In sum, Deut 24:1 is characterized 1) as a concession, 2) which is an accomodation to hard-hearted people, and 3) is at variance with God's creative will.

Verse 9 (= Mark 10:11)

From Mark's instruction of the disciples (Mark 10:10-12), Matthew has borrowed only the first part of Jesus' two-part saying on divorce (Mark 10:11). Undoubtedly he has dropped the second part of the logion, dealing with the case of a woman divorcing her husband, because that situation would not have been germane to the socio-religious condition of the Jewish Christians for whom his gospel was intended.[190] Indeed, there is consistency on this point between Matt 19:9 and Matt 5:32 which likewise speaks only from the perspective of the man.[191]

Confrontation with the Pharisees

Besides restricting the Jesuanic logion to that portion of it which concerns a divorcing husband, Matthew has changed the setting of the logion. In Mark's gospel the logion on divorce is given to the disciples back in the house and in response to the disciples' question (Mark 10:10). It is, therefore, conveyed in the form of a private teaching for the disciples. In Matt 19:9, however, the logion on divorce is presented as being specifically addressed to the Pharisees ("I say *to you*"). Narratively addressed to the Pharisees, the saying of Jesus (Matt 19:9) is, nonetheless, presumably uttered in the presence of the crowds.[192]

Me Against You

From the standpoint of Matthew's narration, the phrase "to you" of verse 9 continues the confrontational stance adopted since verse 7. He portrays an "I versus you" situation. Four pronouns in the second person plural are placed on Jesus' lips by the Matthew who composed verses 8-9: "It was because *you* were so hardhearted that Moses allowed *you* to divorce *your* wives. . . . And I say to *you* . . ."[193] Matthew further sharpens the confrontation by introducing the Jesuanic logion of verse 9 with the emphatic "And I say to you" in place of Mark's third person narrative "but Jesus said to them" (Mark 10:5). In Matt 19:9 the authority of Jesus is presented as sharply antithetical to that invoked by the Pharisees. He rejects out of hand the self-serving interpretation of Deut 24:1 that their question (verse 3) had supposed and presents the teaching of Jesus as being antithetical to the commandment of Moses,[194] as understood by the Pharisees.

A Similar Situation

Matthew's understanding of the Pharisees' interpretation of the Law, so clearly expressed in this discussion with the Pharisees, is also found in Matthew's rendition of Jesus' discussion with the Pharisees on the issue of defilement (Matt 15:1-9). Matthew has also taken this story over from his Markan source (see Mark 7:1-16) and modified it to suits his own editorial needs. Both Matthew's version of the discussion about divorce and his version of the discussion on defilement are narratives written in the form of conflict stories.[195] In both, the Pharisees approach[196] Jesus with a question that pertains to Jewish praxis. In both, there is a scriptural reflection, Isa 29:13 in Matt 15:8-9, Gen 1:27 and 2:24 in

Matt 19:4-5.

An antithetical style characterizes both accounts. In both accounts the Jewish praxis is presented as contrary to the very word of God,[197] rather than to a commandment of Moses.[198] In both accounts a sharp distinction is made between a commandment (Matt 15:3; 19:8) and another authoritative form—an allowance in the case of Matt 19:8, tradition in the case of Matt 15:2, 6. In both accounts the praxis is specifically presented as contrary to a precept of the Decalogue,[199] the fourth commandment, "honor your father and your mother" in Matt 15:4[200] and the sixth commandment, "you shall not commit adultery," in Matt 19:9.[201]

In both accounts the use of the pronoun in the second person plural highlights the second part of the narrative,[202] as the pitch reaches its most confrontational stage. In both accounts, Jesus calls the Pharisees names,—"hypocrites" in Matt 15:7[203] and "hard-hearted" in Matt 19:8—and in both accounts the derogatory epithet receives grammatical emphasis in the Matthean text. In both Matthean accounts, the conflict is apparently, albeit not with explicit narrative mention, played out in the presence of the crowds. Matthew adds to both accounts a reflection directed to the disciples: Matt 15:12-14[204] and Matt 19:10-12. In both Matthean narratives the clarification given by Jesus has to do with his word (*ton logon;* Matt 19:10 and 15:12).

Matthew's version of Jesus' conflict with the Pharisees in regard to defilement is much more coherent and logical than is Mark's.[205] Matthew has aggravated the conflict with the Pharisees,[206] presumably in function of his own community's conflict with the religious leaders of the emerging Jewish establishment. Matthew's narration (Matt 15:1-9 [-20]) not only provides a warrant for a community whose praxis is no longer bound by the tradition of the ancients,[207] it also shows that the Jewish praxis is in violation of the divine command and therefore contrary to God's stated will. A similar motivation, apparent in similar literary techniques and theological argumentation, seems to be the leitmotif of his revision of Jesus' discussion with the Pharisees on the issue of divorce in Matt 19:3-9 (-12).

The Jesuanic Logion

The saying of Jesus in Matt 19:9, "And I say to you, whoever divorces his wife, except for unchastity, and marries another commits adultery," differs from that of its Markan counterpart (Mark 10:11-12) not only by reason of its single thrust and its modified, more confrontational introductory lemma, but also because of the presence of an exceptive clause, "except for unchastity" (*mê epi porneia*), not found in Matthew's Markan source, and the absence of the Markan "against her" (*ep' autên*).

The latter phrase is not found in any versions of Jesus' logion on divorce except Mark 10:11. In its Markan context that phrase is both problematic[208] and innovative. It is, however, part of the Markan text. Matthew, carefully reworking his Markan source, has eliminated the phrase. There is no reason to think that Matthew disagreed with the thrust of its meaning. Indeed, on the basis of Matt 5:27-28 one might proffer the conjecture that the later evangelist would have been in full agreement with Mark. Nevertheless, he has deleted the qualifying phrase from his version of the Jesuanic logion. Why?

By itself, Matthew's tendency to rejudaize[209] the Markan narrative would not sufficiently explain Matthew's deletion of the phrase, "against her." Contemporary Jewish authorities were already speaking about fidelity to one's wife as a quality of a righteous marriage.[210] Rather, a case can be made that it was Matthew's theory of the Decalogue[211] which led to his deletion of the Markan phrase.

It is well known that the Decalogue circulated independently in first-century Judaism[212] and that the Decalogue served the needs of rabbinic catechesis.[213] The evangelist was aware of this use of the Decalogue. He employed the ten commandments as a paradigm for some of the paraenetic elements of his gospel. This is apparent in the great antitheses of the Sermon on the Mount (Matt 5:21-48) and Matthew's reworking of a traditional catalogue of vices in Matt 15:19.[214] While Matt 19:9 does not include a formal citation of the Decalogue, it does make clear allusion to the sixth commandment (Deut 5:18 = Exod 20:14). Elsewhere, Matthew evinces a tendency to make the language of his own text conform to the language of the Greek Bible.[215] It is quite likely that this tendency is also operative in the formulation of the wording of Matt 19:9 from which the evangelist has dropped the "against her" (*ep' autên*), not found in the biblical sixth commandment of the Decalogue.

By adding "*mê epi porneia*-except for unchastity" to the saying of Jesus, Matthew stands over and against the unanimity of other New Testament witness to a saying of Jesus on this subject (Mark 10:11; Luke 16:18; 1 Cor 7:11). He is, however, in agreement with his own previous formulation of that saying (Matt 5:32). The language in which the exception is phrased in Matt 19:9, "*mê epi porneia*-except for unchastity," is, however, different from that of Matt 5:32, "*parektos logou porneias*-except on the ground of unchastity." The grounds for the exception are, nonetheless, the same, namely, "*porneia*-unchastity."

The exception clause found in Matt 19:9 is clearly the product of Matthean redaction.[216] It does not appear in any of the non-Matthean parallel versions of the logion, but it is found in *both* Matthean versions of Jesus' saying on divorce. That the exception appears in both of Matthew's versions of the saying is even more striking when one considers that the two pericopes in which it appears have different literary forms. Matthew's consistency in this regard is quite characteristic of the evangelist, a meticulous redactor who edits his sources with considerable care.[217]

The *lexis* of Matthew's exception is not, however, entirely typical of the evangelist. "*Porneia*-unchastity" appears in Matthew's gospel only in the two exception phrases and in Matt 15:19, where it has been taken over from Mark 7:21.[218] There it appears alongside of "*moicheia*-adultery."[219] The expression "*mê epi*-except" is hapax in Matthew, as is the "*parektos*-except" formulation of Matt 5:32.[220]

Scholars debate among themselves as to the precise import of the Matthean "exception." That issue will be pursued later on in the present study.[221] For the present, it must be noted that the exception is, on the one hand, an editorial insertion on the part of the evangelist and that, on the other hand and from a narrative point of view, it truly responds to the question posed by the Pharisees in verse 3.[222] They asked whether there was any cause which justified a man's action in divorcing his wife; Jesus answers "no" except for unchastity. On a surface reading of the text it would appear that the exception entertained by Matthew's school is adultery.[223] In which case, Matthew's Jesus would appear to be siding with the school of Shammai's less lenient interpretation of Deut 24:1.[224]

The entire Matthean composition (Matt 19:3-12) is a unit of community instruction—Joachim Gnilka calls it "community halakah"[225]—which Matthew has reformulated on the basis of a Markan source. His version of the discussion with the Pharisees and the instruction of the disciples which is appended to it gives to Jesus' teaching on divorce a sharper definition than it had in the Markan text, even if Matthew wrote only about a *man* who divorces his wife. Matthew teaches, furthermore, that God himself will enable Jesus' faithful disciples to abide by the demands of Jesus' radical interpretation of the Decalogue.

There remains, however, the crucial question. What exactly did Matthew mean when he wrote, "whoever divorces his wife, *except for unchastity,* and marries another, commits adultery." To answer that question, we must consider another passage in Matthew's gospel—one already known to the readers of the gospel before they arrive at Matthew's revised version of the tale about Jesus' discussion with the Pharisees over the issue of divorce. That passage is the third of the great antitheses of Matthew's Sermon on the Mount (Matt 5:31-32).

5

An Old Saying

Those who read Matthew's version of Jesus' discussion with the Pharisees on the topic of divorce inevitably experience something of a déjà vu feeling. They inevitably recall that Matthew had previously provided his readers with a more succinct version of Jesus' teaching on divorce (Matt 5:31-32). It appeared in the Sermon on the Mount (Matt 5:1-8:1) as part of a series of passages in which Jesus was contrasting what had been said to the ancients with his own teaching (Matt 5:21-48). This earlier version of Jesus' teaching on divorce shares with the later version (Matt 19:9) a solemn, antithetical introduction, "But I say to you," and the problematic exception clause, "except for unchastity." These two features are so striking in their similarity that, unless one is careful to compare Matthew's divorce texts with one another, the reader of Matthew's gospel might be inclined to think that what is presented as the teaching of Jesus in Matt 19:9 is exactly the same as what is presented as his teaching in Matt 5:32, but that is not the case.

This earlier Matthean version of Jesus' teaching on divorce reads as follows:

> [31]"It was also said, 'Whoever divorces his wife, let him give her a certificate of divorce.' [32]But I say to you that anyone who divorces his wife, except on the ground of unchastity, causes her to commit adultery; and whoever marries a divorced woman commits adultery."

Matthew's Text

Since Jesus' teaching on divorce is found in five different places in the New Testament, it would not be surprising if at least some scribes attempted to harmonize the various forms of the teaching with one another. When we examine the manuscript tradition of Matt 5:31-32, we find that that has indeed proved to be the case. The modern editions of this Matthean passage do not indicate any significant variations in the textual tradition of verse 31, but they do point to two units of variation in verse 32.[1] The first concerns the clause, "anyone who divorces his wife." This is a participial clause in Greek (*pas ho apoluôn*), but a relative clause in most English-language translations of the passage. The fifth-century Codex Bezae Cantabrigiensis (D), a few minuscules,[2] and the Greek text(s) apparently used for several of the ancient versions[3] have a conditional relative clause without the adjective "every" (*pas*) at this place in Matt 5:32. It reads "if any one divorces" (*hos an apolusê*), the wording found in Matt 19:9 and Mark 10:11. Textual critics judge that the reading of Matt 5:32 which includes this relative conditional clause is an accommodation to those other versions of Jesus' teaching on divorce. Thus they reject its claim to be the more original reading. The judgment of the textual critics has been made all the easier insofar as the participial clause, rather than the conditional relative clause, appears in most of the older and generally reliable witnesses to the gospel text.

The second unit of variation in verse 32 concerns the clause "and whoever marries a divorced woman commits adultery." This reading, consisting of a relative conditional clause, "and whoever marries a divorced woman" (*kai hos ean apolelumenên gamêsê*), in the protasis and the simple "commits adultery" (*moichatai*) in the apodosis, is found in the fourth century Codex Sinaiticus, some other important majuscules (especially the Regius, Washingtoniensis, and Koridethi codices), the minuscules of the Lake and Ferrar families, and most of the medieval Greek manuscripts.[4] Nonetheless, the editors of *GNT*[3] admit that there is a considerable degree of doubt as to whether this reading is, in fact, the superior reading.[5]

The Codex Bezae Cantabrigiensis (D), a few other manuscripts, and some of the medieval Greek lectionaries have a reading which includes a participial clause[6] rather than a conditional relative clause, thus, *kai ho apolelumenên gamêsas moichatai,* of which a fluent English translation would also be "whoever marries a divorced woman commits adultery." Modern English finds it difficult to find fluent translations that would adequately render the differences between the two different Greek constructions. In this regard, contemporary English is not much different from some of the languages used in the ancient Christian world. Thus various Old Latin, Vulgate, and Syriac manuscripts offer a translation of Matt 5:32 which does not clearly indicate which of the alternative Greek texts the translators or editors had at hand.

A third possibility is that the problematic phraseology was not present in Matthew's ancient text. Augustine, in fact, comments that the clause "and whoever marries a divorced woman commits adultery" was not present in some ancient Greek and Latin manuscripts.[7] It may not have been present in the Greek New Testament used by Origen.[8] The extant manuscripts which are without the phrase are among the so-called Western witnesses. These include the Codex Bezae Cantabrigiensis and some Old Latin manuscripts. The phrase which has been omitted by these manuscripts is not found in the parallel version of Jesus' teaching on divorce in Matt 19:9. Neither is it found in Matthew's source (Mark 10:11-12) nor in Paul's version of Jesus' logion on divorce (1 Cor 7:10-11). It is, however, found in a version of Jesus' teaching on divorce which appears as an isolated logion in Luke 16:18, albeit with somewhat different wording.

The reading of Matt 5:32 which employs a participial clause (the second possibility above) is most likely a scribal substitution whose intent was to phrase Matt 5:32c in such a way that it was parallel to Matt 5:32b. As for those manuscripts which omit Matt 5:32c, Augustine himself opined, "I believe that it is omitted because the meaning of the sentence could have been thought to have been conveyed by that passage which was written just before it, that is, 'He causes her to commit adultery.' "[9] His view is echoed by modern editors: "The omission . . . may be due to pedantic scribes who regarded them as superfluous, reasoning that if 'everyone who divorces his wife, except on the ground of unchastity, makes her an adulteress [when she remarries']," then it would go without saying that "whoever marries a divorced woman [also] commits adultery."[10]

Thus, on text-critical grounds, it would appear that the text given in N-A[26] is the best attested Greek reading of Matt 5:31-32 and that the translation offered in the NRSV is adequate to this Greek text. Matthew contrasts a two-part saying, about a man divorcing his wife and about a man marrying a divorcée, with what was said of old, "whoever divorces his wife, let him give her a certificate of divorce."

The Context

The saying of Jesus on divorce found in Matt 5:32 is part of a series of six small units of material in which the radicality of Jesus' teaching on the moral life is contrasted with citations taken from the Jewish Scriptures. These six antitheses (Matt 5:21-48) are a significant portion of the larger unit of Matthew's gospel known to Christian tradition as the Sermon on the Mount (Matt 5:1-8:1).

It is well known that, as an evangelist, Matthew was a collector of Christian traditions. He made use of the gospel according to Mark, a collection of sayings of Jesus (Q, also used by Luke), and some material that was apparently known only to himself (M), at least insofar as our New Testament authors are concerned. To a large extent Matthew organized this material into well-organized units and sub-units within his gospel. Thus we have a collection of miracles in chapters 8 and 9 of Matthew and a collection of woes addressed to the scribes and Pharisees in chapter 23.

The Sermon on the Mount

The most striking of Matthew's collections are, however, the five sermons which provide his gospel with its essential structure.[11] These sermons are the Sermon on the Mount (Matt 5:1-8:1), the Missionary Discourse (Matt 10:1-11:1), the Sermon in Parables (Matt 13:1-54b), the Discourse on the Church (Matt 18:1-19:2), and the Eschatological Discourse (Matt 24:1-26:1). Each of these discourses is brought to a close by a characteristic Matthean formula, "When Jesus had finished saying these things," found in virtually the same wording in Matt 7:28; 11:1; 13:53; 19:1; and 26:1. Formally concluding the preceeding discourse, the formula provides an easy transition to the narrative material which is to follow.

The presence of this characteristic formula provides a first bit of evidence that the evangelist has compiled the five sermons in a self-conscious way. That this is indeed the case is most apparent in the case of the first and longest of the five sermons, the Sermon on the Mount. Matthew has not only brought this discourse to a formal close, he has also identified it as a self-contained unit of material by means of the literary device of *inclusio*. No less than five elements of Matthew's introduction to the Sermon (Matt 5:1-2) are repeated in the conclusion to the Sermon (Matt 7:28-8:1): "When Jesus saw the *crowds* (*ochlous*), he *went* up (*anebê*) the *mountain* (*oros*); and after he sat down, his disciples came to him. Then he began to speak, and *taught them* (*edidasken autous*), *saying* (*legôn*) . . . Now when Jesus had finished *saying these things* (*logous*), the *crowds* (*ochloi*) were astounded at his teaching (*didachê*), for he *taught them* (*didaskôn autous*) as one having authority, and not as their scribes. When Jesus *had come down* (*katabantos*) from the *mountain* (*orous*), great *crowds* (*ochloi*) followed him."

Its Setting

The relationship between the crowds and the disciples in Matthew's setting of the Sermon on the Mount is somewhat similar to the relationship between the crowds and the disciples in Matt 19:1-12. The reader has the impression that the crowds are present at the events being narrated, but that instruction is being specifically addressed to Jesus' disciples.[12] One might also note that the phrase, "the crowds were astounded at his teaching, for he *taught them* as one having authority, and not as their scribes," shares many words with Mark 1:22 and most likely represents a Matthean edition of the Markan reflection. Matthew's modification of the verse found in his Markan source are few, but quite significant. He has explicitly introduced the by-now-familiar[13] crowds (*hoi ochloi*) into his scenario. In addition, Matthew has skillfully contrasted Jesus' teaching with the teaching of the scribes by adding "their" (*autôn*) to the wording of his Markan source. This latter addition creates a "we[14] versus them" context for the readers of Matthew's gospel, who were then experiencing the trauma of separation from the Jewish synagogue.

In Mark the crowds are described as being astounded at the teaching given by Jesus in the synagogue of Capernaum (Mark 1:21). A contemporary reader of Mark's text must certainly wonder about the teaching which caused such great amazement, but Mark does not provide his reader with any explicit information about the content of that astonishing teaching. Matthew compensates for the lacuna by providing his readers with three full chapters of Jesus' teaching (Matt 5:3-7:27), which are then brought to a conclusion with the reflection that they caused astonishment among the crowds.

Matthew has, moreover, located this teaching on the mountain rather than in the synagogue at Capharnaum. Much of the material for Matthew's Sermon on the Mount is contained in a parallel section in Luke's gospel (Luke 6:20-7:1a).[15] The Lukan sermon, however, is situated on a plain. Matthew's location of the Sermon on a mountain is probably symbolic.[16] The mountain evokes the memory of Mount Sinai where the Law was given. As the Law set out guidelines for the way of life to be followed by God's people, so the Sermon on the Mount sets out guidelines for the way of life of the church. It is an extended instruction intended for a community that was defining itself and its lifestyle over and against Judaism during the late eighties of the first century, A.D. The authority for the way of life that is exposited in the Sermon is none other than Jesus who sat down and solemnly taught his disciples (Matt 5:1-2).[17]

The Antitheses (Matt 5:21-48)

It is within this sermon, addressed to a group of Christians who were in the process of discerning their identity and the life style appropriate to it, that the six antitheses of Matt 5:21-48 are to be found. They are proceeded by a four-verse introduction which defines the relationship between the teaching of Jesus and the Law:

> [17]"Do not think that I have come to abolish the law or the prophets; I have come not to abolish but to fulfill. [18]For truly, I tell you, until heaven and earth pass away, not one letter, not one stroke of a letter, will pass from the law until all is accomplished. [19]Therefore, whoever breaks one of the least of these commandments, and teaches others to do the same, will be called least in the kingdom of heaven; but whoever does them and teaches them will be called great in the kingdom of heaven. [20]For I tell you, unless your righteousness exceeds that of the scribes and Pharisees, you will never enter the kingdom of heaven." (Matt 5:17-20)

To a large extent this introduction comes from the hand of the evangelist himself.[18] It betrays the fact that Matthew is directing his thoughts in two directions at once. On the one hand, Matthew is trying to define the position of Jesus vis-a-vis the legalism of the Jews. Matthew's *bête noire* is the Pharisees and their scribes, those Pharisees with whom Matthew's own Christian community were in conflict at the time that his gospel was being composed, in the mid to late eighties.[19] On the other hand, Matthew is concerned with his own community. He does not want its members to fall victim to that kind of ethical laxity which people with Matthew's Jewish background so readily attributed to Gentiles.[20]

The six antitheses which follow the general introduction illustrate this double concern. The antitheses are presented according to a regular pattern. After a formal introductory phrase, "you have heard that it was said to those of ancient times,"[21] a passage of Scripture is cited (Exod 20:13 = Deut 5:17 [Matt 5:21]; Exod 20:14 = Deut 5:18 [Matt 5:27]; Deut 24:1 [Matt 5:31]; Lev 19:12[22] [Matt 5:33]; Exod 21:24-25 = Lev 24:20 = Deut 19:21 [Matt 5:38]; Lev 19:18 [Matt 5:43]). After another formal introductory formula, "But I say to you," with an emphatic "I" (*Egô*) and a contrasting particle ("*de*-but"), the teaching of Jesus is presented.

The passive voice of the formula which introduces the scriptural quotation might be interpreted as referring to God or to

Moses, but since what Jesus says is formally contrasted with what has been said to the people of former times, it is more likely that Jewish teachers are implied as the unidentified proponents of the scriptural commandments. On the whole, the antitheses have been formulated by Matthew in order to set in opposition the teaching of Jesus over and against various authoritative teachers within Judaism. Since Matthew's gospel has arisen from a Christian scribal tradition[23] and since his gospel has as its focus not so much the situation of the historical Jesus as it does the historical situation of his own community, one can infer that the antitheses of Matt 5:21-48 basically place Matthew's Christian scribal interpretation in opposition to the scribal tradition of the "Pharisees." An obvious point of confrontation was the interpretation of the Scriptures themselves, particularly the precepts of the Torah.[24]

Before focusing on Matt 5:31-32, the antithesis on divorce, we should take a brief look at the way Matthew has put the antitheses together.[25] The entire Sermon on the Mount is the work of Matthew, redactor of gospel traditions, who has used his editorial skill to weave together into a composite literary and theological whole various traditions coming to him from Mark, the Q-source, and his own special material. Thus, in any analysis of the Sermon it is useful to distinguish four kinds of material: Markan material (Mark), Q-traditions (Q), Matthew's special material (M), and those portions of the Sermon that come from the evangelist's own insights and editorial skill (MtR).[26]

This division of material is also useful in the analysis of the six antitheses. As we look through the antitheses, we find that in the first antithesis, on murder (Matt 5:21-26), some portion of Jesus' teaching is also found in Luke (Luke 12:57-58 = Matt 5:25-26). Presumably, therefore, it comes from their Q-source. In the second antithesis, on adultery (Matt 5:27-30), part of Jesus' teaching is found in Mark (Mark 9:43 = Matt 5:30). In the third antithesis, that on divorce, Jesus' teaching is found in Luke (Luke 16:18 = Matt 5:32, thus Q).[27] There is no Synoptic parallel to the fourth antithesis, on oaths (Matt 5:33-37).[28] As for the fifth antithesis, on retaliation (Matt 5:38-42), part of Jesus' teaching is found in Luke (Luke 6:29-30 = Matt 5:39b-40, 42). As far as the final antithesis, on love of enemy (Matt 5:43-48), is concerned, most of Jesus' teaching is found in Luke (Luke 6:27-28, 32-33, 36 = Matt 5:44-48).

In sum, the content of Jesus' teaching is largely drawn from Matthew's literary sources, Mark and Q. In one instance, however, the antithesis on oaths, the material content of Jesus' teaching comes from Matthew himself, that is, either from his own sources or from his editorial work.[29] As far as the content of Jesus' teaching is concerned, many of the sayings which Matthew attributes to Jesus in the antitheses are similar to sayings attributed to various early rabbis by the Jewish tradition.[30]

On the other hand, although the Jewish tradition frequently portrays the rabbis as explicating the Scriptures and drawing pertinent halakah from them, Matthew's literary sources do not seem to have portrayed Jesus as explicating the six scriptural passages cited in the antitheses. At most, there is the reference to Deut 24:1 in the discussion with the Pharisees on the matter of divorce (Mark 10:4; Matt 19:8) and the use of Lev 19:18 in the discussion on the great commandment (Mark 12:31; Matt 22:39; Luke 10:27). For the rest, the verses of Scripture cited by Matthew in Matt 5:21-48 do not appear in Mark nor in Matthew's Q-source.

The antitheses do not appear in Luke's sermon on the plain, even though the substance of Jesus' teaching in the fifth and sixth antitheses appears in the Lukan sermon (Luke 6:27-30, 32-33, 36 = Matt 5:39b-40, 42, 44-48, albeit in a somewhat different order). As such, then, the antitheses are Matthew's own literary creation.

Whence, then, did Matthew derive the antithetical formulation which provides the consistent structure for the teaching of Jesus given in Matt 5:21-48?

The Antithetical Formulation

It is reasonable to assume that Matthew's Q-source contained the rudiments of a sermon on the basis of which Matthew and, a few years later, Luke formed the sermons which are found in their respective gospels at Matt 5:1-8:1 and Luke 6:17-49.[31] It is also likely that Luke more faithfully reproduced the sequence of material in the Q-sermon than did Matthew.[32] Some authors identify the challenge of Luke 6:27 = Matt 5:43 "I say to you, 'Love your enemies,' " as the heart of the Q-sermon. Matthew used this saying, but deferred its usage until Matt 5:43, where it forms part of the sixth antithesis, the climax of the entire series.[33]

In Matthew's Q-source, this short sentence may have been introduced by the strong adversative conjuction, "but" (*alla*).[34] If so, Matthew's antitheses may have been inspired by an insight which he derived from this Q-source. However, it is not at all certain that the adversative conjunction was part of the Q-text, so it is to elsewhere that we really should look as we try to appreciate Matthew's formulation of the antitheses.

The Dead Sea Scrolls and the discovery of the Nash papyrus[35] show that, among various groups of Jews more or less contemporary with Matthew, copies of the Decalogue existed in a form other than simply as part of a Torah scroll. Taken from their biblical context, the "ten words" of the Decalogue appeared among the Scripture passages chosen for insertion into the phylacteries or tefillim, the small boxes worn on head and arm during morning prayer.[36] Similarly isolated, they were written on the mezuzot, the parchment scrolls affixed to Jewish doorposts.[37] Each day, according to the Talmud,[38] the Decalogue was recited before the Shema, the great confession of Jewish faith.[39] Containing both the Decalogue and the Shema, the Nash papyrus is a monument of popular religion, representing, in the words of Burkitt, a not-yet-Rabbinized Judaism.[40]

The words of the Decalogue were, moreover, explicated by rabbis and philosophers.[41] In other words, during the first century (A.D.), not only did the precepts of the Decalogue enjoy a somewhat independent existence, but there also existed a Jewish tradition of interpreting the precepts of the Decalogue. It is on the basis of that tradition that Matthew probably began his formulation of the antitheses of the Sermon on the Mount.

In first-century Judaism "X says" or "Y says" was a formula used to link the sentence of a master with a portion of Scripture.[42] It is reasonable to assume that Matthew or his predecessors, versed in scribal tradition, linked sayings of Jesus with precepts of the Decalogue by means of a similar formula. This is all the more reasonable insofar as the evangelist made use of the Decalogue[43] and had a particular understanding of the commandments, including the Decalogue.

From his Markan source, Matthew knew of the Christian tradition that Jesus had rejected an understanding of the commandments of the Torah which resulted in their being used in such a way as even to contravene the will of God himself. In his redaction of those Markan passages[44] Matthew refines the Markan narrative so that the contrast between the teaching of Jesus and that of his "opponents" is even more sharply defined than it is in his Markan source. In the sharply antithetical formulations of Matt 5:21-22, 27-28, and 33-34, where precepts of the Decalogue are the counter point of Jesus' teaching, Matthew epitomizes[45] and symbolizes that contrast.

From earlier Christian tradition, Matthew had garnered some insight into the contrast between Jesus' teaching and that of contemporary Judaism. Matthew was familiar with the scribal tradition which used the Decalogue as a teaching device. Elements of various traditions of Jesus' sayings were also available to the evangelist.[46] The use of scribal techniques allowed him to incorporate some of these Jesuanic traditions into his gospel in accordance with the traditional Christian understanding of the contrast between Jesus' teaching and that of various Jewish religious leaders and the consequentially distinctive way of life followed by Jesus' disciples.

The use of the antithetical introductory lemma, "but I say to you," is redactional.[47] Matthew, nevertheless, sharpens the contrast still further by adding an editorial and emphatic "I" (*egô*). The first-person formulation is not only consistent with the evangelist's general presentation of the opposition between Jesus and the Pharisees—a model of the opposition between Matthew's Christian community and its opponents—but also with the fact that the Sermon on the Mount into which these antitheses have been incorporated is presented as a lengthy instruction for the disciples of Jesus.[48]

It is likely that the antithetical formulation was already used in the Matthean church,[49] but we know of its existence only through the evangelist's literary legacy. Matthew, a stylized and systematic author, used the antithetical formulation derived from a tradition of a Christian interpretation of the Decalogue as a structure for presenting some of the sayings of Jesus which he found in the sermon of his Q-source (Luke 6:27-30, 32-33,

36 = Matt 5:39b-40, 42, 44-48). Compiler that he was, the evangelist incorporated into his series of antitheses the Q saying on divorce (Luke 16:18 = Matt 5:32) taken from a different section of the Q material.[50] Its content was related to that of the teaching presented in Matt 5:27-30, the antithesis appearing immediately before the antithesis on divorce in Matthew's editorial layout.

The Antithesis on Divorce

Not only does there exist some similarity of content between Matt 5:27-30 and Matt 5:31-32,[51] but a pair of catchwords links the saying of 5:32 with the saying of 5:28, namely, the verb "*moicheuô*-to commit adultery" and the noun "*gunê*-woman." "*Moicheuô*-to commit adultery" appears in the first part of Matthew's rendition of Jesus' saying on divorce; it also appeared in the preceding commandment and Jesus' commentary on it (5:27, 28). "*Gunê*-woman" is part of that earlier dictum (v. 28). It recurs in Jesus' oblique reference to the biblically sanctioned practice of divorce (v. 31) as well as in Jesus' antithetical commentary on the tradition (v. 32). Use of catchwords like these is one of the literary devices which the evangelist has employed in order to weave the entire Sermon on the Mount into a single literary unit. In the formulation of the first antithesis, for instance, he had used a catchword to link a saying of Jesus with a precept of the Decalogue. In that instance, the catchword was "*krisis*-judgment" (see vv. 21, 22).

While the catchword technique provided Matthew with a ready-made editorial link between verse 32 (on divorce) and verse 27 (on adultery), Matthew's tradition (Mark 10:11-12) had previously identified divorce and remarriage as a violation of the sixth commandment. Thus it is quite reasonable for the evangelist to have introduced the subject of divorce into his presentation of Jesus' interpretation of the commandment. The "*de*-also" which links verse 31 with verse 30 is a textual indication that Matthew is continuing with his train of thought. The connector almost means "by the way, while I am on the topic." Ultimately, a Jewish catechetical tradition may lie behind Matthew's bringing together Matt 5:27-28, 29-30, and 31-32.[52]

Reginald Fuller has called the antithesis on divorce "a supplement" to the previous antithesis.[53] There are, however, some authors who consider the antithesis on divorce to be merely a subsection of the previous antithesis.[54] Arguments can be cited in support of both positions, but on balance it seems preferable to consider the teaching on divorce as an antithesis in its own right. The reference to a different passage of Scripture, the formal introduction of this Scripture,[55] and the use of "but I say to you" to introduce Jesus' interpretive utterance, indicate that the evangelist is taking up a new, albeit related, topic in verses 31-32. In Matt 5:21-48, no one of these three linguistic elements is to be found except as part of the formal introduction to an antithetical saying of Jesus.

Since earlier Christian tradition had linked Jesus' teaching on divorce with Deut 24:1,[56] Matthew[57] had at hand the scriptural passage which he needed for his antithetical presentation of Jesus' teaching on divorce in 5:31-32. Matthew's analysis of the tradition, as reflected in his reworking of it in Matt 19:3-12,[58] sharply contrasted the Pharisees' use of that Scripture with Jesus' teaching.

In short, Matthew 5:31-32 is a piece of work that has come from the evangelist's own hand.[59] He has carefully crafted its principal elements out of bits of various traditions known to him and skillfully woven it into the Sermon on the Mount. In creating the antithesis Matthew has demonstrated both his consistent redactional theology and his customary literary skill.

Matthew's Line of Thought

Since the evangelist has deliberately composed the third antithesis and included it within the series of six antitheses which are a major component of the Sermon on the Mount, the teaching on divorce in Matt 5:31-32 must be read within that context. Matthew's intended readers are the disciples of Jesus. These are not the disciples who appear in the narrative itself (Matt 5:1), but those disciples who belong to Matthew's own Christian community of a later era. These are disciples (*mathêtai,* literally, "those who

have been taught'') because they have been taught by Jesus and
cling to his teaching.

A Point of View

The reader can easily pick up the thread of Matthew's narrative with the evangelist's formal introduction to the series of antitheses:

> [17]Do not think that I have come to abolish the law or the
> prophets; I have come not to abolish but to fulfill. [18]For truly,
> I tell you, until heaven and earth pass away, not one letter, not
> one stroke of a letter, will pass from the law until all is accom-
> plished. [19]Therefore, whoever breaks one of the least of these
> commandments, and teaches others to do the same, will be
> called least in the kingdom of heaven; but whoever does them
> and teaches them will be called great in the kingdom of heaven.
> [20]For I tell you, unless your righteousness exceeds that of the
> scribes and Pharisees, you will never enter the kingdom of
> heaven. (Matt 5:17-20)

This introduction,[60] composed in much the same way as is the
rest of the Sermon on the Mount, begins a new section of the Sermon. It articulates the fact that the author is about to take up
the issue of the relationship between the Law and the prophets,
on the one hand, and Jesus, on the other. It is a matter of defining the relationship between the core of the Jewish tradition and
the focus of the Christian tradition. That relationship must be
considered within an eschatological perspective. Jesus comes as
the eschatological fulfiller. He speaks not only of fulfillment but
also of heaven and earth's passing away. He brings eschatological fulfillment to both Law and prophets. Consequently, says John
Meier, "law is to be understood in relation to, in analogy with
prophecy."[61]
This insight is key to the understanding of what is to follow
in Matthew's gospel. In the antitheses, Jesus will articulate a statement of Law, with regard to which he will make a prophetic challenge. Before spelling out some examples which give flesh to his
basic insight on the relationship between Law and prophecy, the

evangelist reflects that during Jesus' public ministry fidelity to the Torah was demanded, now fidelity to Jesus' prophetic teaching is demanded (v. 19).

What is at stake is *"dikaiosunê-*righteousness." "Righteousness" is one of the evangelist's favorite notions. It evokes the ethical or moral behavior which is in keeping with God's will.[62] The moral life of the Christian is expected to be in conformity with God's will. The Christian is called to be perfect (*teleios*) as the heavenly Father is perfect. In summary fashion, this very challenge concludes the series of antitheses (Matt 5:48). Called to embrace the will of God in its totality, the moral life of the Christian can be compared with but must be superior to that of the Pharisees. Caricaturized by Matthew, the Pharisees' life style is presented as superficial, legalistic, and minimalistic. The Christian is called to live with an interpretation of the Law, enlivened by Jesus' prophetic challenge, so as to be perfect as the heavenly Father is perfect.

A First Example of Matthew's Prophetic Understanding of the Law

From this perspective, Matthew's Jesus begins to pass the precepts of the Decalogue in review. The opening formula, "You have heard that it was said to those of ancient times" (Matt 5:21), introduces the citation of the fifth commandment, "You shall not murder."

"You have heard that it was said to those of ancient times" is a stereotypical formula, similar to formulas frequently used in Jewish circles to introduce scriptural texts.[63] The formula recalls that the Jewish Scriptures were read aloud in the hearing of those who gathered in synagogue. The key phrase, *"errethê-*it was said" contrasts with the patently prophetic "God says." "It was said" was the formula most frequently used in Jewish circles for the citation of scriptural passages. Formulated in the theological passive, the lemma suggests that God has spoken the words to come, but those words do not enjoy the trenchancy and relevance of actual prophetic utterance. Insofar as Matt 5:21 is concerned, the scriptural passage at hand was first spoken to the generation at Sinai.

After the solemn introduction of the Scripture, expanded by "whoever murders shall be liable to judgment," there follows the solemn introduction of Jesus' prophetic utterance, "*Egô de legô humin*-But I say to you." A similar formula was used in rabbinic circles to articulate a teacher's interpretation when that position was in opposition to the doctrinal status quo.[64] This raises a delicate issue. To what is Jesus' prophetic utterance antithetical?

Those who highlight the antithetical nature of the collection of utterances in Matt 5:21-48 draw attention to the rabbinic parallels with the introductory lemmata of both the scriptural citation and the saying of Jesus. Indeed, there are rabbinic formulae similar to those found in Matt 5:21 and 22. "It was said" is comparable to a rabbinic expression meaning "it has been handed down as tradition."[65] "*De*-but" can function as an adversative conjunction. From this point of view, the opposition is not between Jesus and the Scriptures as such, but between the teaching of Jesus and the biblical commandment *as it has been handed down* in Jewish tradition.[66] Indeed, Matthew concludes the Sermon on the Mount with a summary reflection which contrasts the (authoritative) teaching of Jesus with the (Jewish) scribal tradition.[67]

On the other hand, "it was said" is a rather common introduction for a scriptural quotation, indicating that it is the word of God.[68] The Matthean Jesus has just affirmed, in the introduction to the antitheses, "Do not think that I have come to abolish the law. . . . I have come not to abolish. . . . until heaven and earth pass away, not one letter, not one stroke of a letter, will pass from the law." When this is taken into account, it is unlikely that Matthew's Jesus would have relegated passages from the Decalogue—surely highly esteemed among the various passages from the Torah, as their preservation in tefillim and mezuzot clearly shows—to a tradition which has passed away.

Is it the intention of the Matthean Jesus to abrogate the Decalogue by a radical contrast between what God has said and what Jesus has said? Or might it be that Matthew's Jesus is portrayed as getting to the heart of the matter, as radicalizing the demands of that very Law which will not pass away until . . .? In which case, might it not be that the "*de*-but" functions simply as a conjunctive particle?[69]

Indeed, in interpreting the different introductory lemmata, one might ask whether it is a question of "either-or" or "both-and." The thrust of Matthew's introduction to the antitheses is that the Law must be understood prophetically.[70] This is a typically Matthean point of view.

The Law, specifically the Decalogue,[71] is the word of God.[72] Yet the word of God can be made void by the subtleties of self-serving human reason, which then needs to be confronted by Jesus' prophetic utterance.[73] In Matt 15:8-9, a prophetic word (Isa 29:13) is used to confront a practice which deprives the Law of its force. In Matt 12:7, a prophetic word (Hos 6:6)[74] serves to bring judgment to bear upon the Law.[75] The story of the interlocutor who asks what he must do to gain eternal life (Matt 19:16-22)[76] shows that there is more to discipleship than merely observing the demands of the Law. Those demands are not thereby overturned. There is an element of radicality in Matthew's understanding of the Law. On the two great commandments depend all the Law and the prophets.[77]

A clue as to Matthew's understanding of the Law can even be drawn from Matthew's narration of the discussion between Jesus and the Pharisees on the issue of divorce, the subject of the previous chapter. In Matthew's rendition of the debate, radically prophetic statements of Jesus confront a behavioral posture. Although that posture was apparently based on the Scriptures (Deut 24:1), the normative force of the originative word of God is maintained by Jesus.

It is therefore reasonable to assume that in Matt 5:21 the Matthean Jesus is citing the fifth commandment as the word of God. That bit of Law is to be understood in a prophetic mode. As the evangelist composed his Sermon on the Mount, he was looking in two directions at once. To his opponents, whom he caricatures as relying on the letter of the law, Matthew says that the Law must be understood in a prophetic mode. For the benefit of the members of his own community, whose new situation might have induced them to have a certain laxity with regard to moral standards,[78] Matthew's Jesus recalls the Word of God, but accompanies it with an interpretive prophetic challenge.

Since Matthew's formulation of the antitheses portrays them as being addressed to the disciples (Matt 5:1-2), it is probable that, in their literary context, the words "you have heard" in Matt 5:21 refer to the actual experience of Matthew's community. In their synagogal gatherings, those people had heard the Word of God, once spoken to people of former times.[79]

Jesus demands that the Word of God be interpreted prophetically. His "I say to you" is a formula of prophetic utterance.[80] One mode of prophetic interpretation is a radicalization of the demand of the Law. That was the way the fifth commandment was dealt with in the first antithesis. The commandment was interpreted by means of a three-part prophetic statement coming from the lips of Jesus. Part one consists of a general declaration, "if you are angry with your brother or sister" (Matt 5:22a).[81] In Greek, this is a participial phrase: *pas ho orgizomenos*. The second and third parts of the prophetic utterance are conditional statements, "if you insult your brother or sister[82] . . . if you say 'You fool'. . . ." (Matt 5:22b-c). With its spiraling structure, Jesus' utterance demands that his disciples respond to the fifth commandment in a radical way. His hyperbolic rhetoric is a rhetoric of excess.[83]

A Radical Challenge

Radicalization of the demand of the Law is again the mode of prophetic interpretation in the case of the second antithesis (Matt 5:27-30). The sixth commandment is accompanied by a prophetic utterance. Once again the prophetic utterance is phrased in a three-part statement, the first part being a general declaration beginning with a participial clause, "every one who looks" (*pas ho blepôn*). As was the case with the first antithesis, this general declaration is followed by two conditional statements, "if your right eye causes you to sin, . . . if your right hand causes you to sin."

These conditional clauses are apparently phrased in the idiom of oriental hyperbole. They suggest that a wandering eye be pulled out and tossed away, lest the person be cast into hell (*mê holon to sôma sou blêthê eis geennan*). The hyperbole serves to highlight the seriousness of the offense of even a lustful glance. If adultery was a serious offense against the covenant and a capital crime in ancient Israel, leering and covetous glances are likewise subject to irrevocable judgment.

The theme of judgment was first introduced in the conclusion to the general introduction to the entire series of antitheses: "For I tell you, unless your righteousness exceeeds that of the scribes and Pharisees, *you will never enter the kingdom of heaven*" (Matt 5:20). The theme of judgment was continued in the development of the second antithesis with its explicit mention of the judgment (*krisis,* vv. 21 and 22) and received further expression in the notions of the council (*sunedrion*) and the fiery hell (*geenna tou puros*) of verse 22b-c. That same fiery hell is evoked as the threat of judgment which looms over those who commit adultery, not by the physical act of sexual intercourse, but by the covetous glance.

The seriousness of the situation is further accentuated as Matthew introduces a second conditional clause into his antithesis on adultery: "And if your right hand causes you to sin, cut it off and throw it away; it is better for you to lose one of your members than for your whole body to go into hell" (Matt 5:30). Although this logion is parallel in form to verse 29, it would appear to be somewhat extraneous to the evangelist's line of thought. It almost seems as if the evangelist has taken stereotypical material from another source in order to accentuate the seriousness of covetous leering. In fact, Matthew has taken over verse 30 from his Markan source (Mark 9:43) and has patterned verse 29 on his own version of that Markan text.[84] The insertion of verse 30 not only highlights the importance of judgment; it also underscores the traditional notion that there are some patterns of conduct that merit the severest judgment. In the words of Eduard Schweizer, verses 29-30 above all call "attention away from the neighbor who might be injured, focusing it instead on one's own fate at the last judgment."[85]

What is "Adultery"?

In Matt 5:27-30, the evangelist's frame of reference is certainly that of the male.[86] His working notion of adultery seems to be that which was current in traditional Judaism, namely, that a man commits adultery by having sexual intercourse with a married woman. Adultery was not deemed to have been a violation of a man's own marriage; rather, it was the violation of another man's marriage.[87] It was an infringement upon the rights of another man, who alone had the right to sexual intercourse with his wife. Matthew has cited the sixth commandment of the Decalogue in order to set up his second antithesis. After quoting the sixth commandment, Matthew writes about a man who lusts after a woman, presumably a married woman—otherwise, there would be no question of adultery within first-century Judaism. He continues his reflection from a man's point of view in the following antithesis, the third in the series, when he writes about a man who divorces his wife and a man who marries a divorcée.

Matthew's perspective is so thoroughly Jewish. The woman appears to be merely an object in the entire discussion. It is a woman who is leered at, a woman who is divorced, a divorced woman who is married. Matthew seems little concerned with the fate of the aggrieved woman;[88] he is much concerned with the responsibility and eventual fate of the male who might become an aggriever. With their patently male perspective the second and third antitheses seem to evoke the cultural situation of first-century Judaism and are consistent with the Judaic character of the gospel according to Matthew.

A first-century Jewish discussion on male sexuality may provide the background for Matthew's formulation of these two antitheses.[89] Some rabbis had apparently broadened the notion of adultery. In the Mishnah we read: "The hand that oftentimes makes examination is, among women, praiseworthy; but among men—let it be cut off!" (*m. Nid.* 2:1).

In its commentary on this passage, after a discussion on masturbation, the Talmud[90] says:

> R. Eleazar said, "What does Scripture mean in saying, 'Your hands are full of blood?'[91]—These are they who commit adultery with the hand."
> It was taught in the school of R. Ishmael, " 'You shall not commit adultery'[92] means there shall be in you no adultery neither with the hand nor with the foot."
> "In the case of men it is to be cut off."[93] It was asked, "Have we learned here a law or have we learned here a curse? Have we learned a law, as when R. Huna cut off someone's hand, or have we learned a curse?" . . . R. Tarfon said, "A hand

> touching his genitals is to be cut off, his hand upon his stomach! . . . "It is good that his stomach will be split and he will not go down into the pit of destruction."

From this Talmudic passage it is clear that various rabbis had an extended definition of adultery,[94] one in which they included an offense done with the hand. Moreover, they judged such an offense—at least if the text is to be taken literally—as worthy of the punishment of amputation,[95] lest one enter into the pit of destruction. The parallels with Matt 5:30 are apparent. Although the Talmudic passage (*t. Nid.* 13a-b) does not speak of offenses commited with the eye, Jewish sources frequently refer to sexual offenses committed with the eye.[96]

Matthew seems, then, to have drawn from a Jewish catechetical tradition as he formulates the second and third antitheses. His Jesus radicalizes the biblical commandment of adultery by expanding its purview. It is not only sexual intercourse with a married woman that should be considered a violation of the biblical commandment against adultery. Lustful glances, sexual sins committed with the hand, and even a practice permitted under the provisions of Deut 24:1 ought to be considered as adultery.

In Matt 5:27-30, the evangelist has raised the question of what constitutes adultery from the perspective of Jesus' prophetic interpretation of the Law. Continuation of this thought leads Matthew to turn to the topic of divorce in the third antithesis. Earlier Christian tradition had proclaimed divorce with remarriage to be a form of adultery. Matthew begins his discussion of the topic with a syncopated reference to Deut 24:1, introduced by means of a short lemma.[97] Whereas both his own and Mark's version of the discussion between Jesus and the Pharisees on the issue of divorce had referred to the document cited in Deut 24:1 as a certificate of dismissal (*biblion apostasiou*), that legal document is identified in Matt 5:31 simply as an *apostasion,* similarly best translated as "a certificate of dismissal."[98]

A Man's Responsibility

In contrast to the tolerance of divorce provided by the biblical procedure, Matthew's Jesus describes any man who is involved in divorce as one who is responsible for a violation of the sixth commandment: "anyone who divorces his wife, except on the ground of unchastity, causes her to commit adultery; and whoever marries a divorced woman commits adultery." The thought is clear and very Jewish. Everything is uttered from the standpoint of a man's responsibility.[99] Any man who divorces his wife, apart from one specific instance, makes her commit adultery.[100]

This constitutes a radical departure from the provisions set out in Deut 24:1-4. The biblical text expressed a bit of social legislation which both protected a woman and prevented a man from violating a tabu. The necessity that there be specific grounds for divorce protected a wife against arbitrary dismissal by her husband.[101] The certificate of dismissal, the *biblion apostasiou,* was proof that she was free to enter into another marriage.

In a social world where women lived under the tutelage of males,[102] the certificate of dismissal made it possible for a woman who had been dismissed by her husband to find another man as her protector. The words of the Matthean Jesus describe such action on the part of the dismissed wife as adultery,[103] but they state that it is the husband who is responsible for her adultery. Not only that! Any man who dares to marry a divorced woman commits adultery.

In Matthew's social world, the divorced woman was in a very precarious position.[104] Matthew's unstated assumption was that the woman would remarry. If she remarried, she is considered to have committed adultery, *but* her husband is responsible for her sin. Although writing from a manifestly *Jewish* Christian perspective,[105] Matthew should not be considered to be a thoroughgoing anti-feminist. The formulation of verse 32a protects a woman against arbitrary divorce by her husband.[106] Should she nonetheless be divorced, the second part of that verse clearly lays the blame for her seeking the protective environment of a new marriage—apart from the situation of unchastity—on the shoulders of her former husband.

Some authors suggest that verse 32a might have dealt with a real-life situation in the Matthean community, namely, that of the woman who has converted to Christianity after a divorce and remarriage.[107] She is exonerated from crime because it is her former husband who is responsible for her new situation.

These things having been said about the implications of Matthew's formulation of the third antithesis for a woman, there is no doubt that Matthew has formulated the antithesis from a man's perspective. The evangelist's primary consideration is not concern for a woman's social situation. Matthew is writing about the interpretation of the Law, whose provisions were primarily incumbent upon Jewish males, the "sons of the commandment."[108] He was writing in a social world in which men married and women were given in marriage.[109]

In Matt 5:32, Jesus' prophetic utterance, expanding the very notion of adultery, is phrased in a fashion similar to that of the midrashim on the fifth and sixth commandments (vv. 22, 29-30). His first statement is a general pronouncement, whose subject is a generalized participle (*pas ho apoluôn tên gunaika autou,* literally, "everyone divorcing his wife"). The second statement begins with a conditional clause, "whoever marries a divorced woman," more literally, "and if anyone marries a divorced woman" (*kai hos ean apolelumenên gamêsê*). Although there are only two parts in Jesus' utterance—unlike the three-part exposition in the two previous antitheses—the structure of Jesus' prophetic logion is the same: a generalized participial statement, followed by a conditional sentence.[110]

A Matter of Law

Typically, sentences of casuistic law begin with a conditional clause, the apodosis, which specifies the case under consideration. The apodosis of the sentence then gives the penalty. Instances of this type of casuistic law abound in the Hebrew bible. There are, however, other instances of casuistic law in which the protasis enunciates a declaration of guilt rather than the determination of a specific penalty.[111] This is the case in Matt 5:32.

Although Jesus' words have the ring of legal language and appear to have the form of casuistic law,[112] Gerhard Lohfink asks whether they were intended to have the force of legal language. He notes that human language can be used with many different functions and that Jesus occasionally used provocative language.[113] Indeed, Matthew's revised version of the discussion with the Pharisees indicates that Jesus' teaching on divorce provoked not only the Pharisees but also the disciples as well. Can legal language serve a provocative purpose?[114] It is well known that the prophets occasionally used patterns of speech phrased in one specific literary form for a purpose other than that which is normal for that literary form.[115] Thus it is quite conceivable that the Matthean Jesus, adopting the stance of a prophetic interpretation of the Law, used the form of a sentence of law to show that the rigid application of law can serve not justice, but injustice.[116] Matthew's adaptation of a sentence of law for Jesus' teaching on divorce in Matt 5:32 would be a kind of *reductio ad absurdum*. Although formally a sentence of law, it is not used as a sentence of law.

Indeed, in his exposition of the first antithesis Matthew had already employed the form of a sentence of law as a prophetic utterance of Jesus, to wit, "If you are angry with a brother or sister, you will be liable to judgment; and if you insult a brother or sister, you will be liable to the council" (Matt 5:22a-b). The literary form of this prophetic utterance is similar to that of the literary form of Matt 5:32, but its purpose was hardly to promulgate new legislation.[117] Similarly, in Matt 5:32, the evangelist wishes to show that it is absurd for a Christian to make use of the legislation set out in Deut 24:1-4. Both the husband who makes use of this legislation to divorce his wife and a man who marries a woman freed under the provisions of this legislation violate the law. Specifically, they break the sixth commandment.

A Synoptic Reading of Matt 5:31-32

The preceeding narrative reading of Matt 5:31-32 has tried to capture the thrust of Matthew's presentation of Jesus' teaching on divorce in the context of his Sermon on the Mount. It has deliberately avoided any real consideration of the exception ("except on the ground of unchastity," *parektos logou porneias*). This avoidance was intentional. Focusing on the nature of the exception turns many a contemporary reader's attention away from the point that the evangelist was really trying to make. Focusing upon "the exception" treats the logion of Matt 5:32 as if it were really a law, which it is not. It may have the form, but it does not have the force of law.

Our narrative reading of Matt 5:31-32 may well have suggested to the reader of these pages that it would be useful to delve more deeply into the nature of Jesus' teaching on divorce as a prophetic utterance. What might have been the *situation in Jesus' life* which warranted such a prophetic statement? Or is the utterance merely a literary creation of Matthew, the evangelist? We must devote further attention to this matter, but we shall defer the discussion until after we have subjected Matt 5:31-32 to a Synoptic reading.

The principal parallels are with Matt 19:7, 9, and Luke 16:18. We can begin with the Matthean parallel:

Matt 5:31-32

[31]"It was also said, 'Whoever divorces his wife, let him give her a certificate of divorce.' [32]But I say to you that anyone who divorces his wife, except on the ground of unchastity, causes her to commit adultery; and whoever marries a divorced woman commits adultery."

Matt 19:7, 9

[7]They said to him, "Why then did Moses command us to give a certificate of dismissal and to divorce her?" . . . [9]And I say to you, whoever divorces his wife, except for unchastity, and marries another commits adultery."

In terms of their form, the two Matthean pericopes resemble one another because of their antithetical structure. The biblical tradition and the utterance of Jesus are set over and against one another. In both instances, the logion of Jesus (Matt 5:32; 19:9) can be identified as a prophetic statement. The "I say to you" lemma is characteristic of prophetic speech. In both instances, moreover, the saying of Jesus is phrased in a conditional sentence.

The *lexis* or vocabulary in these two passages is remarkably similar. At least nine linguistic expressions appear in both passages, as the following close Synoptic reading of these passages illustrates:

Matt 5:31-32

"It was also said, 'Whoever [1]divorces his wife, let him [2]give her

Matt 19:7, 9

They said to him, "Why then did Moses command us to [2]give a cera certificate of ³divorce.' ⁴But I say to you that anyone who ⁵divorces his wife, except on the ground of ⁶unchastity, causes her to commit adultery; and ⁷whoever ⁸marries a divorced woman ⁹commits adultery.''

tificate of ³dismissal and to ¹divorce her?'' . . . ⁴And I say to you, ⁷whoever ⁵divorces his wife, except for ⁶unchastity, and ⁸marries another ⁹commits adultery.''

The choice of vocabulary for all nine expressions in Matthew's Greek text[118] is the same in both texts, even if the needs of a flowing English-language text have led to their sometimes being translated in different ways. Although the vocabulary is common to both passages, there are some differences in the way that the vocabulary is used. Mention has already been made of the fact that Matt 5:31 uses a simple noun, ³*apostasion,* rather than the expression, *biblion apostasiou,* found in Matt 19:7 and Deut 24:1. Moreover, the sequence of the verbs, to ¹divorce and to ²give, are different in Matt 5:31 from what they are in Matt 19:7 and Deut 24:1.

As far as the expression of Jesus' teaching itself is concerned, the evangelist has incorporated an emphatic "I" (*egô*) into the introductory ⁴lemma of the antithesis. Moreover, the exception clause of verse 32, *parektos logou* ⁶*porneias,* is formulated in a somewhat different fashion from the exception clause of Matt 19:9, *mê epi* ⁶*porneia.*

Between Matthew's two versions of Jesus' teaching on divorce, there are two striking differences in content. First of all, unlike the saying of Matt 19:9, the antithesis of 5:31-32 does not speak of a divorcing husband marrying another woman nor does it say that he commits adultery. It is silent about the possible remarriage of the husband who has divorced his wife. The mere fact that a man has divorced his wife involves her in adultery and makes him liable for her sin, thus putting him in violation of the sixth commandment. This is in accordance with the appreciation of the sixth commandment by some rabbis who noted that the Hebrew text of Exod 20:14, "You shall not commit adultery," could also be pointed as the Hiphil form of the verb so as to be understood, "you shalt not cause adultery to be committed."[119]

Secondly, the antithesis on divorce in Matthew 5 treats the case of a man who marries a divorced woman, convicting him of adultery (v. 32b). Despite the fact that various copyists of the biblical manuscripts, including the majority of medieval scribes, have "completed" Matt 19:9 by adding additional material from Matt 5:32, the issue of a man marrying a divorcée is not addressed in Matt 19:9.[120]

The differences of vocabulary as well as the different thoughts expressed in these two Matthean passages on divorce suggest that Matthew has taken his divorce material from two different sources. Indeed, the mere fact that he treats of divorce on two different occasions suggests that Matthew has made use of different source material as he treats Jesus' teaching on divorce.[121] A glance at Luke 16:18 confirms this initial impression.

Another Synoptic Reading of Matt 5:31-32

Matt 5:31-32

[31]"It was also said, 'Whoever divorces his wife, let him give her a certificate of divorce.' [32]But I say to you that anyone who divorces his wife, except on the ground of unchastity, causes her to commit adultery; and whoever marries a divorced woman commits adultery."

Luke 16:18

[18]"Anyone who divorces his wife and marries another commits adultery, and whoever marries a woman divorced from her husband commits adultery."

Our literary analysis of Matthew's composition of the Sermon on the Mount and its antitheses[122] has indicated that Matthew has skillfully composed both the Sermon on the Mount in general and the antitheses in particular using a variety of pre-existent materials and traditions. Although the evangelist's formulation of Jesus' teaching on divorce in Matt 5:32 is quite different from what he has to narrate about that teaching in Matt 19:9, the wording of 5:32 is quite similar to the wording of Jesus' teaching contained in the isolated logion of Luke 16:18. Both Matt 5:32 and Luke 16:18 are addressed to the husband, both have the phrase "whoever divorces his wife," and both speak about a man marrying a divorced woman.[123] That would seem to suggest that the saying found in Matt 5:32 and Luke 16:18 has been taken over from their Q-source by both evangelists.

That Luke incorporates the logion into his gospel without any narrative context and without either verbal or content links to the preceding saying (Luke 16:16-17) or to the subsequent material (Luke 16:19-31) indicates that the saying found in verse 18 has come from a document whose literary form is that of a collection of sayings.[124] Such collections normally juxtapose sayings one after another, without any narrative context apart from an occasional introductory "he said."[125]

In sum, the presence of an independent saying comparable to Matt 5:32 in Luke 16:18 is an indication that the version of Jesus' teaching on divorce in Matt 5:32 comes from Matthew's Q source. Although based on Aramaic traditions, the Q-source utilized by Matthew in 5:32 was written in Greek, sometime before 60 A.D.[126]

The Lukan Text

Before we consider Q's version of Jesus' teaching on divorce, it might prove useful to bring to closure the Synoptic reading of Matt 5:32 and Luke 16:18 with which we have begun. First of all, a few remarks should be made apropos of the Lukan text itself. The textual apparatus of N-A[26] cites three units of variation. None of the three has been judged sufficiently significant to merit particular treatment in the critical apparatus of *GNT*[3]. Nonetheless, they should be passed in summary review. All three units of variation occur in the second part of the verse (Luke 16:18b).

Insofar as the first variant is concerned, some of the major majuscules (including the Sinaiticus, Alexandrinus, Washingtoniensis, and Koridethi codices) and most of the minuscules (including those of the Lake and Ferrar families) have "*pas*-all" immediately after the "*kai*-and" with which verse 18b begins. In translation, this would give us "everyone who" rather than the NRSV's "whoever." The alternate reading seems to be the result of scribal tendencies to bring the two clauses of verse 18 into greater stylistic balance.

As for the second variant, P⁷⁵, a very important third century papyrus, omits the article (*ho*) which qualifies the participle "*gamôn*-marries," an omission which would not affect the translation of the clause. Apart from P⁷⁵, however, the omission is attested to by relatively few manuscripts. The vast majority of majuscules and minuscules read the text with the definite article.

The fact that "*apo andros*-from her husband" is not found in the Codex Bezae Cantabrigiensis, some few other ancient Greek manuscripts, and some of the ancient versions constitutes the third textual variant in Luke 16:18b. It is likely that this qualifying phrase was dropped by these manuscripts as being unnecessarily redundant. On the other hand, the omission may have been caused by scribal assimilation with the better-known parallel in Matt 5:32, which does not have the explanatory phrase.

Matthew and Luke

The Greek text of Luke 16:18 can thus be assumed to have been such as it appears in N-A²⁶ and *GNT*³. Whatever units of variation are evinced by the manuscript tradition are not particularly important for the understanding of the text. When, however, this text of Luke 16:18 is compared with that of Matt 5:32, it appears that Matthew's version of the saying differs considerably from that of Luke, particularly with regard to the first part of the saying,[127] namely, Matt 5:32a, parallel with Luke 16:18a.

Matthew's version of the saying reads "anyone who divorces his wife, except on the ground of unchastity, causes her to commit adultery" (Matt 5:32a). Luke reads "anyone who divorces his wife and marries another commits adultery" (Luke 16:18a).

There are three major differences between these two versions of the Q logion, that is, the first part of Jesus' saying. First of all, Matthew's version includes the clause, "except on the ground of unchastity," whereas Luke's does not. Secondly, Luke speaks about the remarriage of a husband who divorces his wife "and marries another," whereas Matthew does not. Thirdly, the Matthean text lays blame on the husband because he has involved the wife, whom he has divorced, in adultery. The Lukan text says that the man who divorces his wife [and remarries] commits adultery. This may well be because it was presumed that the divorced husband would remarry and have a sexual relationship with his new wife.

As far as the second part of the saying is concerned, there are again three differences, but they seem not to be as important as are the idiosyncrasies which distinguished Matt 5:32a from Luke 16:18a. First of all, Luke has a participial construction, "*ho* . . . *gamôn*-whoever marries," parallel with verse 18a,[128] whereas Matthew has a conditional clause, "*hos ean* . . . *gamêsê*-whoever marries" (literally, "if anyone marries"). Secondly, Luke has an interpretive phrase "*apo andros*-from her husband" qualifying the verb, "divorce," whereas Matthew does not. Finally, the Lukan verb, "commits adultery," is in the active voice (*moicheuei*), as it is in verse 18a, whereas the verb of the Matthean apodosis is a passive deponent and is, in fact, even a different verb (*moichatai*[129]).

Luke's Version of Jesus' Teaching

Luke has put the Q-saying on divorce to what seems to be strange use in his gospel. Luke has not offered the story of Jesus' discussion with the Pharisees on the topic of divorce (Mark 10:2-12; Matt 19:3-12). That belongs to a section of Mark's narrative which is part of Luke's lesser omission. Luke had been following his Markan source until Mark 9:41. At that point, he diverted from Mark to insert the so-called Lukan travelogue. Luke picks up again the Markan narrative at Mark 10:13, that is, immediately after Mark's narration of the conflict over divorce. By so doing, Luke has omitted the material contained in Mark 9:42-10:12 from his gospel. The fact that Luke has returned to Mark's narrative sequence immediately after the conflict on divorce seems to imply that Luke deliberately and specifically decided not to incorporate the Markan story into his own gospel.

Then, in the middle of his travelogue, Luke abruptly cites a one-verse saying of Jesus on the topic of divorce. One wonders why Jesus' saying on divorce (Luke 16:18)[130] appears at this point and in this context in Luke's gospel. The logion appears as an isolated saying, the last in a group of four sayings that come between two parables: the parable of the unjust steward (Luke

16:1-13)[131] and the parable of the rich man and Lazarus (Luke 16:19-31). Luke's intervenient mini-collection of three or four sayings (Luke 16:14-18) is as follows:

> [14]"The Pharisees, who were lovers of money, heard all this, and they ridiculed him. [15]So he said to them, "You are those who justify yourselves in the sight of others, but God knows your hearts; for what is prized by human beings is an abomination in the sight of God. [16]"The law and the prophets were in effect until John came; since then the good news of the kingdom of God is proclaimed, and every one tries to enter it by force. [17]But it is easier for heaven and earth to pass away, than for one stroke of a letter in the law to be dropped. [18]"Anyone who divorces his wife and marries another commits adultery, and whoever marries a woman divorced from her husband commits adultery."

Luke and his Q-source

There are many scholars who believe that the series of sayings in Luke 16:14-18 were already juxtaposed with one another in Q,[132] and that, in that hypothetical document, verses 17 and 18 especially belonged together.[133]

It is, however, not altogether certain that this was, in fact, the case.[134] Some commentators note that another series of sayings, whose general topic is the same but which appear to have come from different sources (Luke 16:9-13, 15), has been appended to the parable of the unjust steward (Luke 16:1-9). "The upshot," writes Joseph Fitzmyer, "is that there is no clear connection between Jesus' utterance on divorce in v. 18 and the two preceding sayings about the Law and its validity in vv. 16-17. Hence it is far from clear that Luke is citing Jesus on the topic of divorce as an example of his 'challenging' the Mosaic Law."[135]

In an earlier reflection on Luke 16:18, Fitzmyer suggested that the link between this verse and its present literary context (in Luke) might be that, because of the way that a married woman was socially regarded in first-century Palestine, the logion indirectly belongs to a collection of sayings, a topos, dealing with a man's possessions.[136] One might also note that matters of sexual ethics and matters of business or monetary ethics were frequently joined in Jewish tradition[137]—particularly in the Jewish caricature of the Gentiles' way of life.

Luke and the Law

In contemporary studies on the Q document, the predominant view continues to be that the logion on divorce appeared alongside a series of sayings on the Law in the Q-source itself.[138] Kloppenborg, for example, identifies the three sayings found in Luke 16:16-18 as "Q61."[139] The view that Luke 16:18 was juxtaposed with some sayings on the Law in this Q-source has led a number of commentators to suggest that Luke took the group of sayings over as a unit in order to illustrate Jesus' attitude towards the Law.

The commentators, however, have different ideas about how Luke sees the relationship between the Law and the saying on divorce, which has the form of casuistic law.[140] The Lukan saying on divorce has, in this regard, also been taken metaphorically, as if Jesus was condemning those who abandoned the law of Moses in order to pursue a love affair with the world.[141] More commonly, some of those who write about the matter view the saying on divorce as an illustration of the permanence of the Law.[142] Others see it as correcting the Law.[143] According to Marshall, the logion illustrates the continuing validity of the Law but in the new form given to it by Jesus.[144]

The idea that Luke—and Q, if verses 17 and 18 had already appeared together in Q—intended to offer Jesus' teaching on divorce as a challenge to the Law is highly improbable in the light of the fact that verse 17 affirmed, strongly and hyperbolically, the permanent validity of the Law. One must be careful not to interpret Luke in the light of the use that Matthew[145] has made of the Q-saying. The redactional interests of the two evangelists were different. Matthew, despite the use made of Matthew in the later tradition of the church, should not serve as the hermeneutical key for the interpretation of Luke.

On the other hand, it cannot be too readily presumed that Luke has cited verse 18 from his Q-source as an example of the permanency of the Law. Although there is no hint that the formulation of the saying challenges or abrogates the Law of Moses in regard to divorce, it is clear that Jesus' teaching on divorce is *other* than the praxis allowed under the Mosaic Law. The Law of Moses allowed a husband to divorce his wife, provided that certain stipulations be fulfilled. The Law of Moses likewise permitted a man, except for the man who had previously divorced her, to marry a divorced woman. Indeed, the purpose of the certificate of dismissal being handed over to the wife as part of the process of divorce was precisely in order that she could attest to her freedom so that she could be married again. Luke's Jesus, however, tolerated neither a man's divorcing his wife and marrying another woman nor a man marrying a woman who had been divorced.

This does not mean that Jesus' prohibition of divorce is contrary to the Law of Moses. The Law of Moses did not mandate divorce,[146] it merely made provision for divorce in certain circumstances by stipulating that certain conditions be fulfilled. Luke 16:17-18 unambiguously states that the Law of Moses is valid but that divorce is prohibited.

It is not altogether certain that Luke had a sophisticated understanding of the biblical tradition. Despite his manifest desire to portray fidelity to the Mosaic Law in the infancy narratives, Luke evinces some confusion about the Law in his account of the presentation in the temple (Luke 2:22-24).[147]

I would, therefore, albeit with some hesitancy, suggest that verses 17 and 18 were linked in Luke's source and that he may well have cited the teaching of Jesus on divorce as a response to the needs of his community, to be sure, but thinking that it was an example of Jesus' reiterating some demands of the Mosaic Law.[148]

Obviously the needs of a Gentile Christian community were generally such that a reiteration of Jesus' teaching on divorce would be pertinent,[149] but it is difficult to determine why Luke introduced that teaching at this point in his narrative, in such a terse and abrupt fashion, were the logion on divorce not already juxtaposed with the saying on the Law. It is, therefore, quite reasonable to assume that verses 17 and 18 were juxtaposed in Q. One cannot conclusively prove that they were so linked nor can one determine why they were so linked, if indeed they were. However, the juxtaposition of unrelated statements is more consistent with the literary genre of an anthology of sayings than it is with the narrative genre of Luke's gospel.

Luke and Divorce

Although Luke has abruptly introduced Jesus' teaching on divorce from the Q-source into his gospel at 16:18, he has not developed its point any further.[150] Luke may well have reformulated the Jewish expression[151] and point of view of the Q-saying so as to accommodate it to his Hellenistic readership, but he has not significantly expanded the logion, nor has he appended explanatory material to it.

On any reading of the text, Luke's version of Jesus' teaching on divorce is singular. The logion is formulated from the standpoint of the male, presumably the standpoint of the source, and unequivocally condemns any marriage after divorce as adulterous.[152] The man who divorces his wife and remarries commits adultery. The man who marries a divorced woman commits adultery. This presumes a new definiton of adultery[153] and a new understanding of marriage.

Under Jewish law a man could commit adultery only by violating the marriage of another man. In the Lukan version of Jesus' teaching on divorce, as in the parallel Matthean version of the Q-saying (Matt 5:32b), the man who marries a divorced woman is presumed to have offended the marriage of the first husband. That, of course, means that the first marriage continues to exist, despite the divorce procedure. This may well be the point of Luke's, *"apo andros*-from her husband.'' Despite the divorce, he remains *her husband*.

The Lukan logion, moreover, presumes monogamous marriage. Were monogamy not presumed, a man's second marriage would be allowed, whether he had divorced his first wife or not. However, Luke 16:18a clearly states that a husband who divorces his wife and marries another woman commits adultery. Since the new wife is not a divorcée—that case is treated in verse 18b—the husband who divorces and remarries has violated his own marriage. The logion does not specifically state that he has offended his first wife, as does Mark 10:11, but it unequivocally states that he has violated the law of God, that is, the sixth precept of the Decalogue.[154]

This radical condemnation of a second marriage reflects, in the opinion of C. F. Evans,[155] Luke's ascetical interests. Such asceticism would, in any case, be consistent with that late first-century form of Christianity which looked with disdain upon a second marriage, an aversion to which even the Pastoral Epistles may have borne witness.[156] To some extent those Christians shared with the Essenes a fairly rigorous discipline with regard to marriage.[157]

According to Luke, both the man who divorces his wife and the man who marries a divorced woman commit adultery. This puts either of such men in a situation in which they have violated a precept of the Decalogue, one of the Ten Commandments. Luke's understanding of the commandments of old seems to have been neither as precise nor as sophisticated as that of Matthew. Nonetheless, it can be noted that the characters who envelop and intersect with the Lukan story of Jesus' public ministry are presented as those who keep the commandments—Zechariah and Elizabeth in Luke 1:6, the Galilean women in Luke 23:56. The latter are cited as having specifically observed the Sabbath rest, one of the precepts of the Decalogue.

Among the precepts of the Law, the prohibition of adultery seems to enjoy a relatively great importance in Luke's gospel. For example, in response to the ruler's question about eternal life, Jesus cites various precepts of the Decalogue. The prohibition of adultery is named in the first instance (Luke 18:18-25, v. 20). This distinguishes Luke from both Mark and Matthew who cite the prohibition of murder as the first precept of the Decalogue placed on Jesus' lips.[158] The idea that he might be an adulterer stands out in the Lukan Pharisee's caricature of the sinful tax-collector's way of life (Luke 18:11).

There can be no doubt that Luke considered adultery to be a truly serious matter, a violation of the very Law of God. In the isolated saying on divorce which he has taken over into his gospel at 16:18, he affirms that a man who divorces his wife and the man who marries the divorced woman are guilty of that very offense.

The Q-Saying

A comparative reading of Luke 16:18 and Matt 5:32 inevitably leads to the formulation of a series of questions. 1) Did Matthew add the exception to the Q material or did Luke omit it? 2) Did Matthew delete the mention of the husband's remarriage or did Luke add it? 3) Did Matthew omit the interpretive "from her husband," or did Luke add it? 4) Finally, and perhaps the most problematic in this series of questions, did the source speak of the husband's responsibility for his wife's involvement in adultery (Matthew) or did it speak of his own adultery upon his remarriage (Luke). This last question is obviously related to the second, so much so, in fact, that the two questions might be considered as a single unit of variation. Ultimately they cannot be addressed independently of one another.

To answer questions such as these four is to try to reconstitute the Q-form of the saying. Those who deny the existence of Q as a documentary source utilized by the two later evangelists[159] eschew such an effort, but most scholars think that the attempt must be made, no matter how tentative its resolution proves to be. Before treating the issue of the Q-saying itself, it might be useful to recall that both Matthew 5:32 and Luke 16:18 have 1) a two-part saying of Jesus on divorce, 2) from the perspective of the male, and that 3) the second part deals with a man marrying a divorcée.

The Easy Part

In the reconstruction of the Q tradition,[160] one can begin with the elimination of the exception clause from the Q-text. The exception reflects a concern of the Matthean community, and apart from Matthew 19:9 it is not found in the other New Testament witnesses to the teaching of Jesus on divorce.[161] One can also eliminate the Lukan explanatory phrase, "from her husband." Not only is it redundant, but "*anêr*-husband" (literally, "man") is one of Luke's very own favorite words.[162]

Luke

John Kloppenborg opines that the consensus judgment of New Testament scholars is that, apart from the Lukan addition of "from her husband," Luke 16:18 reproduces the Q-text, to wit, "anyone who divorces his wife and marries another commits adultery, and whoever marries a divorced woman commits adultery."[163] Consensus does not mean complete agreement. That portion of Q which represents minimal Q, that is, that part of the extant logion which virtually all authors accept as having belonged to the Q material, is "anyone who divorces his wife commits adultery, and whoever marries a divorced woman commits adultery."[164]

Some scholars think that the clause "and marries another" (*kai gamôn heteran*) is a Lukan addition, perhaps under the influence of Luke's prior reading of Mark.[165] "Another" (*heteros*) is a Lukan term. More than half (fifty out of ninety-eight) of its occurrences in the New Testament are found in Luke-Acts. If the clause is a Lukan addition, it may have been merely an adaptation of the traditional saying to the real conditions of life.[166] Men who divorced normally would have remarried.

Matthew

There are likewise some scholars who think that Matthew's "causes her to commit adultery" (Matt 5:32a) is more faithful to Q[167] than is Luke's "commits adultery" (Luke 16:18a). One might plausibly argue that Luke has simplified the more obtuse language presently found in Matthew, using a verb that he will also employ in verse 18b, but Matthew had an obvious interest in re-judaizing the tradition. Within the Jewish social world, a man could commit adultery only by violating the marriage of another Jewish male. It was Matthew's sensitivity to that situation which most likely prompted him to delete "against her" as he edited Mark 10:11 in Matt 9:9. In Matthew's reformulation of the Markan logion, the divorcing husband's adultery is not construed as an offense against the divorced wife, rather it results from his remarriage (to a divorced woman?).

Had Matthew read "anyone who divorces his wife commits adultery" in the Q source of 5:32a, his tendency to adapt the tradition to the social tradition of his own community would have led him to reformulate "commits adultery" as "causes her to commit adultery."

On the other hand, had Matthew read "anyone who divorces his wife and marries another commits adultery," there would have been little reason for him to alter the verb. "Anyone who divorces his wife and marries another commits adultery" is almost verbally identical to what Matthew says in Matt 19:9. Thus I am inclined to the opinion that the Q source of Luke 16:18a = Matt 5:32a did not include a reference to the divorced husband's remarriage and that there is a very strong possibility that Matthew's "involves her in adultery" better reflects the inflected form of Q's statement about adultery than does Luke's "commits adultery."[168]

Although Polag and Havener believe that the protasis of the second part of the Q saying (Matt 5:32b; Luke 16:18b) was a conditional clause, it seems preferable to maintain—with Kloppenborg—that the protasis was a participial clause. Not only would that provide greater balance between the two parts of the logion, but there is also the fact that the "whoever" of Matt 5:32b is consistent with the redactional language of Matthew's antitheses.[169]

Does the apodosis of the conditional clause have a main verb in the active voice or a verb in the middle voice? It is more likely that the verb of the Q saying was in the active voice. Since the middle voice appears in Matt 19:9-Mark 10:11, Matthew would have had a reason to substitute a middle voice verb for an active voice, had he found the latter in his source. Moreover, if Luke did indeed substitute "commits adultery" for the "involves her in adultery" of his Q-source, it is likely that he would have repeated the final verb of his source in order to create a balance between the apodoses of both parts of the saying.

All things being considered, I would venture to reconstruct the Q-form of Jesus' teaching on divorce as follows: "anyone who divorces his wife involves her in adultery, and whoever marries a divorced woman commits adultery."

6

An Exception

Matthew's version of the old saying which he has taken over from the Q-source and which he has reformulated to meet the needs of his own community is one which contains an exception: "anyone who divorces his wife, except on the ground of unchastity (*parektos logou porneias*), causes her to commit adultery" (Matt 5:32). A similar exception is to be found in the climactic utterance of his version of Jesus' discussion with the Pharisees: "whoever divorces his wife, except for unchastity (*mê epi porneia*), and marries another commits adultery" (Matt 19:9).

An Exceptional Exception

At first glance and upon a second reading as well, these exceptions are striking. A narrative reading of the various antitheses hardly prepares the reader for an exception to be made to any one of Jesus' prophetic statements.

The thrust of the antithesis on divorce (Matt 5:31-32) places Jesus' radical demand for marital fidelity over and against the traditional practice of divorce according to the provisions stipulated in Deut 24:1. The literary form is such that the reader expects to find the contrast drawn with very sharp lines. The formulation of the exception clause in the antithesis on divorce strikes one as the language of casuistry, not the language of antithetical contrast. It breaks the pattern of sharp contrast which otherwise characterizes Matthew's antitheses.

Similarly, a narrative reading of the conflict story in Matt 19:3-9 makes the exception clause stand out as something quite unexpected. The language of controversy is normally the language of black and white; it admits of no grey. The exception cited in verse 9 makes it appear as if Jesus has responded in rather matter-of-fact fashion to the question posed by the Pharisees in verse 3. The Pharisees have set out to test Jesus, and Jesus responds with an answer that was commonly given by the school of Shammai. In the words of Michael Goulder, "the radical Jesus disappears in qualifying phrases, and emerges as a rabbi of the school of Shammai."[1] If Jesus simply responded to the Pharisees' question with an acceptable rabbinic response, there would have been no need for controversy. The conflict interposed between the Pharisees' question and Jesus' response would seemingly be out of place.

As a matter of fact, verse 9's academic response to the Pharisees' academic question seems inconsistent with the Matthean characterization of the Pharisees; elsewhere, they appear as the prototypical opponents of Jesus. Finally, the exception seems to place Jesus in opposition to his own scriptural argumentation. Verse 6 affirms that humans are not to separate what God has joined into one. Jesus' response, with its exception, affirms that there is one situation which allows them to do so.

The literary form and narrative development of each of the two Matthean pericopes on divorce thus suggest that an exception is a bit out of place. A second, or Synoptic, reading of the Matthean texts confirms that the exception clause is indeed rather exceptional. When Matt 5:32 is compared with Luke 16:18 or the reconstituted Q-text of the Jesus' saying, one is struck by the fact that the exception is not found in Luke's parallel saying nor is it—presumably—found in the common source used by both evangelists. When Matt 19:9 is compared with Mark 10:11, one can not help but notice that, once again, Matthew's parallel text, and, in this case, clearly his source, does not have an exception. Moreover, Mark 10:12 seems to be an addition to the traditional logion, an addition presumably made in order to obviate any exceptions to Jesus' call for radical marital fidelity. In short, the exception found in Matthew's two renditions of the Jesuanic logion on divorce is not found in any of the other New Testament traditions of Jesus' teaching on divorce.[2] The absence of an exception clause from the pertinent parallel passage renders it quite unlikely that an exception clause belonged to the earliest tradition of Jesus' saying(s) on divorce.[3]

Today very few scholars would take the approach that the exception was included within the teaching of Jesus on divorce that was handed down by the earliest Christian witness.[4] Redactional analysis of Matthew's gospel generally inclines them towards the view that the exception clause arose as a response to the particular needs of the Matthean community.[5] The fact that it is present in both of Matthew's renditions of the logion on divorce suggests that the way in which the saying of Jesus on divorce was known to Matthew's community—presumably reflecting the discipline in force within that community—included an exception clause.

What did the exception really mean? How did Matthew's community understand Jesus' teaching on divorce? The response to this question is one that is vigorously debated at the present time, as it has been since the dawn of the historical-critical approach to New Testament texts. Before reviewing the various responses to this key question—and they are many—it might be good to recall that exegesis is a matter of the interpretation of texts within their historical context. To some degree, exegesis is a matter of semantics. It is a matter of interpreting the words which an author has used within an historical and literary context. When a critical reader attends to the words in which Matthew has formulated his exception clauses, he or she must recognize that some degree of ambiguity is inherent in the words which Matthew himself has chosen.

A Matter of Semantics

The words under discussion are "*pas ho apoluôn tên gunaika autou parektos logou porneias*-anyone who divorces his wife, except on the ground of unchastity" (Matt 5:32) and "*hos an apolusê tên gunaika autou mê epi porneia*-whoever divorces his wife, except for unchastity" (Matt 19:9). In all, five expressions need to be clarified: 1) "divorces" (from the verb *apoluô*); 2) "his wife" (*tên gunaika autou*); 3) "except" (*parektos,* Matt 5:32, or *mê epi,* Matt 19:9); 4) "unchastity" (*porneia;* Matt 5:32; 19:9); and 5) "ground of unchastity" (*logou porneias,* Matt 5:32).

1) "Divorces" (*apoluôn* or *apolusê*): The verb *apoluô* is a technical term for divorce.[6] On the basis of a study of a Palestinian Greek text on remarriage found in Murabba'at's Cave 2, Fitzmyer believes that the use of *apoluô* in that text was an attempt to render into Greek an Aramaic verb customarily used in Jewish writs of divorce.

While recognizing that *apoluô* does mean "divorce," with the implication that the divorced spouses are free to contract another marriage, it must also be recognized that "divorce" is a specific connotation of a verb whose basic meaning is to dismiss.

Matthew's use of "*apoluô*-divorce" does not, therefore, necessarily imply a formal divorce procedure nor does it necessarily imply that a legal marriage has been contracted. If one were to write about a man's divorcing his wife according to acceptable social practice and the provisions of the Law, the verb *apoluô* would be used. If one were to write about a man's dismissing a concubine, the verb *apoluô* would also be used.

2) "His wife" (*tên gunaika autou*): Of itself the noun *gunê* denotes a mature woman, irrespective of her social status. It means "woman," as distinct from "girl," not specifically a "wife" as distinct from an "unmarried woman." In this respect it is similar to the English "Mr." which designates a man, as distinct from a boy.[7] In one and the other instance it is the context in which the term is used which determines whether the object of the discourse is a married person or not.

The qualified expression, *tên gunaika autou,* literally means "his woman." If there had been a legal marriage, the expression would signify "his wife." If a man and a woman were not legitimately married, this qualified expression would simply imply that the woman somehow belonged to the man. Although *gunê,* in and of itself, does not indicate marital status, it must be granted that within Matthew's cultural situation most adult women were married and that his Hellenistic Greek would have used *gunê* to describe them.

3) "Except" (*parektos* or *mê epi*): Both *parektos* and the expression *mê epi* occur but once in Matthew's gospel, that is, in the passages under present consideration. "*Parektos*-except" is

hapax[8] in Matt 5:32, while "*mê epi-except*" is hapax in Matt 19:9.[9] The components of the latter expression are, however, quite Matthean. According to Morgenthaler's statistics, Matthew uses the particle *mê* 129 times and the preposition *epi* 120 times.[10]

There may be legitimate reasons to think that "*parektos-except*" reflects a pre-Matthean formulation[11] and that "*mê epi-except*" is a Matthean expression, but it does not seem necessary to otherwise distinguish between these two prepositions.[12]

4) "Unchastity" (*porneia*): In classical Greek, *porneia* denoted fornication or prostitution, but in Hellenistic Greek, the noun acquired the general meaning of unchastity.[13] In Hellenistic literature the literary context within which *porneia* is used determines its specific connotation.

In a study of the use of *porneia* and its cognates in the New Testament,[14] Marcel Dumais[15] has suggested that this Greek vocabulary was used of such diverse sexual sins as sexual intercourse with a prostitute, adultery, incest, and possibly pre-marital sex (that is, a woman's sexual intercourse with a man other than her future husband). "*Porneia*-unchastity" appears in the New Testament's catalogs of vices. In these lists, it has a general meaning and can possibly be translated as debauchery. Since marriages within forbidden degrees of kinship were considered to be a source of ritual impurity, the term was also used to describe these incestuous relationships.[16] Finally, the language of *porneia* was used metaphorically of religious infidelity.

5) "Ground of unchastity" (*logou porneias*): This expression, found in the New Testament only in Matt 5:32, is an obvious Semitism. It appears to be a rather literal translation of the *'erwat dâbâr* of Deut 24:1.

The Greek Bible (LXX) uses "*porneia*-unchastity" to translate a variety of Hebrew words.[17] Not once, however, does the Septuagint use "*porneia*-unchastity" to translate *'erwah* (indecency). In the Septuagint, *'erwah* is normally translated by *aschêmon*. Thus in Deut 24:1, as in Deut 23:14, we find the Hebrew Bible's "something objectionable"[18] (*'erwat dâbâr*) rendered as *aschêmon pragma*[19] (literally, "a shameful deed" or "a shameful thing"), words hardly ever used by Matthew. Matthew does not use *aschêmon* ("shameful") or its cognates at all.[20] He uses *pragma* ("deed" or "thing") only in Matt 18:19.

The Historical Context

Since the way that Matthew's exceptive clause is phrased in Matt 5:32 seems to allude to the text of Deut 24:1, it might be useful to examine, if only briefly, the biblical text itself. The discussion is all the more warranted insofar as in each of Matthew's versions of the logion of divorce—with its respective exception clause—the saying of Jesus is antithetically juxtaposed with the biblical text.

Furthermore, most discussions of the historical circumstances in which the Matthean exception clauses developed generally begin with a reference to the difference given to this very passage of Deuteronomy by the disciples of Shammai and those of Hillel, respectively:

> "The school of Shammai say: A man may not divorce his wife unless he has found unchastity in her, for it is written, 'Because he hath found in her *indecency* in anything' And the school of Hillel say: [He may divorce her] even if she spoiled a dish for him, for it is written, 'Because he hath found in her indecency in *anything*.' R. Akiva says: "Even if he found another fairer than she, for it is written, 'And it shall be if she find no favor in his eyes.' " (*m. Giṭ.* 9:10).

The Bible

According to this classic description, the rabbinic debate turned upon the interpretation of Deut 24:1, the very verse to which Matthew makes reference in both Matt 5:31 and 19:7. The verse belongs to a relatively short pericope, Deut 24:1-4:

> [1]Suppose a man enters into marriage with a woman, but she does not please him because he finds something objectionable about her, and so he writes her a certificate of divorce, puts it in her hand, and sends her out of his house; she then leaves his house. [2]and goes off to become another man's wife. [3]Then suppose the second man dislikes her, writes her a bill of divorce, puts it in her hand, and sends her out of his house (or the second man who married her dies); [4]her first husband, who sent her away, is not permitted to take her again to be his wife after

she has been defiled; for that would be abhorrent to the Lord, and you shall not bring guilt on the land that the Lord your God is giving you as a possession.

This pericope is part of a small Deuteronomistic corpus of texts on marriage.[21] It is generally considered to be the basic biblical text for the entire Jewish law on divorce.[22] It is, in fact, the only legislative text in the Bible dealing with divorce, but it must be recognized that the text did not institute the practice of divorce within Judaism. The text presupposes the practice of divorce, which it then regulates in terms of conditions, procedure, and consequences, apparently as a matter of private law.[23]

This Deuteronomic text merits careful study. An in-depth pursuit of that study would take us far beyond what the length and intent of the present book can allow,[24] but a few remarks are certainly in order. To begin, the most primitive form of the text may not have required any formal grounds for the husband's divorce of his wife. Some commentators have suggested that the "something objectionable" formula is a later addition to the text.[25]

As far as the present text itself is concerned, the meaning of the terminology in the "something objectionable" formula, specifying the legitimate grounds for divorce, is not all that clear, as the famous tannaitic discussion between the Hillelites and the Shammites bears witness. For the Deuteronomist, the expression "something indecent" (*'erwat dâbâr,* literally, "the nakedness of a thing") did not necessarily imply a sexual fault. The phrase is used in Deut 23:14 in reference to human excrement. In biblical times it is quite likely that the "something objectionable" of Deut 24:1 referred to something other than adultery.[26] Adultery was a capital crime, punishable by death by stoning (Lev 20:10; Deut 22:22). Dismissal of the adulterous wife from her husband's household and giving her a certificate of dismissal was not a penalty. The certificate gave her the possibility of entering into marriage with a new husband.

On the other hand, some Deuteronomic laws, especially Deut 22:13-18 and Deut 22:28-29, imply that the matter of divorce normally arose when a woman was an adulteress or suspected of being one.[27] Elsewhere in the Septuagint, Dan 13:63—in reference to

Susanna—clearly indicates that adultery was considered to be "something shameful."

In any event, the punishment which had been stipulated for adultery was mitigated during the course of time.[28] The deutero-Isaiah (Isa 50:1), Jeremiah (Jer 3:7-10), and Hosea (Hos 2:4) seem to indicate that mandatory divorce was the punishment for adultery. It is probable that adultery was not punished by the imposition of a death penalty in Palestine during Roman times.[29] Nonetheless, in his exposition of the Law, Josephus explains that the death penalty is inexorable for any who is guilty of the crime of adultery.[30]

While the provisions of Deut 24:1-4 served a social purpose—especially as they came to be understood over the course of the years—in restricting a husband's arbitrary right to divorce his wife and in providing a divorced wife with an attestation of her freedom to be remarried,[31] the final redaction of the text is one which did not allow a husband to remarry a wife whom he has divorced, even after the death of her second husband. Laws of ritual purity[32] are as much at issue as social concerns for the woman who is being divorced—if not more so. Deut 24:1-4 clearly addresses itself to issues of a husband's responsibilities,[33] not to the matter of a wife's care.

The Law in Practice

Under the Law it was only a husband who could legitimately prepare and serve a certificate of dismissal. This seems to be the obvious sense of Deut 24:1-4.[34] Moreover, the verbs which appear in what has been called the "biblical dictionary of divorce terms"—that is, such terms as *garash* (to divorce), *shalaḥ* (to dismiss), *sane'* (to hate)[35] and *azav* (to desert)—are found in sentences in which the husband is the subject and the woman is the object, unless the passive voice is used.[36] Finally, in his explanatory commentary on the Jewish divorce practice, Josephus notes that "it is [only] the man who is permitted to do this" (*andri men gar exesti par' hêmin touto poiein*) and goes on to note that "not even a divorced woman may marry again on her own initiative unless her former husband consents."[37]

On the other hand, wives occasionally left their husbands.[38] In his autobiography Josephus remarks in passing that his own first wife had left him.[39] In first-century Palestine, wives sometimes attempted to divorce their husbands.[40] Josephus reports, for example, that Salome, Herod's sister, had divorced her husband, Costobarus. Apparently she even dared to serve him with a certificate of divorce.[41] This instance may well have been a case of a Hellenistic royal custom being adopted in the culturally less pristine court of Herod.[42] Josephus also reports that Herodias, the daughter of Herod Agrippa, divorced her husband in order to marry her brother-in-law.[43] Notwithstanding the high social positions of these women, Josephus opines that their actions were "contrary to Jewish law" (*ou kata tous Ioudaiôn nomous*).[44]

In some circles, wives seemed, nonetheless, to have benefited from a legal right to divorce provided that such a right had been stipulated in the marriage contract.[45] In the Jewish colony of Elephantine in Egypt (ca. 500 B.C.) some women divorced their husbands. This was most probably due to the influence of the surrounding social environment which made such divorce possible.[46] Although the Elephantine texts do not explicitly mention a certificate of dismissal, divorce—unlike marriage—was a matter of public interest. The party initiating the divorce arose in an assembly, that is, in the presence of witnesses, and declared "hatred" for the repudiated spouse.[47] Among the grounds for divorce are the husband's (or wife's) refusal to have sexual intercourse and the husband's taking a second wife.[48]

Ernst Bammel and Bernadette Brooten cite various other texts that indicate that women did occasionally take the initiative in a divorce. Texts from Murabba'at, the Samaritans, the Jerusalem Talmud,[49] and the Karaite writings are the principal passages which they cite in addition to the Elephantine documentation.[50] Within rabbinic Judaism, rabbis were apparently finally successful in suppressing the practice. Although only a husband could legally deliver a certificate of dismissal—as Josephus reiterates— according to later talmudic legislation an aggrieved wife had the right of appeal to the court which had the power to bring pressure to bear upon an aggrieving husband to prepare the certificate of dismissal.[51] The rabbis also seem to have recognized a pagan divorce obtained by a wife through the practice of the *repudium.*[52]

The Interpretation of the Bible

In the intepretation of the law, the right of a husband to dismiss his wife underwent various restrictions,[53] and the severity of the law was gradually tempered in favor of the woman.[54] The school of Shammai interpreted the "something objectionable" of Deut 24:1 as adultery and as the sole reason justifying divorce.[55] Many New Testament scholars capitalize on the disagreement between the school of Shammai and that of Hillel to affirm that the Matthean Jesus sided with the school of Shammai in interpreting Deut 24:1 in a narrow sense, but there is no certainty that the tradition related in the Mishnah actually reflects the real halakhic situation before the destruction of the temple.[56]

The tannaitic debate between the disciples of Shammai and those of Hillel centered on the applicability of Deut 24:1. In what circumstances *might* a husband legitimately make use of it to divorce his wife? There are, however, other related and more specific questions which were asked. These are questions like "When *must* a husband divorce his wife in accordance with the provisions?" and "When *may* a husband *not* make use of it to divorce his wife?"

As for the first of these related questions, there were some circumstances in which a husband was not permitted to divorce his wife. Two cases are cited in the Bible itself.[57] A man who violated an unbetrothed virgin was required to marry her and was not permitted to divorce her (Deut 22:28-29).[58] A man who falsely accused his wife of not having been a virgin at the time of their marriage was not thereafter allowed to divorce her (Deut 22:18-19).

In addition, under rabbinic law, a man was not permitted to divorce a woman of unsound mind.[59] Nor was he allowed to divorce a wife while she was in a state of captivity.[60] Moreover it was forbidden for a husband to divorce a wife who was too young to understand the certificate of dismissal (and take advantage of the liberty which it afforded her).[61]

On the other hand, there seem to have been circumstances in which, at least under Talmudic law, a husband was obliged to divorce his wife.[62] If a man were to be considered a "just man," one whose "walking" was in accordance with the precepts of the Law as those precepts were interpreted by the legal experts, he was expected to divorce his wife in certain circumstances.

For example, a man who discovered on his wedding night that his wife was not a virgin was to divorce her.[63] A man whose wife had commited adultery was forbidden to him.[64] In this case, the husband was expected to give her a certificate of dismissal and she was apparently allowed to claim divorce if her husband did not do so.[65] A husband was expected to institute divorce proceedings[66] if his marriage was prohibited, irrespective of the spouses' knowledge of the prohibition at the time of their marriage and irrespective of their sexual intercourse after the marriage.[67] Finally, it appears that a man was to divorce his wife if she had not borne him a child within ten years of their marriage, but only if he did not have children by another woman.[68]

An Alternative Lifestyle

The discovery of the Dead Sea Scrolls gives evidence of the fact that at least one group within first-century Judaism, namely, the Essenes, banned divorce. Taking issue with the tolerance of divorce within other strains of Judaism, the Essenes, as has been noted, considered divorce and polygamy, along with incest, to be forms of "whoredom" (*zĕnût*).[69] The community's Halakah required the members "to refrain from whoredom (*hzwnwt*)" (CD 7:1). In a midrashic commentary on Isa 24:17, an unknown Essene author commented upon the havoc wreaked upon Israel by the evil power of Belial and explained what was meant by "whoredom" (*zĕnût*). The prophet had said: "Terror, and the pit, and the snare are upon you, O inhabitant of the earth!" (Isa 24:17, NRSV). The commentator reflected:

> And during all those years shall Belial be let loose upon Israel as He spoke by the hand of the prophet Isaiah son of Amoz, saying: "Fear, and the pit, and the snare are upon thee, O inhabitant of the land." Its explanation: the three nets of Belial,

about which Levi son of Jacob said that he "catches in them the heart [or the house] of Israel: and has made them appear to them as three kinds of righteousness. The first is whoredom (*hazĕnût*) . . . [they] are caught in two respects in whoredom (*bznwt*):
     (a) by marrying two women "in their lifetime," although the principle of nature is: "a male and a female He created them;" and those that were in the ark, "two and two they went into the ark." And about the prince it is written: "Let him not multiply wives unto himself;" but David had not read in the sealed Book of the Law which was inside the ark of the covenant, because it had not been opened in Israel since the day when Eleazar and Jehoshua [and Joshua] and the Elders died, forasmuch as they "worshipped the Ashtoreth," and it was hidden and was not revealed until the son of Zadok arose. And the deeds of David were reckoned as inadvertent sins, except the blood of Uriah, and God allowed them to him.
     Also they convey uncleanness to the sanctuary, inasmuch as they do not keep separate according to the Law, but lie with her that sees "the blood of her flux." (b) And they marry each man the daughter of his brother and the daughter of his sister, though Moses said: 'Thou shalt not approach to thy mother's sister; she is thy mother's kin,' and the rules of incest are written with reference to males and apply equally to women; hence, if the brother's daughter uncover the nakedness of her father's brother, being his kin . . ." (CD 4:12-5:11).[70]

The posture of the Essenes in regard to divorce and polygamy was so radical, indeed countercultural, that they developed a scriptural apologetic in favor of their position.[71] That apologetic made use of biblical texts drawn from the creation and flood narratives as well as the royal law on marriage. As has been already noted, one of the texts used in the scriptural apologetic was Gen 1:27, a text used by both Mark and Matthew in their versions of the conflict story.

On the other hand, the Essenes' radical abhorrence of incest was not countercultural. Their halakah made it clear that the tabu on incestuous relationships extended to women as well as to men, but their strong stance on the prohibition of incest stood well within Jewish tradition. The Holiness Code had spelled out a whole series of relationships (Lev 18:6-23)[72] within which sexual intercourse was considered as something unnatural and forbidden by God.

With regard to the biblical prohibition of incest, it is noteworthy that the encompassing framework (Lev 18: 2b-5, 24-30) is particularly solemn and very striking. It defines incestuous unions as abominations and attributes them to the Caananites (Lev 18:3, 27), who were considered to be especially lubricious and promiscuous. For a Jew to avoid sexual union within the forbidden degrees of relationship was a matter of life (Lev 18:5). The enjoyment of the prohibited sexual intercourse would, on the other hand, bring defilement upon the land. Accordingly, the Jew who violated this ban on incestuous sexual union was to be cut off from the people. As a matter of fact, the abhorrence of incest[73] was so severe that not only the Jew but also the stranger (the *ger*) dwelling in the land of Israel (*eretz Israel*) was also bound to avoid all incestuous relationships (Lev 18:26).

Later Jewish jurisprudence would underscore the importance of the prohibition of incest. Within the classic list of the 613 commandments, the prohibition of the various forms of incest (commandments 331-345) was cited before the prohibition of adultery (no. 347), harlotry (no. 355), remarriage after divorce (no. 356), and the marriage of a eunuch (no. 360).[74] Marriages within the degrees of kinship forbidden by the provisions of the Holiness Code were classified among the *gillui arayot* (*literally, "uncovering of nakedness"*[75]), the sexual sins which, in prior times, under Pentateuchal Law, had been subject to the death penalty. Later jurisprudence considered these forbidden marriages to be not only prohibited but also null.[76]

Roman Law

Still another factor which must be taken into consideration in evaluating the situation in which the Matthean exception clause was formulated, and the situation in which Matthew wrote his Gospel, is the Roman domination of the times. In the Roman year DCCXXXVI, that is 18 B.C., Caesar Augustus had approved the *Lex Iulia de adulteriis coercendis*.[77] The law forbade a husband to kill a wife caught in adultery, but required him to repudiate her and make the situation known to the proper magistrate. As a result of this law, adultery became a delict, a matter of public law rather than being simply an offense against domestic law, as it had been prior to the Augustan legislation. A husband's failure to comply with the provision of the law requiring him to denounce an adulterous spouse made the husband himself liable to being charged with the crime of pandering (*lenocinium*), a capital offense.[78]

The Ecclesial Situation

Since the exceptive clauses are found only in Matthew's renditions of Jesus' teaching on divorce and are not found in any of the other New Testament passages which convey this tradition, it is reasonable to assume that they represent an adaptation of the tradition that specifically pertains to Matthew's own community. Matthew's community was essentially a Jewish-Christian community, to which not a few Gentile Christians belonged.[79] Its radical Judeo-Christian character is reflected in the pervasive Jewish flavor of Matthew's gospel narrative as well as by the evangelist's tendency to re-judaize materials that he has taken over from his Markan source. Its openness to Gentiles is, on the other hand, reflected in the "Great Commission," with which the gospel is brought to its close (Matt 28:16-20)[80] as well as in a variety of editorial modifications which the evangelist has brought to bear on the traditional material which he has used.[81]

Matthew's community was concerned with developing a Judeo-Christian ethos. This specifically Jewish-Christian halakah has been clearly expressed in the Sermon on the Mount (Matt 5-7). The halakah of Matthew's community clearly did not emerge within a vacuum. The community was concerned with its Jewish "opponents," "the Pharisees" whose righteousness was to be exceeded by Christians. These were the religious authorities of the Jewish communities from which Matthew's Jewish-Christian community was painfully separating. On the other hand, it was also concerned with its own members who might tend towards a lax interpretation of traditional Jewish norms.[82] These latter may well have been Gentile Christians, for whom traditional Jewish halakic norms had not been obligatory prior to their entrance into Matthew's Jewish-Christian ecclesial community.

The New Testament offers ample evidence that traditional Jewish norms on sexuality and marital halakah were especially problematic for Gentiles who wished to enter into the church.[83] When Jewish Christians and Gentile Christians co-existed within a same Christian community, questions were raised as to the propriety of certain Gentile sexual practices and marital customs.

Marriages presumed to be incestuous were particularly problematic for Jewish Christians. The so-called apostolic decree of Acts 15:23-29 indicates that among the four commandments of Moses[84] which the Gentile Christians of Antioch, Syria, and Cilicia were expected to observe was the injunction to abstain from *porneia* (Acts 15:29), that is, incestuous relationships.[85] Since the Bible itself had imposed the observance of these commandments on Gentiles living among Jews, Jewish Christians considered that their observance was incumbent upon Gentile Christians in order that there might be *koinônia,* that is, communion or fellowship between the two groups.

A Caution

The apostolic decree represents Luke's ideation of the Church and its unity,[86] but it is not impossible that a similarly problematic situation of marriages judged by some to be incestuous unions existed within Matthew's community. On the other hand, as one attempts to make sense of Matthew's problematic exception clause, the discerning reader should not overlook the fact that much of the older literature dealing with the matter was written before the discovery of the Dead Sea Scrolls. At that time it was all too easy to assume that Matthew's exception clause was formulated within what has sometimes been called "normative" or "mainstream" Judaism.[87] With the discovery of the scrolls, we have learned that first-century Judaism—indeed first-century Palestinian Judaism itself—was far more diversified than had previously been thought.

As a result one cannot simply assume that Matthew's exception clause was formulated within the context of the difference of opinion between the schools of Shammai and Hillel. One cannot, moreover, and without further discussion, simply assume that the tradition related in the Mishnah regarding the interpretation of Deut 24:1 reflects the real halakhic situation at the time of Jesus or at the time of the composition of Matthew's gospel, although this is often presumed to be the case—particularly in the older literature on Matthew's exception clause. Contemporary studies of rabbinic literature call into question this—as so many other— easy assumption(s).

Various Opinions

Within the context of this situation, how did Matthew and his community understand the exception clause? In the history of Christianity, a variety of answers has been given. Some differences of opinion are undoubtedly due to the influence of different practices among the various Christian churches. The development of biblical interpretation has had, however, no small role to play in creating such diversity of opinion as exists at the present time. The consensus two document approach to the Synoptic Problem, the discovery of the Dead Sea Scrolls, and a more sophisticated approach to first century Judaism and rabbinic studies have had their part to play in shaping the contemporary discussion on the matter. There continues to be a remarkable difference of opinion among scholars as to what the exception clause really means. Some of the attempts at explanation undoubtedly belong to what Joachim Gnilka has called "the exegetical curiosity cabinet,"[88] but the bottom line is that the various opinions are many and quite diverse.[89]

1) An ancient opinion, sometimes called the traditional or Catholic opinion, interprets Matthew's problematic phraseology in terms of a legitimate separation from bed and board, without thereby implying that either of the spouses is free to remarry. This opinion goes back to such Fathers of the Church[90] as Jerome,[91] Augustine,[92] and John Chrysostom.[93] As church praxis, it is reflected in the Shepherd of Hermas, a sub-apostolic Christian text.[94] The Ambrosiaster, an anonymous author of the late fourth century, was virtually the only exception to the position which

the Fathers otherwise held in common. The Ambrosiaster held
that adulterous conduct on the part of the wife made it legitimate
for her husband to dismiss her and take another wife.[95] On the
other hand, the Ambrosiaster admitted that a wife could divorce
her husband, but she was not allowed to remarry.[96]

In recent years, the traditional interpretation of the Fathers[97]
has been vigorously proposed by Jacques Dupont as well as by
William A. Heth and Gordon J. Wenham among contemporary
exegetes.[98] Essentially, reasons Dupont, Matthew does not stand
in opposition to the earlier Jesus tradition.[99] Jesus has given a
new meaning to the verb *apoluô*. It does not mean what the Jews
of his time thought it meant. It does not mean divorce with the
right to remarriage; it simply means dismissal.[100] In Matt 5:32
there is no question of remarriage.[101] The logion of Jesus quoted
by Matthew indicates that it is permissible to dismiss one's wife
for reasons of her misconduct, as certain Jews required, but
teaches that any one who marries the divorced woman commits
adultery.

Matthew's version of the conflict story is different from Mark's.
In Mark, the conflict story focuses on the legitimacy of dismissing one's wife, while the instruction for the disciples focuses on
the effects of dismissal, should, by chance, such a dismissal actually take place. Matthew's version of the story concerns only the
reasons for the dismissal. The Pharisees' question in verse 3 is
answered in verse 9. The only legitimate ground for dismissal is
misconduct. A wife's marital misconduct constitutes grounds for
dismissal, but for dismissal only. The exceptive clause, "except
for unchastity," of Matt 19:9 modifies only the verb *apoluô*.[102]
Were the exception clause to have modified both verbs, it should
normally have appeared after the verb "*gamêsê*-marry."

Although the Greek text of Matt 19:9 may not be a model of
clarity, the parallel in Matt 5:32 makes it clear enough that Matthew is stating that dismissing one's wife and remarrying is adulterous conduct, even though circumstances of her misconduct justify
her dismissal. The phraseology of Matt 19:9 might, therefore, be
taken as an attempt on the part of the evangelist to say two things
at once. The obtuse result can be considered as a terse, epigram-
matic summary of the two propositions enunciated in Matt 5:32,
that is, to divorce except for *porneia* is adulterous and to divorce
and remarry is adulterous.[103]

Although this line of approach thoroughly dominated the patristic era, many contemporary exegetes are not, however, happy with the classic solution. They argue that such a separation from bed and board was, at the time, socially impossible.

2) Many biblical scholars, particularly and "traditionally"— but not exclusively—Protestant and Orthodox interpreters, hold that Matthew's exception clause constituted a real exception. There is at least one set of circumstances, that described by Matthew as *porneia,* in which it is legitimate for a man to divorce his wife and remarry. This type of interpretive approach goes back to Erasmus,[104] who held that Matthew's exceptive clause indicated that it was permissible for a man to divorce an adulterous wife and then remarry.

According to this view *porneia* is generally understood to mean "adultery."[105] With regard to this interpretation of *porneia,* one should note that neither in Matt 5:32 nor in Matt 19:9 is the personal pronoun *"autês*-her" used to qualify *"porneia*-unchastity." Rather than specifying the meaning of *porneia* as adultery, some modern translations try to capture the sense of Matthew's exception by rendering Matthew's *"porneia*-unchastity" as "marital unfaithfulness."[106]

From this point of view, the Matthean Jesus essentially endorses an interpretation of Deut 24:1-4 similar to that maintained by the school of Shammai.[107] Divorce is not permitted, except in the case of adultery on the part of the wife. Matt 5:32a strongly emphasizes the husband's responsibility in the matter of divorce. Under Jewish marriage law, an adulterous wife was forbidden to her husband. For all practical purposes she was considered "dead" to her husband.[108] He was not permitted to resume conjugal intercourse with her and was required to divorce her. Some authors[109] also note that, under the Roman *Lex Iulia de adulteriis coercendis,* a husband was legally bound to denounce and divorce an adulterous wife. In the case of a husband who was a Roman citizen, the exceptive clauses would relieve him of the responsibility of violating the law and being subject to its penalty.

In any case, Matthew's exceptive clauses are intended to relieve the husband from responsibility for the divorce and its consequences when the wife has committed adultery. The social conditions of the times were such that the husband who had divorced his wife would remarry.

Among the objections sometimes raised to this point of view is that the Greek language has a specific word for "adultery," namely, *moicheia,* a term used in the New Testament, even by Matthew.[110] Why was this term not used in a text which has the form of casuistic law? Moreover, if *porneia* actually means adultery, what is the meaning of Matt 5:32a? If the grounds for the divorce are adultery, in what sense does a husband involve his already-adulterous wife in adultery?

3) Another popular opinion holds that, in its Matthean context, "*porneia*-unchastity" really connotes marriage within forbidden degrees of relationship. According to this view the relationship would be incestuous and the marriage invalid. Joseph Bonsirven, who proposed this view in 1948,[111] argued that the rabbis used the term *zĕnût* to describe such an illegitimate union. The woman involved in such an incestuous union was called a *zonah*. Bonsirven further argued that the term *porneia* was used in the New Testament to indicate marriages that were contracted in violation of the prescriptions in Leviticus 18 relating to the degrees of kinship within which marriage was not permitted.[112]

According to this view, some Christians might have used the Jesus tradition to their own self-seeking advantage. Some might have employed Jesus' radical call to marital fidelity as a warrant for their continuance in a union that was illicit.[113] Matthew's community counteracted this unfaithful use of the Jesus' tradition by adding the exceptive clauses. Jesus did not allow divorce except if an apparent marital relationship was, in fact, not a licit union. In a variation on this theme, Heinrich Baltensweiler has suggested that the clause was added to clarify the situation of Gentile converts whose marriage would have been considered incestuous from a Jewish point of view.[114]

Bonsirven's proposal gained the support of many exegetes, the majority of whom were Roman Catholic.[115] It is reflected in several recent translations of the New Testament, especially those published under Roman Catholic auspices—for example, the RNAB which renders the problematic clause "unless the marriage is unlawful" and the NJB which translates *porneia* as "illicit marriage,"[116] as well as in the French-language ecumenical translation of the New Testament (*TOB*).[117]

This so-called rabbinic view maintains inviolate Jesus' prohibition of divorce. It also enjoys a certain degree of linguistic and historical plausibility since it is based on the text of Matthew's gospel and capitalizes on its Jewish Christian life situation. Support for its plausibility can be found in the Qumran material,[118] with its manifest abhorrence for incest, a form of *zěnût,* a Hebrew word whose Greek translation would be *porneia.* Finally, this rabbinic solution draws attention to a problem to which the New Testament makes reference, namely, the extent to which the Jewish ethos on marriage must be adopted by those Gentiles who enter the church and are in table fellowship with Jewish Christians.[119]

4) While these three approaches are widely reflected in the current literature on the Matthean exceptive clauses, they are by no means the only opinions that are expressed. Another view, capitalizing on the same literature from Qurman[120] as the rabbinic interpretation, holds that Matthew's *porneia* evokes a specific form of unchastity, not incest, but polygamy. "*Porneia*-bigamy" constitues an affront to Jesus' call for monogamous fidelity on the part of the husband. Divorce is unacceptable for the disciples of Jesus except in the case of bigamy.[121]

5) Yet another opinion takes the exceptive clause to refer to mixed marriages.[122] Since *porneia* ("infidelity") is used of religious infidelity in the Jewish tradition, especially in the prophetic literature, Matthew's exception could refer to those situations in which the partners had been married prior to their conversion to Christianity. After the conversion of one of the spouses, the marriage might be troubled because of the lack of faith of the non-Christian partner. Basically, this approach views Matthew's exception clause as relating to a situation similar to that treated by Paul in 1 Cor 7:12-16.

6) There are, on the other hand, a variety of opinions which take Matthew's *porneia*-clause as a real exception to the ban on divorce and remarriage, but suggest that *porneia* is some form of unchastity on the part of the wife, but not necessarily a single adulterous liaison. André-Marie Dubarle, for example, has proposed that Matthew's *porneia* connotes not a single act of adultery, but a life of harlotry.[123]

7) Another approach to the matter is one which takes *porneia* as a reference to a sexual offense committed by a woman prior to her marriage.[124] This approach differentiates between "*moicheia*-adultery" and "*porneia*-unchastity" and attempts to interpret the latter on the basis of various Jewish traditions and texts.

8) Yet another approach tries to provide some suppleness. It holds that the exceptive clauses express a true exception to God's basic design for the marriage of a man and woman, but is content with the ambiguity of Matthew's choice of vocabulary. According to this view, Matthew has expressed a real exception to the absolute prohibition of divorce. That exception is whatever is meant by *porneia*.[125] For Markus Bockmuehl, it is "*any* kind of obviously unlawful sexual relationship,"[126] while for D. A. Carson it is sexual sin of any sort, including but not limited to adultery.[127]

9) A singular opinion has been expressed by John J. Kilgallen,[128] who claims that the import of the exceptive clause is that it affirms that not every divorce is adulterous—which is not to say that it is thereby permitted. Matthew has made a dramatic exposition of the fundamental reason why divorce is wrong in Matt 19:3-9. The reason is that men and women should not separate what God has joined into one. Matt 19:9 adds and Matt 5:32 states that most (but not all) divorces are also adulterous.

10) Some of this century's Roman Catholic interpreters espoused a position that has been called the inclusive interpretation.[129] Their idea was that Matthew's logia did not permit divorce, not even in the case of *porneia* or adultery. The meaning of verse 9 would be: anyone who divorces his wife—and that includes even the case of her marital misconduct—and marries another commits adultery. A major difficulty with this interpretation is that, on merely linguistic grounds, it is hardly possible.

11) According to what has been called the preteritive or exclusive interpretation, the Matthean Jesus would have left the case of uxorial misconduct outside of consideration.[130] The exceptive clauses are to be interpreted as merely parenthetical remarks.[131] The Matthean Jesus does not address himself to the matter of *porneia*. He does not want to get involved in the legal discussion about the interpretation of the Law. He simply wants to affirm that divorce is contrary to God's creative will.

According to Thomas Fleming[132] Jesus would have superseded Moses by rejecting divorce for any reason other than adultery. Because the Pharisees were hardhearted, and discussion therefore useless, Jesus refused to consider the case of adultery.

This so-called exclusive interpretation falters on the same linguistic grounds as does the inclusive opinion. It is, moreover, hardly imaginable within the context of Matthew's historical circumstances. The pertinent question was precisely what were the legitimate grounds for divorce within the purview of Deuteronomy's *porneia* language.

12) Quite a different approach has been taken by those scholars who consider the exceptive clauses to be glosses added at a late stage of the Matthean text in order to make the saying of Jesus conform to the terms of the debate between the schools of Hillel and Shammai.[133] By means of this gloss on the earlier Matthean tradition, Jesus is portrayed as having made a choice for the more rigorous position. *Porneia* means adultery, but the puzzling exceptive clause is not the result of Matthew's editorial work; rather it stems from a later editor of the Matthean gospel.

This opinion is without support in the manuscript tradition of Matt 19:9. At best, it only exonerates the evangelist himself from responsibility for the confusing expression but leaves the modern interpreter with the difficulty of understanding the expression. In any case, it is the text as handed down by the manuscript tradition that must be interpreted.

A Reflection

Given the plethora of interpretations of Matthew's exceptive clause, it is clear that Matthew's language is not clear—at least its meaning is not self-evident to modern interpreters of his text. The first three approaches summarized above continue to generate the most support among contemporary scholars:[134] the traditional or Catholic position which holds that the Matthean exception indicates that divorce is possible in the case of the wife's marital infidelity, but that it is not permissible for a husband who has divorced his wife in these circumstances to remarry; the so-called Erasmian or Protestant and Orthodox position which holds that Matthew's exception means that a man may divorce an adulterous wife and subsequently remarry; and the so-called rabbinic position which holds that Matthew's exception relates to a particular situation within his church, namely, that of Gentile converts who had married but whose marriage would have been prohibited according to the laws of Leviticus 18 had they been Jews.[135]

In some ways, especially when comparing the traditional with the Erasmian approach, the modern interpreter of Matthew's exception clause is faced with a problem similar to that which faced the ancient rabbis in their interpretation of Deut 24:1. The basic problem is to determine where the emphasis is to be placed. The Mishnah recounts that: "The school of Shammai say: A man may not divorce his wife unless he has found unchastity in her, for it is written, 'Because he hath found in her *indecency* in anything' [with emphasis on *'erwat* in the expression *'erwat dâbâr*]. And the school of Hillel say: [He may divorce her] even if she spoiled a dish for him, for it is written, 'Because he hath found in her indecency in *anything*' [with emphasis upon *dâbâr* in the expression *'erwat dâbâr*]" (*m. Giṭ.* 9:10).

In the past, exegetical opinion was largely divided along confessional lines, for which the justification of current church practice was as much a consideration as was the interpretation of the Matthean text. Thus, Protestant and Orthodox interpreters made an exegesis of Matthew's exceptive clause(s) which justified the practice of divorce (with the possibility of remarriage) in the case of adultery, while Roman Catholics interpreted the problematic expression in such a way that it allowed divorce (that is, separation from bed and board) but not remarriage.

As a result of the recent acceptance of the historical-critical method of biblical exegesis among exegetes of all confessional persuasions, the positions of the various churches with regard to the matter of divorce and remarriage no longer impinge upon the interpretation of the Matthean text as they once did. Now there are evangelicals who espouse the "Catholic" interpretation of Matt 5:32 and 19:9, and there are Roman Catholics who opt for the "Protestant" or Orthodox interpretation of these texts.[136]

That there is such cross-confessional support for both positions indicates that they are not merely confessional positions, but are positions for which some justification can be found in the text—a text that constitutes a *crux,* not only for ecclesial practice but also for biblical interpretation. The meaning of Matthew's text is simply not all that clear. And it is the meaning of Matthew's text as such that occupies the attention of contemporary exegetes.

A Discussion

A Pre-Matthean Formula

There are reasons to believe that Matthew's exception clause reflects the tradition of Matthew's own Christian community. The exception is, in other words, pre-Matthean. From Mark 10:11-12, Matthew knew of a version of the Jesuanic logion on divorce without an exception clause. It is unlikely[137] that the evangelist would have added an exception to the traditional, and wide-spread, logion on his own authority. On the other hand, it is quite clear that Matthew accommodated the received tradition to the needs of his community.

Apart from this general and somewhat a priori consideration, there are serious linguistic grounds which suggest that the exception clause had been received by Matthew from his tradition.[138] In Matt 19:9, Matthew's exception clause, *"mê epi porneia-*except for unchastity,'' is Matthew's editorial addition to Mark 10:11. It is one of the many editorial changes that Matthew has made as he was revising the conflict story. *"Mê epi porneia-*except for unchastity'' is Matthew's formulation of the exception.

This formulation is, however, different from the wording of the exception found in the antithesis, namely, *"parektos logou porneias-*except on the ground of unchastity'' (Matt 5:32). *Parektos* is a word which does not appear elsewhere in Matthew's gospel. In contrast, both *mê* and *epi* are words which appear more than one hundred times in the First Gospel.[139] *Logos* is likewise a common word in Matthew's gospel. It appears thirty-three times. Apart from Matt 5:32, however, *logos* does not mean "thing" or "reality.''[140] In all thirty-two other Matthean uses of the lexeme—that is, in every instance, except for 5:32—*logos* has its usual meaning of "word, statement or address.''[141] Since the language of the exception clause in Matt 5:32 is so unusual, one must conclude that *"parektos logou porneias*-except on the ground of unchastity" reflects the formulation of Matthew's tradition and pre-dates Matthew.

Matthew is, moreover, a skillful editor. He is too fond of his own well-turned expressions[142] to have introduced the clumsy formulation of Matt 5:32, had it not been handed down within the tradition. Matthew's own rendition of the exception clause (Matt 19:9) is an easier formulation, and would likely have been used by the evangelist had not the clumsier formulation not somehow been cast in stone. It would seem, therefore, that the exception was known to Matthew's community prior to Matthew's composition of the gospel and apart from his personal authority within the community. It was the weight of his tradition which led to the retention of the clumsy formulation in Matt 5:32 and the redactional insertion in 19:9.

Deuteronomy 24:1

The clumsy phrasing of the exception, *"logou porneias*-ground of unchastity" in Matt 5:32 is a reference to and perhaps even a free translation of the Bible's "*'erwat dâbâr*-something objectionable." It is also clear that the interpretation of the biblical legislation (Deut 24:1-4) was in a state of flux and that the interpretation of "*'erwat dâbâr*-something objectionable" was a moot issue within Judaism at the very moment that Matthew's Christian community was sundering its links with Judaism. The gospel's witness to the engagement of the Matthean community with the "*'erwat dâbâr*-something objectionable" issue is but one indication of the community's attempt to define itself within formative Judaism.[143]

A Real Exception?

Because he has introduced an exceptive clause into both Matt 5:32 and 19:9, our evangelist has highlighted the fact that the point which he was making by means of this clause was of great importance to himself and the community for which his gospel was immediately intended.

It is also important to note that Matthew has introduced these clauses within a narrative context that gives every evidence of having been carefully composed. It is hardly likely that an author as skillful as the evangelist would derogate from the thrust of his argumentation or render his narrative nonsensical by means of an editorial addition which was contrary to the point that he was making, let alone use his own authority to make an affirmation contrary to the teaching of the Jesus whom he customarily called Lord.

In the antitheses, Matthew has attempted to combat a laxist interpretation of the Law as well as proclaim, as the way to be followed by the members of his community, a form of righteousness that was superior to that of the scribes and Pharisees. Were the exception of Matt 5:32 a real exception to the Jesus tradition on divorce, the righteousness proposed by Matthew would not have exceeded that of the Pharisees. Since the logion of Matt 5:32 proposed a norm of behavior similar to that proclaimed within the school of Shammai,[144] the righteousness to which the disciples of Jesus are challenged in Matt 5:32 exceeds, at best, the righteousness of only some of the Pharisees.

If Matthew's formulation of verse 32 was intended to serve a function of casuistic law, the exception might well have been a real exception. The form of the phrase is indeed that of casuistic law, but its function is prophetic. A real exception would have destroyed the thrust of Matthew's antithetic formulation. A real exception would, moreover, seem to be out of place within the context of the series of antitheses. In the entire unit (Matt 5:21-48) there is no other passage which admits of an exception to Jesus' challenging call for righteousness. Thus, the logion of Matt 5:32 must be seen as a radical challenge to the Christians of Matthew's community.

By their very nature, the antitheses do not really offer casuistry nor do they attempt to set out an entire corpus of material pertinent to marriage. They are a prophetic challenge to the members of Matthew's church to live as Jesus would have them live, especially in the light of the substandard—substandard, that is, by the standards of Matthew's Jesus—practices of Gentiles and Jews with whom Matthew's community was in dialogue. The Gentiles practiced divorce; the "Pharisees" found a warrant for divorce in their interpretation of Deut 24:1-4. Matthew would had none of that for his community.

Indeed, if Matt 5:32a includes a real exception, why is not a similar exception made in verse 32b? If the provisions of Deut 24:1-4 are applicable, albeit limited, for example, to the case of adultery, why is the divorced wife not allowed to remarry? Or was she forbidden to marry only her paramour? The certificate of dismissal constitutes documentary evidence of her freedom to marry.[145]

In short, the thrust of Matthew's emphasis in the antitheses would seem to suggest that there is a situation in which divorce is permissible, but that that situation is not the range of possibilities covered under the then current interpretation of Deut 24:1-4.[146]

When attention is turned to the Matthean revision of Jesus' discussion with the Pharisees, there are once again reasons for suggesting that Matthew's exceptive clause does not constitute a real exception. On the one hand, a real exception would have placed the teaching of Jesus (Matt 19:9) in opposition to the will of God (Matt 19:6). Moreover, even though Matthew has carefully reworked the Markan narrative, he would have created an illogical Jesus. Having drawn a black-and-white conclusion from his scriptural midrash (Matt 19:3-6), the Matthean Jesus would have said that there is at least one gray area (Matt 19:9).

Two other considerations lead us to the conclusion that the exceptive clause in Matt 19:9 does not constitute a real exception. One is that Matt 19:9 appears as the final word in a conflict story. The nature of the genre is such that it presents contrasting positions. Matthew would have respected the laws of the genre only if a sharp contrast is drawn between the position espoused by Jesus and that proposed by his opponents, in this instance, the Pharisees with their recourse to Deut 24:1. In any case, the climax of an argumentative setting is not the place for the introduction of the fine distinctions of casuistic law.

There is, finally, the fact that Matthew has appended the eunuch saying to the conflict story. They both belong to the same narrative unit (Matt 19:3-12). Jesus' utterance created a kind of stumbling block which the eunuch saying seeks to clarify—unless, that is, the disciples of Jesus are viewed by Matthew as being utter laxists with regard to the Law, an interpretation of Matthew's "disciples of Jesus" which does not arise from a reading of his gospel. The eunuch saying shows that Jesus' teaching on divorce is a hard saying. For it to have been such, it must have been radically countercultural. It is apparent that Matthew did not consider his exception to be a real exception. Matthew and his community took exception to the way that Deut 24:1 was being invoked by the "Pharisees" of their day. Their way of interpreting God's word was not God's way. The way in which God's word was to be understood was the way in which it was proclaimed by Jesus. God's word spoke of "*'erwat dâbâr*-something objectionable." Matthew's Jesus explains: in the limited case of *porneia,* when both Jewish practice and Roman law sometime required a man to leave his wife, a man was not to be judged adulterous if he divorced the wife from whom he was required to separate.

A Final Reflection

Matthew's narrative presentation of Jesus' teaching on divorce, even with the exceptive clause, is such that it must be understood as a position that was countercultural to the dominant view of marriage and divorce held by the Jewish opponents of Matthew's community, represented by his Pharisees, with their scribes. Nonetheless, Matthew would have made use of the version of Jesus' teaching known to his community. The community was aware of that teaching in a version which had an exceptive clause, one that had been adapted to the situation of Matthew's Jewish-Christian community.

The formulation of the exceptive clause in Matt 5:32 suggests a pre-Matthean provenance.[147] As such it was most likely known to Matthew and his community in an oral form. We know comparatively little about the early history of the Matthean community, but it may have been, at one time, an exclusively Christian-Jewish[148] community. Whatever its ethnic make-up, why did it modify the traditional logion on divorce? What was the situation (*Sitz-im-Leben*) of the Matthean community as it passed along and adapted the oral tradition of Jesus' saying on divorce?

Might not it have been that the "except on the ground of unchastity," with its somewhat clumsy allusion to Deut 24:1, served to assuage the consciences of Jews who had availed themselves of the liberty accorded to the Jewish faithful under the provisions of the Law to divorce their wives for cause and now wished to associate themselves with the Christian-Jewish community?

Indeed, since it is not unlikely that, at least in certain circumstances, a pious Jew would consider himself bound to write a certificate of dismissal and send an adulterous wife from his household,[149] might not there have been Christian Jews who had divorced their wives because they considered that it was necessary to do so in order to be faithful to God's will? Alexander Sand writes of a *privilegium Judaicum* in that regard.[150] Similarly, might not there have been those in Matthew's community who believed themselves duty-bound under the constraints of the *Lex Iulia de adulteriis coercendis* to divorce their adulterous wives? It is, I believe, situations such as these that led the evangelist to retain the exception clause in the final edition of his gospel.[151] It served as a conscience clause for those who lived in a society ruled by law.

A particular scribal tradition lies behind the gospel.[152] Matthew's scribal tradition stands over and against the interpretive tradition which the evangelist attributes to "their scribes" (Matt 7:29). In first-century Palestine, men were divorcing their wives for reasons that might be considered quite trivial, for any reason whatsoever.[153] The school of Hillel's spoiled meal and Akiva's suggestion that the discovery of a more beautiful woman constituted adequate grounds for divorce can be cited as cases in point. Eventually that position would dominate rabbinic lore, especially after the Hillelite establishment at Jabne.

Matthew's community accepted the Law in its entirety (Matt 5:18). It could not abide the Law being used against itself, to make void the commandment of God or contravene his will. Part of the legacy of the Law was Deut 24:1, a Scripture with which Matthew's community had to seriously deal, as the clumsy formulation of Matt 5:32 seems to indicate. They interpreted its "something shameful" as *porneia,* that is, *zĕnût,* which connoted adultery.[154]

This narrow interpretation of the Deuteronomic prescription was countercultural both as regards the Jews with their increasingly tolerant attitude towards a man divorcing his wife and as regards the surrounding Hellenistic cultural environment. It was part of the distinctive halakah of Matthew's community. The adulterous wife could, and probably should, be dismissed. Forbidden to her husband, she was also forbidden to any other man. The one who dared to marry her was guilty of adultery.

When the evangelist subsequently edited the Markan conflict story, the version of the Jesuanic logion known to him was one that included an exception clause. While editing the story in such a way that it highlighted the fact that the liberal use made of Deut 24:1 was due to the Pharisees' hardheartedness—that is, not the Pharisees of Jesus' time, but those with whom the evangelist and his community were struggling—and modifying the Markan story in such a way that it conformed to his own understanding of the Decalogue, the evangelist introduced into Jesus' final word an exception clause. At this point the evangelist was neither initiating legislation nor promoting a new form of casuistry; he was simply making use of the Jesus tradition he and his community had known. Matthew did not see the exception as a derogation from the challenge of Jesus' word; rather, he saw that word as he had come to know it as a challenge to those who attempted to use God's word against itself.

7

The Development of a Tradition

Anyone who reads the New Testament with an open mind must surely admit that the tradition of Jesus' having uttered a statement on divorce is well attested. It appears in four different books of the New Testament, in five different versions, and in a variety of literary forms, specifically, a conflict story, an isolated saying, and a letter. No matter one's approach to the criterion of multiple attestation, one must acknowledge that the tradition satisfies the requirements of this criterion for an authentic saying of Jesus.

It is, moreover, apparent that Jesus' teaching on divorce was not a commonplace of Jewish lore. One cannot claim that Jesus' teaching was altogether unique in first-century Palestine. There was, after all, the halakic tradition developed by the Essenes. Nonetheless the teaching of Jesus on divorce was unusual—so unusual in fact that two of the evangelists explicitly present Jesus' teaching on divorce as something which distinguished his teaching from typical and traditional Jewish halakah. On the other hand, the diversity of expression given to this saying by the various New Testament authors shows that it was not a saying created by the early church in order to satisfy its internal needs. Rather it is clear that a traditional saying has been variously adapted by the these different writers in order to make the tradition conformable to the real-life situation of the communities for which they were writing. In effect, the tradition of Jesus' teaching on divorce also satisfies the criterion of dual exclusion.[1]

The tradition of Jesus' teaching on divorce seems to enjoy as much claim to authenticity as does any other part of his teaching.[2] Indeed, E. P. Sanders has called it "the most securely attested saying by Jesus."[3] It is, however, one thing to affirm that in dealing with the teaching of Jesus on divorce we are dealing with an authentic element of the Jesus' tradition; it is another thing to reconstitute the original form of that tradition. Each version of the tradition contained within the New Testament has been transmitted within a *Sitz-im-Leben der Kirche,* a concrete ecclesial situation which has preserved, passed along, and shaped that tradition, and a *Sitz-im-Leben des Evangeliums,* the evangelist's own situation, including the literary use to which he has put the tradition on divorce.

Jesus' Saying

The methods of source and redaction criticism are sufficiently refined to allow contemporary scholars to distinguish various pre-literary forms of a tradition contained within the New Testament. When these methods are applied to the the New Testament passages containing Jesus' teaching on divorce, it is clear that in addition to writing about a Pauline, a Markan, a Lukan, and two Matthean versions of the teaching, we must also write about a Q-version, a pre-Markan, and a pre-Matthean version of the tradition. Given this plethora of documentary evidence and hypothetical reconstruction—at least eight versions of the tradition in all—is it possible to identify one of these as reflecting Jesus' teaching in its pristine form? Alternatively, given the diversity of literary attestation to the tradition, is it possible to recover the form in which Jesus' teaching on divorce was originally formulated? Given the diversity of evidence, can we somehow attain to the the *Ur-*tradition, as it were?

The reader of these pages will hardly be surprised to learn that there is no easy answer to this question and that the answers given differ from one author to another. This is partially due to the fact that the answer which is given depends on how one views the relationship between Matthew and Mark, whether or not one accepts the hypothetical existence of Q, and whether one considers

Paul to have been dependent upon a version of the saying presently found in one or another of the gospels.

Some scholars believe that the question is insoluble. *Non liquet,* there is no clear solution, is their reflection. Typical is the opinion proferred by E. P. Sanders who writes: "with regard to *historical authenticity,* we can be sure that Jesus said something about divorce, but we do not know the precise nuance. He was against it. What else?"[4] He comments further to the effect that "On grounds of *what is common* we are inclined to accept the short form[5] in general: remarriage was prohibited. On grounds of *intrinsic probability* the long form[6] looks more likely. We cannot resolve this problem. . . . We have . . . *good general knowledge* about a saying by Jesus, but we do not have the precise nuance, and we cannot be certain of the grounds for his statement."[7]

On the other hand, many scholars believe that, in the history of tradition, Jesus' saying on divorce began life as a radical statement, only to be revised for practicality's sake within various Christian communities.

Some claim that Mark 10:9 apppears to be the most radical form of Jesus' teaching and therefore lies at the origin of the developing tradition. According to Joachim Jeremias, Mark 10:9 contains an apodictic prohibition, later made into a legal resolution with two members, formulated in casuistic terms. He then traced the development of the tradition from Matt 5:32, without the qualification "except on the ground of unchastity" (prohibition of the dismissal of the wife and the wife's remarriage), via 1 Cor 7:10-11 (prohibition of divorce by the wife added in view of the Hellenistic legal situation) and verses 12-16 (exception made for mixed marriages), Luke 16:18 and Mark 10:11-12 (prohibition of remarriage for both parties) to Matt 5:32 and 19:9 (the exception for unchastity).[8]

Another group of scholars believes that it is a Q-form of the logion that has the greatest claim to authenticity and that Luke 16:18 therefore best represents the original saying of Jesus.[9] On the other hand, Gerhard Lohfink opines that Matt 5:32, without the exceptive clause, represents the oldest form of the tradition.[10] Ulrich Luz suggests that it is not possible to decide between these two alternatives but cautions that one ought not let the desire to have a non-Jewish form of the logion (to satisfy partially the criterion of dual exclusion with regard to the authenticity of the saying) lead to an option for the Lukan form.[11]

Quite singular is the opinion of Abel Isaksson who claims that Matt 19:9 represents the most primitive form of the Jesus tradition on divorce.[12] In his view, the saying was subsequently adapted to different situations, to wit, 1) an extension to women (Mark 10:12); 2) a judgment that a divorcing husband commits adultery against his wife (Mark 10:11); 3) the prohibition of a man marrying a divorced woman (Matt 5:32b; Luke 16:18b); and 4) the prohibition of a man divorcing his wife even if he does not remarry (Matt 5:32a).

Similarly singular is the position of Yair Zakovitch. According to Zakovitch, since Mark preserves the only version of the Jesuanic saying according to which a wife might initiate a divorce,[13] the Markan version of Jesus' logion might possibly reflect the original tradition more accurately. It was subsequently modified by Matthew and Luke.[14]

Werner Stenger has offered a very personalized, and rather nuanced opinion as to the development of the logion itself. He begins with the fact that Mark has a two-part statement and the recognition that Mark 10:12 is a Markan adaptation of the logion. Matt 5:32, Luke 16:18, and Q likewise have a double statement, the first part of which speaks of divorce and the second of marriage to a divorcée. Each part of Mark's double statement is, in fact, a double statement which first talks about divorce and then about marriage. The second double statement (Mark 10:12) is redactional.

As for the first (Mark 10:11), Mark has compressed the traditional two-part statement (cf. the Q source) into an elliptical single statement with two parts. The clause of Mark 10:11, "and marries another," represents a condensation of the traditional logion on a second marriage. "Whoever divorces his wife commits adultery against her" should be considered the pre-Markan form of the logion. "Against her" is a pre-Markan redactional element to clarify that the adultery is indeed an offense against an aggrieved wife.

In his reprise of Mark, Matthew has omitted the pre-Markan clarification and the Markan adaptation (Mark 10:12), the latter no longer pertinent to his community. The result is that Matthew's version of Jesus' conflict with the Pharisees has a statement on divorce which is close to the position maintained by the Shammaites.[15] Matthew's desire to teach a righteousness greater than that of the scribes and Pharisees has influenced his formulation of the tradition.

Since Matt 5:32 is different from Matt 19:9, Matt 5:32 must substantially represent the formulation of Matthew's source. Given the manifest similarity between Matt 5:32 and Luke 16:18, that source should be identified as Q. The source, Q, was composed in a situation of imminent eschatological expectation similar to that of Qumran where there was also a concern for ritual purity. The Q saying has been modified by both Luke and Matthew. The latter has put it into an antithetical form which has influenced his formulation of the setting of the logion in Matt 19:9 as well as the incorporation of an exceptive clause into that logion.

Thus, for Stenger, we have: 1) the unknown logion of Jesus; 2) its pre-Markan form, from which derive both 3) its Markan form—close to which is 1 Cor 7:10-11—and 4) its Q-form. The Q- form has been adapted by 5) Luke and by 6) Matthew. The latter's adaptation of the Q-saying, as well as the situation of his own community, have influenced 7) his revision of Mark's logion in the story about Jesus' controversy with the Pharisees over the issue of divorce.[16]

A Prophetic Saying

I think that there is little likelihood that Mark 10:9 best represents the earliest form of the tradition. Although it commends itself by its simplicity and its apodictic form, it would appear to be a Hellenistic formulation and an integral part of the conflict story (Mark 10:3-9) which has been created by a Hellenistic church. While Mark 10:11 is pre-Markan, it may have been subject to some redactional modification, and appears not to have been the earliest form of the tradition.[17]

On the other hand, it is likely that the most primitive form of the saying would have been fairly simple in form. In my judgment it must have been passed down as a prophetic statement rather than as a statement of community halakah.[18] A major reason for this assertion is the difficulty inherent in affirming that the historical Jesus self-consciously intended to form a church and that he set down halakic rules in order to guide the conduct of the members of his community who would survive his death and resurrection. Indeed, as I read the development of the Synoptic tradition, it appears to me that one of the principal reasons why the evangelist Matthew drafted a new edition of the Markan gospel was to provide halakic guidance for a community that was without specific Christian norms in this regard. The gospel of Mark is quite devoid of—which is not to say totally lacking in—community rules.

Isolated logia are easily passed along in the form of prophetic statements. The Q-form of the logion, as preserved in Luke 16:18, suggests that the saying on divorce had an independent existence in the oral tradition of the church.[19] Matt 5:32 indicates that although the Q-saying had the form of casuistic law, it had the function of a prophetic statement. At least Matthew uses it in this way. I would suggest that the saying of Jesus had been transmitted within the church as a prophetic statement, despite and by means of its casuistic form. Subsequently it would have been incorporated within the Q-collection, which included not a few prophetic sayings of Jesus, many of which enjoy a strong claim to authenticity.[20]

Jesus the Prophet

Prophetic statements are consistent with the image of Jesus, the eschatological prophet. The New Testament Scriptures give abundant witness to the role of Jesus as the prophetic figure for the final times. Luke has graphically developed a characterization of Jesus as prophet in his programmatic scene of Jesus in the synagogue of Nazareth (Luke 4:16-30).[21] A confession of faith in Jesus the prophet appears on the lips of the Samaritan woman in John 4:19.[22] Although these are later literary developments within the tradition of the written gospel, they arise from an earlier memory of Jesus as eschatological prophet.

Among the traces of this earlier view of Jesus is the comparison made between Jesus and John the Baptizer, a paradigm of the eschatological prophet in the New Testament. Within the triple tradition a comparison between Jesus and John appears in a short dialogue focusing on the popular opinion about Jesus (Matt 16:14; Mark 8:28; Luke 9:19) as well as in the judgment about Jesus attributed to Herod (Matt 14:2; Mark 6:14,16; Luke 9:7). The Q-source contained a puzzling *mashal* which linked together, albeit in antithetical fashion, John the Baptist and the Son (Matt 11:18-19; Luke 7:33-34).

Another indication of the authenticity of the tradition which held Jesus to be a prophet is the Synoptic Gospels' view that at least some of the people considered Jesus to be a prophet. This popular estimation of Jesus is to be found in Mark 6:15 and Luke 9:8. According to Matthew, the fact that the crowds considered Jesus to be a prophet was even known to the chief priests and Pharisees (Matt 21:46). A similar opinion about Jesus also appears in the disciples' report on what people were saying about Jesus (Matt 16:14; Mark 8:28; Luke 9:19).

What is particularly striking about these reports is that the evangelists clearly distinguish between the views of Jesus' own disciples and the opinions about Jesus maintained by those who are not his disciples. In the dialogue between Jesus and his disciples in the region of Caesarea Philippi, for example, the people's acknowledgment that Jesus was a prophet is sharply contrasted not only with the disciples' confession—expressed by Peter, their spokesperson—that Jesus was the Messiah but also with Jesus' self-revelation as the Son of Man. The primary designation of Jesus as prophet may have been relatively short-lived in the early church precisely because the early church, soon after the death and resurrection of Jesus, came to consider him as much more than a mere prophet.[23] It is, nonetheless, quite likely that Jesus was considered to be a prophet during the time of his historical ministry. In any event, the Markan summary of Jesus' initial proclamation (Mark 1:14-15) clearly bears the mark of prophetic utterance.

Another indication that Jesus was considered to have been a prophet is the existence of a logion attributed to Jesus by all four canonical gospels—one of the few, in fact, to be so attested—namely, the saying about the prophet being without honor in his own country (Matt 13:57; Mark 6:4; Luke 4:24; John 4:44). That the saying is conveyed in somewhat different forms and is presented in different settings within the gospels shows that the logion has had a relatively complex history. It is quite clear, for example, that the saying was used apologetically within the early Church. It could serve to explain why Jesus had not been accepted by his kin and co-religionists. There are, however, many reasons to suggest that the core of the saying goes back to Jesus himself.

The Prophet's Role

One of the classic roles assumed by authentic prophets within the Jewish tradition was criticism of royal activity and the behavior of the powerful when such conduct was judged to be in conflict with God's will for his people even if that activity was not in formal violation of the law. Thus Amos railed against those who profited from the misery of the poor and Malachi cites Yahweh as saying "I hate divorce" (Mal 2:16).

The Synoptic Gospels attest that John the Baptist, commonly revered as a prophet, had criticized the activity of Herod Antipas who had married Herodias, the divorced wife of his half-brother Philip. According to the Synoptists, that criticism directly led to the death of John.[24] Antipas' marital affairs were well known in first-century Palestine and are reported by the Jewish historian Flavius Josephus[25] as well as by the Synoptic authors.

It is not unlikely that Jesus who, as the Baptist, called the people to repentence in view of the impending end time[26] also criticized the tetrarch's marital infidelity.[27] The notariety of the tetrarch's situation at least provides a plausible setting in which Jesus the prophet would have critized divorce.

I would suggest that Jesus' prophetic statement existed as an isolated statement in that form and that it was later incorporated into the Q-source, which included not a few prophetic sayings of the historical Jesus. The Palestinian setting made it likely that the criticism was directed to the male who was involved in a divorce. In this regard it is worthwhile to note that Mark describes John the Baptizer as having directed his condemnation against Antipas, rather than against the machinating Herodias. In contrast, the historian Josephus, clearly writing for a Hellenistic readership, directs his critical remarks against the woman, Herodias.

Indeed, it might be suggested that Matthew's version of the Q-logion, minus the exceptive clause, which I believe to be more faithful to the original version of the Q-logion than is Luke's, which attributes the wrong of divorce to a marriage which takes place after divorce,[28] is one which is quite germane to the situation of Philip, Herodias, and Antipas. I would not want to claim that that particular situation is *the* situation which led to the Q-saying. What I am saying is that there are serious reasons for postulating that the reconstituted Q-saying enjoys the strongest claim to be the oldest form of a logion which is certainly authentic, that serious exegetical arguments can be advanced to suggest that the Q-logion is best reconstituted on the basis of the Matt 5:32 version of the logion, and that such a saying would be appropriate as a prophetic criticism of the marital escapades of Herod and his entourage.

If that were the precise historical situation within which Jesus originally spoke against divorce, his critique would have been of both Philip who divorced Herodias and Antipas who married her. His prophetic utterance condemned as a violation of the Decalogue's prohibition of adultery both the husband who divorces his wife (he involves her in adultery; cf. Matt 5:32a) and the man who marries a divorcée (Matt 5:32b). In any event, the Baptist judged Antipas to have violated the Law (*ouk exestin,*[29] Mark 6:18) because he had married the divorced Herodias.

In sum, I consider that Jesus' saying on divorce was a prophetic utterance, rather than a community regulation. Uttered by Jesus, a prophet from Nazareth in Galilee, it was originally formulated from the point of view of the male. As such, it was part and parcel of his call to repentence in view of the coming of the kingdom. It condemned divorce and its consequences, rather than a second marriage as such. The condemnation proclaimed divorce to be a violation of the Decalogue's prohibition of adultery. And it may have been the well-known situation at the court of Antipas which prompted the condemnation.

The Church's Role

As we look at the historical Jesus and a possible situation in which to place his historic utterance on divorce, it is important to remember that Jesus' entire ministry was re- evaluated and re-interpreted by his disciples in the light of his death and resurrection. The titles that were attributed to him during his lifetime gave way to titles which bespoke the church's confession of faith that Jesus was the risen one. The image of Jesus the prophet gave way to the image of Jesus the teacher.

Indeed, we should even think of the foundation of the church in two distinct moments. At first there was a group of disciples attracted to Jesus the wandering preacher and eschatological preacher. They shared with him an expectation of the coming of the kingdom and apparently awaited its coming with enthusiasm. After the death and resurrection of Jesus, this group of disciples became the earliest core of the church whose faith was grounded on the fact that Jesus had been raised from the dead.

Along with this re-evaluation of who Jesus really was and the new situation of Jesus' disciples as church[30] came a re-evaluation of the tradition of Jesus' sayings. Prophetic sayings of the historical Jesus were re-interpreted in the light of the experience of the church. The sayings of Jesus about the coming Son of Man came to be understood as sayings about the coming of Jesus as Parousiac Lord. The parable of the sower which proclaimed the coming of the kingdom in all its fullness (Mark 4:1-9)[31] was interpreted in allegorical fashion so that it spoke of the church's proclamation and the difficulties experienced by Christian missionaries as they proclaimed God's word (Mark 4:13- 20).[32] An early makarism which proclaimed the happiness of those who were poor (Luke 6:20b)[33] was rephrased in such a way that it proposed poverty of spirit as a quality of discipleship (Matt 5:3).

Jesus' prophetic utterance on divorce was similarly subject to ecclesial re-interpretation in the light of the church's experience after his death and resurrection.[34] What had been a prophetic saying now became a community regulation, promulgated on the authority of the one whom the church recognized as its Lord. Paul's letters are the oldest extant witness to the life and activity of the early church. They make it clear that, from the very beginning, the church's missionary proclamation was accompanied by moral exhortation and community instruction.[35] Those who came to believe that Jesus has been raised from the dead as Lord and Son of God were expected to live as God's people.

Gentile Converts

For Christian Jews, there was initially no problem since the Law of God had been handed down to God's people from the time of Moses. For Gentile Christians there was a problem. To what extent were these Gentile Christians, radically free from the demands of the Law, bound to follow the moral norms observed by Jews and Christian Jews? Twentieth-century Christians make a clear distinction between the Jewish ritual law and the laws of purity and the moral law, but such a distinction was not so patent during the first century. God's people were expected to live in holiness, that is, as God's people with its ritual, customary, and moral ethos. This was the view of Jews and Jewish Christians as well.

Gentile Christians were expected to live in moral fashion, but did that mean that they were expected to live up to the moral standards accepted by Christian Jews? Issues of sexual and familial morality were especially important.[36] On the one hand, Jews had long considered the sexual practices of pagans as particularly abhorrent.[37] Jews expected pagans living in the land of Israel to at least conform to the Jewish norms prohibiting marriages within certain degrees of kinship. Jewish Christians would have held similar expectations of those Gentiles with whom they were to share table fellowship because of their shared belief in Jesus as Lord and their common expectation of his Presence.

On the other hand, the family was not only the basic unit of society, it was also the basic unit of the church. The church was organized on the basis of household units. What affected the Christian household was not only a matter of private or even of social morality (to use contemporary categories!). It touched the very fabric of the Church's existence.

As Christian Jews became aware of the divide which separated them from their fellow Jews when they became Jewish Christians, they, too, had to ask about the relevance of the traditional Jewish Law.[38] If its ritual laws and the demands of ritual purity were no longer obligatory for God's new people, were the community regulations and the moral laws likewise no longer binding for the members of the church?

Such, in brief, was the social situation of the Church during the generations following upon the death and resurrection of Jesus of Nazareth. In addition to the Law, Christians had the memory of a prophetic utterance of Jesus condemning divorce. What did that mean for the new people of God, the Church?

Initially, that meant that divorce was prohibited because divorce was contrary to the teaching of the one who was acknowledged as Lord. Both Paul and Mark, each in his own way, bear witness to this tradition. In 1 Cor 7:10-11 Paul rejects divorce not because it constitutes in some way a form of adultery nor because it is contrary to the creative will of God. Rather, he rejects divorce simply on the authority of Jesus the Lord himself. In Mark 10:10-12, which the history of the tradition allows us to separate somewhat from its present literary context, Jesus' teaching on divorce is presented as the instruction of the disciples by Jesus himself. Mark's instruction is proposed on the authority of Jesus the Teacher, but the authoritative saying continues to retain a verbal reminiscence of Jesus' condemnation of divorce as a form of adultery. The venue of the Markan instruction reflects the situation of the early church which pondered over the meaning of the Jesus tradition as it gathered in home units.[39]

Women

Both Paul's letter to the Corinthians and the gospel of Mark were written for Hellenistic Christian communities. Within Hellenism, both Roman and Greek, women not only left their husbands, as they did in Judaism, but they could actually divorce their husbands.[40] Given the radical equality of men and women within Christianity, it was judged that the prohibition of divorce was as applicable to female Christians as it was to male Christians. Hence, within Hellenistic Christianity the tradition of Jesus' condemnation of divorce was expanded to forbid not only husbands divorcing their wives but also wives divorcing their husbands.

Bernadette Brooten claims that within first-century Judaism some women did divorce their husbands. Accordingly, she has argued that the prohibition of a wife divorcing her husband (1 Cor 7:10b; Mark 10:12) can lay claim to a Palestinian provenance.[41] To the extent that her position is valid, it cannot be excluded that the saying of Jesus on divorce was extended to women within the Palestinian Christian community. I would, nonetheless, argue that such an extension took place on the level of the re-formulation of the logion as a community regulation.[42] In any event, the extension of the ban on divorce to women divorcing is contained in documents which are clearly instructional with regard to the Hellenistic church.

With the extension of Jesus' saying to women, there came into being a new bipartite saying on divorce. Whereas the earlier prophetic statement had condemned both the man who divorces his wife and the man who marries a divorcée, the Hellenistic community regulation forbade a husband to divorce his wife and a wife to divorce her husband (1 Cor 7:10b,11b; Mark 10:11-12).

Despite the pleas of those who believe that Q, and presumably the oral tradition behind it, contains Luke's "and marries another," I believe that it is unlikely that Jesus' prophetic utterance spoke about a man who divorces his wife and marries another woman. Neither Matt 5:32 nor 1 Cor 7:11b suggest that the evil of divorce is to be located in a husband's remarriage. The Matthean text is particularly important in this regard because it condemns a husband's divorce of his wife as a form of adultery. Why would the evangelist have omitted the "and marries another," if it had been in his Q-source? The formula was known to Matthew from Mark 10:11, and is retained by him in his version of the Markan saying at Matt 19:9.

It is difficult to conceive of a reason why either Paul or Matthew, independently of one another and each with an obvious concern to adapt the teaching of Jesus to the situation of their respective churches, would have formulated a more stringent logion had the tradition located the malice of divorce in the husband's remarriage[43] rather than in the divorce itself.[44] Furthermore, the life situation of Jesus' prophetic utterance would have been more congenial to a formulation of the saying without mention of a remarriage than to a formulation which includes a reflection on remarriage, a bit of casuistry that is more appropriate to community regulation than it is to prophetic utterance.

Werner Stenger's argument[45] appears to be quite apropos. He noted that the first part of the traditional saying, which I have called a prophetic utterance, addressed itself to *divorce* and that the second part of the saying addressed itself to the issue of a man's *marriage* to a divorcée. Both divorce and marriage are at issue in the Markan statements pertaining to men (Mark 10:11) and women (Mark 10:12). In effect, the Markan form of Jesus' instruction to his disciples is a bipartite statement, in which each statement has a bipartite protasis (if a man or woman divorces *and* marries, he or she commits adultery). Stenger has suggested that when the traditional logion was extended so as to be applicable to women as well as to men, the second part of the original formulation was compressed and adapted so as to speak of the divorcing person's remarriage.

This formulation may well be due to Mark, the redactor. It is found only in Mark and in texts dependent on Mark.[46] In any case, the balance between Mark 10:11 and Mark 10:12 is a clear-cut instance of Markan duality and would seem to suggest that the formulation is the result of Mark's editorial activity. Mark's compositive narrative continues to reject divorce as such (Mark 10:9); his editorial work has resulted in his offering a version of the tradition which seems to condemn, not divorce as such, but a second marriage, both of the divorcing husband and the divorced wife.[47]

Further Reflection

Mark has "introduced" his expanded version of the traditional logion by means of a conflict story. The story has its origin in a Hellenistic Christian environment and seeks to provide a rationale for the Christian prohibition of divorce. It is an object lesson which uses scriptural reflection to provide a warrant for Jesus' prohibition of divorce. For a Christian Jew, the idea that divorce could be considered a violation of the sixth commandment may well have seemed to be sufficient justification for Jesus to condemn divorce; for a Gentile Christian that may not have been sufficient.

Mark's scriptural reflection grounds Jesus' teaching on divorce in something other than the sixth commandment. It presents Jesus' teaching as based on the will of God, the Creator, as that will has been revealed in the Scriptures. Since the union of husband and wife is the very purpose of creation, no human has the right to separate what God has joined. By appealing to the order of creation rather than to the precept of the Decalogue as the biblical warrant for the church's prohibition of divorce, the conflict story pointedly affirms that not only Jewish Christians, but all men and women are to eschew divorce as contrary to God's will. The Hellenistic formulation of the story's climax, "What God has joined together, let no one separate," poignantly illustrates that human conduct occasionally works in a fashion contrary to the very creation of God itself.

In sum, Mark has created a new paradigm for the teaching of Jesus on divorce. The disciples of Jesus are to look upon marriage in a new light, one somewhat different from the view of marriage commonly held in Jewish and Hellenistic society. Marriage between men and women is the very purpose of God's having created men and women. It is God who has joined together a married couple in one flesh.[48] Consequently divorce contravenes the primal will of God and is inconsistent with the scriptural teaching on the purpose of the sexual distinction between men and women.

Composed primarily for Gentiles, the conflict story also serves to portray the practice of divorce among the Jews as a deviation from God's creative will. If the Mosaic law afforded some tolerance for divorce, that was because of the hardness of heart of God's people. They did not—or perhaps were not able to—fully embrace the will of God. The result was that just as Jewish standards of marital behavior stood over and against the behavioral patterns of Gentiles, so the standard of marital fidelity to which Christians adhered insofar as they were disciples of Jesus set their way of life not only over and against that of Gentiles, but also over and against that of Jews as well. As their mutual love was expected to distinguish Christians from other social groups,[49] so marital fidelity in monogamous marriage was to be a hallmark of the Christian way of life.

The latter point would be underscored with increasing vehemence as Jewish Christians became aware of the differences between themselves and "the Jews." Thus Matthew highlighted the contrast inherent in Mark's conflict story and presented the challenge of Jesus' teaching on divorce as an example of the greater righteousness to which Christians were called—a righteousness that stands in contrast to the hardheartedness that was manifest in an appeal to Deut 24:1-4 as a warrant for divorce.

That Christians were called to a distinctive marital fidelity—a way of conducting themselves as husband and wife different from that existing among Gentiles and Jews—created a distinct challenge for those who would follow after Jesus. The radicalness of Jesus' teaching was such that it might appear preferable not to marry at all. Not only did the Essenes prohibit divorce, some of them also embraced a life of celibacy. Might it not be that the disciple of Jesus ought not to marry at all?

Such a radical position would be at odds with the purpose of God's creation of the sexual differences among human beings. Matthew's appendange of the eunuch saying to the conflict story brings additional theological reflection to bear on the tradition of Jesus' teaching on divorce. As the discipline of the Christian churches was evolving ever more clearly towards the prohibition of a second marriage, the eunuch saying speaks of the gift of God's grace as an enabling force which makes it possible for Christians to accept the hard saying prohibiting divorce and remarriage.

As a community regulation and a moral challenge, Jesus' teaching on divorce seems to admit of no exception. The Christian husband may not divorce his wife; the Christian wife may not divorce her husband. What about a Christian who is married to an unbeliever, someone who has not responded to a call to discipleship? Is the Christian spouse bound to hold the non-Christian partner to a marital union that he or she does not want?

In his first letter to the Corinthians, Paul proffers his personal opinion that the Christian is not so obligated. The non-Christian spouse may be allowed to depart. This does not so much constitute a derogation from Jesus' teaching as it introduces an element of realism. If a non-Christian is not called to discipleship, one can hardly expect that the non-Christian will experience a call to follow the demands of discipleship with regard to marital fidelity.

Exceptional Cases

Are there other exceptional cases? It is not unlikely that Matthew's Jewish-Christian community included some members who had considered it necessary to divorce their wives. According to the prevelant Jewish ethos, a husband was not allowed to live in a sexual union with a wife who had committed adultery. Her adultery had made her tabu to him. He was bound to divorce her. For a similar reason, a man was to divorce his wife if he discovered that she had not been a virgin at the time of their marriage.[50] A Christian who lived under the Roman *imperium* was bound, under penalty of the gravest of consequences, to divorce a wife whom he caught in an adulterous union.

In these situations, the husband who had divorced his wife would usually remarry. While not explicitly stating that remarriage was allowed, Matthew's exception clause, ultimately dependent upon an interpretation of Deut 24:1, may well allow remarriage. By the time that Matthew's gospel was written, however, the popular and self-serving use (of the Hillelites, whose interpretation of halakah was becoming dominant?) of the procedures set down in Deut 24:1 were considered to be a form of hardheartedness and an example of infidelity to God.

The appendage of the eunuch saying to the Matthean version of the discussion with the Pharisees would seem to reinforce the idea that divorce with remarriage—apart from that limited case to which the *porneia*-clause referred—was excluded for Christians of Matthew's community by the time of the redaction of his gospel. Its presence in the Matthean text is yet another indication that early Christians were seriously pondering the significance of the traditional logion on divorce.[51] The appendage bespeaks the seriousness with which early Christians regarded the logion and the severity with which they interpreted it, a kind of severity to which the Shepherd of Hermas also gives very early evidence.[52]

In any event, the fact that the tradition of Jesus' saying on divorce exists in so many different versions and that it is almost impossible to recover the most primitive version of the saying with any surety—even though to do so has been made in the present study—stands as evidence that the first generations of Christians experienced a need not only to pass along Jesus' teaching on divorce but also to adapt it to ever new circumstances. To pass along the tradition, all the while adapting it to the circumstances of later times, is the perennial challenge to those who want to be faithful to Jesus' prophetic witness and to a teaching that concerns not only the lives of specific individuals but also the very existence of the church itself.

NOTES—INTRODUCTION

[1]With regard to the sayings of Jesus on divorce, see especially Heinz Schürmann, "Die Verbindlichkeit konkreter sittlicher Normen nach dem Neuen Testament, bedacht am Beispiel des Ehescheidungsverbotes und im Lichte des
Liebesgebotes," in Walter Kerber, ed., *Sittliche Normen: zum Problem ihrer allgemeinen und unwandelbaren Geltung.* Düsseldorf: Patmos, 1982, pp. 107–123.
With regard to the New Testament logia on violence and peace see Roger Burggraeve, "The Radicalness of the Gospel and the Necessity for a Reflective Ethics
of Peace: In Search of the Specificity of Ethical Pronouncements in the New Testament," in R. Burggraeve and M. Vervenne, *Swords into Plowshares: Theological Reflections on Peace.* Louvain Theological and Pastoral Monographs, 8
(Leuven: Peeters—Grand Rapids, MI: Eerdmans, 1991), pp. 1–63.

[2]This is the second part of Matt 19:6 according to the standard system of ver-
sification, first introduced by Stephanus into his 1551 edition of the text.

NOTES—CHAPTER 1

[1]Cf. 1 Cor 5:1; 11:18.

[2]Cf. 1 Cor 7:1, 25; 8:1, 4; 12:1; 16:1, 12.

[3]Cf. Piet Farla, " 'The two shall become one flesh:' Gen. 1.27 and 2.24 in
the New Testament Marriage Texts," in S. Draisma, ed., *Intertextuality in Biblical Writings: Essays in Honour of Bas van Iersel* (Kampen: Kok, 1989) 67–82,
p. 75. Aristotle's rhetorical theory (see his *Rhetoric* 3.1.1358a), generally followed
by later writers, distinguishes among the epideictic, forensic, and deliberative genres.
While the forensic genre is used to persuade an audience to make a judgment about
the past, and the deliberative to move them to take a given course of action in
the future, the epideictic is used when a communicator wishes to persuade an audience to maintain or reaffirm a point of view at the present time.

[4]Pace Johannes Weiss, *Der erste Korintherbrief.* KEK, 5 (9th. ed.: Göttingen, Vandenhoeck und Ruprecht, 1910) pp. xxxix–xliii, Walter Schmithals, *Gnosticism in Corinth: An Investigation of the Letters to the Corinthians* (Nashville,
TN, Abingdon, 1971) pp. 90–96, and a few other commentators who hold the
view that our extant 1 Corinthians is a compilation of different letters of Paul
to the Corinthians and that the correspondence referred to in 1 Cor 5:9 is not
a previous letter but an extant part of the present 1 Corinthians, I continue to
maintain the *opinio communis,* namely, that 1 Cor 5:9 refers to a now-lost letter
which Paul had sent to Corinth prior to his sending the extant 1 Corinthians.

[5]Thus, 52–58 (A. J. M. Wedderburn, "Keeping Up With Recent Studies, 8:
Some Recent Pauline Chronologies," *ExpTim* 92 [1980] 103–108, p. 107); 52
(maybe 49; Gerd Lüdemann, *Paul, Apostle to the Gentiles: Studies in Chronology*
[Philadelphia: Fortress, 1984] p. 263); 53–54 (C. K. Barrett, *A Commentary on
the First Letter to the Corinthians.* HNTC [New York: Harper & Row, 1968]
p. 8); the winter months of 53–54 (Helmut Koester, *Introduction to the New Testament, 2: History and Literature of Early Christianity* [Philadelphia: Fortress, 1982]
p. 121); the spring of 54 (Jerome Murphy-O'Connor "The First Letter to the Corin-

thians," *NJBC*, pp. 798–815, p. 799); 55 (Robert Jewett, *A Chronology of Paul's Life* [Philadelphia: Fortress, 1979] p. 165; 56 (Hans Conzelmann, *A Commentary on the First Epistle to the Corinthians*. Hermeneia [Philadelphia: Fortress, 1975] p. 120 and William F. Orr and James Arthur Walther, *I Corinthians: A New Translation. Introduction with a Study of the Life of Paul, Notes, and Commentary*. AB, 32 [Garden City, NY: Doubleday, 1976]) p. 120; 57 (Joseph A. Fitzmyer, "Paul," *NJBC*, pp. 1329–1337, p. 1336); spring of 57 (Donald Guthrie, *New Testament Introduction* [4th. rev. ed.: Downers Grove, IL, Intervarsity, 1990] p. 458).

⁶Cf. 1 Cor 7:1, 25; 8:1, 4; 12:1; 16:1, 12. See Ernst Baasland, "Die *perî*-Formel und die Argumentation (ssituation) des Paulus," *Studia Theologica* 42 (1988) 69–87.

⁷Cf. 1 Cor 5:1; 2 Cor 7:12.

⁸Antoinette Clark Wire, "Prophecy and Women Prophets in Corinth," in James E. Goehring, et al., ed., *Gospel Origins & Christian Beginnings: In Honor of James M. Robinson* (Sonoma, CA: Polebridge, 1990) pp. 134–150, p. 138.

⁹Cf. v. 39.

¹⁰On this sub-unit, see the discussion above, pp. 55–57.

¹¹Cf. J. C. Hurd, Jr., *The Origin of 1 Corinthians* (London: SPCK, 1965) pp. 67, 163 with some references to earlier literature; David L. Balch, "Backgrounds of I Cor. vii: Sayings of the Lord in Q; Moses as an Ascetic *theos anêr* in II Cor. iii," *NTS* 18 (1971–1972) 351–364, p. 352; Rodolfo Puigdollers, "Notas para una interpretación de 1 Cor 7," *RCT* 3 (1978) 245–260, pp. 246–247; J. Murphy-O'Connor, "The Divorced Woman in 1 Cor 7:10-11," *JBL* 100 (1981) 601–606, p. 603; William E. Phipps, "Is Paul's Attitude towards Sexual Relations Contained in 1 Cor.7.1?" *NTS* 28 (1982) 125–131; David E. Garland, "The Christian's Posture Toward Marriage and Celibacy: 1 Corinthians 7," *RevExp* 80 (1983) 351–362, p. 351; William A. Heth, *Matthew's "Eunuch Saying" (19:12) and Its Relationship to Paul's Teaching on Singleness in 1 Corinthians 7* (Ann Arbor: U. of Michigan, 1987) p. 209 and *passim;* Frans Neirynck, "Paul and the Sayings of Jesus," in A. Vanhoye, ed., *L'Apôtre Paul: Personnalité, style et conception du ministère*. BETL, 73 (Louvain: University Press, 1986) 265–321, p. 317, n. 283; Dennis Ronald MacDonald, *There Is No Male and Female*. HDR, 20 (Philadelphia: Fortress, 1987) p. 70; R. L. Omanson, "Acknowledging Paul's Quotations," *BT* 43 (1992) 201–213, pp. 207–208; etc. Manuel Orge has, however, argued against this growing consensus of opinion. Cf. M. Orge, "El próposito temático de 1 Corintios 7: Un discernimiento sobre la puesta en práctice del ideal de la continencia sexual y el celibato," *Claretianum* 27 (1987) 5–125, pp. 8–38, with conclusions on pp. 39–40.

¹²Cf. Peter J. Tomson, *Paul and the Jewish Law: Halakha in the Letters of the Apostle to the Gentiles: Jewish Traditions in Early Christian Literature*. CRINT, 3/1 (Assen: Van Gorcum, 1990) p. 105.

¹³See Antoinette Wire, "Prophecy," p. 138, who compares Paul's dealing with this slogan with what he has to say in 6:12, 7:27-28a, 8:1-3; 10:23-24 and 16:12.

¹⁴Cf. P. J. Tomson, *Jewish Law,* p. 104.

¹⁵Cf. 1 Cor 1:12.

[16]Cf. Mary Rose D'Angelo, "Remarriage and the Divorce Sayings Attributed to Jesus," in William P. Roberts, ed., *Divorce and Remarriage: Religious and Psychological Perspectives* (Kansas City, MO: Sheed & Ward, 1990) pp. 78–106, p. 94; P. J. Tomson, *Jewish Law,* p. 117; Antoinette Clark Wire, *The Corinthian Women Prophets: A Reconstruction through Paul's Rhetoric* (Minneapolis, MN: Fortress, 1990), pp. 34, 85; and Margaret Y. MacDonald, "Women Holy in Body and Spirit: The Social Setting of 1 Corinthians 7," *NTS* 36 (1990) 161–181, p. 170. To a large extent MacDonald's study is devoted to the idea that the impulse for celibacy came largely from women. Wire writes of a "tide of women leaving marriage" (p. 34).

[17]Cf. P. J. Tomson, *Jewish Law,* pp. 108, 117–118.

[18]These words are enclosed within parentheses or dashes not only in the NRSV, but also in the RSV, JB, NJB, RNAB, REB, and the original translation by Orr and Walther.

[19]J. K. Elliott has commented that "this to-ing and fro-ing is typical of Paul's often irregular method of presenting arguments." J. K. Elliott, "Paul's Teaching on Marriage in I Corinthians: Some Problems Considered," *NTS* 19 (1972-1973) 219–225, p. 219.

[20]Various other phrases within 1 Cor 7:10-16, the specific passage which deals with the issue of divorce, have been enclosed within parentheses or dashes by the different modern editors and translators of the passage. See, for example, the NAB, the Good News Bible, Philips Modern English, NIV, RNAB, the New Translation, and the Orr-Walther translation.

[21]Frans Neirynck, for example, writes that "the meaning of the parenthesis in 7, 11ab remains uncertain. Paul's insertion is perhaps merely explicative of the radical prohibition." F. Neirynck, "Paul," p. 320.

[22]Johannes Weiss believed that v. 11ab was an interpolation into the text; most scholars, however, attribute the insertion to Paul himself, arguing that the parenthetical remarks interrupt the flow of vv. 10c and 11c, parallel statements which are presumably based on the Word of the Lord. Cf. J. Weiss, *Der erste Korintherbrief,* pp. 178–179; *E contrario,* Heinrich Baltensweiler, *Die Ehe im Neuen Testament: Exegetische Untersuchungen über Ehe, Ehelosigkeit und Ehescheidung.* Zurich: Zwingli, 1967, pp. 187–191.

[23]The *chôristhênai* of v. 10 is the aorist infinitive of *chôrizô* in the passive voice; while the *chôristhê* of v. 11a is the third-person-singular form of the verb in the aorist tense and passive voice.

[24]His arguments are the fact that Paul uses different verbs for the breaking off of an engagement (*luô,* v. 27, hapax in Paul) and the breaking off of a marriage (*aphiêmi,* vv. 11, 12, 13) and that in the Synoptic dispute on divorce (Mark 10:1-12; Matt 19:1-12) *chôrizô* is distinct from the verb *apoluô,* which he takes to be synonymous with Paul's *aphiêmi.* Cf. J. K. Elliott, "Paul's Teaching," p. 224; William F. Luck, *Divorce and Remarriage: Recovering the Biblical View* (San Francisco: Harper & Row, 1987) p. 166.

[25]Cf. *m. Yebam.* 14:1; *m. Ketub.* 7:9-10; *m. Git.* 9:8.

²⁶Cf. E. P. Sanders and Margaret Davies, *Studying the Synoptic Gospels* (London: SCM—Philadelphia: Trinity International, 1989) p. 327; P. J. Tomson, *Jewish Law*, p. 117. Murphy-O'Connor likewise thinks that verse 10b, in opposition to verse 13 which supposes a Greco-Roman cultural setting, "reflects a Jewish milieu in which the right to divorce belonged exclusively to the husband." Cf. J. Murphy-O'Connor, "The Divorced Woman," p. 603. A.-L. Descamps understood *aphiêmi* as a way of speaking about divorce, but opined that it is a mode of expression "which corresponds to the language of the Jews." See A.-L. Descamps, "The New Testament Doctrine on Marriage," in R. Malone and J. R. Connery, eds., *Contemporary Perspectives on Christian Marriage: Propositions and Papers from the International Theological Commission* (Chicago: Loyola University, 1984) pp. 217–273, 347–363, p. 262.

²⁷The issue is discussed at length, and judiciously, in Peter Tomson's *Jewish Law*.

²⁸Apart from 1 Cor 7:11, 12, and 13, Paul uses *aphiêmi* only in Rom 1:27 and 4:7, where it has a more general connotation.

²⁹For example, by Aristotle in *Nichomachean Ethics,* 1163ᵇ22. Cf. LSJ, p. 290.

³⁰The "fragment" is a papyrus from the second century, B.C.E. Cf. MM, p. 97.

³¹Cf. Rudolf Bultmann, *"aphiêmi, ktl,"* TDNT, 1, 509–512, pp. 509, 510; Herbert Leroy, *"aphiêmi, etc.,"* EDNT, 1, 181–183, p. 181.

³²The lexicographers typically cite Herodotus 5.39. See below, n. 52.

³³The "unmarried" (*agamois*) of v. 8 are to be distinguished from the "virgins" (*parthenôn,* a term rendered as "the unmarried" in the RSV and REB and paraphrased as "the question of celibacy" by the NEB and the New Translation) of v. 25. Paired with "widows," the "unmarried" of v. 8 are most likely widowers.

³⁴Cf. P. J. Tomson, *Jewish Law,* pp. 108–109, 118.

³⁵Tomson argues that, whereas Jewish Law provided the background for Paul's command in vv. 10-11, Hellenistic law serves as the context for his exhortation in vv. 12-14. Indications that Paul has a manifestly Hellenistic situation in mind are the fact that the wife has the possibility of taking the initiative in severing the marriage (cf. *"aphiêmi*-divorce" in v. 13) and the use of "unbeliever" (*apistos* in vv. 12-15). Tomson takes *apistos* to mean "pagan," rather than merely "non-Christian," and argues that a Jew would not be married to an *apistos.* Cf. P. J. Tomson, *Jewish Law,* p. 118 and n. 122.

³⁶Cf. R. Pesch, " 'Paulinische Kasuistik.' Zum Verständnis von 1 Kor 7, 10-11," in J. A. Verdes and E. J. A. Hernandez, eds., *Homenaje a Juan Prado: Miscelanea de estudios biblicos y hebraicos* (Madrid: CSIC, 1975) pp. 433–442.

³⁷Literally "the unbelieving one," contextually rendered in the NRSV as "the unbelieving partner."

³⁸In attempting to provide an inclusive translation of Paul's words, the REB offers a paraphrase: "If however the unbelieving partner wishes for a separation, let it be granted." The NIV ("let him do so") and the RNAB ("let him separate") retain a masculine pronoun in the apodosis.

³⁹Cf. Vincent Branick, *House Church in the Writings of Paul*. Zacchaeus Studies: New Testament (Wilmington, DE: Glazier, 1989).

⁴⁰For stylistic reasons, the NRSV has rendered Paul's second use of "*chôrizô*-separate," as "let it be so." Cf. 1 Thess 4:1, where Paul's second use of *peripateô*-live (literally, "walk") is similarly rendered: "you ought to live (*peripatein*) and to please God (as, in fact you are doing [*peripateite*]). In 1 Cor 7:15, both the NJB and the RNAB offer a more literal translation, the RNAB pedantically using "separate" in both instances, the NJB offering a more literary "but if the unbeliever chooses to leave, then let the separation take place"—which, however, renders Paul's second use of the verb as if it were a noun.

⁴¹Including the RSV, JB, NAB, NIV, NEB, RNAB and the New Translation which renders the verb in v. 11a as "if she does," that is, "if she divorces" (cf. v. 10c).

⁴²Cf. Joseph A. Fitzmyer, "The Matthean Divorce Texts and Some New Palestinian Evidence," in *To Advance the Gospel: New Testament Studies* (New York: Crossroad, 1981) pp. 79–111, pp. 81, 89–90, where he writes "that the verb should properly be translated 'be divorced' " and J. Murphy-O'Connor, "The Divorced Woman," pp. 601–602. In "First Corinthians," p. 804, Murphy-O'Connor cites BDF, 314, in support of this meaning of the passive.

⁴³This is the translation given in the REB which attempts to render the Greek middle voice. The NJB's translation of vv. 10c-11a likewise takes the verb as a deponent: "a wife must not be separated from her husband—or if she has already left him . . ." Frans Neirynck has appropriately noted that "The verb *chôrizomai* appears in Mayser's list of 'media passiva' (II/1, 30; 118) and the references to a technical *ap' allêlôn chôristhênai* are listed in Preisigke's *Wörterbuch* (797)." Cf. F. Neirynck, "Paul," p. 318.

⁴⁴That the non-believer is to take the initiative in the case to which Paul refers is highlighted in some translations, for example, the RSV ("desires to separate"), NJB ("chooses to leave"), and REB ("wishes for a separation").

⁴⁵Cf. Hans Lietzmann, *An die Korinther 1-2*. HNT, 9 (14th. ed.: Tübingen, Mohr, 1949) p. 31. Lietzmann is supported by Neirynck ("Paul," p. 318). See also Jacques Dupont, *Mariage et divorce dans l'évangile: Matthieu 19, 3-12 et parallèles* (Bruges: Desclée de Brouwer, 1959) p. 59.

⁴⁶So, Neirynck, "Paul," p. 318.

⁴⁷Donald W. Shaner notes that "in the context it is probably the wife who *separates herself*, in contrast to the action of the husband who puts her away," but adds that the use of the passive voice in vv. 10c and 11a would allow the texts to be intelligible to Jews since "both have the woman as the recipient of the action." Cf. D. W. Shaner, *A Christian View of Divorce According to the Teachings of the New Testament* (Leiden: Brill, 1969) p. 62.

⁴⁸Cf. Wayne A. Meeks, *The First Urban Christians: The Social World of the Apostle Paul* (New Haven-London: Yale University, 1983) p. 161; William A. Heth, *Matthew's "Eunuch Saying,"* p. 241; Christian D. Von Dehsen, *Sexual Relationships and the Church: An Exegetical Study of 1 Corinthians 5-7* (Ann Arbor, MI: UMI, 1987) pp. 171-172.

⁴⁹Cf. H. Conzelmann, *First Corinthians,* p. 120, with references. See also Walter Erdmann, *Die Ehe im alten Griechenland* (Munich: Beck, 1934) pp. 386–403; Hans Julius Wolff, *Beiträge zur Rechtsgeschichte Altgriechenlands und des hellenistisch-römischen Ägyptens* (Weimar: Böhlaus, 1961) p. 203; A. R. W. Harrison, *The Law of Athens: The Family and Property* (Oxford: Clarendon, 1968) pp. 39–44; E. Levy, *Der Hergang der römischen Ehescheidung* (Weimar: Böhlaus, 1925) p. 84; W. Kunkel, "Matrimonium," *PW* (Stuttgart: Metzler, 1930) 14:2, 2259–2286; Max Kaser, *Das römische Privatrecht* (2nd. ed.: Munich, Beck, 1971) pp. 326–328; *Roman Private Law* (3rd. ed.: Pretoria, University of South Africa, 1980) pp. 294–296.

⁵⁰*On Benefits,* 3, 16, 2.

⁵¹In Rom 4:7 Paul's use of *aphiêmi* occurs in a citation of Ps 31:1. The editors of the NRSV offer "giving up" as a translation of *aphiêmi* in Rom 1:27. Although the verb *aphiêmi* is used by Paul only in 1 Cor 7:11, 12, 13, and these two passages in Romans, it occurs fairly frequently in the New Testament with the meaning, "to forgive," a theological meaning which it does not have in Pauline usage. This fact has, apparently, led Leroy to the erroneous affirmation that Paul uses the verb only in Rom 4:7. Cf. H. Leroy, "*aphiêmi,* etc.," p. 182.

⁵²See Herodotus 5.39. Euripides (*Andromache,* 973) used the verb with *gamos* to connote divorce. Cf. LSJ, p. 290.

⁵³Fitzmyer offers Isaeus 8:36, Euripides, *Fr.* 1063:13; Polybius, *Hist.* 31.26.6 as references and cites further such papyrus texts as PSI #166.11-12; GGU #1101:5; #1102:8, #1103:6. Cf. Joseph Fitzmyer, "The Matthean Divorce Texts," pp. 89–90, 107, n. 55.

⁵⁴Strikingly, the *TDNT* does not have an entry for *chôrizô.*

⁵⁵MM, p. 696. See also Jerome Murphy-O'Connor who states that *chôrizô* "is well attested as a technical term for 'divorce' in the strict sense." Cf. J. Murphy-O'Connor, "The Divorced Woman," p. 605. Similar thoughts have been expressed by Bernadette Brooten and Margaret MacDonald. Cf. B. J. Brooten, "Zur Debatte über das Scheidungsrecht der jüdischen Frau," *EvT* 43 (1983) 466–478, p. 475, n. 35; M. Y. MacDonald, "Social Setting," p. 170.

⁵⁶Cf. *Ägyptische Urkunden aus den königlichen Museen zu Berlin: Griechische Urkunden,* 4 (Berlin: Weidmann, 1912) 1102:9.

⁵⁷P. Rylands II, 154:25.

⁵⁸Cf. *Ägyptische Urkunden aus den königlichen Museen zu Berlin: Griechische Urkunden,* 1 (Berlin: Weidmann, 1895) 251:6.

⁵⁹Cf. *Ägyptische Urkunden aus den königlichen Museen zu Berlin: Griechische Urkunden,* 4 (Berlin: Weidmann, 1912) 1045:22.

⁶⁰Pace James A. Fischer who opines that neither *chôrizô* nor *aphiêmi* functioned as a technical term for divorce. J. A. Fischer, "1 Cor. 7:8-24—Marriage and Divorce," *BR* 23 (1978) 26–36, p. 27.

⁶¹Cf. Johannes P. Louw and Eugene A. Nida, eds., *Greek-English Lexicon of the New Testament Based on Semantic Domains,* 1: *Introduction & Domains* (2nd. ed.: New York, United Bible Societies, 1989) p. 457: "Some persons have

attempted to make an important distinction between *aphiêmi* in 1 Cor 7, 11, 13 and *chôrizô* in 1 Cor 7.15 on the assumption that *aphiêmi* implies legal divorce, while *chôrizô* only relates to separation. Such a distinction, however, seems to be quite artificial."

[62]Paul had just used *"agamos*-unmarried" of the previously, but no longer, married in v. 8 (See above, p. 8). Perhaps the point should not be pressed, but the opposite of *agamos*-unmarried is "married." Moreover the general thrust of v. 11b seems to be that the divorced woman should not be married to another man, an impossibility were she not truly divorced.

[63]In my judgment the type of subtle distinction which Tomson introduces between the wife's separation in verse 10c and a wife's divorce in verse 13 seems rather forced. See above, pp. 16–17. On the other hand, Mary Rose D'Angelo's speculation that the woman of vv. 10-11 was married to an unbeliever ("Divorce Sayings," p. 94) and that this gave rise to the stipulations of vv. 12-16 appears rather arbitrary. Were the possibility she suggests well grounded, it would be apparent that "to separate from her husband" (v. 10c) has the same meaning as "to divorce her husband" (v. 13).

[64]Conzelmann notes that, under Greek law, "the authentication of the divorce by an official authority is not necessary, only its registration." See H. Conzelmann, *First Corinthians,* p. 120.

[65]Cf. J. A. Fischer, "1 Cor. 7:8-24," pp. 27, 30.

[66]Cf. D. L. Dungan, *The Sayings of Jesus in the Churches of Paul: The Use of the Synoptic Tradition in the Regulation of Early Church Life* (Oxford: Blackwell/Philadelphia: Fortress, 1971) p. 90. See further J. Murphy-O'Connor, "The Divorced Woman," p. 603, and "First Corinthians," p. 804, Christian D. Von Dehsen, *Sexual Relationships,* pp. 184–186, and P. Farla, "The two," p. 79.

[67]Cf. Norbert Baumert, *Ehelosigkeit und Ehe im Herrn: Eine Neuinterpretation von 1 Kor 7.* FB, 47 (Würzburg: Echter, 1984) p. 66; F. Neirynck, "Paul," p. 320.

[68]It is quite likely that the situation which had been reported to Paul is not that of a man having an incestuous relationship with his own mother.

[69]Murphy-O'Connor suggests that the hint contained in Paul's reversal of his normal order is confirmed by the subsequent parenthetical remark (v. 11ab). Cf. J. Murphy-O'Connor, "The Divorced Woman," p. 602.

[70]So, previously, the RSV and JB.

[71]See also the NAB. On the disruptive nature of Paul's comment, "not I but the Lord," see J. Murphy-O'Connor, "The Divorced Woman," p. 606. For a more extensive treatment of this issue, see Roger L. Omanson, "Some Comments about Style and Meaning: 1 Corinthians 9.15 and 7.10," *BT* 34 (1983) 135–139, pp. 138-139.

[72]Cf. J. Murphy-O'Connor, "The Divorced Woman," p. 605, n. 16.

[73]See F. Neirynck, "Paul," p. 320. Similarly, C. K. Barrett notes that "Paul's specific references to the teaching of Jesus are notoriously few" while Teeple's list of Paul's quotations of the Lord Jesus includes only 1 Cor 7:10-11; 9:14 and

11:23-26. Cf. C. K. Barrett, *First Corinthians,* p. 162; Howard M. Teeple, "The Oral Tradition that Never Existed," *JBL* 89 (1970) 56–68, p. 65, n. 24. See also the discussion in Victor P. Furnish, *Theology and Ethics in Paul* (Nashville, New York: Abingdon, 1968) pp. 51–67, who notes that "one of Paul's sources is the teaching of Jesus—though this is probably not his 'primary' one" (p. 66).

⁷⁴Margaret MacDonald writes: "the fact that the exhortation to females is longer and precedes the corresponding instruction to males . . . suggests that women were the main instigators of the separations." Descamps, however, opined that the sequence adopted by Paul may be because the apostle "remembers that in the Greco-Roman world, contrary to Jewish usage, it is not rare that the woman takes the initiative in the rupture." See M. Y. MacDonald, "Social Setting," p. 170; A.-L. Descamps, "New Testament Doctrine," p. 261.

⁷⁵Cf. F. Neirynck, "Paul," p. 319 and A. C. Wire, *Women Prophets,* pp. 84, 276. Neirynck makes reference to the sixth German-language edition of Georg Winer's classic study of NT grammar (p. 262; see below, note 76).

⁷⁶With regard to conditional sentences, Georg Winer's classic manual states: "Condition with assumption of *objective* possibility, where experience will decide whether the thing is really so or not . . . Here we have *ean* . . . with the conjunctive (= subjunctive)." Winer states that this rule is regularly used in the NT. With regard to the case under consideration Winer comments: "That in 1 C. vii. 11 *ean* refers to a case which (possibly) has already occurred (as Ruckert maintains) is incorrect." See G. B. Winer, *A Treatise on the Grammar of New Testament Greek Regarded as a Sure Basis for New Testament Exegesis* (Edinburgh: Clark, 1882) pp. 365, 367.

⁷⁷J. W. Wenham specifically comments that "the subjunctive is appropriate because of the element of doubt in most future conditions." J. W. Wenham, *The Elements of New Testament Greek* (Cambridge: University Press, 1965) p. 167.

⁷⁸See H. Conzelmann, *First Corinthians,* p. 120.

⁷⁹See Nigel Turner, *A Grammar of New Testament Greek,* 3: *Syntax* (Edinburgh: Clark, 1963) p. 114, and BDF, p. 190.

⁸⁰Cf. BDF, 374; N. Turner, *Grammar,* 3, p. 321.

⁸¹Cf. F. Neirynck, "Paul," p. 319; N. Baumert, *Ehelosigkeit,* p. 66. See also François Stephanus Malan, *Paulus se aanwysings in 1 Korintiërs 7 ten Opsigte van die Huwelik en die ongehude Staat* (D.D. thesis, University of Pretoria, 1980) pp. 143–144.

⁸²J. Murphy-O'Connor, "The Divorced Woman," p. 603.

⁸³1 Cor 4:15, 19; 5:11; 6:4, 18; 7:8, 11, 28, 36, 39, 40; 8:8, 10; 9:16, 10:28; 11:14, 15, 25, 26; 12:15, 16; 13:1, 2 (2x); 3 (2x); 14:6, 8, 14, 16, 23, 24, 30; 16:2, 3, 4, 6, 7, 10.

⁸⁴Rom 2:25, 26; 7:2, 3 (2x); 9:27; 10:9; 11:22; 12:20 (2x, quoting Prv 25:21-22); 13:4; 14:8 (4x), 23; 15:24; 2 Cor 3:16; 5:1; 8:12; 9:4; 10:8; 12:6; 13:2; Gal 1:8; 5:2, 10, 17; 6:1, 7; 1 Thess 2:8; 3:8. *Ean* is not used at all in Phil and Phlm.

⁸⁵The seven letters indisputably attributed to Paul (i.e., the so-called Pauline *homologoumena*) are Rom, 1 Cor, 2 Cor, Gal, Phil, 1 Thess, and Phlm.

[86]D. Dungan, *Sayings,* p. 90.

[87]Thus E.-B. Allo, James Moffatt, Robertson and Plummer, Jeremy Moiser, and Margaret MacDonald. See E.-B. Allo, *Saint Paul: première épître aux Corinthiens.* EB (2nd. ed.: Paris, Lacoffre, 1956) p. 164; J. Moffat, *The First Epistle of Paul to the Corinthians.* MNTC (London: Hodder and Stoughton, 1943) p. 78; A. Robertson and A. Plummer, *A Critical and Exegetical Commentary on the First Epistle of St Paul to the Corinthians.* ICC (2nd. ed.: Edinburgh, Clark, 1967) p. 140; J. Moiser, "A Reassessment of Paul's View of Marriage with Reference to 1 Cor. 7," *JSNT* 18 (1983) 103–122, p. 109; M. Y. MacDonald, "Social Setting," pp. 161–181, esp. p. 170; M. R. D'Angelo, "Divorce Sayings," p. 94. Without specific reference to the problem of divorce, Ralph P. Martin makes mention of women at Corinth who make a "tacit denial of their marital life." Cf. R. P. Martin, *The Spirit and the Congregation: Studies in 1 Corinthians 12-15* (Grand Rapids, MI: Eerdmans, 1984) p. 88.

[88]Essentially this is the position espoused by Norbert Baumert, who, however, denies that the separation has already taken place. See N. Baumert, *Ehelosigkeit,* p. 67.

[89]Cf. W. F. Luck, *Divorce and Remarriage,* pp. 33–34; Ben-Zion Schereschewsky, "Divorce," *EncJud,* 6, 122–135, c. 128.

[90]See J. Murphy-O'Connor, "The Divorced Woman." Murphy-O'Connor has been supported in this approach by D. E. Garland ("The Christian's Posture," p. 355).

[91]B. Byron, "1 Cor 7:10-15: A Basis for Future Catholic Discipline on Marriage and Divorce," *CBQ* 34 (1973) 429–445, p. 430.

[92]See D. L. Dungan, *Sayings,* p. 92; W. F. Luck, *Divorce and Remarriage,* p. 167.

[93]See R. Pesch, *Freie Treue: Die Christen und die Ehescheidung* (Freiburg: Herder, 1971) pp. 60–61; "Paulinische Kasuistik," p. 439.

[94]Cf. Heinz Schürmann, *Neutestamentliche Marginalien zur Frage nach der Institutionalität, Unauflösbarkeit und Sakramentalität der Ehe,* in *Kirche und Bibel* (Paderborn: Schöningh, 1979) pp. 409–430, p. 421; Erhard S. Gerstenberger and Wolfgang Schrage, *Frau und Mann.* Kohlhammer Taschenbücher: Biblische Konfrontationen, 1013 (Stuttgart: Kohlhammer, 1980) p. 236; Helmut Merklein, " 'Es ist gut für den Menschen eine Frau nicht anzufassen.' Paulus und die Sexualität nach 1 Kor 7," in J. Blank, et al., *Die Frau im Urchristentum.* QD, 95 (Freiburg: Herder, 1983) pp. 225–253, p. 236.

[95]But Margaret MacDonald entertains this possibility. Cf. M. Y. MacDonald, "Social Setting," p. 164.

[96]Admittedly this possibility has against it the linguistic difficulty of Paul's use of *can* with the subjunctive. In my mind, however, the grammatical difficulty is not sufficient to make the possibility totally implausible.

[97]Cf. C. D. Von Dehsen, *Sexual Relationships,* p. 186.

[98]See, above, pp. 13–14. See also 1 Thess 4:1-8 and my comments apropos of Paul's authority to speak on an issue of sexual and conjugal morality in *Studies*

on the First Letter to the Thessalonians. BETL, 66 (Louvain: University Press, 1984) pp. 304–305.

[99]Cf. 1 Cor 7:6 (1 Cor 7:25; 2 Cor 8:8).

[100]Used by Paul only in Phlm 8.

[101]In the RSV, *paraggellô* was translated as "I charge." The verb is transitive, requiring a direct object. By translating the verb as "I give this command," thus offering "this command" as the direct object of "give," the NRSV does not sharply distinguish between *epitassô* and *paraggellô,* Greek verbs which—quite obviously—do not have similar linguistic roots.

[102]In addition to verse 10, *paraggellô* is found only in 11:17 and 1 Thess 4:11. In contrast to these three usages, the verb occurs four times in 2 Thessalonians (3:4, 6, 10, 12), a very short letter. In 2 Thess, the use of *paraggellô* is an example of the overbearing style which distinguishes this letter from Paul's authentic letters. Cf. R. F. Collins, *Letters That Paul Did Not Write: The Epistle to the Hebrews and the Pauline Pseudepigrapha.* GNS, 28 (Wilmington, DE: Glazier, 1988) pp. 222–223, 237–238.

[103]See J. A. Fischer, "1 Cor. 7:8–24," p. 26.

[104]Cf. 1 Cor 7:12, "To the rest I say *(legô egô),* not the Lord."

[105]Cf. the REB's "I give this ruling."

[106]As a military officer would pass along orders that originated with some higher authority. In fact, the root connotation of the verb is to transmit a message.

[107]Fischer opines that Paul's usage seems to "fall somewhere between gnomic exhortation and administrative decision," while Baumert has suggested that Paul is offering an instruction *(Weisung)* in the sense of a precise application. "Give this instruction" is, as a matter of fact, the RNAB's translation. See J. A. Fischer, "1 Cor. 7:8–24," p. 26; N. Baumert, *Ehelosigkeit,* p. 63.

[108]On the nature of this phrase as an interruption, see R. L. Omanson, "Comments," pp. 138–139. As a translation of the phrase, Omanson suggests: "I give the order; no, not I, Christ gives it" (p. 139).

[109]Cf. 1 Cor 9:1; 12:3 (comp. Rom 10:9); etc.

[110]Taking a broader view of Paul's allusions to the sayings-of-Jesus tradition than does Neirynck (see above, p. 24.), Joseph Fitzmyer cites 1 Thess 4:2, 14; 5:2, 13, 15; 1 Cor 7:10-11 (cf. v. 25); 9:14; 11:23-25; 13:2; Rom 12:14, 17; 13:7; 14:13, 14; 16:19) as possible instances. Cf. J. A. Fitzmyer, "Pauline Theology," *NJBC,* 1382–1416, p. 1387.

[111]Malan, nonetheless, seems to insist that it is a saying "of Jesus" to which Paul refers in v. 10. See F. S. Malan, *Paulus se aanwysings in 1 Kor 7,* pp. 134, 149.

[112]M. R. D'Angelo, "Divorce Sayings," p. 88.

[113]"Divorce Sayings," p. 87. To a large extent, D'Angelo bases her reflections on Eugene Boring's analyses of early Christian prophecy, especially those which he has developed in "How May We Identify Oracles of Christian Prophets in the Synoptic Tradition? Mark 3:28-29 as a Test Case," *JBL* 91 (1972) 501–521. Boring's ideas on early Christian prophecy have found further expression in his

papers read during the 1973, 1974, 1976, and 1977 meetings of the Society of Biblical Literature and are published in the proceedings for those years, but D'Angelo has not exploited the insights developed in these essays. In "Oracles of Christian Prophets" (p. 504, n. 11), Boring suggests that Paul was dependent upon the traditional words of Jesus for 1 Cor 7:10-11; 9:14 and 11:23-26.

[114]See also 1 Thess 4:15 and my comments on it in *Studies*, pp. 159-162. Regrettably, D'Angelo does not consider 1 Cor 9:14 and 11:23, the other two passages, which commentators generally ascribe to the Jesus tradition.

[115]On the other hand, one can note, with Carolyn Osiek, that Paul "does not claim to be a prophet" and that although "he probably repeats prophetic oracles in his teaching, he never claims to have uttered one." Cf. C. Osiek, "Christian Prophecy: Once Upon a Time?" *CurTM* 17 (1990) 290-297, p. 293.

[116]See above, pp. 218-222. One must not, in any case, overlook "the belief of the earliest Christians that Jesus was the greatest of prophets." Cf. C. Osiek, "Christian Prophecy," p. 290.

[117]It may be that D'Angelo's exegesis of 1 Cor 7:10-11 is biased by a desire to root the tradition of dominical logia on divorce in a prophetic tradition, subject to revision by later prophets. See her conclusion, "New Prophecies," pp. 100-101.

[118]A. C. Wire, "Prophecy," p. 148. Wire makes reference to 1 Cor 7:10; 9:14 and 11:23-25, apropos of the oral tradition about Jesus' words, and to 2 Cor 10:8-9, apropos of Paul's own spiritual experience.

[119]See J. A. Fitzmyer, "Pauline Theology," p. 1395.

[120]This nuance was well understood by that disciple of Paul who wrote the epistle to the Colossians. Although "Christ" is his favorite Christological title, "Lord," without further qualification, appears in his paraenetic contexts. See R. F. Collins, *Letters*, p. 197.

[121]Cf. Elisabeth Schüssler Fiorenza, "Women in the Pre-Pauline and Pauline Churches," *USQR* 33 (1978) 153-166.

[122]For example, Elliott has written that Paul "repeats Jesus' command prohibiting divorce," and again, that Paul "quotes Jesus' words on divorce." See J. K. Elliott, "Paul's Teaching," pp. 219, 223. Quite implausible is Teeple's suggestion that Paul probably received the saying "from the Lord directly, apparently by spiritual revelation." Cf. H. M. Teeple, "Oral Tradition," p. 65, n. 24.

[123]That is, a hypothetical collection of sayings of Jesus, presumably put into writing ca. 50 A.D., which critical scholarship acknowledges to be the principal source of the discourse material common to Matt and Luke (including Matt 5:32 and Luke 16:18).

[124]Cf. Frans Neirynck, "Synoptic Problem," *NJBC*, 587-595.

[125]1 Cor 7:10-11 par. Matt 19:9; 1 Cor 9:14 par. Matt 10:10; 1 Cor 11:23-25 par. Matt 26:26-29. Cf. W. A. Heth, *Matthew's "Eunuch Saying,"* pp. 256-257 (comp. p. 189). For further discussion about the relationship between Paul and Matthew, see F. S. Malan, *Paulus se aanwysings in 1 Kor 7*, pp. 139-140; W. F. Luck, *Divorce and Remarriage*, p. 165.

[126]See below, pp. 184-213.

¹²⁷Cf. A. Mahoney, "A New Look at the Divorce Clauses in Mt 5, 32 and 19, 9," *CBQ* 30 (1968) 29–38, esp. pp. 35–36.

¹²⁸See, for example, Joseph Bonsirven, *Le divorce dans le Nouveau Testament* (Paris: Desclée, 1948) p. 35; Else Kähler, *Die Frau in den paulinischen Briefen: unter Berücksichtigung des Begriffes der Unterordnung* (Zurich: Gotthelf, 1960) p. 26; V. P. Furnish, *The Moral Teaching of Paul* (2nd. rev. ed: Nashville, Abingdon, 1985) p. 39; O. Larry Yarbrough, *Not Like the Gentiles: Marriage Rules in the Letters of Paul.* SBLDS, 80 (Atlanta, GA: Scholars, 1984) p. 111; C. K. Barrett, *First Corinthians*, p. 162; Erich Fascher, *Der erste Brief des Paulus an die Korinther.* THKNT, 7/1 (Berlin: Evangelische Verlagsanstalt, 1975) p. 184; Jozef Załęski, "Nierozerwalnosc małzenstwa według 1 Kor 7, 10–11," *Studia theologica Varsaviensia* 26 (1988) 137–146.

¹²⁹For a summary of these arguments, see C. D. Von Dehsen, *Sexual Relationships*, p. 182.

¹³⁰Without postulating a dependence of Paul on Mark, Bernadette Brooten proposes that both Paul and Mark attest to a Palestinian tradition which spoke of a divorce by the wife as well as divorce by the husband. Cf. Bernadette Brooten, "Konnten Frauen im alten Judentum die Scheidung betreiben? Überlegungen zu Mk 10, 11–12 und 1 Kor 7, 10–11," *EvT* 42 (1982) 65–80, esp. pp. 65–73; "Zur Debatte," pp. 466–478.

¹³¹Cf. Wolfgang Schenk, *Synopse zur Redenquelle der Evangelien: Q-Synopse und Rekonstruktion in deutscher Übersetzung mit kurzen Erläuterungen* (Düsseldorf: Patmos, 1981) p. 116.

¹³²Cf. Christopher M. Tuckett, "1 Corinthians and Q," *JBL* 102 (1983) 607–619, p. 619.

¹³³See, for example, Gordon Fee who deems it "irrelevant" (*The First Epistle to the Corinthians.* NICNT [Grand Rapids, MI: Eerdmans, 1987] p. 292) and David Dungan (*Sayings,* pp. 133–134).

¹³⁴Cf. F. Neirynck, "Paul," p. 315.

¹³⁵Thus, for example, J. A. Fitzmyer, "Pauline Theology," p. 1415. *E contrario,* Murphy-O'Connor thinks that verse 10b, in opposition to verse 13 which supposes a Greco-Roman cultural setting, reflects a Jewish milieu. Cf. J. Murphy-O'Connor, "The Divorced Woman," p. 603.

¹³⁶See, however, B. Brooten, "Frauen;" "Zur Debatte."

¹³⁷Cf. Acts 22:3.

¹³⁸See Birger Gerhardsson, *Memory and Manuscript: Oral Tradition and Written Transmission in Rabbinic Judaism and Early Christianity.* ASNU, 22 (Lund: Gleerup, 1961) p. 312.

¹³⁹See J. Murphy-O'Connor, "The Divorced Woman," p. 606.

¹⁴⁰Compare Paul's technique with that of the rabbis whose teachings appear in the Mishnaic tractate *'Abot* (the Sayings of the Fathers).

¹⁴¹Cf. J. A. Fitzmyer, "Pauline Theology," p. 1387. Analogously, Boring has written apropos the scriptural text used in Christian prophecy that it "is not quoted

as a past authority and then commented upon, but is re-presented as the present word of the living *kurios.*" Cf. M. E. Boring, "Oracles," p. 516.

[142]Cf. N. Baumert, *Ehelosigkeit,* p. 84.

[143]See, for example, D. L. Dungan, *Sayings,* p. 133.

[144]See W. A. Meeks, *Urban Christians,* p. 101.

[145]See, for example, H. Conzelmann (*First Corinthians,* p. 120) and G. D. Fee (*First Corinthians,* p. 292).

[146]See D. L. Dungan, *Sayings,* pp. 92–93, where he states, with emphasis added, "Paul's application is in flat contradiction to the command of the Lord, which is a strict prohibition of divorce" (p. 93). Cf. J. Dupont, *Mariage,* p. 112.

[147]Especially in his use of such significant terms as *paraggelô* ("I give charge") and *Kurios* ("Lord"). See above, pp. 29–31.

[148]Cf. Jeremy Moiser who writes, "The wife should not separate from her husband . . . but if she does she has a choice." J. Moiser, "Reassessment," p. 109; similarly, A.-L. Descamps, "New Testament Doctrine," p. 262; J. Carl Laney, "No Divorce & No Remarriage," in H. W. House, ed., *Divorce and Remarriage: Four Christian Views* (Downers Grove, Ill.: Intervarsity, 1990) pp. 15–54, pp. 41–42, 45, 48.

[149]This weakens Dungan's hypothesis that the woman had divorced because she wanted to marry another man. Presumably the intended marriage would have taken place almost immediately after the divorce. Had the woman entered into another marriage, it would have been impossible for her to be reconciled to her (first) husband (cf. Deut 24:1-4) and he would not have been called *anêr,* her "man" or "husband."

[150]Compare with the use of *parthenos,* which the RSV also translates as "unmarried" in v. 25 and following. It is to be noted that the adjective *agamos,* used of a woman in 1 Cor 7:11b, is in the masculine singular (compare the use of the masculine singular, *apistos,* "unfaithful," to refer to a female unbeliever in 1 Cor 7:12, 14, and its inclusive use in v. 15).

[151]In 1 Cor 7:11b, the woman is *agamos,* that is, not-married, because she has divorced. Paul had previously used the nominal adjective in v. 8 ("to the unmarried"). Because of his use of *agamos* to refer to a divorcée in v. 11b, one should not uncritically presume that Paul is making reference to those who have never been married in v. 8. In both instances, I believe, an *agamos* is one who is no longer married and not yet remarried.

[152]See F. Neirynck, "Paul," p. 319.

[153]See H. Merklein, " 'Es ist gut," p. 236, who is referenced, with apparent approval, by Neirynck, "Paul," p. 319. According to the Shepherd of Hermas, the wife is to repent and return to her husband. In order that he can receive her again as his wife, a husband divorced by his wife is not allowed to remarry. Cf. *Herm. Man.* 4. 1. 8.

[154]Cf. Deut 24:1-4. Cf. Quentin Quesnell, "Made Themselves Eunuchs for the Kingdom of Heaven," *CBQ* 30 (1968) 335–358.

[155]Similarly, A.-L. Descamps, "New Testament Doctrine," pp. 262, 263.

[156]See, for example, Brian Byron who writes, "she must be prepared to return to her husband if the cause of her perhaps legitimate complaint is removed." B. Byron, "1 Cor 7:10-15," p. 430 (cf. p. 439).

[157]After his analysis of some of the problems attendant upon the interpretation of Paul's reflections on divorce, Corrado Marucci emphatically concludes that "the only certain conclusion is that, for Paul the Christian woman can marry only once." Cf. C. Marucci, *Parole di Gesù sul divorzio: Ricerche scritturistiche previe ad un ripensamento teologico, canonistico e pastorale della dottrina cattolica dell'indissolubilità del matrimonio.* Aloisiana, 16 (Naples: Morcelliana, 1972) p. 316.

[158]Cf. Herodotus, 5, 39; Euripides, *Andromache,* 973.

[159]A characteristic "certainly not" (*mê genoito:* cf. Rom 3:4, 6, 31; 6:2, 15; 7:7; 9:14; 11:1, 11; Gal 2:17; 3:21; 6:14) betrays his desire not to be misunderstood. The formula occurs in the Corinthian correspondence only in 1 Cor 6:15, but in a somewhat different usage.

[160]That is, in much the same way that Mark had added Mark 10:12 as an expansion of or an interpretive addendum to the Jesuanic logion reproduced in v. 11.

NOTES—CHAPTER 2

[1]Cf. H. Conzelmann, *First Corinthians,* p. 121; Saeke Kubo, "1 Corinthians vii. 16: Optimistic or Pessimistic?" *NTS* 24 (1978) p. 543; N. Baumert, *Ehelosigkeit,* pp. 92–93; C. D. Von Dehsen, *Sexual Relationships,* p. 189; August Strobel, *Der erste Brief an die Korinther.* Zürcher Bibelkommentare: NT 6/1 (Zurich: Theologischer Verlag, 1989) p. 121.

[2]Cf. C. D. Von Dehsen, *Sexual Relationships,* pp. 189–190.

[3]Within the biblical tradition, see, for example, Deut 7:3 and Neh 13:25.

[4]Cf. C. K. Barrett, *First Corinthians,* p. 165, W. F. Luck, *Divorce and Remarriage,* pp. 168-169, J. Murphy-O'Connor, "First Corinthians," pp. 104–105, and Ernest Best, "1 Corinthians 7:14 and Children in the Church," *IBS* 4 (1990) 158-166, p. 158. Murphy-O'Connor makes reference to 2 Cor 6:14-7:1 in this regard.

[5]Cf. 1 Cor 1:2: "to those sanctified in Christ Jesus, called to be saints" (*hêgiasmenois en Christô Iêsou, klêtois hagiois*).

[6]Cf. 1 Cor 6:11. For one example of the consequences of this distinction in the behavioral sphere, cf. 1 Cor 6:1.

[7]Cf. 1 Cor 5:9.

[8]Cf. 1 Cor 6:15.

[9]Thus H. Conzelmann, *First Corinthians,* p. 121; N. Baumert, *Ehelosigkeit,* pp. 92-93.

[10]Antoinette Wire writes, in this regard, of Paul's "rhetoric of equality." Along with Margaret MacDonald, she suggests that the problem involved mainly the mixed marriages of unbelieving husbands to Christian wives. Cf. A. C. Wire, *Women Prophets,* pp. 84–85; M. Y. MacDonald, "Early Christian Women Married to Unbelievers," *SR* (1990) 221–234, p. 222.

[11]Cf. 1 Cor 5:12a.

[12]Cf. J. Moiser, "Reassessment," pp. 109–110.

[13]In this regard Dungan speaks of Paul's "minimalism" regarding the use of the Lord's commands. Cf. D. Dungan, *Sayings,* p. 98.

[14]Pesch has suggested that Paul's transition to the consideration of mixed marriages was relatively easy insofar as he had—at least in Pesch's understanding of the passage—already treated of a kind of mixed marriage in the parenthesis of verse 11. Cf. R. Pesch, *Paulinische Kasuistik.*

[15]Cf. C. Von Dehsen, *Sexual Relationships,* pp. 187–188.

[16]In Greek, the first person singular is already indicated by the declension of the verb (*legô,* "I say"). The use of a pronoun in the first person singular (*egô,* "I") serves an emphatic function. *Legô egô* really means "I myself say."

[17]Cf. 1 Cor 1:1.

[18]Cf. 1 Cor 7:40. See, likewise, C. D. Von Dehsen, *Sexual Relationships,* pp. 187–188.

[19]Cf. 1 Cor 4:1.

[20]Cf. 1 Cor 14:37.

[21]Cf. J. H. Schütz, *Paul and the Anatomy of Apostolic Authority.* SNTSMS, 26 (Cambridge: University Press, 1975) p. 284.

[22]Ibid.

[23]Thus, G. D. Fee, *First Corinthians,* p. 297. Several, but not all, of the more popular translations of the passage highlight the difference between the verbs *paraggellô* and *legô,* by offering as a translation of the latter something other than the usual "I say." For example, the NJB's "these instructions are my own." See also the REB: "I say this as my own word, not as the Lord's."

[24]It is not uncommon for the Greek particles not to be translated from Greek into English by a specific word. Punctuation and other procedures of translation are generally sufficient to convey their meaning.

[25]Given the difficulty of finding a third group, some translations take *tois loipois* ("to the rest," NRSV) as if it were in the neuter gender. For example, the NAB, "as for other matters," and the NJB, "for other cases." Since the dative masculine plural and the dative neuter plural of *loipos* are both *loipois,* such translations are theoretically possible. In context, however, they are not possible. Paul has clearly arranged the addressees of verses 7, 10, and 12 in a parallel sequence: *legô de tois agamois kai tais chêrais . . . tois de gegamêkosin . . . tois de loipois . . . .*

[26]Cf. P. J. Tomson, *Jewish Law,* p. 118. See above, pp. 17–18.

[27]See D. L. Dungan, *Sayings,* p. 93. He bases his argument upon the fact that in 1 Thess 4:13 and 5:6 *hoi loipoi* are non-believers and cites Robertson-Plummer,

Allo, and Lightfoot as his references. Cf. A. Robertson and A. Plummer, *First Corinthians,* p. 141; E.-B. Allo, *Première épître,* p. 165; J. B. Lightfoot, *Notes on Epistles of St. Paul from Unpublished Commentaries* (London: Macmillan, 1895) p. 225.

²⁸Dungan interprets Paul's *tois loipois* ("concerning the rest") as if the phrase were introduced by a *peri* ("concerning") which, however, does not appear in 1 Cor 7:12. Cf. 1 Cor 7:1, 25; 8:1, 4; 12:1; 16:1, 12.

²⁹Cf. G. D. Fee, *First Corinthians,* p. 298. The New Translation has incorporated an italicized interpretive comment, "to those who are married to unbelievers," into the text of 1 Cor 7:12. One might note that the RNAB's interpretive footnote to 1 Cor 7:12-14, "marriages in which only one partner is a baptized Christian," is particularly significant insofar as the RNAB's translation of *tois loipois* differs from the NAB's "as for the other matters." The NAB translation highlights the fact that Paul is continuing to respond to the issues raised by the Corinthians.

³⁰The adjective "*apistos*-unbeliever" is, in the New Testament, principally a Pauline term. Within Paul's authentic letters, it occurs only in the Corinthian correspondence—eleven times in 1 Corinthians (of which five occurrences are in 1 Cor 7:12-16; cf. 1 Cor 6:6, 7:12, 13, 14 [2x], 15; 10:27; 14:22 [2x], 23, 24) and three times in 2 Cor (2 Cor 4:4; 6:14, 15). Cf. 1 Tim 5:8 and Titus 1:15. The seven other uses of the adjective are scattered throughout the New Testament—once each in Matt, Mark, John, Acts, and Rev, and twice in Luke (cf. Matt 17:17; Mark 9:19; Luke 9:41; 12:46; John 20:27; Acts 26:8; Rev 21:8). Thus fourteen of the twenty-three occurrences of the term are in 1-2 Corinthians, and five of these fourteen are to be found in 1 Cor 7:12-16.

³¹Cf. 1 Cor 14:22-24.

³²Cf. D. Daube, "Pauline Contributions to a Pluralistic Culture: Re-creation and Beyond," in D. G. Miller and D. Y. Hadidian, eds., *Jesus and Man's Hope,* 2 (Pittsburgh: Theological Seminary, 1971) pp. 223-245, p. 233. Quite implausible is the interpretation of Josephine Massyingberde Ford who takes the *apistos* ("unbelievers") of vv. 12-16 as a reference to a Jew "of doubtful stock." See J. M. Ford, " 'Hast Thou Tithed Thy Meal?' " and "Is Thy Child Kosher (1 Cor. x. 27 ff and 1 Cor. vii, 14), *JTS* 17 (1966) 71-79, pp. 76-79; *A Trilogy on Wisdom and Celibacy* (Notre Dame, IN: Notre Dame University Press, 1967) pp. 73-82.

³³That is, those called saints (*klētoi hagioi;* 1 Cor 1:2). Cf. Rom 1:7.

³⁴Cf. 1 Cor 7:39, *gameô en kuriô.* Comp. 1 Cor 11:11 which Orr and Walther consider an extension of the "uxorial sanctification," proposed by Paul in 1 Cor 7:12-16. Cf. W. F. Orr and J. A. Walther, *1 Corinthians,* p. 263.

³⁵Yarbrough's view that the marital partners to which vv. 10-11 make reference are Jews and that the dominical logion is binding upon only Jews (presumably Jewish Christians?) is, in my judgment, quite implausible. See O. Larry Yarbrough, *Not Like Gentiles,* p. 111, n. 68.

³⁶Cf. D. L. Dungan, *Sayings,* pp. 98-99; F. Neirynck, "Paul," p. 320; and the footnote in RNAB *ad locum.*

[37]Brian Byron has stated that verses 12-13 "do actually reflect the Lord's teaching" (1 Cor 7:10-15, p. 430), but most commentators, a bit more prudently and, in my judgment, a bit more correctly, consider that Paul's teaching is in continuity with the Christian tradition prohibiting divorce. Cf. B. Gerhardsson, *Memory and Manuscript,* pp. 312-314; Béda Rigaux, "Réflexions sur l'historicité de Jésus dans le message paulinien," in *Studiorum paulinorum congressus internationalis catholicus 1961,* 2. AnBib, 18 (Rome: Pontifical Biblical Institute, 1963) 265-274, p. 270; H. Conzelmann, *First Corinthians,* p. 121, n. 25; D. Dungan, *Sayings,* p. 98; etc.

[38]Called a "brother" (*adelphos*) in 1 Cor 7:12. This term was virtually used as a technical term in the Pauline correspondence to designate a Christian. Used in this sense some nineteen times in 1 Thessalonians, it occurs thirty-nine times in 1 Corinthians. In this letter Paul twice uses the cognate expression "sister" (*adelphê,* 1 Cor 7:15; 9:5) to designate a Christian woman. He uses "sister" in the present context (v. 15) but has chosen to balance the "brother" of 1 Cor 7:12 with "woman" (*gunê*) in the parallel statement of verse 13. The choice of "woman" (*gunê*) as a designation of the subject of the verb in verse 13 may have been influenced by the appearance of "wife," (*gunaika,* literally, "woman") in verse 12.

[39]Cf. 1 Cor 7:2, 3.

[40]The phrase *gameô en kuriô* ("marry in the Lord") is used by Paul in 1 Cor 7:39 of a baptized Christian being married to a baptized Christian. In my judgment, however, the phrase, in a passive participial form, would likewise be applicable to the marriage of two pagans, both of whom subsequently became Christian.

[41]On the use of analogy, and the restrictions on its use, in the exposition of *halakah,* see Moses Mielziner, *Introduction to the Talmud* (4th. ed.: New York, Bloch, 1968) pp. 178-181.

[42]Dungan writes about the "particular 'minimalism' of Paul's regarding the actual use of the commands of the Lord," which he deems "worthy of the most careful consideration." See D. L. Dungan, *Sayings,* p. 99.

[43]Cf. Matt 5:21-48.

[44]Cf. the tractate *'Abot* in the Mishnah. On the Talmud as a process of accretion, see Robert Goldenberg, "B. M. Lewin and the Saboraic Element," in J. Neusner, ed., *The Formation of the Babylonian Talmud: Studies in the Achievements of Late Nineteenth and Twentieth Century Historical and Literary-critical Research.* SPB, 17 (Leiden: Brill, 1970) pp. 51-60; Terry R. Bard, "Julius Kaplan, Hyman Klein, and the Saboraic Element," *Ibid.,* pp. 61-74.

[45]Cf. C. D. Von Dehsen, *Sexual Relationships,* pp. 188-189.

[46]He cites the phrase "a sister as wife" (*adelphên gunaika*) in 1 Cor 9:5 as an indication of the norm. Cf. W. A. Meeks, *Urban Christians,* p. 101.

[47]That there was some misunderstanding of Paul's apostolic authority at Corinth is clear from 1 Cor 1:12-14. That there was an inappropriate invoking of Paul's authority by some Corinthians does not establish as fact that his authority had been specifically misused in regard to divorce in a situation of a mixed marriage.

Nonetheless Meeks' suggestion enjoys some attraction and is quite plausible in and of itself.

In any event, Paul was aware that some of his teaching was apt to be misunderstood. His use of the rhetorical question followed by the expression "by no means" (*mê genoito*) in the letter to the Romans provides clear evidence that the apostle knew that his teaching could be misunderstood. Cf. Rom 6:1-2; 7:7, etc. Postpauline evidence of the misconstrual of Paul's thought is to be found in 2 Thess 2:2; 2 Pet 3:16, etc.

⁴⁸See George A. Kennedy, *New Testament Interpretation Through Rhetorical Criticism* (Chapel Hill, NC—London: University of North Carolina Press, 1984) p. 16.

⁴⁹Pace Gordon Fee who opines that the three verses (vv. 12-14) form a perfect triple chiasm. See G. D. Fee, *First Corinthians,* p. 299, n. 14.

⁵⁰Cf. 1 Cor 11:2-10.

⁵¹The translations found in the NIV, NJB, RNAB, and the New Translation are rather similar, as are those of the earlier RSV and NAB.

⁵²In N-A²⁶ the Greek of verse 14a reads *hêgiastai gar ho anêr ho apistos en tê gunaiki,* but several manuscripts, particularly D, F, G and other witnesses of the Western textual tradition, have added an interpretive gloss, *"tê pistê*-who is a believer," to Paul's *"gunaiki*-wife." See Bruce M. Metzger, *A Textual Commentary on the Greek New Testament: A Companion Volume to the United Bible Societies' Greek New Testament* (London—New York: United Bible Societies, 1971) p. 554.

⁵³The Greek term is actually *"tô adelphô*-the brother," the term found in verse 12. Although this Greek word is found in the most ancient Greek manuscripts and in those generally considered to be most reliable, other Greek manuscripts, including the majority of medieval Greek manuscripts (and the "corrected" Sinaiticus and Claromontanus codices), read *andri,* literally, "man" or "husband." This creates a perfect balance between verse 14a and verse 14b, but the reading is not well attested. One might also note that the fourteenth-century minuscule 629, Tertullian, and the Ambrosiaster have added an interpretive *"tô pistô*-who is a believer" to *andri* in a fashion similar to their addition of the interpretive *tê pistê* in verse 14a. See above, n. 52. Cf. B. M. Metzger, *Textual Commentary,* p. 555.

⁵⁴Similarly, the NEB which, however, spoke of "the heathen husband" and the "heathen wife."

⁵⁵Compare with the Good News Bible's "For the unbelieving husband is made acceptable to God by being united to his wife, and the unbelieving wife is made acceptable to God by being united to her Christian husband."

⁵⁶This translation reflects an old opinion, cited by Thomas Aquinas, that the Christian spouse should live with the non-Christian partner in the hope that the latter will convert to Christianity. As a variant on this theme, see D. Daube, "Pauline Contributions," pp. 234–235. 1 Pet 3:1 (cf. Tit 2:5) suggests that the conduct of Christian wives might be a motivating force in the conversion of their husbands.

[57]To the list of eight interpretations cited in Gerhard Delling's 1958 survey of the mid-twentieth-century literature on the topic in a 1958 article, Murphy-O'Connor has added a ninth and tenth type of interpretation. Cf. G. Delling, "Nun aber sind sie heilig," in *Studien zum Neuen Testament und zum hellenistischen Judentum. Gesammelte Aufsätze 1950-1968* (Göttingen: Vandenhoeck & Ruprecht, 1970) pp. 257-269, pp. 257-260; J. Murphy-O'Connor, "Works without Faith in I Cor., VII, 14," *RB* 84 (1977) 349-361, p. 349.

[58]Cf. J. C. O'Neill, "1 Corinthians 7, 14 and Infant Baptism," in A. Vanhoye, ed., *L'apôtre Paul, personnalité, style et conception du ministère.* BETL, 73 (Louvain: University Press, 1986) pp. 357-361. O'Neill has argued that the verb in the perfect tense has a future sense and that, on the basis of v. 16, the believer who remains in a mixed marriage will lead his or her spouse to baptism and sanctification.

[59]Cf. G. Delling, "Sind sie heilig," pp. 87-88.

[60]See J. Murphy-O'Connor, "Works," p. 349, with reference to H. Conzelmann, *First Corinthians,* p. 122.

[61]See, for example, E.-B. Allo, *Première épître,* pp. 166-167. Allo cites Chrysostom, Jerome, and Augustine as patristic witnesses in favor of this opinion.

[62]Murphy-O'Connor notes that "this hypothesis underlies a wide variety of opinions stretching from the concept of 'holiness' as a spiritual substance or power to that of 'holiness' as an objective relationship to the Christian partner, or to God, or to sanctity itself." Cf. J. Murphy-O'Connor, "Works," p. 351.

[63]See J. Murphy-O'Connor, "Works," p. 352. In this article Murphy-O'Connor provides a good summary of the Pauline notion of holiness. See also Horst Balz, "*hagios,* etc.," *EDNT,* 1, 16-20, esp. pp. 19-20.

[64]Cf. J. Murphy-O'Connor who has written that "the simplest [interpretation] is that Paul considered the unbeliever holy because, by deciding to maintain the marriage, he or she is acting in conformity with the divine plan (Gen 2:24 = 1 Cor 6:17) and the dominical directive in 7:10-11." J. Murphy-O'Connor, "First Corinthians," p. 805. Although the Irish Dominican considers this to be the simplest solution to the crux, it is not one of the eight which Delling has passed in review and would constitute an addition to Murphy-O'Connor's expanded list of the interpretations of holiness in 1 Corinthians 7. In a fashion somewhat similar to that of Murphy-O'Connor, Malan states that the non-Christian spouse is acceptable to God insofar as he or she remains united in marriage to the Christian spouse. Cf. F. S. Malan, *Paulus se aanwysings in 1 Kor 7,* p. 165.

[65]Pace C. K. Barrett who states that "some measure of instrumentality is implied." See C. K. Barrett, *First Corinthians,* p. 164; cf. Josef Blinzler, "Zur Auslegung von I Kor 7, 14," in J. Blinzler, O. Kuss, F. Mussner, eds., *Neutestamentliche Aufsätze. Festschrift für Prof. Josef Schmid zum 70. Geburtstag* (Regensburg: Pustet, 1963) pp. 23-41, p. 37.

[66]Murphy-O'Connor correctly suggests that "we have to be content with a translation which expresses a vague relationship." Cf. J. Murphy-O'Connor, "Works," p. 358.

⁶⁷F. F. Bruce, *1 and 2 Corinthians*. NCB (London: Oliphants, 1971) p. 69. As illustrations of the principle he cites Exod 29:37, "seven days you shall make atonement for the altar, and consecrate it, and the altar shall be most holy; whatever touches the altar shall become holy," and Lev 6:18, "anything that touches them shall be holy." Ernest Best writes about moral and spiritual qualities being transferred from one person to another (cf. 1 Cor 12:26; 2 Cor 1:3-7; 4:12), noting that Paul is "influenced by two currents of thought, one associating holiness with people and the other viewing people as affecting one another by their actions and the way they live." Cf. E. Best, "1 Corinthians 7:14," pp. 164–165.

⁶⁸Similarly, G. D. Fee, *First Corinthians*, pp. 300–301, and Michael Lattke, "Holiness and Sanctification in the New Testament," in E. W. Conrad and E. G. Newing, eds., *Perspectives on Language and Text: Essays and Poems in Honor of Francis I. Andersen's Sixtieth Birthday* (Winona Lake, IN: Eisenbrauns, 1987) pp. 351–357, p. 354 [= "Heiligkeit III," *TRE*, 14, pp. 703–708, p. 705]. Lattke, borrowing an expression from Nathan Söderblom, writes in this regard of the "contagious character of holiness."

⁶⁹Cf. Evald Lövestam, "Divorce and Remarriage in the New Testament," *The Annual Jewish Law Annual* 4 (1981) 47–65, p. 64.

⁷⁰This affirmation is one of the major interpretive cruces in this passage. The discussion turns to a large degree on the extent to which Paul is dependent on Jewish usage as he makes this affirmation.

⁷¹See, for example, Kurt Aland, *Did the Early Church Baptize Infants?* The Library of History and Doctrine (London: SCM, 1963); Oscar Cullmann, *Le baptême des enfants et la doctrine biblique du baptême*. Cahiers théologiques de l'actualité protestante, 19/20 (Neuchatel-Paris: Delachaux & Niestlé, 1948) esp. pp. 37–39; *Baptism in the New Testament*. SBT, 1 (Chicago: Regnery, 1950); Joachim Jeremias, *Infant Baptism in the First Four Centuries*. The Library of History and Doctrine (London: SCM, 1960) esp. pp. 44–48; *The Origins of Infant Baptism: A Further Study in Reply to Kurt Aland*. SHT, 1 (Naperville, IL: Allenson 1963) esp. pp. 35–38; G. R. Beasley-Murray, *Baptism in the New Testament* (London: Macmillan, 1963) pp. 192–199; Georg Walther, "Übergreifende Heiligkeit und Kindertaufe im Neuen Testament," *EvT* 25 (1965) 668–674.

⁷²Cf. Gerhard Delling, "Lexikalisches zu *teknon*," in *Studien zum Neuen Testament*, pp. 270–280; "Sind sie heilig," pp. 266–269.

⁷³Cf. G. Delling, "Sind sie heilig," pp. 261–269; "Zur Exegese von I. Kor. 7, 14," in *Studien zum Neuen Testament*, pp. 281–287, p. 283.

⁷⁴Cf. 1 Cor 5:9-11; and especially, 2 Cor 6:14-18. Cf. G. Delling, "Sind sie heilig," pp. 261–262.

⁷⁵Cf. J. Jeremias, *Infant Baptism*, p. 46; J. M. Ford, "Is Thy Child Kosher?" p. 76; G. D. Fee, *First Corinthians*, p. 301.

⁷⁶Cf. G. Delling, "I. Kor. 7, 14," p. 283.

⁷⁷Murphy-O'Connor notes that *hēgiastai* "carries a temporal connotation." See J. Murphy-O'Connor, "Works," p. 357.

⁷⁸Murphy-O'Connor believes that it seems most natural to understand "your children" as referring to children who had not reached maturity. He further opines

that they may not be described as "unbelievers" (*apistoi*) because faith (*pistis*) requires the maturity needed for a confession of faith (see Rom 10:9-10) and unbelief (*a-pistis*) implies the possibility of a choice. Cf. J. Murphy-O'Connor, "Works," p. 360.

⁷⁹This understanding of the situation of these children seems, however, to fly in the face of Paul's understanding of the term "*hagios*-holy." It is unfortunate that the word "*akathartos*-unclean" is not very often used by Paul. In the extant and certainly authentic Pauline corpus it is found only in verse 14 and in 2 Cor 6:17, where it appears in a citation of Isa 52:4.

⁸⁰In agreement with Albrecht Oepke, Delling, for example, suggests that v. 14cd excludes the idea that the baptized children of a mixed marriage are somehow contaminated by their non-Christian parent in addition to its rejection of the idea that non-baptized adult children somehow contaminate their Christian parents. Cf. A. Oepke, "Urchristentum und Kindertaufe," *ZNW* (1930) 81-111, p. 86; G. Delling, "I. Kor. 7, 14," p. 283. See, further, J. Blinzler, "I Kor 7, 14," pp. 29-31.

⁸¹Cf. J. C. O'Neill, "1 Corinthians 7, 14," pp. 360-361; E. Best, "1 Corinthians 7:14," p. 159. O'Neill, however, argues that just as an unclean child is lead to baptism and sanctification by the believing parent, so an unclean husband or wife may be lead to sanctification by the believing partner. According to O'Neill, sanctification entails baptism and children were baptized as a matter of course.

⁸²Cf. W. F. Orr and J. A. Walther, *1 Corinthians,* p. 213; G. D. Fee, *First Corinthians,* pp. 301-302. Antoinette Wire offers this opinion: "Women married to nonbelievers would have sought assurance that their children were holy because Greek children shared their father's political and religious identity; hence reference to that issue suggests an address to women" (*Women Prophets,* p. 85).

⁸³Cf. *m. Qidd* 1:2; *m. Ketub.* 4:4.

⁸⁴This is the contention of J. Murphy-O'Connor, in "Works," p. 361.

⁸⁵See D. Daube, "Pauline Contributions," pp. 233-235.

⁸⁶With regard to this optimistic interpretation of v. 16, see above, pp. 60-62.

⁸⁷Daube opines that the *hagiazô* of vv. 14-15 reflects the Hebrew *qiddesh,* that is, "to consecrate the wife." Cf. G. Daube, "Pauline Contributions," p. 236. See, also, above, p. 48 and n. 56.

⁸⁸Thus, for example, Eduard Lohse who writes "in this case, the Christian partner should not refuse a divorce, but agree to the dissolution of the marriage, for 'it is to peace that God has called you' (v. 15)." See E. Lohse, *Theological Ethics of the New Testament* (Minneapolis, MN: Fortress, 1991), p. 28.

⁸⁹"Pauline Contributions," p. 235.

⁹⁰Victor Hasler notes that "marital relationships (7:12ff.) are to fall under the sway of peace." Cf. V. Hasler, "*eirênê, ktl.,*" *EDNT,* 1, 394-397, p. 396. This is true even if, as some commentators see things, v. 15c serves, in the first instance, as the Pauline argument which provides a warrant for a Christian's toleration of the departure of an unbelieving spouse. It may be, however, that v. 15c bears more upon the pericope (vv. 12-16) as a whole than it does upon v. 15ab.

See the discussion above, p. 64. In which case, the call to peace serves the purposes of Paul's argumentation primarily as a reason why Christians should remain in marital unions with non-Christian spouses.

[91]Cf. 1 Cor 7:12c, 13b: "*suneudokei*-consents to live with."

[92]Cf. 1 Thess 5:23 (comp. Rom 15:13), as well as the opening and final greetings of Paul's letters (Rom 1:7; 1 Cor 1:3; 2 Cor 1:2; Gal 1:3; Phil 1:2; Phlm 3; Rom 15:33; 16:20; 2 Cor 13:11; Gal 6:16; Phil 4:9).

[93]The NRSV's "It is to peace that God has called you" translates the Greek text of 1 Cor 7:15c, *en de eirênê keklêken humas ho theos*, somewhat tendentiously. The particles *en* and *de* are generic, but the NRSV translates the first as if the preposition had been *eis* with a connotation of purpose ("to peace"). Lietzmann explicitly makes such a claim. Cf. Hans Lietzmann, in Hans Lietzmann and W. G. Kümmel, *An die Korinther 1-2.* HNT, 9 (4th. ed.: Tübingen, Mohr, 1949) p. 31. See also Werner Foerster, "*Eirênê,*" *TDNT,* 2, 400–420, p. 416, n. 95. The NRSV, moreover, takes the mild conjunctive *de* as if it had been an explanatory *gar* ("for"). With regard to the latter, it is interesting to note that although the NEB had translated the conjunctive *de* as "for," the REB has foregone the use of a conjunction in its translation, preferring instead to bring v. 15b to closure with a period and translating verse 15c as an independent sentence.

[94]There is a text-critical problem affecting verse 15c. A footnote to the NRSV serves as a reminder "that other ancient authorities read *us*" (cf. the RSV's "For God has called us to peace"). Among those ancient witnesses which read "*humas*-you," the reading adopted by the editors of N-A[26], are the Codex Sinaiticus, the Codex Alexandrinus, the Codex Ephraemi Rescriptus and minuscules 81, 326, and 2127 as well as the Coptic Bohairic text. The editors of N-A[26] considered that the "us" reading was better attested by the manuscript tradition (the witnesses include P[46], dating from about 200 A.D., and the fourth-century Codex Vaticanus), but judged that the "*humas*-you" reading enjoyed a somewhat stronger claim to authenticity because of scribes' common tendency to generalize aphorisms. Cf. B. M. Metzger, *Textual Commentary,* p. 555. Among modern English translations, the NJB and RNAB adopt the "you" reading, while the NIV and the New Translation read "us." The REB's paraphrase obviates the necessity to make a choice between the two pronouns.

[95]1 Cor 7:15c, REB.

[96]Cf. Gerhard von Rad, "*Shalôm,*" in "*Eirênê,*" *TDNT,* 2, 400–422, pp. 402–404.

[97]1 Cor 7:15.

[98]The "each . . . to which God called" (*hekaston hôs keklêken ho theos*) of verse 17 has a clear parallel, in word and thought, in verse 24, "each . . . in which you were called" (*hekastos en hô eklêthê*).

[99]Compare 1 Cor 7:25 and 1 Cor 7:12.

[100]See also 1 Cor 7:26-27.

[101]See " 'But if you can gain your freedom' (1 Corinthians 7:17-24)," a study of this general rule by Gregory W. Dawes in *CBQ* 52 (1990) 681-697. Manuel

Orge calls this rule the "pastoral principle" of the status quo. Cf. M. Orge, "El próposito temático," *Claretianum* 31 (1991), p. 125.

[102]See, for example, J. Weiss, *Der erste Korintherbrief*, p. 183, and C. K. Barrett, *First Epistle*, p. 167. Similarly, M. Orge, "El próposito temático," *Claretianum* 27 (1987) pp. 94–95 with, however, a somewhat different implication. Orge claims that they refer back to verse 15ab. Conzelmann, however, opines that the entire discussion is an "idle matter" since the *ei mê* (the NRSV's "however") can be taken either as a reference to what has preceded or as a reference to what follows. Cf. H. Conzelmann, *First Corinthians*, p. 125. Taking *ei mê* as equivalent to "but" (*alla*), Orr and Walther suggest the possibility that 1 Cor 7:17-24 may be a commentary on the "*eirênê-peace*" of verse 15. Cf. W. F. Orr and J. A. Walther, *1 Corinthians*, pp. 215–216.

[103]Cf. Gal 3:28, "there is neither Jew nor Greek, there is neither slave nor free, there is neither male nor female; for you are all one in Christ Jesus." See also Col 3:11 and my comment in this regard in *Letters*, p. 202.

[104]See especially F. Stanley Jones, *"Freiheit" in den Briefen des Apostels Paulus: Eine historische, exegetische und religionsgeschichtliche Studie*. GTA, 34 (Göttingen: Vandenhoeck & Ruprecht, 1987), pp. 27–69, 158–192.

[105]Cf. F. Stanley Jones, *Freiheit*, p. 36, who reflects that the Lord may be considered their redeemer. As such He is their "patron."

[106]The paradoxical formulation of verse 22 would seem to be an ad hoc formulation on the part of Paul. The expression, "*doulos Christou*-slave of Christ," is, in any case, hapax in the New Testament. On the other hand, Paul often writes about serving God (*douleuô theô*). Cf. 1 Thess 1:9; Rom 1:22; 12:11; 14:18 (cf. Rom 7:6; 16:18).

[107]This is the interpretation of the passage given by most commentators, and, most recently, by G. W. Dawes ("But if you can gain your freedom," pp. 689–693). This interpretation is reflected in the translations offered by the RNSV, NIV, REB, and the New Translation. Zerwick and Grosvenor note, however, that the sentence, whose main verb is without an explicit object, can be understood in another way, i.e., "but even though you have the possibility of becoming free, suffer it (slavery) rather." Cf. Max Zerwick and Mary Grosvenor," *A Grammatical Analysis of the Greek New Testament,* 2 (Rome: Biblical Institute, 1979), p. 510. This alternative translation is reflected in the NJB's "even if you have a chance of freedom, you should prefer to make full use of your condition as a slave." The RNAB offers a confusing mediation between the two interpretations: "Do not be concerned but, even if you can gain your freedom, make the most of it."

[108]See Dawes, "But if you can gain your freedom," p. 690.

[109]Similarly, Antoinette Wire, *Women Prophets*, pp. 86–87.

[110]In my *Letters,* I have dealt with the actualization of the Pauline tradition.

[111]Norbert Baumert has suggested that, although the church at Corinth was of relatively recent foundation when Paul wrote this letter, the mission to the Gentiles had been in existence for a longer period of time. Consequently, Paul would have had the opportunity and occasion to develop the kind of response that he has presented here. Cf. N. Baumert, *Ehelosigkeit*, p. 75.

[112]It has been noted that the verb *aphiêmi,* which occurs three times in this context, is a technical term for divorce (see above, p. 238, n. 55). This technical meaning is, however, a specific connotation of a word which has a more general connotation. In the letter to the Romans, Paul uses the verb in passages where it bears other connotations. Cf. Rom 1:27 and 4:7 (a citation of Ps 32:1). It would be incorrect to think that the trust of Paul's exhortation in 1 Cor 7:12-14 is merely the prohibition of Christians (formally) divorcing their non-Christian spouses. His argument is that Christians must not sever the marital relationship provided that their unbelieving partners consent to a continuance of the marriage. Depending on the context, the verb *aphiêmi* can be translated as "abandon" or "dismiss" just as, in context, it can be translated as "divorce."

[113]Orge likewise cites 1 Cor 7:15-16 as an example of the pastoral principle of the status quo. Cf. M. Orge, "El próposito temático," *Claretianum* 31 (1991), p. 125.

[114]The NRSV gives a fairly literal translation of verse 15. Other modern versions (including the RSV) attempt to refine Paul's language. Compare, for example, the NJB's "But if the unbeliever chooses to leave, then let the separation take place: in those circumstances, the brother or sister is no longer tied. But God has called you to live in peace." and the REB's "If however the unbelieving partner wishes for a separation, it should be granted; in such cases the Christian husband or wife is not bound by the marriage. God's call is a call to live in peace."

[115]See above, p. 19 and p. 237, n. 44.

[116]Used absolutely as a nominal adjective in verse 15 (*ho apistos,* literally, "the unbelieving [one]"), *apistos* is used as a qualifying adjective in verses 12 and 13 (*gunaika apiston* [unbelieving wife] and *andra apiston* [unbelieving husband]). Although masculine in form, "the unbelieving one" refers to either the unbelieving husband or the unbelieving wife. In verse 12 the descriptive adjective also has a masculine form even though it qualifies a female.

[117]Note the use of the adversative "*de*-but." See above, n. 116.

[118]Byron's statement that "Paul seems to suggest that the Christian need not go to too much trouble to dissuade the unbeliever from going: 'let it be so' " ("1 Cor 7:10-15," p. 430) seems to be something of an overstatement. Paul has said too much about the quality of the marital relationship in verses 1-14 for him to have espoused such a cavalier position in verse 15.

[119]Byron correctly notes the significance of exceptional situations for both Paul and Matthew. Cf. B. Byron, "1 Cor 7:10-15," p. 438.

[120]Although the verb *chôrizô* denotes separation, it also had the technical meaning "to divorce." See the discussion above, p. 21. Barrett, however, offers the opinion that in verse 15 the choice of term implies something more than a refusal to have sexual intercourse but something less than divorce. Cf. C. K. Barrett, *First Corinthians,* p. 166. See also R. L. Roberts, "The Meaning of *chorizo* and *douloo* in 1 Cor 7:10-17," *ResQ* 3 (1965) 178-184.

[121]Similarly, N. Baumert, *Ehelosigkeit,* p. 83.

[122]See Paul's "*en tois toioutois*" in v. 15. Following the RSV, the NRSV renders Paul's Greek generically as "in such a case." Most modern editors, however, prefer

to respect the plural number of Paul's expression and render the phrase "in such cases" (RNAB, REB, The New Translation, The Living Bible, The Good News Bible, and the remark in Zerwick-Grosvenor's *Grammatical Analysis,* p. 510) or "in such circumstances" (NIV; similarly, "in these circumstances" of JB and NJB). It is grammatically possible, but less likely, that the antecedent of Paul's plural demonstrative is personal. Were that to be the case, v. 15b should be translated "the brother or sister is not bound to such persons," that is, to unbelieving partners.

[123]This is clearly the meaning of the term in Paul's four other uses of it (Rom 6:18, 22; 1 Cor 9:19; Gal 4:3).

[124]Cf. Rom 7:2; 1 Cor 7:27, 39.

[125]See above, n. 122.

[126]So, for example, C. K. Barrett, *First Corinthians,* p. 166; H. Lietzmann and W. G. Kümmel, *An die Korinther,* p. 31.

[127]Cf. W. Foerster, *"Eirênê,"* p. 416, and C. Von Dehsen, *Sexual Relationships,* p. 193, who cites Robertson and Plummer, *First Corinthians,* p. 143 and Dungan, *Sayings,* p. 96.

[128]Cf. H. Conzelmann, *First Corinthians,* p. 123, n. 42.

[129]Cf. W. Schenk, *Synopse zur Redenquelle,* p. 116.

[130]According to Fischer, the formula is "not strictly a proverb, but it at least has the pithiness of proverbial form and embodies the unexpectedness which is found in proverbs." Cf. J. A. Fischer, "1 Cor 7:8-24," p. 29.

[131]Cf. Rom 15:33; 16:20; 1 Cor 14:33; 2 Cor 13:11; Phil 4:9; 1 Thess 5:23. Cf. 2 Thess 3:16.

[132]Cf. 1 Cor 1:3 and Rom 1:7; 2 Cor 1:2; Gal 1:3; Phil 1:2; 1 Thess 1:1; Phlm 3.

[133]Cf. 1 Thess 5:24.

[134]Cf. W. Foerster, *"Eirênê,"* p. 416.

[135]A remark by James Fischer seems to tend, however, in this direction: "The cause of the marriage problem is not stated, but the invocation of the God of peace in verse 15b [our 15c] suggests that such a serious rift has taken place that a minimally peaceful coexistence is no longer possible." Cf. J. A. Fischer, "1 Cor. 7:8-24," p. 31.

[136]Thus, Orr and Walther, *I Corinthians,* p. 212.

[137]See, for example, the title of Sakae Kubo's article, "I Corinthians vii. 16: Optimistic or Pessimistic?" in *NTS* 24 (1978) 539-544. See also the discussion in F. S. Malan, *Paulus se aanwysings in 1 Kor 7,* pp. 183-186.

[138]J. Jeremias, "Die missionarische Aufgabe in der Mischehe (1.Kor. 7, 16)," in *Neutestamentliche Studien für Rudolf Bultmann zum siebzigsten Geburtstag.* BZNW, 21 (Berlin: Töpelmann, 1954) pp. 255-260. Jeremias' study has influenced the commentaries on this verse in the commentaries of Barrett (*First Corinthians,* p. 167), Bruce (*Corinthians,* p. 70), and Murphy-O'Connor ("First Corinthians," p. 805). See also J. C. O'Neill, "1 Corinthians 7, 14," pp. 359-360, and Antoinette Wire, *Women Prophets,* p. 85.

¹³⁹Among the Fathers who favored this interpretation, Thomas Considine quotes several Fathers who have left us a commentary on 1 Corinthians, namely, Chrysostom (PG 61, 156); Ambrosiaster (PL 17, 218); Cyril of Alexandria (PG 74, 876); Theodoret (PG 82, 276) and John Damascene (PG 95, 624), as well as several who have made reference to this verse, including Tertullian (*Ad uxorem:* PL 1, 1289), Basil (*Ep.* 188; PG 32, 677), Augustine (*Sermon on the Mount,* 1, 16; PL 34, 1251), and Jerome (*Adversus Jovinianum,* I, 1, 10; PL 22, 233). J. C. O'Neill refers to passages of Theodore of Mopsuestia and Theodoret preserved in the Catena. Cf. T. P. Considine, "The Pauline Privilege (Further examination of 1 Cor. vii, 12-17)" *AusCR* 40 (1963) 107–119, pp. 111–113; J. C. O'Neill, "1 Corinthians 7, 14," pp. 359–360. Not all of Considine's referents are as crystal clear as that of John Damascene who interprets 1 Cor 7:16 as an exhortation to "remain . . . counsel . . . persuade" (*paramene . . . sumbouleue . . . peithe*).

¹⁴⁰Cf. 1 Pet 3:1-2.

¹⁴¹That is, in addition to the extended dominical logion, the holiness of the unbelieving partner, peace, and social stability. See the discussion of this varied argumentation in the earlier pages of this chapter.

¹⁴²Similar translations are found in the NIV, NJB, RNAB and the New Translation, although the last version qualifies the translation somewhat by rendering the verbal expression as "how do you know whether or not . . ."

¹⁴³This approach has been vigorously argued by Sakae Kubo whose study is essentially an attempt to refute Jeremias. Kubo's work has been explicitly rejected by Murphy-O'Connor, "First Corinthians," p. 805. Hans Conzelmann, whose work in this regard has been favorably cited by Orr and Walther, has also taken issue with Jeremias. Cf. H. Conzelmann, *First Corinthians,* pp. 123–124; W. F. Orr and J. A. Walther, *I Corinthians,* p. 212. See, further, W. F. Luck, *Divorce and Remarriage,* p. 172, and the brief discussion by D. E. Garland, who opts for the pessimistic approach, in "The Christian's Posture," p. 356.

¹⁴⁴The tension between an optimistic reading of verse 16 and the patent meaning of verse 14 is the reason why Orr and Walther believe that the "saving" mentioned in verse 16 is the "healing" of the marriage. Cf. W. F. Orr and J. R. Walther, *1 Corinthians,* p. 214.

¹⁴⁵Ibid.

¹⁴⁶See the suggestion above, pp. 54–55.

¹⁴⁷It is translated as "for" in the RSV and the New Translation, as "but" in the NJB.

¹⁴⁸Dungan also takes verse 15c as an introduction to verse 16. Cf. D. Dungan, *Sayings,* pp. 96–97.

¹⁴⁹One could also speak of an *inclusio* formed by verse 17a and verse 24. The verb *kalein* occurs eight times within verses 17a-24 indicating that the "call" is the theme which imparts thematic unity to this section of the letter. It has, however, been argued that the disquisition on "the call" is an aside whose purpose is to support the Pauline teaching that one should remain *socially* as one was at the time of one's baptism and, therefore, one should remain in one's marriage,

even if that marriage is a mixed marriage. In any case, this section of Paul's letter interrupts the general presentation of the chapter which is the relationship between men and women (cf. v. 1b). At the conclusion of the interlude, Paul takes up a new subject (1 Cor 7:25). The turning of Paul's attention to a different facet of the male-female relationship is clearly indicated by his use of the *peri* ("concerning") formula.

[150]That is, of course, the burden of Paul's further reflections on the call in verses 17-24.

[151]For example, Mary Rose D'Angelo, who writes: "the believer is 'not bound';— i.e., is free to marry again" ("Divorce Sayings," p. 81). See further W. F. Orr and J. A. Walther, *1 Corinthians*, p. 214; B. Byron, "1 Cor 7:10-15," p. 109; J. Moiser, "Reassessment," p. 109; etc.

[152]Cf. E. Lövestam, "Divorce and Remarriage," p. 65, n. 86; C. Von Dehsen, *Sexual Relationships*, p. 195; etc.

[153]Admittedly the extant texts are a bit more recent than 53-57 A.D.

[154]Cf. *PW* 5, 1241-1245, 2011-2013; *m. Git.* 9:3 and the brief discussion by J. Murphy-O'Connor, "First Corinthians," p. 805. See further our discussion, above p. 95 and below, p. 322, n. 145.

[155]Cf. B. Byron, "1 Cor 7:10-15," p. 430.

[156]See also the parenthetical remark of v. 11. There Paul describes the divorced woman as an "*agamos*-unmarried." Because she is such, there is the possibility of her marriage to another man, a possibility from which Paul dissuades her. He desires that she be reconciled to her husband.

[157]Cf. 1 Tim 5:11-15.

[158]Cf. George W. MacRae, "New Testament Perspectives on Marriage and Divorce," in L. G. Wrenn, ed., *Divorce and Remarriage in the Catholic Church* (New York-Paramus-Toronto: Paulist, 1973) pp. 8-9.

[159]Cf. 1 Cor 7:7.

NOTES—CHAPTER 3

[1]Apart, that is, from such small units as Mark 3:19b-21, 4:26-29, 7:31-37, 8:22-26, 9:49; 14:51-52.

[2]For a synthetic overview of the problem, see Frans Neirynck, "Synoptic Problem," *NJBC*, pp. 587-595 or my own *Introduction to the New Testament* (Garden City: Doubleday, 1983), pp. 126-135.

[3]The opposite tack is taken by Harold Riley in *The Making of Mark: An Exploration* (Macon, GA: Mercer University Press, 1989) pp. 115-117. W. F. Luck, whose work is to a very large extent directed against the analyses of Heth and Wenham, provides "a conflate reading as a solution to the synoptic problem." Cf. W. F. Luck, *Divorce and Remarriage*, pp. 129-131.

⁴Cf. John 6:60.

⁵Similar to the translation found in the AV, NEB, NIV, RNAB, REB, and the Phillips Modern English version.

⁶And the earlier JB as well.

⁷But not RNAB. See above, n. 5.

⁸Mark 10:7-8a in the NJB.

⁹Other manuscripts which omit the Genesis clause from Mark 10:7-8 are an eighth-(ninth?) century majuscule (044), a ninth-century gospel minuscule (892), "corrected" at some later point in time, a Greek-language lectionary dating from 1055 (l^{48}), an ancient Syriac version (syr^s, the Syriac Sinaiticus), and the ancient Gothic version of the text. Marucci deems the absence of this clause from the Sinaiticus and Vaticanus codices (his "neutral text") as sufficient warrant to conclude that the words did not belong to the original text of the gospel. Cf. C. Marucci, *Parole di Gesù,* p. 251.

¹⁰The great nineteenth-century German textual critic, Constantin Tischendorf (1815–1874) considered the Codex Sinaiticus, which he had discovered in 1859, to be the most reliable witness to the text of the New Testament. The great nineteenth-century British textual critics, Brooke Foss Westcott (1828–1892) and Fenton John Anthony Hort (1928–1892), considered that the text type represented by the Sinaiticus and the Vaticanus was a "neutral text." Because of the authority accorded to the two manuscripts by these text critics, the text of Nestle's *Novum Testamentum Graece* did not include the phrase *kai proskollêthêsetai pros tên gunaika autou.*

¹¹That is the text found in Kurt Aland, Matthew Black, Carlo M. Martini, Bruce M. Metzger, and Allen Wikgren, eds., *The Greek New Testament* (3rd. corrected ed.: Stuttgart, United Bible Societies, 1984) as well as in Kurt Aland, *Novum Testamentum Graece* (2nd. ed. of the 26th. ed.: Stuttgart, Deutsche Bibelgesellschaft, 1985). Cf. H. Zimmermann, *Neutestamentliche Methodenlehre: Darstellung der historisch-kritischen Methode* (7th. ed., reworked by Klaus Kleisch: Stuttgart, Katholische Bibelwerk, 1982) pp. 104–105.

¹²Cf. Matt 19:5.

¹³There is the possibility that the eye of the scribe passed from the *kai* ("and") at the beginning of v. 7b to the *kai* at the beginning of v. 8. Such a movement of the eye is technically known as a parablepsis, due to homeoarchton (a "similar beginning"). See B. M. Metzger, *Textual Commentary,* p. 104.

¹⁴The members of the committee were Münster's Kurt Aland, Saint Andrews' Matthew Black, Rome's Carlo Martini, Princeton's Bruce Metzger, and Chicago's Alan Wikgren. The use of the brackets indicates that, in the judgment of the committee, the enclosed text is to be regarded as disputed. The committee has assigned to the disputed clause only a D rating. This indicates "that there is a very high degree of doubt concerning the reading selected for the text."

¹⁵See above, notes 6 and 7.

¹⁶Along with the units of variation cited in the critical apparatus prepared by Barbara Aland for N-A²⁶, there is a variant for the word order of "one flesh"

in v. 8 and another form of the expression "in the house" in v. 10. Cf. C. Marucci, *Parole di Gesù*, p. 251.

[17]Cf. Matt 19:7.

[18]For the sake of good sense, most contemporary English-language translations of verse 6 have "God" as the subject of the verb "made." In Greek, however, the verb does not require an explicit subject and does not have one in verse 6. The verb *epoiêsen* itself means "he made." Good grammatical style and the presence of an explicit subject in the text of Genesis have led the translators to insert "God" as the explicit subject of the verb "made." Cf. AV, NEB, JB. NAB, NIV, NJB, RNAB, and Phillips Modern English, in addition to the RSV and NRSV.

[19]Manuscript evidence for all six units of variation is cited in Kurt Aland, et al., *Novum Testamentum Graece. GNT*[3] and Metzger's commentary on it cites only the introduction to v. 1, *kai proselthontes Pharisaioi*, the insertion of *ho theos* in v. 6, and the Gen 2:24 citation in v. 7 as significant units of variation.

[20]As they are in the minuscules of the Lake family.

[21]This reading is accepted by Robert W. Herron. See R. W. Herron, "Mark's Jesus on Divorce: Mark 10:1-12 Reconsidered," *JETS* 25 (1982) 273-281, pp. 277-279. See also the discussion by W. D. Davies, who rejects the reading, in *The Setting of the Sermon on the Mount* (Cambridge: University Press, 1966) pp. 462-463. Manuscripts with this reading include the Codex Bezae Cantabrigiensis and the minuscules of the Ferrar family and, with minor variations, Codex Koridethi. This reading, along with that commonly found in the medieval Greek minuscules, "if a woman divorces her husband and is married to another" (*apolusê ton andra autou kai gamêthê allô*), diminishes the legal autonomy of the woman. The legal status of women in antiquity suggests that these readings are accomodated readings and establishes "if she divorces her husband and marries another" as the *lectio difficilior* and most probable reading of the text.

[22]The manuscript evidence for this reading is relatively weak: the fifth-century Codex Washingtoniensis (W; 032), a twelfth-century minuscule (1), a few other Greek manuscripts, and the Syriac Sinaiticus. The editors of *The Greek New Testament* have judged this unit of variation to be so insignificant that they have not included it in their textual apparatus.

[23]Dibelius distinguished the conversation both from the "dispute" and the "paradigm." Cf. M. Dibelius, *From Tradition to Gospel* (New York: Scribner's, n.d.) pp. 221-223. The original German work appeared in 1919. The English translation is of the second revised edition of 1933.

[24]The original German term was *Streitgespräch*. Cf. Martin Albertz, *Die synoptischen Streitgespräche. Ein Beitrag zur Formgeschichte des Urchristentums* (Berlin: Trowitzsch, 1921) pp. 39-41.

[25]See R. Bultmann, *The History of the Synoptic Tradition* (Oxford: Basil Blackwell, 1963) pp. 39-54, esp. pp. 49-50. Cf. Klaus Berger, *Die Gesetzesauslegung Jesu: ihr historischer Hintergrund im Judentum und im Alten Testament*, 1: *Markus und Parallelen*. WMANT, 40 (Neukirchen-Vluyn: Neukirchener Verlag, 1972) pp. 533, 552; Joachim Gnilka, *Das Evangelium nach Markus (Mk 8, 27-16, 20)*.

EKKNT 2/2 (Zurich: Benziger—Neukirchen-Vluyn: Neukirchener Verlag, 1979) p. 70.

[26]Taylor identifies the unit as consisting of verses 1-9, and labels it a pericope "on adultery." Cf. V. Taylor, *The Gospel According to St. Mark* (2nd. ed.: London, Macmillan, 1966) pp. 78–79. On p. 415, however, he identifies the pronouncement story on adultery as vv. 2-9.

[27]Albertz (*Streitgespräche*, p. 40) suggests that the controversy dialogue attracted other material on the same theme. Dibelius (*Tradition to Gospel*, p. 221) describes the instruction as "esoteric teaching."

[28]Among the more important recent literary approaches to Mark, see David Rhoads and Donald Michie, *Mark as Story* (Philadelphia: Fortress, 1982); David Barrett Peabody, *Mark as Composer*. New Gospel Studies, 1 (Macon, GA: Mercer University Press, 1987); and Mary Ann Tolbert, *Sowing the Gospel: Mark's World in Literary-Historical Perspective* (Minneapolis, MN: Fortress, 1989).

[29]In a brief essay, Barbara Green has identified six "patterns" of Markan construction present in Mark 10:1-12, namely, Jesus' enigmatic speech, chiastic structure, indications of time, indications of space, "in the house privately," and the controversy genre. Cf. B. Green, "Jesus' Teaching on Divorce in the Gospel of Mark," *JSNT* 38 (1990) 67-75.

[30]Cf. Mark 2:18; 8:16.

[31]Mark 5:9; 7:5, 17; 8:23, 27, 29; 9:11, 16, 21, 28, 32, 33; 10:2, 10, 17; 11:29; 12:18, 28, 34; 13:3; 14:60, 61; 15:2, 4, 44.

[32]That is eight times by Matthew, eighteen times by Luke in the Gospel and Acts, twice by the fourth evangelist, and twice by Paul. Cf. Matt 12:10; 16:1; 17:10; 22:23, 35, 41, 46; 27:11; Luke 2:46; 3:10, 14; 6:9; 8:9, 30; 9:18; 17:20; 18:18, 40; 20:21, 27, 40; 21:7; 22:64; 23:6, 9; Acts 5:27; 23:34; John 9:23; 18:7; Rom 10:20; 1 Cor 14:35.

[33]Namely, Matt 17:10, 22:23, 35; 27:11; Luke 8:30; 9:18; 20:27; 21:7. Thus Markan usage (in the gospel itself, or in passages of Matthew or Luke dependent on Mark) represents 68% of the uses of the verb *eporôtaô* in the New Testament. One might also note that Matthew and Luke occasionally use the simple *erôtaô* in passages dependent on Mark where Mark uses the compound verb *eporôtaô*. See Matt 21:24; Luke 9:45; 20:3; 23:3.

[34]Among other indications, see also D. B. Peabody, *Mark as Composer*, p. 62, table 84; Rainer Riesner, *Jesus als Lehrer. Eine Untersuchung zum Ursprung der Evangelien-Überlieferung*. WUNT, 2, 7 (2nd ed.: Tübingen, Mohr, 1984) pp. 435–440.

[35]Used twice in Mark 10:1—unusual even for Mark—and once in Mark 10:10, it occurs 28 times in Mark, as compared with 17 times in Matthew and only three times in Luke. On the Markan use of this adverb, see E. J. Pryke, *Redactional Style in the Marcan Gospel: A Study of Syntax and Vocabulary as Guides to Redaction in Mark*. SNTSMS, 33 (Cambridge: University Press, 1978) pp. 96–99 and D. B. Peabody, *Mark as Composer*, pp. 115–141.

³⁶Cf. Mark 7:14, 17; 4:1-2, 10; 9:14, 28. See D. B. Peabody, *Mark as Composer,* p. 139 and p. 162, where he writes of Mark 10:10 as being in relationship with Mark 10:1.

³⁷See also Mark 4:10, where the simple verb *erôtaô,* to ask, is used. In Mark 4:10, the inquiry does not take place in the house, but it does take place when Jesus was "alone" (*kata monas*) with the Twelve and other disciples. Cf. Mark 4:34, which forms an *inclusio* with 4:10. The verse which concludes the pericope does indeed suggest that some of the Markan Jesus' discourse was indeed esoteric teaching directed to the disciples alone.

³⁸Cf. D. B. Peabody, *Mark as Composer,* p. 47, table 42; my "House Churches in Early Christianity," *Tripod* 55 (1990) 38-44, esp. pp. 43-44; and B. Green, "Jesus' Teaching," pp. 70-71. Riesner suggests that the function of the domestic localization is "to isolate Jesus from the masses." Cf. R. Riesner, *Jesus als Lehrer,* p. 437.

³⁹Cf. Heinrich Greeven, "Ehe nach dem Neuen Testament," *NTS* 15 (1968-1969) 365-388, p. 376.

⁴⁰Cf. D. B. Peabody, *Mark as Composer,* pp. 137-141, 162.

⁴¹Cf. Frans Neirynck, *Duality in Mark: Contributions to the Study of the Markan Redaction.* BETL, 31 (Rev. ed.: Louvain, University Press, 1988) p. 95.

⁴²Cf. F. Neirynck, *Duality,* p. 132.

⁴³Mark 3:8; 10:1.

⁴⁴Matt 4:15, 28; 19:1.

⁴⁵Cf. Eduard Schweizer, *The Good News According to Mark* (Richmond, VA: John Knox, 1970) p. 50.

⁴⁶See above p. 73 and note 42.

⁴⁷The nine different types of expression of daulity represented in Mark 10:1-12 are among thirty types of Markan duality identified by Neirynck. Cf. F. Neirynck, *Duality,* pp. 75-136. Neirynck recapitulates the dualistic features of Mark 10:1-12 on page 168 of his work.

⁴⁸This citation is followed by: "R. Akiva says: Even if he found another fairer than she, for it is written, *And it shall be if she find no favour in his eyes. . . .*" These are the last words of the tractate. Cf. *m. Git.* 9:10. Akiva was one of the outstanding tannaim and probably the foremost scholar of his age. He is credited with the organization of the Mishnaic halakoth, but his principal activity as a sage was subsequent to the composition of Mark's gospel. In this book, passages from the Mishnah are cited according to Danby's edition (Herbert Danby, *The Mishnah Translated from the Hebrew with Introduction and Brief Explanatory Notes* (Oxford: Clarendon, 1933). For another translation and additional commentary on *m. Git.* 9:10, see Philip Blackman, *Mishnayoth, 3: Order Nashim* (London: Mishna, 1953), p. 444.

⁴⁹The issue of divorce was not among them.

⁵⁰Cf. Mark 7:1-3 and Matt 15:1.

[51]In Greek, *anthrôpos* is used, not the gender specific *anêr* implied by the traditional, "let no man put asunder."

[52]Cf. Euripides, *Alcestis,* 166; Xenophon, *Oeconomicus* 7:30. See also Josephus, *Antiquities of the Jews,* 6, 13, 8.

[53]Cf. Euripides, *Alcestis,* 314, 342 and *T. Reub.* 4:1, cited below, pp. 98–99. Other references are indicated in BAGD, 783.

[54]Cf. Plato, *Leges,* 930[b]; Aristotle, *Politika* 1253[b], 10; 1335[a], 10.

[55]Aeschylus, *Choephori,* 599.

[56]Cf. Euripides, *Alcestis,* 921.

[57]Cf. Stobaeus, 2, 7, 3a.

[58]Cf. Josephus, *Ant.,* 4, 8, 23; Aristotle, *Politika,* 2, 7, 5; and Plato, *Leges,* 6, 784. Cf. Philo (*Spec. Leg.,* 3, 11, 70) where the verb is used with reference to the dissolution of a marriage through death.

From the standpoint of the present study the text of Josephus is particularly interesting since it continues with requirements imposed by Deut 24:1-4: "He who desires to be divorced from the wife who is living with him for whatsoever cause (*gunaikos de tês sunoikousês boulomenos diazeuchthênai kath' asdêpotoun aitias*)—and with mortals many such may arise—must certify in writing (*grammasi*) that he will have no further intercourse with her; for thus will the woman obtain the right to consort with another, which thing ere then must not be permitted. But if she be maltreated by the other also or if upon his death the former husband wishes to marry her, she shall not be allowed to return to him."

[59]Eduard Lipinski, nonetheless, cites a sixteenth-century B.C. West Semitic text in which "to yoke" appears to be used obliquely as a metaphor for marriage. Cf. E. Lipinski, "The Wife's Right to Divorce in the Light of an Ancient Near Eastern Tradition," *The Jewish Law Annual* 4 (1981) 8–27, p. 17.

[60]Cf. 1 Cor 7:10, 11, 15.

[61]Cf. Isaeus 8, 36; Polybius 31, 26. See above, p. 21.

[62]There we find the verbs *apoluein* (1 Esdr 9:36), *ekballein* (Lev 21:14; 22:13; Num 30:10), and *exapostellein* (Deut 24:1, 3, 4; Jer 3:8; Mal 2:16).

[63]Cf. Klaus Beyer, *Semitische Syntax im Neuen Testament.* SUNT, 1 (Göttingen: Vandenhoeck und Ruprecht, 1962) pp. 167–168.

[64]Cf. R. F. Collins, *Introduction,* pp. 123–124.

[65]The importance of distinguishing among these three life situations for a correct understanding of the gospels has been endorsed in significant texts emanating from the magisterium of the Roman Catholic Church. See the Instruction of the Pontifical Biblical Commission Concerning the Historical Truth of the Gospels (*Sancta Mater Ecclesia,* April 21, 1964) and Vatican Council II's Dogmatic Constitution on Divine Revelation (*Dei Verbum*), 18–19. Cf. James J. Megivern, *Bible Interpretation.* Official Catholic Teaching (Wilmington, NC: McGrath, 1978) pp. 393–396, 414–415.

[66]The technical German language term, occasionally found in English language exegetical literature, is *Sitz-im-Leben.* Accordingly, German scholars write about

the *Sitz-im-Leben Jesu,* the *Sitz-im-Leben der Kirche,* and the *Sitz-im-Leben des Evangeliums.*

⁶⁷The writing of any one of the gospels was a one-time event. Thus it is only by extension that one can use the expression "the evangelist's life situation" (*Sitz-im-Leben des Evangeliums*). Nonetheless, even that specific situation can be analyzed by means of broader sociological categories.

⁶⁸That is, one type of situation differs from another type of situation.

⁶⁹Cf. R. F. Collins, *Introduction,* pp. 163–166, 172–177.

⁷⁰Cf. Arland J. Hultgren, *Jesus and His Adversaries: The Form and Function of the Conflict Stories in the Synoptic Tradition* (Minneapolis, MN: Augsburg, 1979) pp. 119–123, 143–146.

⁷¹Cf. A. J. Hultgren, *Jesus,* p. 54 who cites Mark 12:13-14 and Matt 22:34-35 in addition to Mark 10:2 (comp. Matt 22:41).

⁷²Cf. *m. Giṭ.* 9:10 (see above, p. 75), where three opinions are given, that of the school of Shammai, that of the school of Hillel, and that of Rabbi Akiva, a second-century Hillelite.

⁷³Hultgren, however, notes that the dominical saying may be followed by closing remarks or an additional brief narration. Cf. A. J. Hultgren, *Jesus,* p. 57.

⁷⁴Hultgren notes that in five instances the saying of Jesus is articulated in parallel fashion, either synonymous or antithetic. Cf. Mark 2:17a, 27; 3:4; 7:8 *and* Mark 10:9.

⁷⁵In somewhat similar fashion, but without detailed analysis, Barbara Green identifies "Mark's controversy pattern" as "consistent in the Gospel." She finds examples of Mark's use of the "controversy genre" present in 2:1–3:6; 7:1-23; 10, 12, 14. The presence of the pattern in Mark 10:1-12 is a "compelling" indication of its Markan composition and of singular importance for the interpretation of the pericope. Cf. B. Green, "Jesus' Teaching," p. 71.

⁷⁶All eleven of the Markan conflict stories have been taken over by Matthew and Luke, with the exception of the conflicts on the tradition of the elders and the issue of divorce which have parallels only in Matthew (cf. Mark 7:1-8; 10:2-9; Matt 15:1-9; 19:3-9).

⁷⁷Hultgren has noted that, in addition to the Markan material, there are other conflict stories in the Synoptic tradition, namely, a story from Q (Luke 11:14-23 = Matt 12:22-32), two stories in Luke's special material (Luke 13:10-17; 14:1-6), three stories in Matthew based partially on his Markan source and partially on Q (Matt 12:38-42, 22:34-40, 22:41-46), and one story in Luke based partially on the Markan source (Luke 7:36-50). In all, there are eighteen conflict stories preserved in the Synoptic tradition.

⁷⁸Mark 2:18-20; 3:1-5; 11:27-33; 12:13-17. Cf. Luke 7:36-40. See Hultgren, *Jesus,* pp. 67 99.

⁷⁹Therefore, it is only the unitary conflict stories that can *possibly* come from the earliest stage of tradition and can *possibly* preserve the memory of a real conflict between Jesus and an adversarial party. Cf. A. J. Hultgren, *Jesus,* p. 67.

[80]Cf. A. J. Hultgren, *Jesus,* p. 100.

[81]Cf. p. 82.

[82]Verse 12, however, takes the reader beyond the question of verse 2. It touches upon the issue of a woman's divorcing her husband, an issue not raised in the Pharisees' gender-specific question, is it lawful for a *man* to divorce . . . (*ei exestin andri . . .*).

[83]One can note the use of a different verb (*chôrizô,* cf. *apoluô,* in v. 2) and the absence of an explicitly legal perspective in v. 9.

[84]Cf. A. J. Hultgren, *Jesus,* p. 131.

[85]Along with those who, sometimes vigorously, defend the hypothesis of Matthean priority and Markan dependence, there are those who are open to or at least tolerant of this position. E. P. Sanders, for example, who gives evidence of a fair amount of sympathy for those who defend the priority of Matthew over and against that of Mark, "thinks" that Matthew used Mark. Cf. E. P. Sanders and M. Davies, *Studying,* p. 116. Sanders' views on the Synoptic Problem are contained in chapter two of this work (pp. 51-119), a chapter which is principally the work of Sanders rather than that of Davies.

[86]James R. Mueller, "The Temple Scroll and the Gospel Divorce Texts," *RevQ* 38 (1980) 247-256, p. 255. See further R. W. Herron, "Mark's Jesus," pp. 275-276; J. Fitzmyer, "The Matthean Divorce Texts," p. 98. Mueller's study of the implications of the discovery of the Qumran scroll known as *11 Q Temple* for an understanding of the New Testament's divorce passage identifies, as the first of these implications, that it supports the priority of the Markan form of the Pharisees' questions or at least makes it comprehensible in a first-century Jewish and Palestinian setting.

[87]This is the translation given in Johann Maier, *The Temple Scroll: An Introduction, Translation & Commentary.* JSOTSup, 34 (Sheffield: University of Sheffield, 1985) p. 50. For a seminal discussion of the passage, see Yigael Yadin, "L'attitude essénienne envers la polygamie et le divorce," *RB* 79 (1972) 98-100 and *Megillat ha-Migda,* 1 (Jerusalem: The Israel Exploration Society and the Shrine of the Book, 1977) pp. 272-274; ET: *The Temple Scroll,* 1. Jerusalem: The Israel Exploration Society and the Shrine of the Book, 1983, pp. 355-357. For a facsimile of the text, see Yadin, *The Temple Scroll,* 3, plate 72; for a transcription and translation, *The Temple Scroll,* 2, p. 228.

[88]Cf. *t. Sahn.* 4:2, where it is mentioned that "the king chooses for himself wives from wherever he wishes: the daughter of priests, Levites or Israelites." See J. Maier, *The Temple Scroll,* pp. 126-127. See, further, the discussion on the requirement that the king marry within his own clan by Yigael Yadin in *The Temple Scroll: The Hidden Law of the Dead Sea Sect* (London: Weidenfeld and Nicolson, 1985) p. 199.

[89]Apropos of Deut 17:17, the "royal law" on marriage, *m. Sanh.* 2:4 comments: "*Nor shall he multiply wives to himself*—eighteen only R. Judah says: He may multiply them to himself provided that they do not turn away his heart." The Tosepta comments: "Nor shall he multiply wives to himself like Jezebel, but like Abigail it is permissible says Rabbi Judah" (*t. Sanh.* 4:5). Cf. Y. Yadin, *Hidden Law,* p. 201.

[90]Cf. Y. Yadin, *Hidden Law,* p. 200.

[91]Cf. J. D. Amusin, *Kumranskaja obš ina* (Moscow: Izdatel'stvo 'Nauka', 1983), whose position is summarized in Zdzislaw J. Kapera, "A Review of East European Studies on the Temple Scroll," in G. J. Brooke, ed., *Temple Scroll Studies.* JSOTSup, 7 (Sheffield: JSOT, 1989) pp. 275-286, p. 281.

[92]Cf. J. R. Mueller, "Temple Scroll," p. 251.

[93]Julius Kravetz also mentions that similar views are expressed in the Book of Jubilees, the text of which was also discovered at Qumran. Cf. J. Kravetz, "Divorce in the Jewish Tradition," in J. Freid, ed., *Jews and Divorce* (New York: KTAV, 1968) pp. 149-157, p. 153.

[94]Cf. Solomon Schechter, *Fragments of a Zadokite Work.* Documents of Jewish Sectaries, 1 (Cambridge, MA: University Press, 1910).

[95]Some manuscript fragments of the text published by Schechter were discovered among the Dead Sea Scrolls. While the nature of Schechter's "Zadokite Work" was in much dispute for the first half of this century, the discoveries at Qumran point to its Essene origin.

[96]I.e., a person called "Vanity."

[97]Cf. Chaim Rabin, *The Zadokite Documents* (Oxford: Clarendon, 1954) pp. 16-19.

[98]Cf. Philip R. Davies, *The Damascus Covenant: An Interpretation of the "Damascus Document."* JSOTSup, 25 (Sheffield: JSOT, 1983) pp. 108-119; Jerome Murphy-O'Connor, "An Essene Missionary Document? CD II, 14-VI, 1," *RB* 77 (1970) 201-229.

[99]J. Murphy-O'Connor, "Missionary Document," p. 220. Criticism is sometimes addressed to practices which those outside of the community consider to be consistent with the Law, rather than a violation of it. Cf. P. R. Davies, *The Damascus Covenant,* p. 115 (cf. p. 109).

[100]Thus C. Rabin, *The Zadokite Documents,* p. 17, n. 21.1 and Geza Vermes, "Sectarian Matrimonial Halakhah in the Damascus Rule," *JJS* 25 (1974) 197-202. Other references are given by Paul Winter, "Sadoqite Fragments IV 20, 21 and the Exegesis of Genesis I 27 in Late Judaism," *ZAW* 68 (1956) 71-84, p. 76. Rabin argues, on the basis of CD 13:17, that the sect permitted divorce. The passage cited by Rabin is, however, fragmentary and appears in Rabin's own translation only as "And likewise with regard to him who divorces his wife, and he . . ." (pp. 66-67).

[101]Thus, S. Schechter, *Fragments,* pp. xvii, xxxvi; P. Winter, "Sadoqite Fragments," pp. 71-84; J. Murphy-O'Connor, "Missionary Document," p. 220; J. R. Mueller, "Temple Scroll," p. 253; and P. R. Davies, *The Damascus Covenant,* p. 116. Although Davies speaks of this passage as condemning any second marriage, 1 Q Temple 56:17-19 specifically provides for the remarriage of the king after the death of his spouse. Hence the condemnation of a man having two wives in CD 4:19-21 should be understood as a condemnation of polygamy and divorce, but not as a condemnation of a man's remarriage after the death of his spouse.

[102]For a discussion of the significance of the male suffix on the Hebrew term, see J. A. Fitzmyer, "The Matthean Divorce Texts," p. 96 and Y. Yadin, *Hidden Law,* pp. 200-201; *The Temple Scroll,* 1, p. 356.

[103]It is interesting to note that CD 5:2-5 exonerates David from having consciously violated the ban on divorce. Rabbinic lore specifically cites the example of David as a warrant for royal polygamy, with specific mention of his marriage to Abigail. Cf. *t. Sanh.* 4:5 (above, p. 266, n. 89).

[104]Joseph M. Baumgarten, however, takes the disputed expression as a reference to the husband's lifetime and offers a rather strict interpretation of the text: "The law therefore prohibits not merely polygamy, but even the remarriage of a widower. In that respect CDC goes beyond Mark 10:2 ff. which only condemns marriage after divorce, although both restrictions are derived from the same source, Gen. 1:27. As far as the validity of divorce, itself, is concerned, it is possible that the sectarians recognised it, as suggested by the fragmentary text in CDC 13:17." Cf. J. M. Baumgarten, *Studies in Qumran Law.* SJLA, 24 (Leiden: Brill, 1977) p. 34, n. 80.

[105]Cf. Deut 17:17; 24:1-4. Lev 18:8, 9, 11 proffers legislation which supposes polygamy, while divorce is taken for granted by Lev 21:4, 7; 22:13; Num 30:10; Deut 22:19, 29.

[106]Maier, with reference to an article by Ze'ev W. Falk (see *Sinai* 83 (1977–1978) 30–41, pp. 35–36), notes that since the formulation of 11 Q Temple 57:17-18 follows Lev 18:18, that is, an incest law for which the sectarians had their own interpretation—they took the text to refer to an Israelite woman rather than to a blood sister—"the prohibition against the king's taking a second wife (who would have to be from his own family) in addition to the first should be understood not so much in terms of monogamy as of an extended sexual taboo." J. Maier, *The Temple Scroll,* p. 127.

[107]Cf. J. A. Fitzmyer, "The Matthean Divorce Texts," pp. 93, 96; J. R. Mueller, "Temple Scroll," p. 251.

[108]Mueller, "Temple Scroll," p. 251, n. 22, makes reference to David Daube and Joseph Fitzmyer in this regard.

[109]Reference is also made to Deut 17:17 in 11 Q Temple 56:18: "And he shall not acquire many wives, lest they turn his heart away from me." Here the biblical text has been modified ("*they turn* his heart away" instead of the biblical "*his* heart will turn away") so as to provide an explanation for the ban that is in keeping with sectarian attitudes.

[110]Cf. J. R. Mueller, "Temple Scroll," p. 252; J. Maier, *The Temple Scroll,* p. 136.

[111]Cf. J. R. Mueller, "Temple Scroll," p. 251; Y. Yadin, *The Temple Scroll,* pp. 201–202.

[112]Cf. CD 5:2.

[113]Cf. CD 4:21; 5:1.

[114]He calls this the "long form" of Jesus' teaching on divorce in contrast to the "short form" (Matt 5:31-32; Luke 16:18; 1 Cor 7:10-11). Cf. E. P. Sanders and M. Davies, *Studying,* pp. 325–326; E. P. Sanders, "When Is a Law a Law? The Case of Jesus and Paul," in Edwin B. Firmage, Bernard G. Weiss and John W. Welch, eds., *Religion and Law: Biblical-Judaic and Islamic Perspectives*

(Winona Lake, Ind.: Eisenbrauns, 1990), pp. 139–158, p. 149; *Jesus and Judaism* (London: SCM, 1985) p. 260.

¹¹⁵If, indeed, it is legitimate to make a distinction between social acceptability and religious acceptability in a context of first-century Palestinian Judaism.

¹¹⁶Cf. E. P. Sanders, *Jesus,* p. 257; and E. P. Sanders and M. Davies, *Studying,* p. 328. Sanders' resolution of the issue is more tentative in the latter work than it is in the former.

¹¹⁷Cf. CD 4:14-18. For Sanders' evaluation of the importance of this passage, see *Jesus,* pp. 257–259, and *Studying,* p. 328. It allows him to contend that Jesus' prohibition of divorce was part of an appeal to the new age. Cf. "When Is a Law a Law?" pp. 149–150.

¹¹⁸By his own admission, Sanders has not analyzed the tradition on divorce from a form-critical point of view. Cf. E. P. Sanders, *Jesus,* p. 256.

¹¹⁹Cf. A. J. Hultgren, *Jesus,* p. 39, who writes that "the conflict stories . . . have no formal dependence on other literary or popular forms of the period." See also p. 88 in specific regard to the unitary conflict stories.

¹²⁰This issue is clearly addressed in the gospel according to Matthew, especially in his use of the citation formulae, and in the Fourth Gospel with its motif of the replacement-fulfillment of Jewish institutions. It is also reflected in Luke's theological understanding of history. The issue is neither so clearly nor so systematically addressed in the gospel according to Mark as it is in the later texts which come from a time in which the church's separation from Judaism had reached a decisive stage. Nonetheless certain passages in Mark suggest that the matter was already an issue at the time when his gospel was being composed. See, for example, Mark 11:12-25. It is of course not only the canonical gospels which bear witness to the church's need to clearly articulate the relationship between itself and Judaism. Various aspects of the matter find expression in Paul's letters, most systematically in Rom 9-11.

¹²¹Cf. A. J. Hultgren, *Jesus,* p. 88.

¹²²Ibid., p. 133. Hultgren is very guarded in his reflections on the life situation of the non-unitary conflict stories. He regards them all as church compositions, but is disinclined to identify a typical situation which provides the *Sitz-im-Leben* for *all* the conflict stories. Admittedly problematic is the Beelzebul controversy (Mark 3:22-30), clearly a case apart. For the rest Hultgren identifies an ecclesial response to a Palestinian Jewish criticism (Mark 2:1-12, 15-17, 23-28), an ecclesial response to Hellenistic Jewish criticism (Mark 7:1-8), and the church's response to Gentile converts as occasions for non-unitary conflict stories. What all three narratives have in common is that they articulate the church's response to something Jewish. The Beelzebul pericope is problematic, but the Palestinian tradition about Jesus, the exorcist, was generally problematic for the early church. In this regard it can be noted that Mark 3:21 is one of the very few verses in Mark that is reprised by neither Matthew nor Luke and that the Fourth Gospel does not contain a single story about Jesus' activity as an exorcist.

¹²³Mary Rose D'Angelo, with reference to E. P. Sanders, *Jesus,* pp. 291–292, and Morton Smith, *Jesus the Magician* (New York: Harper and Row, 1978),

pp. 153–157, notes: "Scholars have become increasingly aware that on some level debates between Jesus and the Pharisees reflect the interests and struggles of the early churches face to face with the Judaism of their day" ("Divorce Sayings," p. 89).

[124]Cf. A. J. Hultgren, *Jesus,* pp. 122–123, 132–133.

[125]See his arguments on pp. 122–123.

[126]See, especially, Jan Lambrecht, "Jesus and the Law: An Investigation of Mk 7, 1-23," in J. Dupont, *Jésus aux origines de la christologie.* BETL, 40 (New expanded edition: Louvain, University Press, 1989) 358–415, 428–429. Lambrecht speaks of the "Pharisees" as "more as symbols" (p. 402). For the gist of his conclusions as to the situation in light of the discussion, see pp. 399, 401–402.

[127]A conflict, in which the Hellenistic church was engaged, over the issue of divorce was, in other words, part of the tradition out of which Mark composed his gospel story. In "Jesus and the Law" (p. 400), Lambrecht attempts to recapture the main lines of the conflict story behind Mark 7:1-23.

[128]Lev 18:1-2, 6, 22. Cf. Lev 20:13; 1 Kgs 14:24. I have treated some elements of the biblical tradition's distinction between the understanding of sexuality and sexual behavior in Judaism and that of non-Jews in chapter seven of *Christian Morality: Biblical Foundations* (Notre Dame, IN: Notre Dame University, 1986), pp. 151–182, "Human Sexuality in the Jewish Scriptures."

[129]In addition to these works one might also cite Wisdom and Tobit, works which belong to the biblical canon according to the Roman Catholic tradition. For a study of some of the pertinent references, see. O. L. Yarbrough, *Not Like Gentiles,* pp. 8–18.

[130]Cf. *Ep. Arist.,* 151, 152; *Sib. Or.,* 591–599; *Ps.-Phoc.,* 3, 190; Philo, *Spec. Leg.* 3, 8, 22-25, 37-42; *Hypoth.,* 7, 1; Josephus, *Apoin.,* 2, 199.

[131]Ibid., pp. 18–28.

[132]b. *'Erub.* 21b. Cf. Louis M. Epstein, *Sex Laws and Customs in Judaism* (New York: KTAV, 1967) p. 6.

[133]Cf. George P. Carras, "Jewish Ethics and Gentile Converts: Remarks on 1 Thess 4, 3-8," in R. F. Collins, ed., *The Thessalonian Correspondence,* BETL, 87 (Louvain: University Press, 1990), pp. 306–315. See also B. S. Easton, "New Testament Ethical Lists," *JBL* 51 (1932) 1-12; H. D. Betz, *Galatians: A Commentary on Paul's Letter to the Church in Galatia.* Hermeneia (Philadelphia: Fortress, 1979) pp. 281–286; Siegfried Wibbing, *Die Tugend- und Lasterkataloge im Neuen Testament und ihre Traditionsgeschichte unter besonderer Berücksichtigung der Qumran-Texte.* BZNW, 25 (Berlin: Töpelmann, 1959) 77–78; Hans Conzelmann, *First Corinthians,* pp. 100–107; Erhard Kamlah, *Die Form der katalogischen Paränese im Neuen Testament.* WUNT, 7 (Tübingen: Mohr, 1964) p. 176.

[134]Cf. R. F. Collins, *Studies,* pp. 229–335; O. L. Yarbrough, *Not Like Gentiles,* pp. 65–87; H. Ulonska, "Christen und Heiden: Die paulinische Paränese in 1 Thess 4, 3-8," *TZ* 43 (1987) 210–218; G. P. Carras, "Jewish Ethics," and Norbert Baumert, "Brautwerbung—das einheitliche Thema von 1 Thess 4, 3-8," in R. F. Collins, ed., *Thessalonian Correspondence,* pp. 316–339.

[135]Cf. Helmut Koester, "1 Thessalonians—Experiment in Christian Writing," in *Continuity and Discontinuity in Church History: Essays Presented to George Huntston Williams on the Occasion of his 65th Birthday.* Studies in the History of Christian Thought, 19 (Leiden: Brill, 1979) pp. 33-44, p. 42; R. F. Collins, *Studies*, pp. 422-423; G. P. Carras, "Jewish Ethics," p. 306.

[136]The expression comes from O. L. Yarbrough, *Not Like Gentiles,* p. 5.

[137]Cf. 1 Thess 1:9.

[138]Cf. 1 Thess 4:2. See R. F. Collins, *Studies,* pp. 324-325. Yarbrough suggests that the occasion for Paul's instruction of the Thessalonians in regard to the sexual standards that they were expected to maintain was baptismal catechesis. Cf. O. L. Yarbrough, *Not Like Gentiles,* p. 120.

[139]On God's will in the Pauline letters, cf. Victor Paul Furnish, "Der 'Wille Gottes' in paulinischer Sicht," in D.-A. Koch, et al., *Jesu Rede von Gott und ihre Nachgeschichte im frühen Christentum: Beiträge zur Verkündigung Jesus und zum Kerygma der Kirche. Festschrift für Willi Marxsen zum 70. Geburtstag* (Gütersloh: Mohn, 1989) pp. 208-221.

[140]Cf. R. F. Collins, "The Unity of Paul's Paraenesis in 1 Thess 4, 3-8: 1 Cor 7, 1-7, a Significant Parallel," in *Studies,* pp. 326-335.

[141]The husband (vv. 2, 3, 4, 10, 11, 13, 14, 16, 35, 39) and the wife (vv. 2, 3, 4, 10, 11, 12, 13, 14, 16, 27, 29, 33, 39), the unmarried (vv. 8, 32) and the married (vv. 10, 33), the unmarried woman (v. 34) and the married woman (v. 34), the virgin (vv. 25, 34, 36, 37, 38) and the widow (v. 8), the unbeliever (vv. 12, 13, 14, 15) and the believer (= "brother" or "sister," vv. 12, 15, 24, 29), the uncircumcised (v. 18) and the circumcised (v. 18), the slave (vv. 21, 22, 23) and the free person (v. 22). Note also the disjunctive language of vv. 30-31a.

[142]Unfortunately Gerd Theissen does not treat of this topic in his sociological reflection on 1 Corinthians. Cf. G. Theissen, *The Social Setting of Pauline Christianity: Essays on Corinth.* Studies of the New Testament and Its World (Philadelphia: Fortress, 1982). Similarly silent is Richard A. Horsley who cites 1 Cor 1-2, 10, and 12-14 relative to "the absolute importance of political events and of social interaction in concrete communities." Cf. R. A. Horsley, *Sociology and the Jesus Movement* (New York: Crossroad, 1989) p. 3.

[143]See also 1 Cor 5:1-5; 6:15-20.

[144]See the use of the authoritative term *Kurios*-Lord in 1 Cor 7:10, 12, 17, 22, 25, 32, 34, 35, and 39.

[145]See the use of God-talk (*theos*) in 1 Cor 7:7, 15, 17, 19, 24 and 40.

[146]Cf. 1 Cor 7:14, 34.

[147]See, for example, Ernst Haenchen, *The Acts of the Apostles: A Commentary* (Oxford: Basil Blackwell, 1971) p. 449.

[148]See above, pp. 202-203.

[149]Note the use of "*oun*-therefore" in v. 9.

[150]Cf. *b. Šabb.* 63a, *b. Yebam.* 24a.

¹⁵¹"Jewish teachers," write Newman and Stine, "affirmed that when two passages of Scripture were in conflict, the earlier passage was to be regarded as superior." Cf. Barclay M. Newman and Philip C. Stine, *A Translator's Handbook on the Gospel of Matthew*. Helps for Translators (London-New York-Stuttgart: United Bible Societies, 1988) p. 609. Thus Paul has argued in both Romans and Galatians (cf. Rom 4:3; Gal 3:6) that the plain sense of Gen 15:6, apropos of Abraham's justification cannot be derogated by the dispensation of the Law.

¹⁵²The phrase comes from Barnabas Lindars. Cf. B. Lindars, *New Testament Apologetic: The Doctrinal Significance of Old Testament Quotations* (London: SCM, 1961) p. 13.

¹⁵³B. Lindars, *New Testament Apologetic*, p. 19.

¹⁵⁴Cf. B. Lindars, *New Testament Apologetic*, p. 30.

¹⁵⁵Interestingly, Lindars who has devoted his entire book to the New Testament's scriptural apologetic, does not treat of the use of Scripture in Mark 10:3-9 and Matt 19:3-9. His sole reference to the Markan narrative is a footnote which supports the affirmation that "in Mark all the Pentateuchal quotations belong to the legal class." Cf. B. Lindars, *New Testament Apologetic*, p. 273, n. 1.

¹⁵⁶Note that Matthew separates the two scriptural citations by means of the introductory lemma, "*kai eipen*-and said" in Matt 19:5.

¹⁵⁷Mark 10:7 omits the "*autou*-his" found before "*metêra*-mother" in Rahlfs' edition of the Septuagint. The *autou* is, nonetheless, found in the Sinaiticus and Bezae Cantabrigiensis codices (see above, p. 69). However, the critical edition of the Septuagint edited by John William Wevers omits the *autou* from Gen 2:24. See J. W. Wevers, *Septuaginta: Vetus Testamentum Graecum auctoritate Academiae Scientiarum Gottingensis editum,* 1: *Genesis* (Göttingen: Vandenhoeck & Ruprecht, 1974) p. 88.

¹⁵⁸That is, the Masoretic text (and the Onkelos Targum) does not have the equivalent expression. It is, however, found in the Targum of Jonathan, a fact which led T. W. Manson to presume that it was present in Mark's Hebrew text. Cf. T. W. Manson, "The Old Testament in the Teaching of Jesus," BJRL 34 (1951-1952) 312-322, pp. 315, 317; Krister Stendahl, *The School of St. Matthew and its Use of the Old Testament.* ASNU, 20 (Uppsala: Almqvist & Wiksells, 1954) p. 144.

¹⁵⁹Even the truncated version of Gen 2:24 found in some manuscripts of Mark 10:7 (see above p. 67-68) retain the *hoi duo* of the LXX in the Markan text.

¹⁶⁰Cf. K. Berger, *Die Gesetzesauslegung,* pp. 508, 539, 547. See also pages 540 and 542, where Berger indicates that it is only on the basis of the Greek text that Moses can be portrayed as commanding divorce.

¹⁶¹Cf. Mark 3:8. "*Peran*-beyond" is a Markan term. Within the Synoptic tradition, all the occurrences of *peran* are in Mark (cf. Mark 3:8; 4:35; 5:1, 21; 6:45; 8:13; 10:1) or in passages dependent on Mark (Matt 4:25; 8:18, 28; 14:22; 16:5; 19:1; Luke 8:22), with the exception of Matt 4:15, where Matthew quotes the Greek text of Isa 9:1.

[162]Cf. Elizabeth Struthers Malbon, *Narrative Space and Mythic Meaning in Mark* (San Francisco: Harper & Row, 1986) pp. 41–42.

[163]Another example of Markan duality. See above, pp. 73–74.

[164]Cf. Bas van Iersel, *Reading Mark* (Edinburgh: T. & T. Clark, 1989) pp. 127–128. Van Iersel notes that "immediately" occurs almost forty times in the first half of the Markan composition, but only ten times in the second. On Mark's use of "*euthus*-immediately," see, further, E. J. Pryke, *Redactional Style*, pp. 87–96.

[165]In Mark the verb "*didaskô*-to teach" has only Jesus as its grammatical subject. Cf. E. Schweizer, *Mark*, p. 50.

[166]Cf. Vernon K. Robbins, *Jesus the Teacher: A Socio-rhetorical Interpretation of Mark* (Philadelphia: Fortress, 1984) pp. 163, 198. Riesner, however, notes that as teacher, Jesus is nonetheless distinct from the other teachers of his days. Cf. R. Riesner, *Jesus als Lehrer, passim*, p. 499.

[167]Cf. V. K. Robbins, *Jesus the Teacher*, p. 163. Robbins notes, among other features of the narrative, the interspersing of Jesus' public teaching and his program of instruction for his disciple-companions. Barbara Green also notes the importance of teaching in Mark's narrative context. According to Green the context is 9:14–10:45 which she analyzes by means of a chiastic structure of which 10:1-12 is the hinge and focus. Cf. B. Green, "Jesus' Teaching," p. 75.

[168]Cf. Mark 9:17, 38; 10:17, 20, 35.

[169]Cf. Mark 8:31; 9:31; 10:1.

[170]The question is placed on the lips of the Pharisees. Hultgren opines that the introductory phrase, "some Pharisees came, and" was due neither to Mark's tradition nor to his own editorial work. He suggests that the phrase is a later interpolation into the Markan composition as a result of the textual influence of Matt 10:2. Cf. A. Hultgren, *Jesus*, pp. 119–120. Hultgren's opinion in this regard is without foundation. The textual tradition bears witness to a variety of different readings, including the six cited by Kurt Aland, et al. in *The Greek New Testament* (p. 163). None of these six exactly reproduce Matthew's "and Pharisees came." Matthew has a verb in the indicative (*prosêlthon*), whereas Mark uses a participle (*proselthontes*). Moreover, the manuscripts which omit mention of the Pharisees altogether are few in number and not very significant.

[171]Cf. Mark 8:27, 29; 9:11, 16, 21, 33; 10:36, 38. Comp. 9:28.

[172]Cf. Mark 9:28.

[173]See, for example, Rudolf Pesch, *Das Markusevangelium*, HTKNT 2/2 (Freiburg: Herder, 1984) p. 121.

[174]Cf. 1 Esdr 9:36.

[175]"Is it lawful" (*exestin*) is the impersonal form of the verb *exeinai*, used only in the impersonal. The lexicographers translate *exestin* as "it is allowed," "it is permitted," or "it is possible." This usage is found in Euripides and Herodotus, as well as in koine Greek. In the Synoptics, the term is found not only in Mark and the passages dependent on Mark (Mark 2:24, 26; 3:4; 6:18; 10:2; 12:14; Matt

12:2, 4, (10), 12; 14:4; 19:3; 22:17; Luke 6:2, 4, 9; 20:22), but also in Matthew's and Luke's special material (Matt 20:15; 27:6; Luke 14:3). In Mark the term seems to enjoy a legal connotation.

[176]This is the only time that Pharisees (*Pharisaioi*) appears in Mark without the definite article. Cf. Mark 2:16, 18 (2x), 24; 3:6; 7:1, 3, 5; 8:11, 15; 9:11; 12:13.

[177]Cf. Mark 8:11 and 12:15 (cf. Mark 1:13). The verb "to test" (*peirzaô*) is a Markan expression. Ten of its twelve occurrences in the Synoptics occur in Mark or texts influenced by Mark (Mark 1:16; 8:11; 10:2; 12:15; Matt 4:1; 16:1; 19:3; 22:18; Luke 4:2; 11:16; cf. Matt 3:1; 22:35).

[178]Cf. C. S. Mann, *Mark: A New Translation with Text and Commentary.* AB, 27 (Garden City, NY: Doubleday, 1986) p. 390.

[179]Cf. Mark 6:17-18.

[180]Cf. E. P. Sanders, *Jesus,* p. 256; "When Is a Law a Law?," pp. 147-148.

[181]Mark 6:37 provides another example of the Markan Jesus' turning the tables on his interlocutors.

[182]See also Mark 10:5, "for your (*humôn*) hardness of heart he wrote you (*humin*) this commandment." In the Greek text the two pronouns are separated by a single word (*humôn egrapsen humin*).

[183]In this regard, Pesch speaks of a "distanciation" (*eine Distanzierung*) placed on the lips of Jesus. Cf. R. Pesch, *Markusevangelium,* 2, p. 122.

[184]*Epitrepsen* (used elsewhere by Mark only in 5:13) rather than *eneteilato.* Robert Banks suggests that the use of the verb "*epitrepô*-allow" tallies with the later rabbinic attitude according to which divorce was regarded as sanctioned for Israelites but not for others. Cf. R. Banks, *Jesus and the Law in the Synoptic Tradition.* SNTSMS, 28 (Cambridge: University Press, 1975) p. 147. In the Markan narrative (10:5) Jesus himself is presented as considering the divorce procedure as a commandment.

[185]Gnilka speaks of the "anti-Jewish character of the controversy," while Berger writes of the "anti-Jewish scriptural proof." Cf. J. Gnilka, *Markus (Mk 8, 27-16, 20),* p. 71; K. Berger, *Die Gesetzesauslegung,* p. 536. See also K. Berger, "Hartherzigkeit und Gottes Gesetz. Die Vorgeschichte des antijüdischen Vorwurfs in Mc 10 5," *ZNW* 61 (1970) 1-47.

[186]Mark's Greek text does not give a direct object for this transitive verb.

[187]Cf. Jer 3:8.

[188]Apart from Mark 10:4 and Matt 19:7, *apostasion,* the term used for divorce in the technical expression *biblion apostasiou,* "certificate of dismissal," is used elsewhere in the New Testament only in Matt 5:31, the other Matthean context in which mention is made of divorce. In classical Greek the term was used of the action taken against a freedman for having forsaken his protector (*prostates*). Cf. Demosthenes 25:65; Aristotle, *Athenaion Politeia,* 58:3. In the papyri, the term was used of the abandonment of one's claim to property after its sale. From this secular usage one might infer that the connotation of the biblical expression (LXX) was both that the wife had in some way affronted her husband and that he had abandoned any claims that he might have had over her.

[189]Cf. H. Danby, *The Mishnah,* pp. 307–321; Str-B, 1, pp. 303–312.

[190]*m. Giṭ.* 9:3. The Mishnah continues: "R. Judah says, 'Let this be from me thy writ of divorce and letter of dismissal and deed of liberation, that thou mayest marry whatsoever man thou wilt.' The essential formula in a writ of emancipation is, 'Lo, thou art a freedwoman: lo, thou belongest to thyself.'" Strack and Billerbeck cite the text of a bill of divorce, witnessed by Reuben b. Jacob and Eleazar b. Gilead, in which this essential formula is found verbatim. Cf. Str-B, 1, p. 311.

[191]Cf. A. D. H. Mayes, *Deuteronomy.* NCB (Grand Rapids, MI: Eerdmans, 1979) p. 322 who refers to T. R. Hobbs, "Jeremiah 3, 1–5 and Deuteronomy 24, 1–4," *ZAW* 86 (1974) 23–29.

[192]Where the setting free of a woman by divorce is paralleled with the manumission of a female slave. See above, note 188. See also Josephus, *Ant.,* 4, 8, 23.

[193]This is the kind of interpretation of Deut 24:1 cited by most New Testament commentators. See, for example, K. Berger, *Die Gesetzesauslegung,* p. 509, R. Pesch, *Markusevangelium,* 2, pp. 122–123, and C. S. Mann, *Mark,* p. 391.

[194]Cf. J. Gnilka, *Markus (Mk 8, 27–16, 20),* p. 72; R. Pesch, *Markusevangelium,* 2, p. 123; K. Berger, *Gesetzesauslegung,* pp. 268–269, 538, 541–542.

[195]Reginald Fuller interprets the concession from a manifestly Christian standpoint. He writes that the Mosaic permission of divorce "is viewed as a temporary concession, now abrogated with the advent of the Reign of God." Cf. R. H. Fuller, "The Decalogue in the New Testament," *Int* 43 (1989) 243–255, p. 249.

[196]Cf. Deut 10:16; Jer 4:4; Sir 16:10. The term is hapax in Mark. See, however, Mark 16:14, where the term is used apropos of the disciples of Jesus. Outside of Mark, and Matthew's appropriation of the expression in Matt 19:8, the term is not found in New Testament literature. Cf. J. Behm, *"sklērokardia,"* TDNT, 3, 613–614. On the Markan use of "hardhearted," see K. Berger, "Hartherzigkeit," and F. W. Danker, "Hardness of Heart: A Study in Biblical Thematic," *CTM* 44 (1973) 89–100.

[197]Cf. Rom 1:21 where Paul writes, "their senseless minds (*kardia,* literally, the "heart") were darkened" and then proceeds to speak of the consequences, specifically the sexual deviation which follows. See also K. Berger, *Gesetzesauslegung,* p. 538.

[198]For a study of the use of Gen 1:27 and 2:24 in Jewish literature until the time of the New Testament, see K. Berger, *Gesetzesauslegung,* pp. 521–533.

[199]One might note, however, that in the texts cited in the biblical catena, it is God who has created (Gen 1:27) but humans who have joined together (Gen 2:24). According to the logion of verse 9, it is God who has joined together.

[200]Cf. R. Pesch, *Markusevangelium,* 2, p. 123 and K. Berger, *Gesetzesauslegung,* who cites *Jubilees* 3:8, 30; 4:4–6, 31; and 41:25 as instances of the practice (pp. 543–544). He cites 1 Tim 2:13 as another New Testament witness to the practice.

[201]As a reference to creation, "from the beginning" (*ap' archēs*) is found in Wis 6:22; 9:8; 14:13; 24:14; Sir 15:14; 16:26; 24:9; 39:25; Prov 8:23; Qoh 3:11). Cf. P. Farla, "The two," p. 69. Whether Mark's "of creation" (*ktiseōs*) should

be construed as an epexegetical genitive or as a term in apposition is a moot issue without great consequence for the understanding of the Markan text. Francesco Vattioni has, in any event, correctly noted that the expressions should not be so construed as if it were intended to say that creation began with the creation of humans. Cf. F. Vattioni, "A propos de Marc 10, 6," *ScEs* 20 (1968) 433–436.

[202]Elisabeth Schüssler Fiorenza takes the citation of Gen 1:27 to mean that God did not create or intend patriarchy but created persons as male and female human beings. She then translates v. 8a as "the two persons—man and woman—enter into a common human life and social relationship because they are created as equals." Cf. E. Schüssler Fiorenza, *In Memory of Her: A Feminist Theological Reconstruction of Christian Origins* (New York: Crossroad, 1983) p. 143.

[203]Gaster's translation. Cf. Theodor H. Gaster, *The Dead Sea Scriptures in English Translation with Introduction and Notes* (3rd. ed.: Garden City, NY, Doubleday, 1976) p. 71.

[204]See the *heneken toutou,* the NRSV's "for this reason," with which v. 7 begins.

[205]Cf. 1 Cor 6:16-17. Apropos of "one flesh," see also K. Berger, *Gesetzesauslegung,* pp. 550–552, and Evald Lövestam, "Divorce and Remarriage," p. 51. Lövestam writes: "This expression does not only refer to the sexual relationship nor to the unity that comes from having children together. It refers to man and woman's entire concrete existence as human beings where they—in their unity with each other—with their different qualifications (*ish-ishah/zakhar-nekevah*) complement each other and live together as parts of the same body."

[206]Similarly, Mark had not focused on sexual distinction in his use of Gen 1:27 in v. 6.

[207]See above, p. 91.

[208]Cf. K. Berger, *Gesetzesauslegung,* pp. 549–550; J. Gnilka, *Markus (Mk 8, 27-16, 20),* p. 73; R. Pesch, *Markusevangelium,* 2, pp. 123–124.

[209]David Daube explains the Markan text on the basis of the myth of the androgynous man (Adam), but his theorizing has been rightly criticized and rejected by Berger. Cf. D. Daube, *The New Testament and Rabbinic Judaism* (London: Athlone, 1956) pp. 71-83; K. Berger, *Gesetzesauslegung,* pp. 526–527, 550, n. 1. Also, J. Gnilka, *Markus (Mk 8, 27-16, 20),* p. 74 and E. Schüssler Fiorenza, *Memory,* p. 143, 211. For Jewish references to the myth, see Str-B, 1, 801-802.

[210]See above, pp. 67-68.

[211]If the clause were not in the Markan text, the conclusion drawn from that portion of Gen 2:24 cited in Mark 10:7 would be tighter than it is on the basis of the longer reading of Gen 2:24. In such a case, however, that portion of Gen 2:24 cited in Mark 10:8 would need a somewhat circuitous explanation.

[212]Cf. the causal *oun* in verse 9. Berger identifies verse 9 as one of a series of gnomic sayings in Mark (cf. 2:17a, 19, 27; 3:4b; 7:15; 12:17; and 10:9) to which he ascribes an early postpaschal but Hellenistic setting. Cf. K. Berger, *Die Gesetzesauslegung,* pp. 576–580.

[213]Cf. Mal 2:15-16.

[214]Cf. D. Daube, *Rabbinic Judaism,* pp. 368-369.

[215]See above, p. 76.

[216]See above, p. 21.

[217]Examples of this usage are to be found in Matt 19:9; 1 Cor 7:10, 11, 15.

[218]The present tense of the imperative has, in this instance, a conative sense. No one should purposely separate what God has joined. Of itself the prohibition does not imply that it is impossible to separate what God has joined. See the brief discussion of the important distinction between "cannot" and "may not" in Jan Lambrecht, *The Sermon on the Mount: Proclamation & Exhortation.* GNS, 14 (Wilmington, DE: Glazier, 1985) pp. 103–104; George R. Ewald, *Jesus and Divorce: A Biblical Guide for Ministry to Divorced Persons* (Waterloo, Ont.—Scottdale, PA: Herald, 1991) p. 69; and F. X. Durrwell, "Indissoluble et destructible mariage," *Revue de droit canonique* 36 (1986) 214–242, esp. pp. 227–236, 240.

[219]Cf. Mal 2:15-16.

[220]Cf. K. Berger, *Gesetzesauslegung,* p. 536.

[221]Cf. Mark 10:1, 17. The hiatus also includes the blessing of the children (Mark 10:13-16). It should, however, be noted that the focus of that scene is Jesus' rebuke to the disciples and also that his words pertain to the same general subject matter (the family) as the instruction of Mark 10:11-12.

[222]Cf. Mark 10:1 where "again" occurs twice. "Again" (*palin*) is a Markan term. Of its forty-eight occurrences in the Synoptics, twenty-eight are in Mark. Matthew contains the word but twenty times (five times in dependence on Mark) and Luke has it only three times (once in dependence on Mark). Cf. F. Neirynck and F. Van Segbroeck, *New Testament Vocabulary: A Companion Volume to the Concordance.* BETL, 65 (Louvain: University Press, 1984) p. 300.

[223]Cf. Mark 7:17.

[224]Green comments: "When, in the house, the disciples push for precision, Jesus supplies it, but the precision is not so easily matched with the teaching he gave outside." Earlier in her study, she had suggested that the teaching of Jesus was perhaps flattened out in the appended instruction. Cf. B. Green, "Jesus' Teaching," pp. 73, 71.

[225]Cf. Mark 7:1-13, where the practice of Corban dedication is criticized by means of the fourth commandment. In this regard, see my comments in *Christian Morality,* pp. 73-74, 91-92.

[226]Other Christian traditions enumerate "Neither shall you commit adultery" as the seventh commandment. This enumeration is, in fact, my own preference. See *Christian Morality,* p. 52.

[227]Cf. R. Pesch, *Markusevangelium,* 2, p. 125.

[228]Note the use of *apoluō* ("divorce") in vv. 11-12 and v. 2. Cf. K. Berger, *Gesetzesauslegung,* pp. 557 and 559. Comparing the Markan version of the Jesuanic logion with its Matthean counterpart, Yadin has noted that: "The version of Mark, banning divorce outright, follows the rule set by the Temple scroll and the Damascus Document." Cf. Y. Yadin, *The Temple Scroll,* p. 202.

[229]Pace Berndt Schaller, "Die Sprüche über Ehescheidung und Wiederheirat in der synoptischen Überlieferung," in E. Lohse, ed., *Der Ruf Jesu und die Ant-*

wort der Gemeinde. Exegetische Untersuchungen Joachim Jeremias zum 70. Geburtstag gewidmet von seinen Schülern (Göttingen: Vandenhoeck und Ruprecht, 1970) 226–246, pp. 240–244. Cf. R. Pesch, *Markusevangelium*, 2, p. 125; J. Gnilka, *Markus (Mk 8, 27-16, 20)*, p. 74.

[230]This is implicitly recognized in the interpretive saying attributed to R. Akiva apropos of Deut 24:1: "Even if he found another fairer than she, for it is written, 'And it shall be if she find no favor in his eyes . . .' " (*m. Giṭ.*, 9:10).

[231]Cf. Nigel Turner, "The Translation of *Moixatai ep' Autên* in Mark 10:11," BT 7 (1956) 151–152. Nigel remarks that the other Markan uses of the preposition *epi* are not of much help in determining the precise nuance of the phrase.

[232]Proponents of the translation, "with her," implying that a husband who dismisses his first wife and marries a second commits adultery by virtue of his sexual intercourse with the second wife, include Nigel Turner ("Translation," pp. 151–152); *e contrario*, Peter Katz ("Mark 10, 11 Once Again," BT 11 [1960] 152), B. Schaller ("Ehescheidung und Wiederheirat," esp. pp. 238–243; " 'Commits adultery with her,' not 'against her,' Mk 10:11," *ExpTim* 83 [1972] 107–108), and Joachim Gnilka (*Markus [Mk 8, 27-16, 20]*, p. 75). For a brief discussion of the issues, both of interpretation and of translation, see Robert G. Bratcher and Eugene A. Nida, *A Translator's Handbook on the Gospel of Mark*. Helps for Translators, 2 (Leiden: Brill, 1961) p. 313.

[233]Cf. Mark 3:24, 25, 26; 13:12; 14:48.

[234]Cf. K. Berger, *Gesetzesauslegung*, p. 559; R. Pesch, *Markusevangelium*, 2, p. 126; Werner Stenger, "Zur Rekonstruktion eines Jesusworts anhand der synoptischen Ehescheidungslogion (Mt 5, 32; 19, 9; Lk 16, 18; Mk 10, 11f.)," in *Strukturale Beobachtungen zum Neuen Testament*. NTTS, 12 (Leiden: Brill, 1990) pp. 104–118, p. 115. Reginald Fuller notes that in verse 11 the sixth commandment "is reinterpreted positively to mean life-long matrimonial fidelity and is grounded in God's loving purpose in creation." Fuller adds: "The multiple attestation of this tradition and its consistency with Jesus' characteristic radicalism argue for its authenticity." Cf. R. H. Fuller, "The Decalogue," p. 250.

[235]See my *Christian Morality*, pp. 58–59.

[236]Cf. Sjef van Tilborg, "Mattheüs 19, 3-12 en het onontbindbare huwelijk," in Th. A. G. van Eupen, ed., *(On) ontbindbaarheid van het Huwelijk*. Annalen van het Thijmgenootschap, 58/1 (Hilversum: Brand, 1970) pp. 23–34, p. 26, and F. Neirynck, "De Jezuswoorden over Echtscheiding," in *Evangelica: Gospel Studies—Études d'évangile*. BETL, 60 (Louvain: University Press, 1982) pp. 821–834, p. 825. Neirynck holds that "*ep' autên*-against her" is a redactional addition to an older saying, added most probably at the same time as v. 12.

[237]Cf. Klaus Beyer, *Semitische Syntax*, p. 145. Although N-A[26] has a participal conditional clause in v. 12, the Codex Alexandrinus and the *Textus Receptus*, along with the vast majority of the minuscule manuscripts, have a compound conditional clause.

[238]Cf. 1 Cor 7:28, 34, 39; 1 Tim 5:11, 14.

[239]See, however, B. Brooten, "Frauen" and "Zur Debatte."

[240]Cf. E. Schüssler Fiorenza, *Memory*, p. 143.

NOTES—CHAPTER 4

¹Cf. Benedict T. Viviano, "The Gospel According to Matthew," *NJBC,* pp. 630–674, p. 631.

²Critical scholarship has, by and large, rejected the opinion that the gospel according to Matthew was written by one of the Twelve. Reliant on Mark, Matthew's narrative is not an eye-witness account. A few scholars, however, hold that Matthew, one of the Twelve, was somehow the source of this gospel's tradition, particularly if it was Matthew who first gathered together a collection of Jesus' sayings. That originative figure is distinct from the evangelist who wrote the extant and canonical gospel of Matthew. In any event, we must distinguish between Matthew, one of the Twelve, and "Matthew," traditional nomenclature for the anonymous author of the first gospel. Making use of the tradition, I will continue to use "Matthew" as a code name for the evangelist, but I make no claim that the evangelist was one of the Twelve.

³See, especially, Edouard Massaux, *L'influence de l'Évangile de saint Matthieu sur la littérature chrétienne avant saint Irenée.* BETL, 75 (Louvain: University Press, 1986).

⁴That is, Matthew was read more frequently than Mark, Luke, and John combined.

⁵There are, nonetheless, some inconsistencies within the narrative. See, in this regard, B. Viviano, "Matthew," p. 631.

⁶The Sermon on the Mount, a literary creation by the evangelist, is an integral part of the evangelist's literary work. Prior to the Sermon on the Mount, Matthew had already begun to make use of and adapt the gospel according to Mark, the principal literary source for the gospel according to Matthew.

⁷Cf. B. M. Metzger, *Textual Commentary,* pp. 47–48. Of the fourteen units of variation in Matt 19:3-9—there are an additional three units of variation in vv. 10-12—only six are cited in the critical apparatus of *The Greek New Testament* (3rd. ed.: Stuttgart, United Bible Societies, 1975). These are the six variants commented upon by Metzger, to wit, those identified as numbers 1, 3, 5, 9, 12, and 13 in the list which follows.

⁸A unit of variation may sometimes consist of an expression rather than a single word for which variant readings exist in the manuscript tradition.

⁹A dative of advantage in Greek grammar.

¹⁰This is the reading of the *GNT*³-N-A²⁶. The editors reasoned that *andri* was introduced into the text by way of assimilation to Mark 10:2, while the shorter reading was basically found in the manuscripts that belong to the Alexandrine family.

¹¹The NRSV employs a relative clause, "the one who made them" to translate the Greek *ho ktisas,* a participle which has no direct object in Greek. The NRSV is a translation based on the Greek text of *GNT*³-N-A²⁶, but its rendering of the participle in v. 3 might lead one to suppose that the donor Greek text reads "*poiêsas-*

making" rather than "*ktisas*-creating." More felicitously, the REV renders the participle "*ktisas*-creating" as "the Creator."

Although "*poiêsas*-making" is supported by several excellent witnesses, including the Sinaiticus, the majuscules, C, D, W, and the minuscules of the Lake family, the *GNT* [3] committee judged that this reading was a scribal modification introduced in order to accomodate the Matthean text to that part of the LXX version of Gen 1:27, "made them male and female," cited in v. 4. According to Marucci, since *poiêsas* is the classic reading of the Genesis text, *ktisas* is the *lectio difficilior* and therefore the reading which enjoys the stronger claim. Cf. C. Marucci, *Parole di Gesù,* pp. 252-253.

[12]In addition to the single unit of variation cited in the textual apparatus of the diglot *Greek-English New Testament* edition of N-A[26], Marucci discusses *heneken* as a variant in place of *heneka* and a "*autou*-his" found in some manuscripts after both "father" and "mother." These variants are cited in the *Synopsis of the Four Gospels* edition of N-A[26], but are not found in the simple bilingual edition of the text.

[13]Including the Codex Sinaiticus.

[14]The compound verb may be a harmonization with the LXX text of Gen 2:24, although some see it as a harmonization with the parallel Markan text, i.e., the longer reading of Mark 10:7. In sum, three of the units of variation in Matt 19:5 might be the result of assimilation with the Markan reading, namely, the *heneken,* the *autou* after *patera,* and the compound verb. All three of these variant readings are found in the fifth-century Codex Ephraemi Rescriptus and the minuscules of the Lake family.

[15]Most manuscripts read these words in the sequence "flesh, one" (*sarx mia*) but the Codex Sinaiticus and the Codex Bezae Cantabrigiensis read "one flesh" (*mia sarx*), the reading found in the parallel text, Mark 10:8.

[16]This is the reading in *GNT*[3]-N-A[26], but text critics debate whether it is a clarifying addition to a text which lacked a direct object or whether the text without the direct object is a result of a deletion of the direct object in order to make Matt 19:7 more conformable with Mark 10:4.

[17]Including the fourth-century codex Vaticanus, the minuscules of the Lake and Ferrar families, and the Coptic Bohairic text. As a result of his study of the patristic authors—especially Origen's important commentary—who cite this verse of Matthew and its parallel in Matt 5:32, Henri Crouzel has proposed that the reading of the Codex Vaticanus represents the original reading of the text. Cf. H. Crouzel, "Le texte patristique de Matthieu V.32 et XIX.9," *NTS* 19 (1972-73) 98-119. Crouzel's analysis of the patristic evidence has been criticized, correctly in my view, by Jean Duplacy and Corrado Marucci. Cf. J. Duplacy, "Note sur les variantes et le text original de *Matthieu* 19, 9," in *Études de critique textuelle du Nouveau Testament.* BETL, 78 (Louvain: University Press, 1987) 387-412, pp. 390-395; C. Marucci, "Clausole Matteane e critica testuale: In merito alla teori di H. Crouzel sul testo originale di Mt 19, 9" *RivB* 38 (1990) 301-325. See also the discussion by Michael W. Holmes in "The Text of the Matthean Divorce Passages: A Comment on the Appeal to Harmonization in Textual Decisions," *JBL* 109 (1990) 651-664, pp. 657, 660-661.

[18]Marucci describes this finale as "tormented" (*tormentata*). Cf. C. Marucci, *Parole di Gesù,* p. 253.

[19]B, C*, W, θ, 078, *f* [1, 13] and the majority of the later minuscules. The fourth-century P[25] has a slightly different wording of this additional clause. The longer reading was adopted by Augustin Merk. Cf. A. Merk, *Novum Testamentum Graece et Latine* (8th. ed.: Rome, Pontifical Biblical Institute, 1957) p. 64.

[20]That is, a movement of the eye from the "*moichatai*-commits adultery" at the end of Matt 19:9 to the *moichatai* at the end of the disputed clause. This would represent a classic case of homeoteleuton. According to Duplacy, this possibility is a bit more plausible than is the possibility that the disputed clause was added by way of accommodation to Matt 5:32. Cf. J. Duplacy, "Notes sur les variantes," p. 411.

[21]According to Metzger (p. 48) the fact that B, C*, *f* [1], and others read but a single *moichatai,* namely, at the end of the combined clauses, is an indication of the probablity of the insertion.

[22]As well as the RSV, JB, NIV, NJB, RNAB, REB, and Phillips Modern English.

[23]The longer reading is not, however, found in RNAB. The RSV, REB, and NRSV make reference to the longer reading in a footnote. See the discussion in Holmes, "Text of the Matthean Divorce Passages," pp. 661–663, who concludes that the longer reading is the "original text" of 19:9.

[24]The longer reading appears in Weber's edition of the Vulgate but is not to be found in the *Nova Vulgata* authorized by Vatican Council II and promulgated by Pope John Paul II. Cf. Robertus Weber, *Biblia Sacra iuxta vulgatam versionem,* 2 (Stuttgart: Wurttembergische Bibelanstalt, 1969) p. 1555; *Nova Vulgata Bibliorum Sacrorum Editio* (Vatican City: Libreria Editrice Vaticana, 1979) p. 1806.

[25]The Sermon on the Mount (Matt 5-7), the Missionary Discourse (Matt 10), the Sermon in Parables (Matt 13), the Community Instruction (Matt 18), and the Eschatological Discourse (Matt 24-25).

[26]Matt 7:28 (cf. 8:1); Matt 11:1a (cf. 11:1b); Matt 13:53a (cf. 13:53b); Matt 26:1.

[27]Having completed the discourse to the disciples, Matthew returns to Mark's narrative sequence, the sequence which he will basically follow until the end of the gospel story. Cf. Daniel J. Harrington, *The Gospel of Matthew.* Sacra Pagina, 1 (Collegeville, MN: Liturgical Press, 1991) p. 274.

[28]Cf. Jack Dean Kingsbury, *Matthew as Story* (2nd. rev. ed.: Philadelphia: Fortress, 1988) p. 60 and *passim.*

[29]So Michael D. Goulder, *Midrash and Lection in Matthew* (London: SPCK, 1974) p. 376. In fact the verb *metairô* is used only twice in the NT, namely in Matt 13:53 and 19:1, where we find the same identical clause.

[30]Cf. B. M. Newman and P. C. Stine, *Matthew,* pp. 604–605.

[31]Cf. Matt 4:23; 9:35 (comp Matt 11:1). Cf. J. D. Kingsbury, *Story,* pp. 68–70.

[32]Cf. Matt 14:13-14; 15:30-31, where the crowds following and Jesus' healing their sick is the Matthean setting for the narrative account of the feeding of the thousands.

[33]Cf. Matt 4:25; 8:1; 12:15; 14:13; 19:2; 20:29; 21:9. Cf. Georg Strecker, *Der Weg der Gerechtigkeit: Untersuchung zur Theologie des Matthäus.* FRLANT, 82 (Göttingen: Vandenhoeck & Ruprecht, 1962) pp. 230–231; J. D. Kingsbury, *Story,* pp. 24–25. On Matthew's characterization of "the crowds," see further, Michael J. Wilkins, *The Concept of Disciple in Matthew's Gospel: As Reflected in the Use of the Term Mathētēs.* NovTSup, 59 (Leiden: Brill, 1988) pp. 137–141, 148–150, 157–158, and especially 170–171.

[34]Cf. Matt 3:7; 5:20; 9:11, 14, 34; 12:2, 14, 24, 38; 15:1, 12; 16:1, 6, 11, 12; subsequently in Matt 21:45; 22:15, 34, 41; 23:2, 13, 14, 15, 26; 27:62. Cf. J. D. Kingsbury, *Story,* pp. 17–24, 115–127. George Ewald, who considers Matthew's text to be prior to Mark's and who has an historicizing approach to the narrative, ponders whether Matthew had Shammaites or Hillelites in mind as he wrote about the Pharisees and concludes that "the concerns seem to be more Shammaite in character." Cf. G. R. Ewald, *Jesus and Divorce,* pp. 64–65.

[35]Cf. J. D. Kingsbury, *Story,* pp. 19–24.

[36]Cf. Matt 16:1; 22:18, 35.

[37]Matthew's Greek text has a kind of verbal hendiadys: *peirazontes auton kai legontes,* literally "testing him and saying," a typically Semitic type of expression. Matthew's language clearly shows that it is the testing which is the most significant element in the description of the Pharisees. Their asking the question merely specifies their putting Jesus to the test. Cf. Matt 16:1.

[38]Cf. the NIV's "for any and every reason" and the NJB's "on any pretext whatever."

[39]Cf. Robert G. Bratcher, *A Translator's Guide to the Gospel of Matthew.* Helps for Translators (London-New York: United Bible Societies, 1981); Eduard Schweizer, *The Good News According to Matthew* (Atlanta, GA: John Knox, 1975) p. 381; Alejandro Díez Macho, *Indisolubilidad del matrimonio y divorcio en la biblia. La sexualidad en la biblia* (Madrid: Fe catolica, 1978) pp. 223–230; D. A. Carson, "Matthew," in *The Expositor's Bible Commentary,* 8 (Grand Rapids, MI: Zondervan, 1984) pp. 3–599, p. 411.

[40]*Antiquities,* 4, 253.

[41]Jesus' quotation of Gen 1:27c is in verbatim agreement with the text found in the Greek Bible (LXX).

[42]Albert van Gansewinkel interprets this phrase in terms of first principles rather than temporally. It can be rendered "basically" or "fundamentally." Cf. Albert van Gansewinkel, "Ursprüngliche oder grundsätzliche Unauflösbarkeit der Ehe," *Diakonia* 3 (1972) 88–93.

[43]Cf. Wis 6:22; 9:8; Sir 15:14; 16:26, etc. See above, p. 97.

[44]The subject of "*kai eipen*-and said" is "the one who made them," not Jesus. It is part of Jesus' response, not the introduction to a second response.

[45]See the "so-*hôste*" of v. 6.

[46]Gnilka notes that the Greek verb *sunezeuxen* indicates not only the difficulty of marriage but also the common task to be accomplished. Cf. J. Gnilka, *Das Matthäusevangelium.* HTKNT 1/2 (Freiburg-Basel-Vienna: Herder, 1988) p. 153.

⁴⁷Note the use of *oun,* "therefore," in v. 6b.

⁴⁸On *epetrepsen,* see above, pp. 94–95.

⁴⁹Gnilka correctly observes that the prepositional phrase is not to be interpreted in a final sense, as if Deut 24:1 had been given in order to harden people's hearts. Cf. J. Gnilka, *Matthäusevangelium,* 2, p. 153.

⁵⁰Cf. Jer 4:4 (with a noun; cf. Deut 10:16; Sir 16:10) and Ezek 3:7 (with an adjective; cf. Prov 17:20; Sir 16:9). The combination of the verb *sklêrunô,* "to harden," and the noun *kardia* "heart," is, of course, well known in biblical usage. Cf. Exod 4:21; 7:3, 22; 8:19; 9:12, 35; 10:1, 20, 27; 14:4, 8, 17; 2 Chr 30:8; Ps 94:8 (LXX); Isa 63:17.

⁵¹See the Mishnaic summary, *m. Giṭ.* 9:10, above, p. 75.

⁵²The word *aitia,* found in Matt 19:3 and 10, but not present in the Markan account, is also found in Josephus' summary description of Deut 24:1-4 in *Antiquities* XV, 7, 10. In his autobiography Josephus mentions that he divorced his second wife because he was displeased at her behavior (*tên gunaika mê areskomenos autês tois êthesin apepempsamên, Vita,* 76).

⁵³Cf. the rabbinic *midrashim* and the Qumran *pesharim.*

⁵⁴For example, Ezek 20:25. Cf. J. Gnilka, *Matthäusevangelium,* 2, p. 153; A. Sand, *Das Evangelium nach Matthäus.* RNT (Regensburg: Pustet, 1986) p. 390. See above, p. 96.

⁵⁵Cf. Rom 7:7, 13; 1 Tim 1:8-11.

⁵⁶There are four words in Greek. Cf. Matt 19:3, *apolusai tên gunaika autou;* Matt 19:9, *apoluse tên gunaika autou.*

⁵⁷The *legô* of verse 3, found in the participial form, *legontes,* is translated by the editors of the NRSV as "asked." Such a translation is demanded by the good flow of the English-language text. It detracts, however, from the sharply antithetical stance of Matthew's Greek narrative.

⁵⁸Cf. Matt 12:39; 16:4.

⁵⁹See chapter six, below, pp. 184–213.

⁶⁰"But" may be a better translation of the adversative *de* in Matt 19:9 than is the NRSV's "and." The NIV, NJB, and RNAB leave the particle without explicit translation, thereby achieving a greater contrast between Jesus' logion and the words of the Pharisees. The NJB has attempted to capture the contrast by translating the lemma, "Now I say this to you."

⁶¹The contrast between the Pharisees' statement (v. 3) and that of Jesus in verse 9 would be even sharper if verse 3 were to be read with the *autô,* "him," found in D, W, Δ, and various minuscules. See above, p. 107.

⁶²Cf. Matt 5:1-2; 7:28-29.

⁶³Cf. Gerhard Barth, "Matthew's Understanding of the Law," in G. Bornkamm, G. Barth, and H. J. Held, *Tradition and Interpretation in Matthew.* NTL (London: SCM, 1963) pp. 58-164, esp. pp. 64-73.

⁶⁴Cf. M. D. Goulder, *Midrash and Lection,* pp. 18-19, 291.

⁶⁵Evilness is their root trait, says Kingsbury. Cf. J. D. Kingsbury, *Story,* pp. 19, 115. See, further, pp. 17-24 and 115-127 for the evangelist's consistent portrayal of the Pharisees in the light of this trait.

⁶⁶Here the reference to the Pharisees is clearly due to Matthean redaction. Cf. Luke 3:7.

⁶⁷In Matt 12:34, the derogatory epithet is a rebuttal to the derision of v. 24. The language used by Matthew reflects the acrimony of the debate between Christians and adherents to the Jewish synagogue at the time that he was composing his gospel. Calling someone or a group of people the children of animals was then, as it is now, "street language." Matthew's "brood of vipers" has a quite adequate analogue in the slang of contemporary English.

⁶⁸Cf. Matt 12:39.

⁶⁹Cf. M. D. Goulder, *Midrash and Lection,* p. 291; E. Schweizer, *Matthew,* p. 381; J. Gnilka, *Matthäusevangelium,* 2, p. 152; B. Viviano, "Matthew," p. 662; etc.

⁷⁰See, for example, G. Giavini, "Nuove e vecchie vie per la lettura delle clausole di Matteo sul divorzio," *ScuolCatt* 99 (1971) 83-93; M. D. Goulder, *Midrash and Lection,* p. 291; Eduardo de La Serna "¿Divorcio en Mateo?" *RevistB* 51 (1989) 91-110, p. 106; Y. Yadin, *The Temple Scroll,* p. 202. See further, below p. 145.

⁷¹Of the twenty-six occurrences of "the Pharisees" in Matthew, sixteen are the result of Matthean redaction: Cf. Matt 3:7; 5:20; 9:34; 12:24; 15:12; 16:11, 12; 21:45; 22:34, 41; 23:2, 13, 14, 15, 26; 27:62.

⁷²Cf. J. Gnilka, *Matthäusevangelium,* 2, p. 150. See also p. 156.

⁷³The expression comes from Gnilka. Cf. J. Gnilka, *Matthäusevangelium,* 2, p. 156.

⁷⁴Paul does something similar in 1 Corinthians 7.

⁷⁵Cf. Matt 19:1-2.

⁷⁶Compare Matt 19:10 with Mark 10:10, where there is a change of setting as the disciples are introduced.

⁷⁷Cf. M. J. Wilkins, *Disciple,* pp. 171, 221-222.

⁷⁸Cf. Matt 18:1, "the disciples came to Jesus and asked . . ." (*proselthon hoi mathētai tō Iēsou legontes*) and Matt 19:3, "Pharisees came to him and . . . asked" (*proselthon autō Pharisaioi . . . legontes*). Since it is not said that the disciples approach Jesus (cf. Matt 5:1; 13:10, 36; 14:15; 15:12; 17:19; 18:1; 26:17), Matthew's narrative must presume that they are associated with the crowds in following Jesus (Matt 19:2). A formal mention of the disciples' approach and of their saying something is Matthew's typical introduction to an instruction for the disciples. This stylistic feature of the gospel is consistent with Matthew's understanding of discipleship. Whereas Mark presents the disciples as those who follow a kerygmatic preacher and teacher, Matthew presents the disciples in a more rabbinic-like cast, that is, as those who come to the teacher to learn from him.

⁷⁹See M. J. Wilkins, *Disciple,* pp. 126-172.

⁸⁰The flat figure is one that embodies a single trait. The terminology comes from Edward Morgan Forster, *Aspects of the Novel* (reprinted: New York, Penquin, 1962) pp. 73, 81.

⁸¹See Matthew's characterization of the disciples as people "of little faith" in Matt 6:30; 8:26; 14:31; 16:8. Apart from Matthew, "*oligopistos*-of little faith" appears in the New Testament only in Luke 12:28.

⁸²Cf. M. J. Wilkins, *Disciple,* p. 136.

⁸³The Greek word *aitia* appears in both Matt 19:3 and Matt 19:10, but it has a somewhat different meaning in the two instances. Cf. A. Sand, *Matthäus,* p. 392. Blass-Debrunner-Funk explain the use of *aitia* in v. 10 as a Latinism. Cf. BDF, 5 (3).

⁸⁴See above, p. 113.

⁸⁵Note the use of the adversative particle *de* in both introductory clauses. From the rhetorical standpoint, however, the third-person narrative (v. 11) does not have the same adversative force as does the first-person narrative (v. 9).

⁸⁶Cf. BDF 130 (1), 313; ZBG, 236.

⁸⁷Note the use of the explanatory "*gar*-for" in v. 12.

⁸⁸The metaphorical meaning of the term in Hellenistic Greek, as in the LXX and the NT. Cf. Herodotus, Aristotle, Gen 39:1; Acts 8:27; etc.

⁸⁹Here, "the kingdom of heaven," as is common in Matthew. Cf. Matt 3:2; 4:17; 5:3, 10, 19 (2x) 20; 7:21 (2x); 8:11; 10:7; 11:11, 12; 13:11, 24, 31, 33, 44, 45, 47, 52; 16:19; 18:1, 3, 4, 23; 19:12, 14, 23; 20:1; 22:2; 23:13; 25:1.

⁹⁰The remark is without verbal parallel in Matthew. In form and function, however, the final exhortation is similar to the "Let anyone with ears listen!" of Matt 11:15, 13:9, and 13:43. This latter is a redactional insertion by the evangelist as is the insertion of the same phrase in Luke 14:35 (cf. A. Polag, *Fragmenta Q: Textheft zur Logienquelle* (Neukirchen-Vluyn: Neukircher, 1979) p. 72; I. Havener, *Q: The Sayings of Jesus.* GNS, 19 (Wilmington, DE: Glazier, 1987) p. 142. Matthew 13:9 and Luke 8:8 agree with one another over and against Mark 4:9 in the use of this exhortatory remark. This is one of the so-called minor agreements which, together, constitute a major difficulty for the resolution of the Synoptic Problem.

⁹¹As an example of Matthew's ideological point of view being reflected in his editorial work, one might note that Matthew systematically eliminates (pace Matt 13:36, which comes from MtR) the Markan theme of Jesus' being "at home" with his disciples. Mark's references to Jesus' being at home in Mark 2:1; 3:20; 5:19; 7:17, 24; 9:28, 33; 10:10; (13:34) have been omitted from the Matthean revision.

Matthew's use of the Markan parable of the unknown day and hour (Mark 13:32-37) is striking. Matthew has used much of the material to provide a transition (Matt 25:13-15) between the parable of the ten maidens and the parable of the talents, but at 25:14 he deletes Mark's reference to a home (cf. Mark 13:34). Some material in the Markan parable seems to be the source of Matthew's rendition of the parable of the flood and the exhortation to watchfulness in Matt 24:37-44. Matt 24:42 is dependent upon Mark 13:35, but Mark's "master of the house" is replaced by a Matthean "Lord."

In similar fashion, Matthew has systematically deleted all but one of Mark's references to the disciples asking Jesus a question (*eperôtaô*, with disciples as the subject: cf. Mark 7:17; 9:11 [retained in Matt 17:10]; 9:28; [9:32]; 10:10; 13:3). This is consistent with the higher estimation of the disciples' faith which is characteristic of the first gospel. Often Matthew replaces Mark's question (*eperôtaô*) with a statement by the disciples: cf. Matt 15:12, 17:19; 24:3. Comp. Matt 13:36 (MtR).

⁹²The three occurrences of the noun in Matt 19:12 represent its only New Testament usage apart from Acts 8 (vv. 27, 34, 36, 38, 39).

⁹³Used twice in Matt 19:12, but not otherwise used in the New Testament.

⁹⁴Cf. Deut 23:1; *b. Yebam.* 63b. See J. Blinzler, " 'Zur Ehe unfähig . . .'— Auslegung von Mt 19:12," in J. Blinzler, *Aus der Welt und Umwelt des Neuen Testaments. Gesammelte Aufsätze,* 1 (Stuttgart: Katholisches Bibelwerk, 1969) pp. 20–40, esp. p. 23, n. 12.

⁹⁵Benoit and Boismard opine that Matthew has reproduced a saying originally appearing in a more ancient text, which they call document A, or a collection of sayings of Jesus. Cf. P. Benoit and M.-E. Boismard, *Synopse des Quatre Evangiles en français* (Paris: Cerf, 1980) p. 309. The fact that some of the Fathers of the Church have a slightly different version of the saying can be cited as argument that the saying pre-dates Matthew and was appropriated by him from the tradition. Cf. J. Blinzler, "Justinus Apol. I, 15, 4 und Matthäus 19, 11-12," in A. Descamps and A. de Halleux, eds., *Mélanges bibliques en hommage au R. P. Béda Rigaux* (Gembloux: Duculot, 1970) pp. 45–55, "Zur ehe unfähig," pp. 34–35, n. 47.

⁹⁶Compare Matt 19:10 with Matt 19:25. Constantin Daniel has suggested that the disciples are, in effect, endorsing the celibate status of the Essenes, a practice with which Jesus takes issue (cf. Matt 19:12c, "made eunuchs by others"). Cf. D. Daniel, "Esséniens et eunuques (Matthieu 19, 10-12)," *RevQ* 6 (1968) 351–379, esp. pp. 356 and 364. See also M. J. Wilkins, *Disciple,* p. 136.

⁹⁷See above, p. 117.

⁹⁸One should also note that in Matt 5:30 and 18:6 "*sumpherei*-it is better" is a redactional emendation of the Markan "*kalon estin*-it is/would be better" (cf. Mark 9:43 and 9:42) and that Matt 5:29 (MtR) is based on 5:30. Matthew also uses Mark 9:43 in 18:8, where it is sequentially parallel to his Markan source. In this instance, however, Matthew retains the Markan "*kalon estin*-it is better."

⁹⁹Note the presence of the explanatory *gar* at the beginning of v. 12: *For* there are eunuchs . . ." That v. 12 is an explanation of v. 11 has seemingly been overlooked by G. D. Kilpatrick who suggests that vv. 10-11 refer to marriage and v. 12 refers to celibacy. According to Kilpatrick vv. 10-11 represent an early Christian response to the rigid teaching of Mark 10:11-12—an even greater relaxation than the relaxation of the exception clause in Matt 19:9 and 5:32. Verse 11 relegates Jesus' teaching on divorce to the status of a "counsel of perfection." Cf. George D. Kilpatrick, *The Origins of the Gospel According to St. Matthew* (Oxford: Clarendon, 1946), p. 83. In my estimation this view is almost totally without exegetical foundation.

¹⁰⁰"Men" (*andres* or *anthrôpoi*) does not appear in Matthew's Greek text.

[101]The REB's translation of v. 11, "That is a course not everyone can accept, but only those from whom God has appointed it," has changed the register of the discourse by rendering the verse in such a way that it has reference not to a teaching which is difficult to accept, but to a way of life which is difficult to lead. While *logos* may signify a thing or a reality (cf. Matt 5:32), it normally means a word, an utterance, a discourse. It is with this semantic reference that the *logos* of v. 11 should be interpreted. By rendering *ton logon touton* as "this teaching," the editors of the NRSV have apparently endorsed an interpretation of the phrase which takes it to be a reference to Jesus' teaching on divorce, the position which I adopt.

[102]Walter Bauer's classic overview of the patristic exegesis of Matt 19:12, "Matth. 19, 12 und die alten Schriften," appeared in *Neutestamentliche Studien Georg Heinrici zu seinem 70. Geburtstag dargebracht von Fachgenossen, Freunden und Schülern*. UNT, 6 (Leipzig: Hinrichs, 1914) pp. 235-244. Some modern commentators, including Schniewind, Lohmeyer, Johnson, Schmid, Schnackenburg, and Gnilka, maintain a similar position. Cf. J. Schniewind, *Das Evangelium nach Matthäus*. NTD, 2 (5th. ed.: Göttingen, Vandenhoeck und Ruprecht, 1950) p. 204; E. Lohmeyer, *Das Evangelium des Matthäus*. KEK 1/2 (11th. ed.: Göttingen: Vandenhoeck und Ruprecht, 1951) p. 283; S. E. Johnson, "The Gospel According to Matthew," *IB*, 7, p. 482; J. Schmid, *Das Evangelium nach Matthäus*. RNT, 1 (3rd. ed.: Regensburg, Pustet, 1956) p. 280; W. D. Davies, *Setting*, pp. 393-395; Heinrich Greeven, "Ehe," p. 370; Rudolf Schnackenburg, *Matthäusevangelium*. Die Neue Echter Bibel, 1/2 (Würzburg: Echter, 1987), p. 180; J. Gnilka, *Matthäusevangelium*, 2, p. 155. Gnilka bases his argument on a reading of Matt 19:10 without the demonstrative "this" (*touton*), omitted by the Codex Vaticanus, minuscule 892, and the minuscules of the Lake family. For a more popular, but synthetic, overview of this interpretation, see P. E. Dinter, "Disabled for the Kingdom: Celibacy, Scripture & Tradition," *Commonweal* 117 (1990) 570-577.

[103]Cf. Isa 56:3-5 and various Qumran texts. Cf. A. Sand, *Reich Gottes und Eheverzicht im Evangelium nach Matthäus*. SBS, 109 (Stuttgart: Katholisches Bibelwerk, 1983).

[104]BDF 290 (3). Cf. Peter Ketter, " 'Nicht alle fassen dieses Wort.' Bemerkungen zu Mt 19, 10-12," *Pastor bonus* 49 (1938-39) 311-323, esp. p. 117; J. Dupont, *Mariage*, pp. 162-164; J. Blinzler, "Zur Ehe unfähig," p. 32, n. 43, followed by G. R. Ewald, *Jesus and Divorce*, p. 78; Pierre-René Coté, "Les eunuques pour le Royaume (Mt 19, 12)," *EglTh* 17 (1986) 321-334, p. 325; Stephenson H. Brooks, *Matthew's Community: The Evidence of His Special Sayings Material*. JSNTSup, 16 (Sheffield: JSOT, 1987), p. 107; D. J. Harrington, *Matthew*, p. 274. Blinzer offers the opinion (see pp. 32-34) that v. 11 was once the conclusion to the three-part eunuch saying. Matthew transposed the conclusion to provide a smooth transition with the preceding material (introducing the *gar* ["for"] at this point) and then formed from the vocabulary of v. 11 a Matthean-type conclusion for the eunuch saying (v. 12d). Given the relative paucity of occurrences of *chôreô* in Matthew, the semantic differences between its use in 19:11-12 and its redactional use (MtR) in 15:17, and the redactional framework within which Matthew has encompassed the eunuch saying, Blinzer's suggestion seems quite plausible.

¹⁰⁵As RNAB would have it. See the footnote on v. 11. See also T. W. Manson, *The Sayings of Jesus* (London: SCM, 1949) p. 215 and W. D. Davies, *Setting,* pp. 393–394; D. A. Carson, "Matthew," p. 419.

¹⁰⁶Cf. Matt 5:48; 23:8-12; etc. See Thaddée Matura, "La célibat dans le Nouveau Testament d'après l'exégèse récente," *NRT* 97 (1975) 481–500, 593–604, p. 481 ("Celibacy in the New Testament," *TD* 24 [1976] 39–45, p. 40) and W. A. Heth, *Matthew's "Eunuch Saying,"* pp. 162–163. Matura cites Joachim Jeremias in support of his position, while Heth cites Gerhard Barth. See J. Jeremias, *New Testament Theology,* 1: *The Proclamation of Jesus.* NTL (London: SCM, 1971) pp. 203–230; G. Barth, "Matthew's Understanding of the Law," p. 96. Robert H. Stein claims, nonetheless, that Matt 19:11-12 is the only passage in the gospel where Matthew distinguishes between two groups of disciples. Cf. R. H. Stein, *The Method and Message of Jesus' Teachings* (Philadelphia: Westminster, 1978) p. 91.

¹⁰⁷Note the use of *contradictio* as a stylistic feature, and the use of the verb "to give" (*didōmi*). These stylistic and lexigraphical features recur in Matt 19:11. It should also be noted that Matthew has replaced Mark's apocalyptic "secret" (*mustērion*) with a plural (*mustēria*) which seems to suggest "particular teachings." See, further, W. A. Heth, *Matthew's "Eunuch Saying,"* pp. 184–185.

¹⁰⁸With regard to these two points, see Quentin Quesnell, "Made Themselves Eunuchs," pp. 342–344. As an additional argument in support of the view that Matt 19:10-12 is not per se an exhortation to celibacy, Quesnell notes that Matthew systematically deletes from his gospel material relating to a call to virginity or celibacy such as is found in Luke or Mark.

¹⁰⁹Q. Quesnell, "Made Themselves Eunuchs," p. 343.

¹¹⁰Cf. not only Matt 19:25, 27, but also Matt 15:12, 15-16. Wilkins has noted that, in comparison with Mark, Matthew has softened the obduracy and ignorance of Mark's disciples and that he has done this "by accentuating the teaching of Jesus as the means by which the disciples gain further understanding." Cf. M. F. Wilkins, *Disciple,* p. 143.

¹¹¹Cf. Francis J. Moloney, "Matthew 19, 3-12. A Redactional and Form Critical Study," *JSNT* 2 (1979) 42–60, p. 46.

¹¹²Between the two passages there is only the short account of the blessing of the little children (Matt 19:13-15), a passage appended to the discussion on divorce in Matthew's Markan source (Mark 10:1-16).

¹¹³One might also note that the hard saying of Matt 19:6 is elucidated by the equally hard saying of the formally introduced logion of verse 9. In similar fashion, the hard saying of Matt 19:21 is "clarified" by the formally introduced logion in verses 23-24.

¹¹⁴On the composition of the redactional framework, see above, p. 287, n. 104. Among the Synoptics, "*chōreō*-accept" (elsewhere in the NT, only in John 2:6; 8:37; 21:25; 2 Cor 7:2; 2 Pet 3:9) is used four times by Matthew (15:17; 19:11-12 [3 times]) and once by Mark (2:2), but Matthean usage evinces a nuance somewhat different from that of Mark. Although "*dunamai*-can" often appears in Matthew's Markan (8:2; 9:15; 12:29; 17:19; 19:25; 20:22; 26:9; 27:42), Q (3:9;

6:24 [2x], 27), and M (5:14, 36; 7:18; 26:53) sources, nine of its appearances in the gospel come from Matthew's editorial hand (9:28; 10:28; 12:34; 16:3; 17:16; 22:46; 26:42, 61; and 19:12).

[115]Cf. Matt 15:17. See also Schnackenburg who suggests that the term implies as much a readiness to "make room for" as it does an intellectual understanding. Cf. R. Schnackenburg, *Matthäusevangelium*, 2, p. 180. Sand notes that the principal connotation of the term includes its locative sense. Cf. LSJ, 2015; A. Sand, *Matthäus*, p. 392.

[116]Cf. Matt 5:1-2; 7:24-27; 16:20, etc.

[117]Cf. Matt 5:20.

[118]Cf. Matt 7:29, where Matthew's tell-tale addition of *autôn* ("their") to Mark 1:22 distinguishes the scribal tradition of his community from that of *their* scribes.

[119]Cf. BDF, 130, 313.

[120]Note the use of the root *dun-* (denoting ability or power) in Matt 19:25 and 26 as well as in 19:12d.

[121]Cf. the introductory lemma of v. 9, "but I say to you." The point is made even more clearly in Matt 5:31-32. See below, pp. 150–151, 156.

[122]Moloney calls it a "graced situation." Cf. F. J. Moloney, "Matthew 19, 3-12," p. 47.

[123]F. J. Moloney, "Matthew 19, 3-12," p. 48. Zimmermann likewise interprets vv. 10-12, along with the exception clause, as well as "for any cause" in v. 3, as an historicizing addition on the part of Matthew. He contends, however, that the addition of vv. 10-12 (cf. Matt 22:11-14) has changed the total thrust of the narrative. Marriage is presented as being of great value in vv. 3-9 in order to introduce the real point of Matthew's compositive narrative, namely, that celibacy is of even greater value (vv. 10-12). Cf. H. Zimmermann, *Methodenlehre*, pp. 242-244. In my estimation, Zimmerman has drawn a false conclusion from Matthew's redactional technique. Sand likewise interprets vv. 10-12 as a Matthean addition, occasioned by a precise situation in Matthew's community. He, however, opines that the situation is the celibate state of some members of the community. Since that life style was a social scandal, Matthew pleads (cf. Matt 19:12d) that it be appreciated by all members of the community and even embraced by some. Cf. A. Sand, *Matthäus*, p. 392.

[124]See my *Studies*, pp. 321-322, 324.

[125]My interpretation of verses 10-12 has taken its inspiration from the earlier studies of Dupont and Quesnell. I find their approach more acceptable than that of Heth. Heth interprets Matt 19:10-12 as a teaching on celibacy, used rhetorically in the context of Matt 19:3-9 as an argument from the greater to the lesser. According to Heth, vv. 10-12 define a new demand, that is, the demand incumbent upon some to live celibately. God enables some people to live in this fashion. If God enables some people to live totally without marriage, then, a fortiori, he can enable those who are married to stay married and those separated to remain single despite their broken marriage. Cf. W. A. Heth, *Matthew's "Eunuch Saying,"* pp. 190, 193.

[126]The explanatory *gar*. See above, p. 286, n. 99.

[127]Cf. J. Dupont, *Mariage*, p. 191; F. J. Moloney, "Matthew 19, 3-12," p. 50; J. Gnilka, *Matthäusevangelium*, 2, p. 155; Francisco Marín, "Un recurso obligado a la tradición presinóptica," *EstBib* 36 (1977) 205-216." According to Albright-Mann, however, the three-part saying really describes only two classes of men, those physically incapable of marriage (either from birth or because others have made them incapable of marriage) and those who have renounced marriage (either by self-mutilation or voluntary celibacy). Cf. W. F. Albright and C. S. Mann, *Matthew: Introduction, Translation, and Notes.* AB, 26 (Garden City, NY: Doubleday, 1971) p. 227.

[128]Cf. *m. Yebam.* 8:4-6; *m. Zabim* 2:1. See Str-B, 1, pp. 805-806. Taking Isa 56:4 as his starting point, Daniel, however, has argued that all three categories of eunuchs employ the term "eunuch" in a metaphorical sense, that is, simply as a reference to those who are not married. Cf. C. Daniel, "Esséniens et eunuques."

[129]That is, the ritual of removing the brother-in-law's shoe by the widow (cf. Deut 25:5-10).

[130]*m. Yebam.* 8:4.

[131]Newman and Stine correctly note that the expression probably refers to those who have renounced sexual activity rather than to men who have mutilated themselves. Cf. B. M. Newman and P. C. Stine, *Matthew*, p. 613.

[132]This phrase is not included in Zimmermann's reconstruction of the "original logion." Cf. H. Zimmermann, *Methodenlehre*, pp. 240-241.

[133]Exceptional instances of "kingdom of God" are found in Matt 12:28; 19:24; 21:31, 43. Apart from these instances, the periphrastic "kingdom of heaven" is used by Matthew altogether some thirty-three times.

[134]Cf. C. H. Dodd, *The Parables of the Kingdom* (London: Nisbet, 1935) pp. 34-35 and J. Jeremias, *The Proclamation of Jesus*, p. 98.

[135]See BDF, 222.

[136]The RNAB takes *gar* in a final sense. The editors explain: "*for the sake of the kingdom*, i.e., to devote themselves entirely to its service.

[137]Pace J. Dupont, *Mariage*, p. 201. Cf. J. Blinzler, "Zur Ehe unfähig," p. 28, n. 27; Roger Balducelli, "The Decision for Celibacy," *TS* 36 (1975) 219-242, pp. 226-227; T. Matura, "Le célibat," p. 488; Jerome Kodell, "The Celibacy Logion in Matthew 19:12," *BTB* 8 (1978) 19-23, p. 21; F. J. Moloney, "Matthew 19, 3-12," p. 49; D. A. Carson, "Matthew," p. 419.

[138]See above, p. 119, on the use of the word "eunuch." Cf. S. H. Brooks, *Matthew's Community*, pp. 107-108, and J. P. Meier, *A Marginal Jew: Rethinking the Historical Jesus*, 1. ABRL (Garden City: Doubleday, 1991) p. 343.

[139]*Apol.* I, 15. PG 6, 349.

[140]See, especially, Josef Blinzler, *"Eisin eunouchoi;"* and "Justinus." Cf. J. Gnilka, *Matthäusevangelium*, 2, p. 151.

[141]See my *Introduction,* p. 20. Among the authors who argue that *Apol.* I, 15, is indeed dependent on Matt 19:12 are Edouard Massaux and Arthur J. Bellinzoni. Cf. E. Massaux, *L'influence,* pp. 469–70; A. J. Bellinzoni, *The Sayings of Jesus in the Writings of Justin Martyr.* NovTSup, 17 (Leiden: Brill, 1967), pp. 60–61.

[142]Cf. J. Dupont, *Mariage,* pp. 191–196; F. J. Moloney, "Matthew 19, 3-12," p. 50.

[143]J. Kodell, "The Celibacy Logion," p. 19. He refers to Matura for support of this statement. Cf. T. Matura, "Le célibat." Matura's study presents a good defense of the authenticity of the logion contained in verse 12.

[144]Cf. Rudolf Bultmann, *Tradition,* pp. 26, 76, 81, J. Jeremias, *The Proclamation of Jesus,* pp. 31, 33, 224, and J. Gnilka, *Matthäusevangelium,* 2, p. 156. In the literature dealing specifically with Matt 19:10-12, see Abel Isaksson, *Marriage and Ministry in the New Temple: A Study with Special Reference to Mt. 19, 3-12 and 1 Cor. 11, 3-16,* ASNU, 24 (Lund: Gleerup, 1965) p. 148 and, especially, Joseph Blinzler (see "Zur Ehe unfähig," pp. 35–38), as well as such scholars as F. J. Moloney ("Matthew 19, 3-12," pp. 51–52), T. Matura ("Le célibat," pp. 488–491, 496; "Celibacy," pp. 40–41), P.-R. Coté ("Les eunuques," p. 326), Piet Farla ("The two," pp. 70–71) and J. P. Meier (*A Marginal Jew,* pp. 344–345). Francisco Marín ("La tradición presinóptica") agrees that the logion is Jesuanic, but holds that its inspiration is to be found in Jeremiah. In his opinion the logion spoke of interior virginity as a characteristic of eschatological Israel.

[145]Matt 12:2; Mark 2:24; Luke 6:2.

[146]Cf. Matt 9:14; Mark 2:18; Luke 5:33.

[147]Cf. Matt 15:2; Mark 7:5; comp. Luke 11:38.

[148]Matt 11:19 (= Luke 7:34), a Q saying. Cf. Matt 9:11, from Mark (2:16). Comp. Luke 5:30.

[149]John 8:48.

[150]Cf. J. Blinzler, "Zur Ehe unfähig," pp. 35–38; F. J. Moloney, "Matthew 19:3-12," pp. 51–52; P.-R. Coté, "Les eunuques," p. 326.

[151]Cf. Luke 7:31-34.

[152]See Joachim Jeremias, *The Parables of Jesus* (Rev. ed.: London, SCM, 1963) pp. 124–146.

[153]Cf. Luke 11:20 = Matt 12:28, a saying which both evangelists have taken over from their Q source.

[154]Cf. Luke 6:22.

[155]In effect, he would have used the tradition of Jesus' sayings in much the same way that he used biblical citations.

[156]It is clear that Matthew used sayings of Jesus which came to him from the Q source in this fashion (e.g., the beatitudes of Matt 5:3-6). Thus there is no reason to doubt that Matthew might have used Jesus' sayings coming from his special material (M) in similar fashion.

[157]The line of reasoning which I have presented (see my *Christian Morality,* pp. 187–188) generally follows the position developed by Dupont, endorsed and somewhat modified by Quesnell and Moloney. Among others endorsing this line of approach are Robin Scroggs, Bruce Vawter, G. J. Wenham, John Pilch, G. Bromiley, K. Condon, and W. J. O'Shea. Cf. W. A. Heth, *Matthew's "Eunuch Saying,"* p. 184, n. 87. An overview of the recent discussion is given by L. Barni in "Il recente dibattito sul 'logion' degli eunuchi (Mt 19, 10-12)," *StudPat* 34 (1987) 129–151. Barni, however, criticizes Dupont's line of approach because he cannot accept the idea that the "eunuch" can apply to a married person. While taking a somewhat different tack from Dupont et al., A. M. Dubarle also holds that vv. 10-12 do not directly pertain to voluntary celibacy. See A. M. Dubarle, "Les textes évangéliques sur le mariage et le divorce," in H. Cazelles, ed., *La vie de la Parole: De l'Ancien au Nouveau Testament. Études d'exégèse et d'hermeneutique bibliques offertes à Pierre Grelot* (Paris: Desclée, 1987) pp. 333–344, pp. 342–343.

The editors of the NAB have apparently reversed their interpretation of the Matthean addendum. In a footnote to Matt 19:12 (NAB), the editors state: "While there is no consensus on its meanings, *some* [my emphasis] exegetes understand it to refer to voluntary and perpetual celibacy for members of the Christian community who wish to dedicate themselves completely to the kingdom of God." In a footnote to Matt 19:12, RNAB reads: "*Some* [my emphasis] scholars take the last class to be those who have been divorced by their spouses and have refused to enter another marriage. But it is more likely that it is rather those who have chosen never to marry, since that suits better the optional nature of the decision: *whoever can . . . ought to accept it.*"

[158]Matthew's final exhortation, "Let anyone accept this who can" (NRSV), consists of just four words in the Greek text: *ho dunamenos chôrein chôreitô.* In addition to the article which qualifies the participle, there are three verbs: a present participle in the middle/deponent voice (*dunamenos*), a present active infinitive (*chôrein*) and a present active imperative (*chôreitô*). Neither of the two forms of "*chôreô*-accept" has an expressed direct object.

[159]Note the resumptive *palin,* "again," in Mark 10:10.

[160]This is, in fact, the point of view adopted in this study.

[161]Zimmermann suggests that Matthew had written a livelier and a more historicized narrative than did Mark. Cf. H. Zimmermann, *Methodenlehre,* p. 111.

[162]Cf. E. Schweizer, *Matthew,* p. 381 and A. Sand, *Matthäus,* p. 389. The latter identifies the Matthean pericope as a controversy dialogue (*Streitgesprach*) whereas he classes Mark 10:2-12 as community paraenesis (*Gemeindeparanëse*). The composite Markan unit (Mark 10:2-12) has a literary form similar to those of some stories told about the rabbis, where there is 1) a public and provocative questions, 2) the rabbi's response, 3) a private question of a disciple, and 4) the rabbi's private instruction. Cf. D. Daube, *Rabbinic Judaism,* pp. 141–150; H. Zimmermann, *Methodenlehre,* pp. 100–111.

[163]The comments below on Matthew's editorial reworking of Mark 10:2 in Matt 19:3 show how Matthew has in fact intensified the confrontational aspect of the encounter between Jesus and the Pharisees.

[164]Cf. Matt 15:34 (Mark 8:5); 16:25 (Mark 8:35); etc.

[165]This use of *ei* occurs only three other times in Matthew (Matt 12:10; 26:63; 27:49), but it occurs five times in Mark in addition to its occurrence in Mark 10:2 (Mark 3:2; 9:23; 15:36, 44 [2x]).

[166]Note the verbal hendiadys, *peirazontes . . . kai legontes,* modifying the principal verb *"prosēlthon-*came," in place of Mark's use of *epērōtōn-*asked," modified by two participles, as a principal verb. Mark holds the second participle, *"peirazontes-*to test" in reserve until the end of the sentence in such a way that it serves to interpret the scene which he has just described.

[167]Although Matthew uses *anēr* more often than does Mark, i.e., eight times (Matt 1:16, 19; 7:24, 26; 12:41; 14:21, 35; 15:38) as compared to four times (Mark 6:20, 44; 10:2, 12), he has retained only one of Mark's four usages, that of Mark 6:44 taken over in Matt 14:21.

[168]This is most apparent in those passages in which Matthew employs the stylistic device of the fulfillment citation (Matt 1:22-23, etc.). Cf. George M. Soares Prabhu, *The Formula Quotations in the Infancy Narrative of Matthew: An Enquiry into the Tradition History of Mt 1-2.* AnBib, 63 (Rome: Biblical Institute, 1976) pp. 160–161.

[169]Cf. E. De La Serna, "¿Divorcio en Mateo?" p. 96.

[170]For a brief discussion of Matthew's text of Gen 1:27, cf. R. H. Gundry, *The Use of the Old Testament in Matthew's Gospel with Special Reference to the Messianic Hope.* NTSup, 18 (Leiden: Brill, 1967) pp. 16–17.

[171]According to Schnackenburg, Jesus' scriptural response "takes the wind out of the sails" of the Pharisees' question. Cf. R. Schnackenburg, *Matthäusevangelium,* 2, p. 179.

[172]Cf. Gen 1:1; John 1:1.

[173]Cf. Matt 12:3, 5; 22:31.

[174]See the discussion above, p. 69.

[175]This is consistent with a redactional technique commonly employed in the First Gospel. Compare, for example, Matt 3:17 with Mark 1:11 and Matt 5:3-6 with Luke 6:21-22a.

[176]Matthew would obviously have been unaware that the two texts derive from the author of Genesis' priestly and elohist sources, respectively, and that they came from different eras.

[177]Cf. *kai eipen,* "and he said" in Gen 1:3, 6, 9, 14, 20, 24, 26, 29.

[178]As to the sequence of these words in Mark's Greek text, see above, p. 260, n. 16.

[179]Cf. G. A. Kennedy, *New Testament Interpretation,* p. 25.

[180]The present tense of the Greek *legousin* is an historical present.

[181]We have already noted Matthew's omission of the pronoun "to them" (*autois*) from v. 4.

[182]Cf. LSJ, 2, pp. 1271–1272.

[183]Since Mark presents the Pharisees as answering Jesus' question with an affirmative statement, the *ti oun* has no place in his account.

[184]With a verb in the historical present and the use of the recitative *hoti,* literally, "he is saying to them that."

[185]Cf. Gijs Bouwman, *"epitrepô,"* *EDNT,* 2, 43-44. Marucci suggests that, at this point, Matthew is correcting Mark or their common source. Cf. C. Marucci, *Parole de Gesù,* p. 277.

[186]The second person plural pronoun appears three times in this verse, "for *your (humôn)* hardness of heart Moses allowed *you (humin)* to divorce *your (humôn)* wives." Bratcher comments: "Jesus is talking to the Pharisees, but the *you* includes all the Jews, and not just the Pharisees." Cf. R. G. Bratcher, *Matthew,* p. 233. His comment hardly takes sufficient account of the narrative function of the Pharisees in Matthew's gospel nor the circumstances of its composition.

[187]For stylistic reasons, the NRSV's "because you were so hard-hearted" appears at the beginning of Jesus' statement in both Mark 10:5 and Matt 19:8, but the placement of the phrase is somewhat different in the Greek texts of the two gospels. One might note that the NRSV's translation of the phrase *pros tên sklêrokardian humôn* in Matt 19:8 is somewhat different from what it is in Mark 10:5. The Greek text is, however, the same in both instances. Matthew has borrowed the expression from Mark, but has imparted to it his own meaning.

[188]The *ap' archês,* with ellipsis (cf. Matt 24:21), also appears in Matt 19:4, the proper parallel to Mark 10:6.

[189]Cf. H. Zimmermann, *Methodenlehre,* p. 112, and, following him, C. Marucci, *Parole de Gesù,* p. 277.

[190]See also D. J. Harrington, *Matthew,* pp. 274-275.

[191]Matt 5:32 speaks not only of the man who divorces his wife but also of the man who marries a divorced woman. Some manuscripts of Matt 19:9 likewise make reference to that second situation, undoubtedly under the influence of Matt 5:32. On the textual tradition, see above, p. 108.

[192]The crowds following Jesus have been left in the air since Matt 19:2. They reappear in Matt 20:29 at a rather lengthy narrative distance from the present pericope.

[193]In the parallel Markan texts, the second-person plural pronoun occurs but twice, "for *your* hardness of heart he wrote *you* this commandment" (v. 5).

[194]Cf. H. Zimmermann, *Methodenlehre,* p. 112.

[195]Schnackenburg suggests that these two pericopes contain the sharpest examples of Jesus' criticism of the Jewish practice of the Law. Cf. R. Schnackenburg, *Matthäusevangelium,* 1. Die Neue Echter Bibel: NT (Würzburg: Echter, 1985) p. 141.

[196]Note the use of the verb *proserchomai* in Matt 15:1 as in Matt 19:3.

[197]See "and he said" (*kai eipen*) of Matt 19:5 in comparison with the "God commanded" (*eipen*) of Matt 15:4 and "the word of God" (*ton logon tou theou*) of Matt 15:6.

¹⁹⁸Cf. "from the beginning" in Matt 19:8 and Matt 15:4's substitution of "God" (*theos*) for Mark 7:10's "Moses."

¹⁹⁹Gnilka describes the Corban tradition as a "contrary commandment" (*Gegengebot*). Cf. J. Gnilka, *Matthäusevangelium*, 2, p. 22.

²⁰⁰Krämer suggests that the wording of Matt 15:6a (in Greek), "that person need not honor the father," is a modification of the Markan text so as to make very explicit the contravention of the fourth commandment. Cf. H. Krämer, "Eine Anmerkung zum Verständnis von Mt 15, 6a," *Wort und Dienst* 16 (1981) 67–70. Likewise, A. Sand, *Matthäus*, p. 311. Similarly Albright-Mann, Schweizer, Gnilka, and Schnackenburg suggest that Matt 15:19's revision of Mark 7:22 results from an assimilation to the Decalogue. Cf. W. F. Albright and C. S. Mann, *Matthew*, p. 185, E. Schweizer, *Matthew*, p. 325; J. Gnilka, *Matthäusevangelium*, 2, pp. 19, 20; and R. Schnackenburg, *Matthäusevangelium*, 1, p. 141. For another aspect of the Decalogue's influence on Matthew's formulation of the episode, see my *Christian Morality*, p. 73.

²⁰¹On the enumeration of the precepts of the Decalogue, see *Christian Morality*, pp. 51–52.

²⁰²Note the three-fold use of the second-person plural pronoun in Matt 15:5-7, especially the emphatic *humeis* in v. 5.

²⁰³In the New Testament this is a term for the Pharisees which Matthew has truly made his own. It is hapax in Mark (at Mark 7:6, whence it is taken over at Matt 15:7) and occurs but three times in Luke, namely at 6:42 (cf. Matt 7:5), 12:56 (unusually omitted from Matt 16:3), and 13:15 (the passage has no Matthean parallel). Thus it occurs only once in his Markan source and once in Q, but Matthew employs the term fourteen times: Matt 6:2, 5, 16; 7:5; 15:7; 22:18; 23:13, 14, 15, 23, 25, 27, 29; 24:51.

²⁰⁴In this regard, Matthew is following Mark's two-part schema. In Mark, the further instruction is given directly to the disciples who ask Jesus about the matter under discussion (Mark 7:17), just as they do in Mark 10:10, with regard to divorce. In the Matthean parallel to Mark, there is likewise a shift of audience before the interpretive addendum is given. In Matthew, the shift is to the crowds (*ton ochlon*, Matt 15:10) rather than to the disciples in the house (*eis oikon apo tou ochlou . . . hoi mathêtai*, Mark 10:17). In Matthew, the instruction of the disciples (cf. Matt 15:12) appears within a larger narrative unit (see the *inclusio*, Matt 15:10 and 20). The Matthean redaction is obviously shaped by Matthew's theory of discipleship.

²⁰⁵Cf. Gregory Murray, "What Defiles a Man?" DR 106 (1988) 297–298, p. 298, and R. Schnackenburg, *Matthäusevangelium*, 1, p. 140. Murray, however, draws an implausible conclusion from the observation, namely, that Mark used the gospel according to Matthew as the basic source material for his own work. The greater coherence and logic of Matt 15:1-20 over and against its Markan source is a trait which this narrative also shares with Matt 19:3-9.

²⁰⁶Cf. E. Schweizer, *Matthew*, p. 326.

²⁰⁷Cf. J. Gnilka, *Matthäusevangelium*, 2, p. 20.

²⁰⁸See above, p. 101.

²⁰⁹See above, pp. 104, 128, 182.

²¹⁰See above, p. 101.

²¹¹See R. F. Collins, "Commandment," *Anchor Bible Dictionary,* 1, pp. 1097-1099.

²¹²The Nash papyrus and various phylacteries found in Qumran bear witness to this. Cf. D. Barthélemy and J. T. Milik, eds., *Qumran Cave I.* DJD, 1 (Oxford: Clarendon, 1955) pp. 72-74; M. Baillet, J. T. Milik, and R. de Vaux, eds., *Les "petites grottes" de Qumran.* DJD, 3 (Oxford: Clarendon, 1962) pp. 149-150, 153-155.

²¹³Cf. F. E. Vokes, "The Ten Commandments in the New Testament and First Century Judaism," *SE,* 5 (= TU 103) (Berlin: Akademie, 1968) pp. 146-154.

²¹⁴See above, p. 295, n. 200.

²¹⁵Cf. Matt 15:6, 19. See p. 295, n. 200. See also p. 293, n. 168.

²¹⁶Ben Witherington has suggested that the exceptive clauses, here and in Matt 5:32, "may be the original words of Jesus that the First Evangelist includes because of their relevance for his own audience." While I agree that Matthew has added the exceptive clause, I cannot accept the contention that the exception derives from Jesus. Neither can I accept Luck's contention "that Mark eliminated the exception clause for the sake of brevity." Cf. Ben Witherington, "Matthew 5.32 and 19.9—Exception or Exceptional Situation?" *NTS* 31 (1985) 571-576, p. 572; W. F. Luck, *Divorce and Remarriage,* p. 154.

²¹⁷For another example of the consistency of Matthew's editorial work, see Matt 9:9 and 10:3. Matthew's theory of discipleship led him to substitute the name of Matthew for the name of Levi, found in his Markan source (Mark 2:14; cf. Luke 5:29) and then add "the tax collector" to the name of Matthew in the list of the Twelve (Matt 10:3; cf. Mark 3:18; Luke 6:15; Acts 1:13). See my *These Things Have Been Written: Studies on the Fourth Gospel.* LTPM, 2 (Louvain: Peeters— Grand Rapids, MI: Eerdmans, 1990) p. 76.

²¹⁸The only usage of *porneia* in the Synoptic Gospels.

²¹⁹Cf. Mark 7:22. Mark 7:22 and Matt 15:19 are the only two Synoptic passages in which the word "adultery" occurs.

²²⁰It appears elsewhere in the NT only in Acts 26:29 and 2 Cor 11:28. It also appears in some manuscripts of Matt 19:9 in place of the "except-*mê epi*" formulation. See above, p. 108.

²²¹See below, pp. 184-213.

²²²Leopold Sabourin has suggested that "the introduction of a qualified solution had been prepared by the addition of 'for any cause' to the question of the Pharisees" in v. 3. Cf. L. Sabourin, "The Divorce Clauses (Mt 5:32; 19:9)," *BTB* 2 (1972) 80-86, p. 81.

²²³Among the commentators, M. D. Goulder, E. Schweizer, J. Gnilka, et al., suggest that adultery is the exception which Matthew intends to cite by means

of his use of the generic *porneia*. Cf. M. D. Goulder, *Midrash and Lection*, p. 291; E. Schweizer, *Matthew*, p. 383; J. Gnilka, *Matthäusevangelium*, 2, p. 157.

²²⁴Cf., for example, E. Schweizer, *Matthew*, p. 382.

²²⁵Cf. J. Gnilka, *Matthäusevangelium*, 2, pp. 151, 156.

NOTES—CHAPTER 5

¹The variant readings in the transmission of the text are reflected neither in the translations nor in the footnotes of the principal contemporary English versions of the New Testament. Cf. NRSV, RSV, NEB, JB, NAB, NIV, NJB, RNAB, REB, and Phillips Modern English.

²Notably the eleventh-century minuscule, 28, and the twelfth-century minuscule, 1010.

³Including the Vetus Latina as well as old Syriac and old Coptic manuscripts.

⁴With regard to this reading, several of the various manuscripts have minor variations from a basically similar text.

⁵They give the reading a C rating.

⁶See also Luke 16:18.

⁷*De Conjugiis Adulterinis*, I, 10 (PL 40, 458).

⁸See also Henri Crouzel, "Quelques remarques conçernant le texte patristique de Mt 19, 9," *BLE* 82 (1981) 83–92.

⁹Ibid.

¹⁰B. M. Metzger, *Textual Commentary*, p. 14.

¹¹Pace the efforts of Kingsbury to use the phrase "from that time Jesus began" (Matt 4:17; 16:21) as key to the major articulations of the first gospel. Cf. J. D. Kingsbury, *Matthew as Story*.

¹²Cf. B. T. Viviano, "Matthew," p. 639; Robert A. Guelich, *The Sermon on the Mount: A Foundation for Understanding* (Waco, TX: Word, 1982) pp. 59–60. John P. Meier specifically notes that the antitheses are addressed to Christian disciples. Cf. J. P. Meier, *Law and History in Matthew's Gospel: A Redactional Study of Mt. 5:17-18*. AnBib, 71 (Rome: Pontifical Biblical Institute) p. 161, n. 82.

¹³Cf. Matt 4:25; 5:1.

¹⁴The evangelist himself might well be characterized as a Christian scribe. Cf. Matt 13:52. See B. Viviano, "Matthew," p. 630; K. Stendahl, *School*.

¹⁵For a synoptic reading of this comparative material, see Jan Lambrecht, *Sermon*, pp. 234–238.

¹⁶Cf. B. T. Viviano, "Matthew," p. 639. Guelich (*The Sermon*, pp. 54–59) takes issue with a symbolic understanding of the mountain. He sees it as having primarily a literary function. While Guelich obviously wishes to distance himself from earlier and simplistic ideas relative to Matthew's characterization of Jesus

as well as from B. W. Bacon's classic comparison between Matthew's five ser-mons and the five books of Moses in the Torah, he seems not to have sufficiently taken into account the evangelists' symbolic use of geography as a redactional device. A classic exposition of this use of topography is to be found in Willi Marx-sen's *Mark the Evangelist: Studies on the Redaction History of the Gospel* (Nash-ville, TN: Abingdon, 1969) pp. 37-38, 54-94.

[17]The Sermon on the Mount deserves and has earned extensive study. See, for example, the extensive bibliography given by Warren S. Kissinger, *The Sermon on the Mount: A History of Interpretation and Bibliography.* ATLA Bibliography Series, 3 (Meteuchen, NJ: Scarecrow, 1975).

This limited scope of the present work permits only a very sketchy overview of an approach to the Sermon. Several of the key elements in this approach de-mand additional reflection and nuance, especially the symbolic use of topographical references, the relationship between Matthew's community and contemporary Juda-ism, the relationship between the Sermon and contemporary Jewish halakah, and Matthew's understanding of the relationship between Jesus and Moses. For an overview of one of these issues, Matthew and contemporary Judaism, see G. N. Stanton, "The Origin and Purpose of Matthew's Gospel: Matthaean Scholarship from 1945 to 1980," ANRW II/25, 3, 1889-1951, pp. 1910-1921; see also J. Andrew Overman, *Matthew's Gospel and Formative Judaism: The Social World of the Matthean Community* (Minneapolis, MN: Fortress, 1990).

[18]Cf. J. Lambrecht, *Sermon,* pp. 80-90.

[19]For W. D. Davies, the Sermon on the Mount was a kind of Christian coun-terpart to the Mishnaic formulation that was in the process of taking place at Jabneh. Cf. W. D. Davies, *Setting,* p. 315 and *passim.*

[20]This double front is clearly seen in Matthew's introduction to the Lord's prayer as well. Cf. Matt 6:5-8.

[21]The introductory formula admits of some variation.

[22]This is the only one of the six antitheses in which a passage of Scripture is not cited verbatim. Matthew's language reflects the language of several scriptur-al passages, among which Lev 19:12 is one. It can be suggested that Matthew chose phraseology intended to echo yet another precept of the Decalogue, that on false oaths (Exod 20:16 = Deut 5:20). Cf. Reginald H. Fuller, "The Decalogue," p. 247.

[23]Cf. Matt 7:29; 13:52.

[24]Cf. Matt 4:1-11.

[25]See also M. Jack Suggs, "The Antitheses as Redactional Products," in Luise Schottroff, et al., *Essays on the Love Commandment* (Philadelphia: Fortress, 1978) pp. 93-107.

[26]For Matthew, the redactor.

[27]See also Mark 10:10, Matt 19:9. Since however the logion of Matt 5:32 ap-pears in the gospel without an immediate narrative context and since it exists as an isolated saying in Luke, it is most probable that the version of the logion on divorce in Matt 5:32 derives from Matthew's Q source.

²⁸There is, however, a parallel with Jas 5:12. Cf. Patrick J. Hartin, "James and the Q Sermon on the Mount/Plain," in David J. Lull, ed., *Society of Biblical Literature 1989 Seminar Papers* (Atlanta, GA: Scholars, 1989) pp. 440–456, esp. pp. 455–456; *James and the Q Sayings of Jesus.* JSOTSup, 47 (Sheffield: JSOT, 1991). With regard to the antitheses on murder (Matt 5:21-26) and adultery (Matt 5:27-32), Hartin notes, "in a similar context James has reference to the breaking of the Law by quoting the examples of adultery and murder, but in the reverse order to Matthew" ("James," p. 452). The context to which he refers is Jas 2:11, but see also Jas 1:19-20 and 4:11.

²⁹Compare Matt 5:34-35 with Matt 23:20-22.

³⁰An anthology of many of these parallels can be found in Str-B, 1, pp. 254–386. See also Herbert Braun, *Spätjüdisch-häretischer und frühchristlicher Radikalismus*, 2. BHT, 24 (Tübingen: Mohr, 1957) pp. 10–11. Braun indicates that the kind of midrash on the Torah found in the antitheses has late-Jewish paraenesis as its proper context.

³¹Cf. J. Lambrecht, *Sermon*, p. 35.

³²Kloppenborg cites Catchpole, Crossan, Grundmann, Guelich, Hunter, Jacobson, Lührmann, Manson, Muller, Polag, Schürmann, Streeter, and Worden as authors who favor the Lukan order in addition to himself. Cf. John S. Kloppenborg, *Q Parallels: Synopsis, Critical Notes, and Concordance*. Foundations and Facets: New Testament (Sonoma, CA: Polebridge, 1988) p. 30.

³³Cf. Matt 19:19b where Matthew has placed (cf. Mark 10:19) the love commandment climactically at the end of a presentation of the Decalogue.

³⁴Thus, Lambrecht, *Sermon*, p. 98. Kloppenborg considers the "but" to be part of the "generally accepted extent of Q" (*Q Parallels*, p. 28), but it is not found in the reconstruction of Q offered by Polag (*Fragmenta Q*, p. 34) and Havener (*Sayings*, p. 124).

³⁵Cf. F. E. Vokes, "Ten Commandments," pp. 147-148; Ferdinand Dexinger, "Der Dekalog im Judentum," *BLit* 59 (1986) 86–95, pp. 87–88.

³⁶Cf. D. Barthélemy and J. T. Milik, *Qumran Cave I*, pp. 72-74, plate 14; M. Baillet, et al., *Les "petites grottes,"* pp. 150, 153-154; *Les "petites grottes" de Qumran: Planches*. DJD, 3 (Oxford: Clarendon, 1962), plate 32; Heinrich Schneider, "Der Dekalog in den Phylakterien von Qumran," *BZ* 3 (1959) 18–31. Barthélemy comments (p. 72) that the most remarkable feature of the contents of the phylactery is the presence of the Decalogue according to the text of Deuteronomy.

³⁷Cf. Exod 12:7.

³⁸Cf. *m. Tamid.* 5:1; *b. Ber.* 12a; *y. Ber.* i, 3c. The practice was eventually abandoned because of objections arising from Christians(?) or Liberal Jews ("because of the claim of the Minim"). Cf. Geza Vermes, "The Decalogue and the Minim," in M. Black and G. Fohrer, eds., *In Memoriam Paul Kahle*. BZAW, 103 (Berlin: Töpelmann, 1968) pp. 232–240.

[39]Deriving its name from the first word of Deut 6:4, *"Hear,* O Israel,'' this twice-daily declaration of the Lord's unity consisted, at least as early as the second century A.D., of Deut 6:4-9, Deut 11:13-21, and Num 15:37-41.

[40]Cf. F. C. Burkitt, ''The Hebrew Papyrus of the Ten Commandments,'' *JQR* 15 (1903) 392-408, pp. 402, 405.

[41]The best-known example is probably Philo's *De Decalogo.* For Philo, the Decalogue supplied ten headings under which the Law could be arranged. Apparently some rabbis shared this view of the Ten Commandments. Cf. F. E. Vokes, ''Ten Commandments,'' p. 150, with reference to Charles Taylor, *Sayings of the Jewish Fathers* (2nd. ed.: Cambridge, University Press, 1897) p. 108.

[42]Cf. Jacob Neusner, *The Memorized Torah: The Mnemonic System of the Mishnah.* BJS, 96 (Chico, CA: Scholars, 1985) pp. 6, 9-10. Neusner notes the unusual use of the present-tense participle of the verb ''to say'' in this regard. Although different linguistic structures are involved, this may be compared with Matthew's formulaic use of ''but I say to you'' *(egō de legō humin,* Matt 5:22, 28, 32, 34, 39, 44; cf. Matt 5:26).

[43]In addition to Matt 5:21, 27, (33), see Matt 15:4, 19; 19:18.

[44]Cf. Mark 7:8-13 (Matt 15:1-6); Mark 10:2-9 (Matt 19:3-9). Note the use of the formula *''humeis de legete-*but you say'' in Mark 7:11 = Matt 15:5.

[45]Another example of Matthew's use of epitome as an editorial technique is Matt 5:10. This ''eighth Beatitude'' is at once a digest of Matt 5:11-12 and an adaptation to the formulaic presentation of the Beatitudes in Matt 5:3-9. In the light of our discussion on the provenance of the antitheses, one might note that some of the Beatitudes in Matt 5:3-10 are the result of Matthew's adaptation of traditional source material (Q) while others derive from the evangelist (MtR) or his particular sources (M).

[46]Jesus' sayings utilized by Matthew in conjunction with the use of the Decalogue in the antitheses come from Q, Mark, and M. See above, pp. 153-154.

[47]Cf. Matt 19:8.

[48]See the comparable use of the first person in Matt 18:3; 19:10.

[49]Cf. R. H. Fuller who opines that we cannot be certain whether the antithetical formulation is pre-Matthean or redactional but suggests that, ''at the very least the antitheses represent the *Wirkungsgeschichte* of Jesus' authentic teaching.'' Cf. R. H. Fuller, ''The Decalogue,'' p. 248.

[50]Matthew's classic five sermons amply attest to the fact that compilation was one of his editorial techniques. So, too, does the collection of miracle stories in chapters 8 and 9 and the series of seven woes in chapter 23. Vincent Taylor offered some reflections on the way in which Matthew utilized the Q material in his various collections in ''The Order of Q'' and ''The Original Order of Q'' *(New Testament Essays* [London: Epworth, 1970] pp. 90-94, 95-118).

[51]In Matt 19:3-12, the evangelist has also brought together material from different sources on the basis of their general similarity of content. Newman and Stine discern a similarity of content between Matt 5:27-30 and 5:31-32 insofar as ''the protection of the woman,'' the original point of Deut 24:1-4 (cf. v. 31), is Jesus'

purpose in verse 28. I find this much too precise a specification of the similarity. Cf. B. M. Newman and P. C. Stine, *Matthew,* p. 144.

⁵²Cf. Will Deming, "Mark 9.42-10.12, Matthew 5.27-32, and *B. Nid.* 13b: A First Century Discussion of Male Sexuality," *NTS* 36 (1990) 130-141.

⁵³Cf. R. H. Fuller, "The Decalogue," p. 247. See also S. H. Brooks, *Matthew's Community,* pp. 34-35. Brooks writes of "subordination or a parenthesis."

⁵⁴Among such authors are Floyd V. Filson, Walter Grundmann, John J. Kilgallen, Walter Kirchschläger, and, apparently, Joachim Gnilka. Cf. F. V. Filson, "Broken Patterns in the Gospel of Matthew," *JBL* 75 (1956) 227-231, p. 229; W. Grundmann, *Das Evangelium nach Matthäus.* THKNT, 1 (Berlin: Evangelische Verlaganstalt, 1968) pp. 158-159; J. J. Kilgallen, "To What are the Matthean-Texts (5, 32 and 19, 9) an Exception?" *Bib* 61 (1980) 102-105, p. 103; W. Kirchschläger, *Ehe und Ehescheidung im Neuen Testament. Überlegungen und Anfragen zur Praxis der Kirche* (Vienna: Herold, 1987) pp. 65-66; J. Gnilka, *Matthäusevangelium,* 1, p. 164. See also, B. Viviano, "Matthew," p. 642.

⁵⁵I agree with Fuller that the truncated introduction, *"errethê de*-it was also said," indicates that Matt 5:31-32 really is a separate antithesis. The truncation, however, is part of the problem. It is the shortest introduction to any of the antitheses. Cf. "you have heard that it was said to those of ancient times" (vv. 21, 33) and "you have heard that it was said" (vv. 27, 38, 43). Moreover, in the other five antitheses the Scripture is cited verbatim (according to the LXX), while in Matt 5:31 there is only an *allusion* to the biblical text.

⁵⁶Cf.Mark 10:2-12, esp. vv. 3-4, reworked by Matthew in Matt 19:3-12, esp. vv. 7-8. Klaus Berger calls the reference to Deut 24:1 in Matt 5:31 a "free rendering," while Hans-Theo Wrege remarks that the use made by Matthew of Deut 24:1 in Matt 5:31 reflects Hellenistic Christian tradition. Cf. K. Berger, *Die Gesetzesauslegung,* p. 516; H.-T. Wrege, *Die Überlieferungsgeschichte der Bergpredigt.* WUNT, 9 (Tübingen: Mohr, 1968) p. 53.

⁵⁷Eduardo De La Serna is of the opinion that the collection of antitheses were originally five in number and that a final redactor (Matthew himself?) added this present third antithesis at the time when he was revising the text of Mark 10 in the light of the situation of the community to which he belonged. Cf. E. De La Serna, "¿Divorcio en Mateo?" p. 104.

⁵⁸See above, pp. 108-145.

⁵⁹Cf. R. Bultmann, *Tradition,* pp. 135-136; R. A. Guelich, "The Antitheses of Matthew v. 21-48: Traditional and/or Redactional," *NTS* 22 (1975-1976) 444-457; M. J. Suggs, "Antitheses."

⁶⁰Cf. G. Barth, "Matthew's Understanding of the Law," pp. 64-73 and J. P. Meier, *Law and History,* pp. 41-124.

⁶¹J. P. Meier, *Law and History,* p. 123.

⁶²Cf. J. P. Meier, *Law and History,* p. 77. Meier cites Georg Strecker and Jacques Dupont in support of this position. Cf. G. Strecker, *Der Weg der Gerechtigkeit,* pp. 149-158; J. Dupont, *Les Béatitudes,* 3. EBib (Paris: Gabalda, 1973) pp. 211-384.

⁶³Guelich has reviewed some of the specificities of the various rabbinic parallels to this formula. Cf. R. A. Guelich, *The Sermon*, pp. 180–181.

⁶⁴Eduard Lohse has pointed out that a "but I say to you" formula was used in scribal discussions when a predominant doctrinal point of view was being contradicted. Cf. E. Lohse, "Ich aber sage euch," in E. Lohse, ed., *Der Ruf Jesu und die Antwort der Gemeinde. Exegetische Untersuchungen Joachim Jeremias zum 70. Geburtstag von seinen Schülern* (Göttingen: Vandenhoeck und Ruprecht, 1970) pp. 189–203.

⁶⁵Cf. Str-B, 1, pp. 253–254.

⁶⁶See, for example, J. Lambrecht, *Sermon*, pp. 93–94.

⁶⁷Cf. Matt 7:29: "he taught them as one having authority, and not as *their* scribes."

⁶⁸Cf. B. M. Newman and P. C. Stine, *Matthew*, p. 145.

⁶⁹While *de* is a conjunctive particle with adversative force, it is not as strong as "*alla*-but." In fact *de* is sometimes used merely to pass from one thing to another. When *de* is used in this way, as it sometimes is in the New Testament, it often appears in English translation as "and," but sometimes it is not translated or is replaced by a punctuation mark.

⁷⁰Within the New Testament "the Law and the prophets" is a typically Matthean expression (see Matt 5:17; 7:12; 11:13; 22:40), apparently taken from his Q-source (Matt 11:13 = Luke 16:16). Apart from Matthew, it is used four times by Luke in Luke-Acts (Luke 16:16; 24:44 [with the psalms]; Acts 13:15; 28:23 [cf. 24:14]) and once by Paul (Rom 3:21).

⁷¹See also my *Christian Morality*, pp. 69–74.

⁷²See Matt 15:6 (cf. Matt 5:21, 27, [33]) apropos the fourth commandment.

⁷³Cf. Matt 15:1-9; 19:3-9.

⁷⁴Cf. Matt 9:13.

⁷⁵Lev 24:5-9, to which reference is made in Matt 12:4.

⁷⁶Cf. Mark 10:17-22; Luke 18:18-23.

⁷⁷Cf. Matt 22:40.

⁷⁸Cf. Matt 5:19a; Matt 22:11-14.

⁷⁹Cf. J. P. Meier, *Law and History*, pp. 131-133.

⁸⁰Cf. Richards A. Edwards, *A Theology of Q: Eschatology, Prophecy, and Wisdom* (Philadelphia: Fortress, 1976) p. 48. The formula means "that the speaker does not speak on his own but rather under the influence of inspiration."

⁸¹The Greek has *adelphô*, literally "brother," but rendered as "brother or sister" by the NRSV.

⁸²Literally, "if anyone says to his brother, 'Raca.' "

⁸³Cf. Frank Kermode, "Matthew" in Robert Alter and Frank Kermode, eds., *The Literary Guide to the Bible* (Cambridge, MA: Harvard University Press, 1987) pp. 387-401, p. 391; James G. Williams, "Paraenesis, Excess, and Ethics: Mat-

thew's Rhetoric in the Sermon on the Mount," *Semeia* 50 (1990) 163–187, pp. 174–175.

⁸⁴See above, p. 153 and S. H. Brooks, *Matthew's Community,* p. 34.

⁸⁵E. Schweizer, *Matthew,* p. 122. Schweizer's reflections on the extraneous nature of verses 29-30 are quite common in the exegetical literature, although many commentators would find only verse 29 to be properly extraneous.

⁸⁶Cf. Gerhard Lohfink, "Jesus und die Ehescheidung. Zur Gattung und Sprachintention von Mt 5, 32," in Helmut Merklein and Joachim Lange, eds., *Biblische Randbemerkungen: Schülerfestschrift für Rudolf Schanckenburg zum 60. Geburtstag* (2nd. ed.: Würzburg, Echter, 1974) pp. 209–210; W. Kirchschläger, *Ehe und Ehescheidung,* pp. 66–67; Marc Christiaens, "Pastoraal van de echtscheiding volgens Matteüs. Vragen rond de 'ontuchtclausule,' " *TvT* 23 (1983) 3–23, pp. 6–7, etc. Christiaens draws an interesting conclusion from the evangelist's male perspective. He considers that the Matthean formulation is concerned with the situation of a pagan divorced woman who has converted to Christianity. From a Christian perspective she would be considered an adulteress, but Matthew exculpates her, laying the blame on the divorcing husband.

⁸⁷Cf. Israel Abrahams, *Studies in Pharisaism and the Gospels,* 1 (Cambridge: University Press, 1917) p. 73. In contrast, a married woman who had sexual intercourse with any man was considered to have committed adultery. She had violated the marriage rights of her own husband.

⁸⁸Pace C. F. Evans who writes that Matt 5:32 "can be construed as a single continuous statement primarily concerned with the consequences of divorce for the woman." Cf. C. F. Evans, *Saint Luke.* TPINTC (London: SCM— Philadelphia: Trinity Press International, 1990) p. 609.

⁸⁹Cf. Will Deming, "A First-Century Discussion." Without adducing comparative material, Mary Rose D'Angelo claims that Matthew betrays an intensification of interest in sexual purity ("Divorce Sayings," p. 98). The written form of the rabbinic materials is admittedly late, but Deming argues that "it is quite possible that we are dealing here with materials from around the middle of the first century" ("A First-Century Discussion," p. 136; cf. pp. 135–136).

⁹⁰*t. Nid.* 13a-b.

⁹¹Isa 1:15.

⁹²Exod 20:14.

⁹³*m. Nid.* 2:1.

⁹⁴It is also to be noted that the return of a woman dismissed by her husband contrary to the provisions of Deut 24:1-4 was also assumed to be a form of adultery. Cf. Yari Zakovitch, "The Woman's Rights in the Biblical Law of Divorce," *The Jewish Law Annual* 4 (1981) 28 46, p. 32.

⁹⁵Even at the present time, in some Moslem cultures, amputation continues to be the punishment meted out for various infractions of Sharia, the religious law of Isalm.

⁹⁶Cf. Str-B, 1, pp. 298-301; W. Michaelis, *"opthalmos,"* TDNT, 5, p. 376; G. F. Moore, *Judaism in the First Century of the Christian Era: The Age of the Tannaim,* 2 (Cambridge, MA: Harvard University Press, 1950) pp. 267-268.

⁹⁷See above, p. 301, n. 55.

⁹⁸Matt 19:7 and Mark 10:4 use the expression *biblion apostasiou* to refer to this document. A similar expression, *apostasiou suggraphê* is found in various Hellenistic papyri. So far as I have been able to discover, Matt 5:31 represents the only known use of *apostasion* alone to refer to a document.

⁹⁹In his reflections on Matt 19:1-12, Ewald focuses sharply upon the Matthean emphasis on the man. Cf. G. R. Ewald, *Jesus and Divorce,* pp. 68-72.

¹⁰⁰It might even be suggested that Matthew's "makes her an adulteress" (*poiei autên moicheuthênai*) is to be interpreted as "makes her resort to prostitution," that is, as a means of economic support. See the discussion of Judg 19:2 and 1 Kgs 3:16-27 in Y. Zakovitch, "Woman's Rights," pp. 38-40.

¹⁰¹Until very recent times, some cultures permitted a husband to divorce his wife merely by repeating "you are no longer my wife."

¹⁰²Josephus even reports that a divorced woman may not marry again on her own initiative unless her former husband consents. See *Antiquities* XV, 7, 10. This is obviously a reference to Deut 24:1-4 which lays responsibility for the issue of the certificate of divorce, establishing the repudiated wife's right to remarriage, upon the husband who divorces her.

¹⁰³Matthew uses the aorist passive infinitive, *moicheuthênai,* to describe what the husband has made her do. The aorist, an oblique tense in Greek, is used of a single (rather than a past or repeated) action. Cf. BDF, 318. "Makes her an adulteress" is the translation found in the RSV, JB, and NJB. The NEB and the REB render the Greek *poiei autên moicheuthênai* as "involves her in adultery." The NIV, RNAB, and NRSV translate the phrase "causes her to commit adultery," a bit less forceful than the NAB's "forces her to commit adultery." Matthew's somewhat convoluted Greek phraseology comes from the fact that he is expressing a reality within the Jewish social world. A man cannot commit adultery against his own marriage. Cf. Ulrich Luz, *Matthew 1-7: A Commentary* (Minneapolis, MN: Augsburg, 1989) p. 300. The sense of Matthew's phrase might be retained if it were said that a man who divorces his wife "causes adultery to be committed with her." The NEB-REB translation perhaps best reflects the passive voice of Matthew's verb.

¹⁰⁴Davies and Allison cite Ruth 1:20-21; Ps 94:6; and Isa 1:23; 10:2 and 54:4 as biblical evidence for the difficulties faced by a single woman. Cf. W. D. Davies and Dale C. Allison, *A Critical and Exegetical Commentary on the Gospel According to Matthew,* 1. ICC (Edinburgh: T. & T. Clark, 1988) p. 528.

¹⁰⁵See, especially, D. J. Harrington whose commentary on Matthew is entirely written from the perspective of Matthew's "Jewishness." Cf. D. J. Harrington, *Matthew,* pp. 1-3.

¹⁰⁶Cf. G. Lohfink, "Jesus und die Ehescheidung," p. 211.

¹⁰⁷This is Christiaens' position. See above, p. 303, n. 86.

¹⁰⁸*Bar miswah,* son of the commandment.

¹⁰⁹Cf. Matt 22:30, "neither marry nor are given in marriage," more literally, "neither marry (*gamousin,* in the active voice) nor are married (*gamizontai,* in the passive voice)."

¹¹⁰Luz identifies it as a mashal in synthetic parallelism. Cf. U. Luz, *Matthew,* p. 299.

¹¹¹Cf. Lev 17:3-4; 20:9, 11, 12, 13, 16, 27; Num 35:16, 17, 18, 20-21.

¹¹²Cf. R. Bultmann, *Tradition,* p. 132; H.-T. Wrege, *Die Überlieferungeschichte,* p. 67; K. Haacker, "Ehescheidung und Wiederverheiratung im Neuen Testament," *TQ* 151 (1971) 28-38, p. 30; Siegfried Schulz, *Q. Die Spruchquelle der Evangelisten* (Zurich: Theologischer Verlag, 1972) p. 116; G. Lohfink, "Jesus und die Ehescheidung," pp. 207-217, pp. 212-213. Gnilka, however, identifies Jesus' first utterance as a sentence of apodictic law. Cf. J. Gnilka, *Matthäusevangelium,* 1, p. 164. In the light of Alt's magisterial study of the use of apodictic law in Israel ("The Origins of Israelite Law," in *Essays on Old Testament History and Religion* [Garden City, NY: Doubleday, 1967] pp. 79-103), it would seem that apodictic law is an improper category within which to categorize Jesus' first statement. Although making use of a participial phrase, the sentence envisions a specific case. Cf. Gen 9:6.

¹¹³For example, Matt 19:24, "Again I tell you (*palin de legō humin*), it is easier for a camel to go through the eye of a needle than for a rich man to enter the kingdom of God." Cf. G. Lohfink, "Jesus und die Ehescheidung," p. 217.

¹¹⁴Similarly, A. E. Harvey, *Strenuous Commands: The Ethic of Jesus* (London: SCM.—Philadelphia: Trinity International, 1990) pp. 85-86, 88.

¹¹⁵Lohfink cites Isa 14:4-21, a dirge used not to mourn, but to mock a foreign king and make known his premature death. In the New Testament, "sentences of holy law" serve as a form of prophetic proclamation. Cf. Ernst Käsemann, "Sentences of Holy Law in the New Testament," in *New Testament Questions of Today.* NTL (Philadelphia: Fortress—London: SCM, 1969) pp. 66-81; R. A. Edwards, *A Theology of Q,* pp. 40-41.

¹¹⁶Cf. Mark 7:9-13; par. Matt 15:4-9.

¹¹⁷Lohfink asks to which local council would the person be subject who is angry with his brother. Is it likely that a person who insults his brother would really be hauled before the Sanhedrin in Jerusalem? See G. Lohfink, "Jesus und die Ehescheidung," p. 214.

¹¹⁸1) *apolusē, apolusai;* 2) *dotō, dounai;* 3) *apostasion, apostasiou;* 4) *egō de legō humin hoti, legō de humin hoti;* 5) *apoluōn tēn gunaika autou, apolusē tēn gunaika autou;* 6) *porneias, porneia;* 7) *hos an, hos an;* 8) *gamēsē, gamēsē;* 9) *moichatai, moichatai.*

¹¹⁹Cf. E. Lövestam, "Divorce and Remarriage," p. 53, who cites *t. Šebu'ot* 47b as an example.

¹²⁰See the textual discussion above, p. 108.

¹²¹See my *Introduction,* p. 123.

[122]See above pp. 149-157.

[123]Cf. W. D. Davies and D. C. Allison, *Matthew,* 1, p. 527; M. A. D'Angelo, "Divorce Sayings," pp. 84-85.

[124]Luke 16:15-18 contains three or four sayings of Jesus in rapid succession. The sayings on the Law and the prophets (v. 15), the Law (v. 17) and divorce (v. 18) have parallels in Matt (11:12-13; 5:18; 5:32) and may be presumed to come from Q. The subsequent passage begins "There was a rich man." This is a classic opener for a narrative, but it is an aporia with regard to the preceding collection.

[125]In this respect, the Coptic Gospel of Thomas is a classic example of the genre. Although this Gnostic text contains 114 sayings of Jesus, many of which are parallel to sayings of Jesus contained in the Synoptic Gospels, the Gospel of Thomas does not contain the Jesuanic logion on divorce.

[126]Cf. Dieter Lührmann, "The Gospel of Mark and the Sayings Collection Q," *JBL* 108 (1989) 51-72, p. 59. Havener offers "before the year 70 A.D." as the date of Q's composition. Cf. I. Havener, *Sayings,* p. 45.

[127]Cf. F. Neirynck, *Q-Synopsis: The Double Tradition Passages in Greek,* Studiorum Novi Testamenti Auxilia, 13 (Louvain: University Press, 1988) pp. 56-57; J. S. Kloppenborg, *Q Parallels,* p. 180.

[128]The parallelism would be even more complete were "*pas*-all" the preferable reading of the text.

[129]From *moichaô,* to have dalliance with. When used in the passive, the verb has the meaning "to commit adultery." Cf. LSJ, 2, p. 1141. In the New Testament this verb is used only in Matt 5:32 and 19:9 and Mark 10:11, 12.

[130]Borge Krag Diderichsen once attempted to prove that the saying in Luke 16:18 was not originally a prohibition of divorce. He suggested that the verb "to divorce" (*apoluein,* literally, "to dismiss") simply meant leaving one's wife. In his view, the original context of the saying would have been that of a man leaving his wife in order to be a disciple of Jesus. Should he then marry another woman, his situation would be considered adulterous. Cf. B. K. Diderichsen, *Den markianske skilsmisserperikope: Dens genesis og historiske placering* (Aarhuus: Gyldendal, 1962), esp. pp. 20-247, 62-76, 347. On the other hand, the verb in question was used as a technical term for divorce even in at least one Greek-language Palestinian document. Cf. E. Lövestam, "*Apoluein* en gammalpalestinensisk skilsmässoterm," *SEA* 27 (1962) 132-152.

[131]The parable itself is found in vv. 1-9, to which have been added a series of sayings loosely connected by the theme of riches.

[132]See especially Heinz Schürmann, *Traditisonsgeschichtliche Untersuchungen zu den synoptischen Evangelien.* Kommentare und Beiträge zum Alten und Neuen Testament (Düsseldorf: Patmos, 1968) pp. 132-134, but also the earlier works of Rodenbusch, Taylor, Easton, and Daube, and the later commentary of I. H. Marshall: E. Rodenbusch, "Die Komposition von Lukas 16," *ZNW* 4 (1903) 243-254; Vincent Taylor, *Behind the Third Gospel: A Study of the Proto-Luke Hypothesis* (Oxford: Clarendon, 1926) pp. 156-158; B. S. Easton, *The Gospel according to St. Luke: A Critical and Exegetical Commentary* (Edinburgh: Clark,

1926) pp. 247–248; D. Daube, *The New Testament and Rabbinic Judaism* (London: Athlone, 1956) pp. 292–293; I. H. Marshall, *The Gospel of Luke: A Commentary on the Greek Text.* NICNT (Grand Rapids, MI: Eerdmans, 1978) pp. 626–627.

[133]Cf. I. H. Marshall, *Luke,* p. 627.

[134]Cf. Paul Hoffmann, *Studien zur Theologie der Logienquelle.* NTAbh, NF, 8 (Münster: Aschendorff, 1972) pp. 53–56; J. A. Fitzmyer, *Luke the Theologian: Aspects of His Teaching* (New York-Mahwah: Paulist, 1989) pp. 179–180.

[135]J. A. Fitzmyer, *Luke the Theologian,* p. 180.

[136]Cf. J. A. Fitzmyer, *The Gospel According to Luke X-XXIV.* AB 28A (Garden City, NY: 1985) p. 1119.

[137]Cf. *T. Jud.* 18:2, "Beware therefore, my children, of fornication, and the love of money." The pairing of these two themes in Judaism is so common that many commentators interpret the exhortation "that no one wrong or exploit his brother or sister in this matter" (1 Thess 4:6a) of the sin of avarice. See the discussion in my *Studies,* pp. 317–319.

[138]There is some discussion whether Luke 16:16, undoubtedly a Q-saying, originally (that is, in Q itself) belonged to this collection of sayings on the Law. Cf. J. S. Kloppenborg, *The Formation of Q: Trajectories in Ancient Wisdom Collections.* Studies in Antiquity & Christianity (Philadelphia: Fortress, 1987) pp. 112–115; *Q Parallels,* p. 56.

[139]See Kloppenborg, *Q Parallels,* pp. 180–181. Polag and Havener identify these logia as sayings 62-63-64 in the Q document. Cf. A. Polag, *Fragmenta Q,* p. 74, and I. Havener, *Sayings,* p. 143.

[140]See above, pp. 168–169 and also Luke T. Johnson who identifies this as "the real problem." Cf. L. T. Johnson, *The Gospel of Luke.* Sacra Pagina, 3 (Collegeville, MN: Liturgical Press, 1991) p. 251.

[141]Cf. Claude Sélis, "La répudiation dans le Nouveau Testament," *Lumière et vie* 206 (1992) 39–49, p. 47.

[142]For example, Eduard Schweizer in *The Good News According to Luke* (Atlanta: GA: John Knox, 1984) p. 258.

[143]Cf. Stephen G. Wilson, *Luke and the Law.* SNTSMS, 50 (Cambridge: University Press, 1983) pp. 43–51.

[144]I. H. Marshall, *Luke,* p. 631.

[145]Pace Michael D. Goulder who opts for the dependence of Luke on Matthew and therefore suggests that Matthew has influenced the thread of Luke's thought. Cf. M. D. Goulder, *Luke—A New Paradigm,* 2. JSNTSup, 20 (Sheffield: JSOT, 1989) pp. 630–631.

[146]Cf. Mal 2:14-16.

[147]Cf. J. A. Fitzmyer, *The Gospel According to Luke (I-IX),* AB, 28 (Garden City, NY: Doubleday, 1981) pp. 421, 424.

[148]Acts 15:19-21, 28-29 demonstrates the Lukan view that some demands of the Mosaic Law are incumbent even upon Gentile Christians.

¹⁴⁹Cf. 1 Cor 7:10-11 and Mark 10:1-12.

¹⁵⁰Cf. J. M. Creed, *The Gospel According to St. Luke: The Greek Text with Introduction, Notes and Indices* (London: Macmillan, 1930) p. 206.

¹⁵¹See the discussion, pp. 181-182.

¹⁵²For Evans, the logion is "not a verdict on divorce as such, but a condemnation of second marriage." Cf. C. F. Evans, *Luke,* p. 610.

¹⁵³Cf. C. F. Evans, "adultery must therefore have some other meaning than the legal" (*Luke,* p. 610).

¹⁵⁴Cf. Luke 18:20.

¹⁵⁵Evans cites the addition of "the wife" to Mark 10:29 in Luke 18:29 as an example of Lukan asceticism. Cf. C. F. Evans, *Luke,* p. 610.

¹⁵⁶See the discussions of 1 Tim 3:2, 12 and Tit 1:6 in the various commentaries and monographs.

¹⁵⁷Cf. Abel Isaksson, *Marriage and Ministry.* In this regard one might also note the dualism (esp. vv. 34-35) of Luke's version of the discussion with the Sadducees (Luke 20:27-40). This dualism is not dissimilar to some of the dualism found in the Dead Sea Scrolls.

¹⁵⁸Cf. Mark 10:19; Matt 19:18.

¹⁵⁹They are relatively few in number, but they do exist. For example, Sanders and Davies take this position in *Studying.*

¹⁶⁰See, principally, S. Schulz, *Die Spruchquelle,* pp. 116-117; A. Polag, *Fragmenta Q,* pp. 74-75; I. Havener, *Sayings,* pp. 142-143; and J. Kloppenborg, *Q Parallels,* pp. 180-181.

¹⁶¹Cf. Joseph A. Fitzmyer, *Luke (X-XXIV),* p. 1120, who writes: "in both instances of the Matthean doublet Matthew has secondarily introduced an exceptive clause . . . to meet a new contingency in the early Christian community for which he composed his Gospel—phrases which were scarcely part of the otherwise authentic saying of Jesus prohibiting divorce, ultimately derived from Stage 1 of the gospel tradition."

¹⁶²Of the 216 times that "*anēr*-man" occurs in the New Testament, 27 are in Luke and 100 in Acts. In comparison, the word appears in Matthew and in the Fourth Gospel only eight times each, while in Mark it occurs four times.

¹⁶³Kloppenberg calls this "the generally accepted extent of Q" (*Q Parallels,* p. xxiii). See, for example, Eduard Schweizer who says that Luke 16:18 "is added in its Q form" and Frans Neirynck who speaks of Luke 16:18a as "the more primitive logion." Cf. E. Schweizer, *Luke,* p. 258; F. Neirynck, "De Jezuswoorden," p. 834.

¹⁶⁴For the expressions "commits adultery" (*moicheuei*) and "marries" (*gamōn*), there is agreement upon the choice of word, not upon its inflected form. Neirynck (*Q Synopsis,* pp. 56-57) would note that, in addition, the root *moich-* in the "adultery" of Luke 16:18b is an element that is common to both Matthew and Luke. Hence it, too, deserves to receive the status of minimal Q.

¹⁶⁵So, Siegfried Schulz, I. Howard Marshall, Michael Goulder, C. F. Evans, and Werner Stenger. Cf. S. Schulz, *Die Spruchquelle,* p. 117; I. H. Marshall, *Luke,* p. 631; M. D. Goulder, *Luke,* 2, p. 632; C. F. Evans, *Luke,* p. 609; and W. Stenger, "Zur Rekonstruktion eines Jesusworts," p. 118. In his 1907 study, Adolf von Harnack also opined that this clause did not belong to Q, as did Josef Schmid in his 1930 study of Q (cf. A. Polag, *Fragmenta Q,* 75). Polag, however, followed by Havener, qualifies this clause as an expression that probably belonged to Q. My colleague, Jan Lambrecht, whose working hypothesis is that "Mark used Q" (see J. Lambrecht, "Q-Influence on Mark 8, 34-9, 1," in Jöel Delobel, ed., *Logia: Les paroles de Jésus—The Sayings of Jesus.* BETL, 59 [Louvain: University Press, 1982] pp. 277–304, p. 278), has expressed to me his opinion that the "*kai gamêsê allên*-and marries another" of Mark 10:11 is an indication that reference was made to re-marriage in Q. In addition, he has suggested that the convoluted phrasing of Matt 5:32a (see above, p. 304, nn. 100, 103) may be due to Matthew's omission of "*gamôn*-marries" in his use of Q.

¹⁶⁶Cf. Paul Hoffmann, "Jesu Stellungnahme zur Ehescheidung und ihre Auswirkungen in Urchristentum," in P. Hoffmann—V. Eid, *Jesus von Nazareth und eine christliche Moral.* QD, 66 (Freiburg-Basel-Vienna: Herder, 1975), p. 112. Hoffman, himself, is unsure as to whether or not "and marries another" belongs to the original Q saying (cf. pp. 110, 113).

¹⁶⁷Especially von Harnack and Schulz. Hans-Theo Wrege considers this formulation to be pre-Matthean, but nonetheless secondary. Cf. H.-T. Wrege, *Die Überlieferungsgeschichte,* p. 68.

¹⁶⁸I generally concur with Schulz in this regard. See also Werner Stenger, "Zur Rekonstruktion eines Jesusworts," p. 105. With regard to Exod 20:14, see above, p. 171.

If Matthew's version of the Q saying better reflects the ancient version of the tradition than does Luke's, the early tradition calls to mind the Markan version of the Jesuanic logion in which divorce is castigated as "adultery against her" (Mark 10:11).

Paul Hoffmann, however, thinks that the Matthean formulation is the result of Matthew's editorial work. Since Deut 24:1, to which Matt 5:31 makes reference, speaks of the consequences for the wife who is divorced, so Matt 5:32a takes up the issue of the consequneces of divorce for the divorced wife. Cf. P. Hoffmann, "Jesu Stellungnahme," p. 111.

¹⁶⁹Cf. Matt 5:19, 22, and, especially, 31.

NOTES—CHAPTER 6

¹M. D. Goulder, *Midrash and Lection,* p. 18.

²Nor is it found in 1 Cor 7:10c-11.

³From a text-critical point of view Michael Holmes finds it "amazing that the 'Matthean exception' . . . is not known to occur in any Marcan manuscript." See M. W. Holmes, "Text of the Matthean Divorce Passages," p. 659.

⁴One of the few recent scholars to do so is Abel Isaksson. Cf. A. Isaksson, *Marriage and Ministry,* pp. 72, 74, 102, etc. See also Bruce Vawter, "The Divorce Clauses in Mt 5, 32 and 19, 9," *CBQ* 16 (1954) 155-167, p. 166; Manfred R. Lehmann, "Gen 2, 24 as the Basis for Divorce in Halakhah and New Testament," *ZAW* 72 (1960) 263-267, p. 266; Tarcisio Stramare, "Matteo divorzista?" *Divinitas* 15 (1971) 213-235, pp. 234-235; W. F. Luck, *Marriage and Divorce,* passim. See also Ben Witherington, "Matthew 5.32 and 19.9—Exception or Exceptional Situation," *NTS* 31 (1985) 571-576, p. 572.

⁵This point is strongly urged by E. De La Serna, "¿Divorcio en Mateo?" *passim,* but especially pp. 105-107. De La Serna writes of a "Matthean privilege" (p. 109), parallel to the "Pauline privilege," and of an exception for a local situation (p. 107).

⁶See the earlier discussions of this verb, above, p. 227, n. 208; p. 306, n. 130, and J. Fitzmyer, "The Matthean Divorce Texts," pp. 89-91.

⁷In contrast, "Mrs." designates a female with regard to her marital relationship rather than with regard to her age or maturity.

⁸It occurs only two other times in the New Testament (Acts 26:29 and 2 Cor 11:28).

⁹According to Morgenthaler's statistics, Matthew uses the particle *mê* 129 times and the preposition *epi* 120 times.

¹⁰Cf. Robert Morgenthaler, *Statistik des neutestamentlichen Wortschatzes* (Zurich: Gotthelf, 1958).

¹¹See above, pp. 207-208.

¹²Michael Holmes, "Text of the Matthean Divorce Passages," p. 659, finds it interesting to note that the formulation of the exception clause in Matt 5:32 is without variation.

¹³See the entry *porneia* in BAGD and LSJ as well as Friedrich Hauck and Siegfried Schulz, *"porneia, ktl.,"* *TDNT,* 6, 579-595 and Horst Reisser, *"porneuô,"* in Lothar Coenen, Erich Beyreuther, Hans Bietenhard, eds., *Theologisches Begriffs-lexikon zum Neuen Testament,* 2/2 (Wuppertal: Brockhaus, 1971) pp. 1506-1509.

¹⁴*Porneia* itself is used twenty-five times in the New Testament. Its cognates appear some thirty times.

¹⁵Cf. M. Dumais, "Couple et sexualité selon le Nouveau Testament," *EglT* 8 (1977) 47-72, pp. 48-56.

¹⁶See especially Acts 15:20, 29, but also the discussions on 1 Cor 5:1 and Heb 12:16.

¹⁷One of which is *zânâh* (cf. Jer 2:20; Ezek 16:41; Mic 1:7 [twice]).

¹⁸The NRSV translation of *'erwat dâbâr.* The RSV has "some indecency;" the NAB, "something indecent;" the NJB, "some impropriety;" and the NEB, "something offensive."

¹⁹The formulation of Deut 23:14 is but slightly different, to wit, *aschêmosunê pragmatos.*

[20]The New Testament use of these words is basically Pauline. Apart from Rev 16:15, the root *aschêmon* is found in Rom 1:27 and 1 Cor 7:36; 12:23; 13:5.

[21]Cf. Deut 22:13-21, 22, 23-27, 28-29; 24:5; 25:5-10.

[22]Cf. J. Kravetz, "Divorce in the Jewish Tradition," p. 149; Ulrich Nembach, "Ehescheidung nach alttestamentlichem und jüdischem Recht," *TZ* 26 (1970) 161-171, p. 163; Dale Patrick, *Old Testament Law* (Atlanta: John Knox, 1985) p. 134. Biblical texts which refer to the certificate of divorce mentioned in Deut 24:1 are Jer 3:8, Isa 50:1, and Sir 25:26.

[23]Cf. C. Marucci, *Parole di Gesù*, p. 49.

[24]For an analysis of this text and pertinent bibliography (cf. p. 47, n. 1), see C. Marucci, *Parole di Gesù*, pp. 47-67. In addition to Ludwig Blau's classic analysis of the text and its consequences (*Die jüdische Ehescheidung und der jüdische Scheidungsbrief. Eine historische Untersuchung*, 1, 2. *Jahresbericht der Landes-Rabbinerschule in Budapest für das Schuljahr 1910-1911* [Budapest, 1911, 1912. Republished: Westmead, Gregg, 1970]), see, on the use of the text within Judaism until New Testament times, K. Berger, *Die Gesetzesauslegung*, pp. 509-220.

[25]Cf. Rosario Pius Merendino, *Das deuteronomische Gesetz. Eine literar-kritische, gattungs- und überlieferungsgeschichtliche Untersuchung zu Dt 12-26.* BBB, 31 (Bonn: Hanstein, 1969) p. 297; C. Marucci, *Parole di Gesù*, p. 51.

[26]Cf. S. R. Driver, *A Critical and Exegetical Commentary on Deuteronomy.* ICC (Edinburg: T. & T. Clark, 1895) p. 271; Carl Steurenagel, *Das Deuteronomium.* HAT (Göttingen: Vandenhoeck und Ruprecht, 1898) pp. 87-88; Peter C. Craigie, *The Book of Deuteronomy.* NICOT (Grand Rapids, MI: Eerdmans, 1976) p. 305; A. D. H. Mayes, *Deuteronomy*, p. 322; Joseph Blenkinsopp, "Deuteronomy," NJBC, 94-109, p. 105; Reuven Yaron, "The Restoration of a Marriage," *JJS* 17 (1966) 1-11; D. Patrick, *Old Testament Law*, p. 135; J. Carl Laney, "Deuteronomy 24:1-4 and the Issue of Divorce," *BSac* 149 (1992) 3-15, pp. 5-6.

[27]Cf. Y. Zakovitch, "Woman's Rights," p. 32.

[28]Cf. Josef Blinzler, "Die Strafe für Ehebruch in Bibel und Halacha. Zur Auslegung von Joh. VIII. 5," *NTS* 4 (1957-1958) 32-47; Henry McKeating, "Sanctions Against Adultery in Ancient Israelite Society," *JSOT* 11 (1979) 57-72.

[29]Pace John 7:53-8:11, a late addition to the Fourth Gospel. Cf. E. Lövestam, "Divorce and Remarriage," p. 59.

[30]See *Contra Apion* II, 24: *oudemia thanatou paraitêsis.*

[31]Flavius Josephus interpreted the legislation in this sense: "He who desires to be divorced from the wife who is living with him for whatsoever cause—and with mortals many such may arise—must certify in writing that he will have no further intercourse with her; for thus will the woman obtain the right to consort with another, which thing ere then must not be permitted. But if she be maltreated by the other also or if upon his death her former husband wishes to marry her, she shall not be allowed to return to him." (*Antiquities*, 4, 253). Cf. Jer 3:1.

[32]Yaron and Wenham consider that the reason why a man's resumption of marriage with his former wife, after she had been the wife of another man, is an abomination to the Lord is that it is tantamount to incest. Cf. R. Yaron, "The Restoration

of a Marriage"; G. J. Wenham, "Restoration of Marriage Reconsidered," *JJS* 30 (1979) 36–40; and C. J. Laney, "Deuteronomy 24:1-4," who deals approvingly with Wenham on pp. 10–11, 13. See also ZBG, 458.

[33]In somewhat similar fashion, Matt 5:32, which makes at least oblique reference to Deut 24:1 speaks of a man's responsibilities, but clearly goes beyond what is stipulated in Deut 24:1-4.

[34]Cf. Louis Epstein, *The Jewish Marriage Contract* (reprinted: New York, Arno, 1953) p. 128.

[35]*Śena'* (to hate) and *tarak* (to expel, equivalent to the Hebrew *garash*) are found in the Elephantine divorce lexicon. Yaron is of the opinion that the former, used with respect to both a divorcing husband and a divorcing wife, may have originally expressed the motive for divorce, but it came to acquire the secondary meaning of "divorce." In the marriage contracts, its use allowed for the *formula contraria* (cf. Hos 2:4) to be dispensed with. The technical sense of *śena'* is reflected in such technical expressions as "divorce money" (*kesaf śin'ah*) and "divorce law" (*din śin'ah*). Cf. Reuven Yaron, *Introduction to the Law of the Aramaic Papyri* (Oxford: Clarendon, 1961) p. 55; Bezalel Porten, *Archives from Elephantine: The Life of an Ancient Jewish Military Colony* (Berkeley and Los Angeles: University of California, 1968) p. 210.

[36]Cf. Y. Zakovitch, "Woman's Rights," pp. 34–35.

[37]Cf. Josephus, *Antiquities,* XV, 7, 10. Note the use of the explanatory "*gar*-for."

[38]Biblical warrant for wives leaving their husbands in some circumstances is provided by Exod 21:7-11, but the Bible does not record any case of a wife repudiating her husband.

[39]*Vita,* 75.

[40]See the discussion by Bernadette Brooten in "Frauen," pp. 65–73; "Zur Debatte," pp. 466–478.

[41]See *Antiquities,* XV, 7, 10. Josephus notes that Salome sent "a document" (*grammateion*) to Costobarus. Later in the same passage he writes of Salome having "separated" (*apostēnai*) from her husband. The document in question is likely to have been a certificate of dismissal (the Septuagint's *biblion apostasiou*) which Josephus calls "a written text" (*grammasi*) in *Antiquities,* IV, 8, 23.

[42]Cf. Ernst Bammel, "Markus 10:11f. und das jüdische Eherecht," *ZNW* 61 (1970) 95–101, p. 96. Bammel makes reference to Hans Volkmann's 1935 study, *Zur Rechtsprechung im Principat des Augustus. Historische Beiträge* (Munich: Beck, 1935), p. 151.

[43]See *Antiquities,* XVIII, 5, 4. Cf. Matt 14:3-4; Mark 6:17-18; Luke 3:19.

[44]*Antiquities,* XV, 7, 10. A bit later Josephus adds that Salome "did not choose to follow her country's law but acted on her own authority" (*ou mēn hē Salōmē ton eggenē nomon, alla ton ap' exousias helomenē*). See also *Antiquities,* XVIII, 5, 4: "taking it into her head to flout the way of our fathers" (*epi sunchusei phronēsasa tōn patrōn*).

⁴⁵Among the Elephantine documents, the three marriage contracts included a provision for divorce, but it is not stipulated that a certificate of divorce be written. Cf. E. Bammel, "Das jüdische Eherecht," pp. 96-97; R. Yaron, *Aramaic Papyri*, pp. 53-54; B. Porten, *Archives*, p. 209; E. Lipinski, "The Wife's Right to Divorce," pp. 21-23. Lipinski offers a selective bibliography on the Elephantine marriage texts on p. 21, n. 47.

⁴⁶Cf. R. Yaron, *Aramaic Papyri*, p. 53.

⁴⁷Cf. B. Porten, *Archives*, p. 210.

⁴⁸Ibid., p. 224. These grounds are mentioned in but one of the three extant marriage contracts. Some commentators suggest that "no fault" divorce was essentially the situation envisioned in the contracts.

⁴⁹Cf. *y. ketub.*, 10b; *y. B. Bat.*, 16c.

⁵⁰Cf. E. Bammel, "Das jüdische Eherecht," pp. 96-100, and B. Brooten, "Frauen" pp. 70-71. To a large extent Brooten's work is dependent upon the evidence cited by Bammel. See also Ruthild Geiger, "Die Stellung der geschiedenen Frau in der Umwelt des Neuen Testament," in J. Blank, et al., *Die Frau im Urchristentum*. QD, 95 (Freiburg-Basel-Vienna: Herder, 1983) pp. 134-157, esp. pp. 140-142.

⁵¹The grounds were the physical defects of her husband or his conduct towards her, especially the refusal to have sexual intercourse. Cf. Ben-Zion Schereschewsky, "Divorce," cols. 126-128.

⁵²Cf. Boaz Cohen, "Concerning Divorce in Jewish and Roman Law," *Proceedings of the American Academy for Jewish Research* 21 (1952) 3-34.

⁵³Cf. Mal 2:14-16; Sir 7:26.

⁵⁴Cf. Menachem M. Brayer, "The Role of Jewish Law Pertaining to the Jewish Family, Jewish Marriage and Divorce," pp. 1-43, esp. p. 6, in J. Freid, ed., *Jews and Divorce* (New York: KTAV, 1968); Nathan Goldberg, "The Jewish Attitude Toward Divorce," pp. 44-90, esp. pp. 47-48; and J. Kravetz, "Divorce in the Jewish Tradition," pp. 153-157. See also Y. Zakovitch, "Woman's Rights," pp. 28-46.

⁵⁵Cf. J. Kravetz, "Divorce in the Jewish Tradition," p. 152. D. A. Carson claims, however, that Shammai and his followers interpreted the expression to refer to gross indecency, though not necessarily adultery. Cf. D. A. Carson, "Matthew," p. 411.

⁵⁶Cf. M. N. A. Bockmuehl, "Matthew 5.32; 19.9 in the Light of Pre-rabbinic Halakah," *NTS* 35 (1989) 291-295," p. 291.

⁵⁷Cf. John H. Otwell, *And Sarah Laughed: The Status of Women in the Old Testament* (Philadelphia: Westminster, 1971) p. 121, and Julius Kravetz who comments that: "From this we may infer that divorce was permitted in all other cases." Cf. J. Kravetz, "Divorce in the Jewish Tradition," p. 150.

The two precepts are enumerated as numbers 218 and 219 in the classic list of the 613 commandments. Cf. Abraham Hirsch Rabinowitz, "Commandments, the 613," *EncJud*, 5, 760-783, col. 770.

⁵⁸Cf. Exod 22:16-17. It might be noted that the Exodus formulation seeks to protect the rights of the woman's father, while that of Deuteronomy seems to be more concerned about the woman herself. Cf. Y. Zakovitch, "Woman's Rights," p. 30.

⁵⁹Cf. *m. Yebam.* 14:1. See B.-Z. Schereschewsky, "Divorce," col. 130.

⁶⁰Cf. *m. Ketub.* 4:9.

⁶¹Cf. *m. Giṭ.* 6:2.

⁶²The biblical evidence itself is not entirely clear. In his study of "Divorce in the Jewish tradition," Julius Kravetz has written that in the classic documents of Judaism, one encounters "extreme and contradictory points of view" (p. 149). He further notes that "the Bible records no actual cases, but the statements of Isaiah (50:1), and Jeremiah (3:7-10), indicate clearly that adultery made divorce compulsory where the offence did not lead to the capital punishment of the sinful parties" (p. 150), but also that "an unbiased perusal of the Biblical text shows that divorce was not mandatory" (p. 151).

With regard to Jewish tradition, which was constantly in a state of evolution, it must be noted that not all of the pertinent texts are clear as to the extent of the husband's obligation. Moreover, it is not at all certain that the Talmudic regulations were in force during the first century. In addition, one must ask whether the discipline in force in the Diaspora was the same as the discipline in force in *eretz Israel.*

⁶³Cf. *m. Ketub.* 1:1: "A virgin should be married on a Wednesday and a widow on a Thursday, for in towns the court sits twice in the week, on Mondays and on Thursdays; so that if the husband would lodge a virginity suit he may forthwith go in the morning to the court." Apropos of this passage, Isakkson comments, "a Jewish husband . . . was not to overlook his wife's not having been a virgin but was to accuse her in court and divorce her." Cf. A. Isakkson, *Marriage and Ministry,* p. 137. Rabbinic halakah in regard to this practice as well as with regard to the dismissal of an adulterous wife is pertinent to the interpretation of Matt 1:19 (see the discussion, brief as it is, in Raymond E. Brown, *The Birth of the Messiah: A Commentary on the Infancy Narratives in Matthew and Luke* (Garden City, NY: Doubleday, 1972) p. 128. Matt 1:19 need not detain us here, but it serves as an indication of Matthew's awareness of Jewish procedures on divorce.

⁶⁴Ulrich Nembach cites *m. Ketub.* 7:6; *b. Giṭ.* 90b, *b. Yebam.* 63b, *y. Ketub.* 34b, 52, *y. Giṭ.,* 9, 50d, 29 as indications of this legislation. Cf. U. Nembach, "Ehescheidung," pp. 163-168. See also Sir 7:26 and the pertinent commentary apropos of this text by C. Marucci, *Parole di Gesù,* pp. 93-94.

⁶⁵Cf. B.-Z. Schereschewsky, "Divorce," col. 129. Under rabbinic law, however, she was not allowed to marry the paramour with whom she had committed adultery.

⁶⁶The wife was also allowed to petition the court to compel her husband to divorce her in this situation.

⁶⁷Cf. B.-Z. Schereschewsky, "Divorce," col. 130; "Marriages, Prohibited," *EncJud,* 11, 1051-1054. In the case of those marriages prohibited by Leviticus

18 and that were considered capital crimes in Israel, the marriage was considered to have been null and void. In the case of marriages prohibited by rabbinic law, the marriage was dissolved by the divorce procedure.

⁶⁸Cf. *Shulḥam Arukh,* EH 154:11 and the glosses (*Rema* EH 1:3) by Moses ben Isaac Isserles. The *Shulḥam Arukh* ("The prepared table"), prepared by the medieval halakhist, Joseph ben Ephraim Caro, became the authoritative code of Jewish Law for Orthodox Jewry. See further, B.-Z. Schereschewsky, "Divorce," col. 130.

⁶⁹The Hebrew *zěnût* would normally be rendered as *porneia* in Greek.

⁷⁰Cf. Chaim Rabin, *The Zadokite Documents,* pp. 16–19. The significance of this passage from the Cairo Damascus Document for the understanding of Matthew's exceptive clause was noted as long ago as 1968 by Mariano Diekhans, "Mt 19, 9 (5, 32)" *REB* 28 (1968) 425–427.

⁷¹See not only CD 4:12–5:11 but also 11 Q Temple 57:17-19. See the discussion above, pp. 80–85.

⁷²Cf. Martin Noth, *Leviticus: A Commentary.* OTL (London: SCM, 1965) pp. 132-136.

⁷³Claude Lévi-Strauss has correctly noted that the prohibition of incest is the most universal of marriage regulations. He writes, for example, that "The incest prohibition is not a prohibition like the others. It is *the* [his emphasis] prohibition in the most general form, the one perhaps to which all others . . . are related as particular cases. The incest prohibition is universal like language, . . ." Cf. C. Lévi-Strauss, *The Elementary Structures of Kinship* (rev. ed.: Boston, Beacon, 1969) p. 493.

⁷⁴Cf. A. H. Rabinowitz, "Commandments," col. 782.

⁷⁵The use of the term usually implies sexual intercourse, but not always so (cf. Exod 20:23; Isa 47:3; etc.) Sometimes the term simply suggested improper conduct of a sexual nature.

⁷⁶Cf. B.-Z. Schereschewsky, "Marriages, Prohibited," col. 1052.

⁷⁷Cf. Percy Elwood Corbett, *The Roman Law of Marriage* (2nd. ed.: Aalen, Scientia, 1979) pp. 133-146, esp. p. 142; Joseph Moingt, "Le divorce 'pour motif d'impudicité' (Matthieu 5, 32; 19; 9)" *RSR* 56 (1968) 337-384, pp. 363-364; C. Marucci, *Parole di Gesù,* pp. 383-395.

⁷⁸*Herm. Man.* 4. 1. 5. similarly states that a husband who does not divorce an adulterous wife is an accomplice to her sin.

⁷⁹Cf. B. T. Viviano, "Matthew," p. 631. This description of the nature of the Matthean community merits further analysis, but it is beyond the scope of the present work to enter into a discussion of the various issues. While Matthew's community seems to be Jewish-Christian in its origins, Georg Strecker has systematically exploited its openness to the Gentiles in his *Der Weg der Gerechtigkeit,* as had Wolfgang Trilling in *Das wahre Israel. Studien zur Theologie des Matthäus-Evangeliums* (3rd. ed.: Munich, Kösel, 1964) pp. 124-140. Some elements of the discussion, with particular emphasis on the relationship between Matthew's "church" and the "synagogue" and the ethnic character of the gospel's author,

are discussed, with references, by J. P. Meier, in *Law and History,* pp. 9–21, and *The Vision of Matthew: Christ, Church and Morality in the First Gospel.* Theological Inquiries (New York—Ramsey—Toronto: Paulist, 1978) pp. 15–23.

[80]See also Matt 2:1-12.

[81]Compare, for instance, Matt 21:43 with Mark 12:9-10 (cf. Luke 20:16-17).

[82]See our summary reflections on Matthew's introduction to the antitheses, above, pp. 151–152.

[83]Cf. 1 Thess 4:1-8, with its exhortation to Gentile Christians to abstain from *porneia* (v. 3). Some commentators suggest that this Pauline paraenesis on marriage and sexuality constitutes Paul's response to the lack in the faith of the Thessalonians (cf. 1 Thess 3:10).

[84]Cf. Acts 15:21.

[85]See also Acts 15:20. Cf. Ernst Haenchen, *Acts,* pp. 449, 451; Str-B, 2, p. 729.

[86]Haenchen suggests that Luke might have been describing a living tradition which was probably traced back to the apostles. Cf. E. Haenchen, *Acts,* pp. 470–471.

[87]Cf. George F. Moore, *Judaism.*

[88]J. Gnilka, *Matthäusevangelium,* 1, p. 168.

[89]Surveys of some of the representative literature are offered, among others, by Leopold Sabourin, Emiliano Vallauri and Corrado Marucci. See L. Sabourin, "The Divorce Clauses"; E. Vallauri, "Le clausole matteane sul divorzio. Tendenze esegetiche recenti," *Laurentianum* 17 (1976) 82–112; C. Marucci, *Parole di Gesù,* pp. 333–383; and G. R. Ewald, *Jesus and Divorce.* A 1975 article by Jose Alonso Díaz, provides an historical overview of the situation beginning with an interpretation of Deut 24:1-4 in Judaism. Cf. J. Alonso Díaz, "La indisolubilidad del matrimonio o el divorcio hoy visto por escrituristas y téologos," *Studium Ovetense* 3 (1975) 203–226.

[90]The patristic literature has been thoroughly studied by Henri Crouzel. See, especially, *L'église primitive face au divorce du premier au cinquième siècle.* Théologie historique, 13 (Paris: Beauchesne, 1971); "Le texte patristique;" "La indisolubilidad del matrimonio en los padres de la iglesia," in T. G. Barberena, *El vínculo matrimonial. ¿Divorcio o indisolubilidad?* BAC, 395 (Madrid: La editorial catolica, 1978) pp. 61-116; "Quelques remarques." Cf. Pierre Nautin, "Divorce et remariage dans la tradition de l'église latine," *RSR* 62 (1974) 7–54.

One of the oldest patristic texts to speak about divorce is the Shepherd of Hermas. *Herm. Man.* 4. 1. 6. contains a teaching on divorce that is quite similar to Matt 19:9. The text *requires* a husband to divorce but does not allow him to remarry. The Shepherd, however, does not make any explicit reference to sayings of the Lord.

[91]*Ep.* 77, 3, 1. PL 22, 691.

[92]*De sermone Domini in monte,* 1, 37-50; PL 34, 1247-1255; *De bono conjugali,* 7, 6-7; PL 40, 378-379. Dupont notes that this is the early exegesis of Augustine. Cf. J. Dupont, *Mariage,* p. 137, n. 2.

[93] *Homily on Matt 17:4;* PG 57, 260.

[94] Mark Molldrem notes that the Shepherd interpreted divorce in the situation cited by Matthew as a reference to bed and board separation. Cf. M. J. Molldrem, "A Hermeneutic of Pastoral Care and the Law/ Gospel Paradigm Applied to the Divorce Texts of Scripture," *Int* 45 (1991) 43–54, p. 46.

[95] Cf. H. Crouzel, *L'église primitive,* pp. 24, 267–274, 359 and *passim,* "La indisolubilidad," pp. 104–106; P. Nautin, "Divorce et remariage," pp. 27–30; and Peter J. Huizing, "Huwelijk, scheiding en hertrouw in de oude kerk (eerstevierde eeuw)," in P. J. Huizing, M. J. M. Hageman, et al., *Wat God verbonden heeft . . .: Beschouwingen over Huwelijk, Echtscheiding en Kerkrecht* (Nijmegen: Baarn, 1991) 39–70, p. 45.

The Ambrosiaster is, with the exception of Basil of Caesarea (ca. 330–379), the only Church Father who held that both husband and wife had the right to separate from an adulterous spouse. Nautin believes that the Ambrosiaster was not an innovator in this regard, but that he took the idea from a source which was also used by Hilary. According to Nautin, that source was, most probably, a commentary on Matthew by Victorinus of Pettau.

[96] Fornication, apostasy, and sexual abuse were the reasons which the Ambrosiaster cites as justifying a wife's divorcing her husband. That a wife does not enjoy the right to remarry, as does a husband, is based on Ambrosiaster's interpretation of 1 Cor 7:10–11.

[97] It is noteworthy that an evangelical like William Heth writes: "It is significant that those who had the closest contact with the language and culture of the New Testament did not regard the exception to apply to remarriage." Cf. W. A. Heth, "Divorce, but No Remarriage," in H. Wayne House, ed., *Divorce and Remarriage: Four Christian Views* (Downers Grove, IL: Intervarsity, 1990) pp. 73–129, p. 38.

[98] See J. Dupont, *Mariage,* pp. 136–157; R. Schnackenburg, *The Moral Teaching of the New Testament* (Freiburg: Herder—London: Burns & Oates, 1965) pp. 135–141, esp. p. 141; Gordon J. Wenham, "May Divorced Christians Remarry?" *Churchman* 95 (1981) 150–161; "Matthew and Divorce: An Old Crux Revisited," *JSNT* 22 (1984) 95–107; "The Syntax of Matthew 19.9," *JSNT* 28 (1986) 17–23; W. A. Heth, "Another Look at the Erasmian View of Divorce and Remarriage," *JETS* 25 (1982) 263–272; W. A. Heth and G. J. Wenham, *Jesus and Divorce: The Problem with the Evangelical Consensus* (Nashville, TN: Thomas Nelson, 1985), esp. chapter 6; W. A. Heth, "Divorce, but No Remarriage," esp. pp. 93–107; M. Bockmuehl, "Matthew 5.32; 19.9," p. 295.

Dupont's work was carefully analyzed, and criticized, by Frans Neirynck in "Huwelijk en Echtscheiding in het Evangelie," *Collationes Brugenses et Gandavenses* 6 (1960) 123–130. Wenham's 1981 article, to which David Atkinson responds on pp. 153–162, is essentially a critique of the position systematically developed by Atkinson (no. 2 in our exposition of the various interpretations of the exceptive clause) in *To Have and to Hold: The Marriage Covenant and the Discipline of Divorce* (Grand Rapids, MI: Eerdmans, 1979) pp. 99–133.

[99] Heth spells out "six major reasons" why he does not believe "that Jesus' authoritative pronouncement in Matthew 19:9 was ever intended to single out 'mar-

ital unfaithfulness' or some other sexual sin as the one exception to his absolute prohibition of remarriage after divorce." See "Divorce, but No Remarriage," pp. 94–107.

[100]Cf. J. Dupont, *Mariage,* pp. 143–146.

[101]See, among others, H. G. Coiner, "Those 'Divorce and Remarriage' Passages (Matt. 5:32; 19:9; 1 Cor. 7:10-16), With Brief Reference to the Mark and Luke Passages," *CTM* 39 (1968) 367–384. One should note, in any case, that Matt 5:32b does not explicitly address itself to the issue of a man's second marriage. The only second marriage that is evoked is that of the woman who had been previously married.

[102]See Dupont, *Mariage,* pp. 148–149. The point is also made by Heth and Wenham, *Jesus and Divorce,* p. 118, and by Heth in "Divorce, but No Remarriage," pp. 104–105. The grammatical arguments have been criticized by Phillip H. Wiebe in "Jesus' Divorce Exception," *JETS* 32 (1989) 327–333. The logic of Wiebe's own argumentation was subsequently criticized by Stanley E. Porter and Paul Buchanan in "On the Logical Structure of Matt 19:9," *JETS* 34 (1991) 335–339.

[103]Cf. G. J. Wenham, "Syntax."

[104]Cf. V. Norskov Olsen, *The New Testament Logia on Divorce: A Study of their Interpretation from Erasmus to Milton.* BGBE, 10 (Tübingen: Mohr, 1971).

[105]Horst Reisser states that this is the most common translation of *porneia* in Matthew's exception clauses. Cf. H. Reisser, *"porneuô,"* p. 1508.

Among recent studies, see F. Neirynck, "Het evangelisch Echtscheidingsverbod," *Collationes Brugenses et Gandavenses* 4 (1958) 25–46, esp. pp. 44–46; T. V. Fleming, "Christ and Divorce," *TS* 24 (1963) 106–120, p. 109; Alexander Sand, "Die Unzuchtsklausel in Mt 5, 31, 32 und 19, 3-9," *MTZ* 20 (1969) 118–129; *Matthäus,* pp. 119, 390; K. Haacker, "Ehescheidung;" J. R. W. Stott, "The Biblical Teaching on Divorce," *Churchman* 85 (1971) 165–174; D. Atkinson, *To Have and To Hold,* pp. 99–133; M. D. Goulder, *Midrash and Lection,* p. 18; A. E. Przybyła, "List rozwodowy w prawie Mojzesźa," *Zycie i Myśl* 26 (1976) 54–63; A.-L. Descamps, "New Testament Doctrine," esp. pp. 247–249, 257, 270; Phillip Sigal, *The Halakah of Jesus of Nazareth according to the Gospel of Matthew.* Ph.D. thesis, University of Pittsburgh, 1979, pp. 130–142; Phillip H. Wiebe, "The New Testament on Divorce and Remarriage: Some Logical Implications," *JETS* 24 (1981) 131–138; "Jesus' Divorce Exception," p. 333; Y. Zakovitch, "The Woman's Rights," p. 33; E. Lövestam, "Divorce and Remarriage," pp. 56–61; Gottfried Fitzer, *"Porneia," EWNT,* 3, pp. 328–333, esp. pp. 329–330; W. Stenger, "Zur Rekonstruktion eines Jesusworts," p. 109; U. Luz, *Matthew,* pp. 304–306; C. Marucci, *Parole di Gesù,* pp. 262–406; R. Schnackenburg, *Matthäusevangelium,* 1, p. 57; W. D. Davies and D. C. Allison, *Matthew,* pp. 530–531; J. Gnilka, *Matthäusevangelium,* 1, pp. 168–169; 2, p. 167; E. De La Serna, "¿Divorcio en Mateo?," p. 103; Thomas R. Edgar, "Divorce & Remarriage for Adultery or Desertion," in H. Wayne House, Ed., *Divorce and Remarriage,* pp. 155–169; Craig L. Blomberg, "Marriage, Divorce, Remarriage and Celibacy," *Trinity Journal* 11 (1990) 161–196; etc.

¹⁰⁶Thus, the NIV. Somewhat similar are the translations found in Phillips Modern English ("except on the ground of unfaithfulness") and the Good News Bible ("and she has not been unfaithful").

¹⁰⁷Cf. F. Neirynck, "Het evangelisch Echtscheidingsverbod," p. 45; I. J. du Plessis, "The Ethics of Marriage according to Matt. 5:27-32," *Neot* 1 (1967) 28-34; G. Giavini, "Nuove e vecchie"; Y. Yadin, *The Temple Scroll*, p. 202; M. D. Goulder, *Midrash and Lection*, p. 291; W. D. Davies and D. C. Allison, *Matthew*, p. 530; E. De La Serna, "¿Divorcio en Mateo?," p. 106; D. J. Harrington, *Matthew*, p. 275; etc. Davies-Allison and De La Serna suggest that the option expressed in the exceptive clause is more restrictive than the dominant, Hillelite opinion which countenanced divorce in any number of situations.

¹⁰⁸Cf. Willy Rordorf, "Marriage in the New Testament and in the Early Church," *JEH* 20 (1969) 193-210; M. Christiaens, "Pastoraal van de echtscheiding."

¹⁰⁹See especially C. Marucci, *Parole di Gesù*, pp. 383-395. A. E. Przybyla also writes about a husband's obligation to hand an adulterous wife over to the authorities. Cf. A. E. Przybyla, "List rozwodowy," and C. Sélis, "La répudiation," p. 42.

¹¹⁰Cf. Matt 15:19. Cf. Mark 7:22 (John 8:3).

¹¹¹Cf. J. Bonsirven, *Mariage*, pp. 46-60. He called the exceptive clause a "negative precision." The approach had previously been proposed, but not developed at length, by W. K. Lowther Clarke in "The Excepting Clause in St. Matthew," *Theology* 15 (1927) 161-162, and *New Testament Problems* (New York: Macmillan, 1929) pp. 59-60. A summary of the principal arguments in favor of this interpretation can be found in W. D. Davies and D. C. Allison, *Matthew*, pp. 529-530, but these authors ultimately espouse the Erasmian interpretation.

¹¹²Cf. Acts 15:20, 29; perhaps 1 Cor 5:1 and Heb 12:16 as well.

¹¹³Matt 5:18-19; 7:21; and 22:11-14 seem to indicate that Matthew had to counteract certain laxist tendencies within the community.

¹¹⁴Cf. Heinrich Baltensweiler, "Die Ehebruchklauseln, 340-356; *Die Ehe*, pp. 87-102.

¹¹⁵For example, M. Zerwick, "De matrimonio et divortio in Evangelio," *VD* 4 (1960) 193-212; J. B. Bauer, "De coniugali foedere quid edixerit Matthaeus?" (Mt 5, 31s; 19, 3-9)," *VD* 44 (1966) 74-78; Ralph P. Martin, "St. Matthew's Gospel in Recent Study," *ExpTim* 80 (1969) 132-136, p. 136; E. Danieli, " 'Eccetto in caso di fornicazione' (Mt. 5, 32; 19, 9)," *PalCler* 48 (1969) 1297-1300; F. F. Bruce, *New Testament History* (Garden City, NY: Doubleday, 1969) p. 287; B. Byron, "The Brother or Sister Is Not Bound. Another Look at the New Testament Teaching on the Indissolubility of Marriage," *New Blackfriars* 52 (1971) pp. 514-521; Antonio Vargas-Machuca, "Los casos de 'divorcio' admitidos por S. Mateo (5, 32, y 19, 9). Consecuencias para la teología actual," *EstEcl* 50 (1975) 5-54; "Divorcio e indisolubilidad del matrimonio en la Sagrada Escritura," *EstBib* 39 (1981) 19-61; J. A. Fitzmyer, "The Matthean Divorce Texts;" John P. Meier, *Law and History*, pp. 147-150; *The Vision of Matthew*, pp. 248-257; Jack Dean Kingsbury, *Matthew*. Proclamation Commentaries (Philadelphia: Fortress, 1977) pp. 83-84;

A. Díez Macho, "Cristo instituyo el matrimonio indisoluble," *Sef* 37 (1977) 261-291; *Indisolubilidad,* pp. 217-222, 230-239, 242-251, 252-257; Henry Wansbrough, "Divorce in the New Testament," *Ampleforth Journal* 83 (1978) 57-63; Augustine Stock, "Matthean Divorce Texts," *BTB* 8 (1978) 24-33, esp. pp. 25-28; John R. Donahue, "Divorce: New Testament Perspectives," *Month* 154 (1981) 113-120; Gerard Caron, "Did Jesus Allow Divorce? (Mt. 5:31-32). A Preaching Problem" *AFER* 24 (1982) 309-316; Charles C. Ryrie, "Biblical Teaching on Divorce and Remarriage," *GTJ* 3 (1982) 177-192, esp. pp. 188-189, 191; B. N. Wambacq, "Matthieu 5, 31-32. Possibilité de divorce ou obligation de rompre une union illégitime," *NRT* 104 (1982) 34-49; B. Witherington, "Matthew 5.32 and 19.9'"; D. E. Garland, "A Biblical View," pp. 425-426; B. M. Newman and P. C. Stine, *Matthew,* pp. 145-146; George T. Montague, *Companion God: A Cross-Cultural Commentary on the Gospel of Matthew* (New York—Mahwah: Paulist, 1989) pp. 76-77, 211; S. H. Brooks, *Matthew's Community,* pp. 33, 134; B. T. Viviano, "Matthew," p. 643; C. Sélis, "La répudation," p. 46; etc.

[116]Similarly, Vaccari's "eccetto in caso di concubinato" and Mateos-Camacho's "uníon ilegal." Arguments for this kind of translation are presented in the footnotes to Matt 5:32 by NJB and RNAB and to Matt 19:9 by NAB, NJB, and RNAB, and in J. Mateos-F. Camacho, *Mateo,* pp. 62-63, 190.

[117]"Sauf en cas d'union illégale." The German-language *Einheitübersetzung,* however, translates the clause more generally as "obwohl kein Fall von Unzucht liegt," literally, "provided that there is no situation of unchastity." The *Traduction oecuménique de la Bible* offers the rationale for its translation in a footnote appended to Matt 5:32; but the *Einheitübersetzung* does not justify its translation.

[118]The point is vigorously made by Joseph Fitzmyer in "The Matthean Divorce Texts." See also J. R. Mueller, "Temple Scroll," pp. 255-256.

[119]While that is the specific problem envisaged in Acts 15, it is not certain that this is specifically a problem for Matthew's Jewish Christian community.

[120]Specifically CD 4:19-21; cf. *b. Ketub.* 62b.

[121]M. Diekhans, "Mt 19, 9 (5, 32);" L. Ramaroson, "Une nouvelle interprétation de la 'clausule' de Mt 19, 9," *ScEs* 23 (1971) 247-251.

[122]Cf. T. P. Considine, "Except it be for Fornication," *AusCathRec* 33 (1956) 214-223; A. Mahoney, "A New Look;" A. P. da Silva, "Ainda uma teoria sobre Mt 5, 32 e 19, 9? (No atual debate sobre o divórcio)," *RCB* 11 (1974) 112-119; T. Stramare, "Clausole di Matteo e indissolubilità del matrimonio," *BeO* 17 (1975) 65-74.

[123]Cf. A.-M. Dubarle, "Mariage et divorce dans l'Evangile," *OrSyr* 9 (1964) 61-74, "Les textes évangéliques," p. 343, and H. Reisser, "*porneuô,*" p. 1508, who says that it is not an easy matter to decide between "adultery" and "prostitution" as the correct meaning for *porneia,* even though he eventually opts for "adultery" as the more likely meaning. So far as I have been able to determine, Dubarle's suggestion has not received much backing among exegetes.

[124]Cf. A. Isaksson, *Marriage and Ministry,* pp. 135-141; Mark Geldard, "Jesus' Teaching on Divorce: Thoughts on the Meaning of *porneia* in Matthew 5:32 and 19:9," *Churchman* 92 (1978) 134-143; Marcel Dumais, "Couple et sexualité,"

p. 53; A.-M. Dubarle, "Les textes évangéliques," 335–339. Isaksson's exposition was not only novel but also significant, particularly in the light of his use of Qumran materials. As a result, his work was widely reviewed, most often rather critically. See, for example, the review of Josephine Massingberd Ford in *JTS* 18 (1967) 197–200.

[125]Cf. Albert van Gansewinkel, "Grundsätzliche Unauflösbarkeit," pp. 89–92. Van Gansewinkel argues that Matt 19:3-9 presents indissolubility as God's basic plan for the marriage of the humans whom he has created. There are, however, exceptions, three of which are stipulated in the Scriptures, Deut 24:1-4, 1 Cor 7:15, and Matthew's *porneia,* which van Gansewinkel does not further specify. See further B. W. Powers, "Marriage and Divorce: The Dispute of Jesus with the Pharisees, and its Inception," *Colloquium* 5 (1972) 34–41 and D. A. Carson, "Matthew," pp. 417–418. Powers, criticized by J. D. McCaughey in the same issue of *Colloquium* (pp. 42–43), identifies the Matthean *porneia* with the biblical *'erwat dâbâr,* while Carson does not.

[126]Cf. M. Bockmuehl, "Matthew 5.32; 19.9," p. 295.

[127]According to Carson, Jesus abrogrates Deut 24:1 only insofar as the text was considered to countenance divorce for a reason other than sexual sin. See Carson, "Matthew," pp. 417–418.

[128]J. J. Kilgallen, "The Matthean Exception-Texts," pp. 102–105.

[129]See, especially, Joseph Sickenberger, "Die Unzuchtsklausel im Matthäusevangelium," *TQ* 123 (1942) 189–206, pp. 198–199 and Michael Brunec, "Tertio de clausulis divortii Mt 5, 32 et 19, 9," *VD* 27 (1949) 3–16. Its classic exposition had been developed by Anton Ott in *Die Auslegung der neutestamentlichen Texte über die Ehescheidung.* NTAbh, 3 (Münster: Aschendorff, 1911) pp. 298–299. On pages 230–289 of this work Ott gives a survey of the nineteenth-century positions relative to the exceptive clause. For other references to the inclusive position, see A. Isaksson, *Marriage and Ministry,* p. 129, n. 1.

[130]Cf. A. Ott, *Die Ehescheidung im Matthäusevangelium* (Würzburg: Rita, 1939) pp. 29–30; Bruce Vawter, "The Divorce Clauses," pp. 155–167; "Divorce and the New Testament," *CBQ* 39 (1977) 528–542; reprinted in *The Path of Wisdom: Biblical Investigations.* Background Books, 3 (Wilmington, DE: Glazier, 1986) pp. 238–256; T. V. Fleming "Christ and Divorce," Robert Banks, *Jesus and the Law,* pp. 156–157.

[131]A possibility implied for the exceptive clause in Matt 19:9 by JB and NJB (whose French "prostitution" has been translated into English as "illicit marriage") and for both Matt 5:32 and 19:9 by NAB, which translates the clause as "lewd conduct is a separate case." Somewhat similar is the translation, "no hablo de unión ilegal" found in Juan Mateos and Fernando Camacho, *El Evangelio de Mateo: Lectura comentada* (Madrid: Cristianidad, 1981) p. 189.

[132]Cf. T. V. Fleming, "Christ and Divorce," pp. 111–112.

[133]Thus M'Neille speaks of a gloss, and the footnote to Matt 19:9 in NJB mentions an addition by "one of the last editors." M. R. Lehmann suggests that the excepting clause "is generally considered a scribal gloss which should be disregarded." See M. R. Lehmann, "Gen 2, 24," p. 264. The literature simply does

not support Lehmann's evaluation of the situation. He himself, however, considers that the clause goes back to Jesus and is readily explicable in the light of the Talmudic background on the divorce laws.

[134]See B. Viviano, "Matthew," p. 643, as well as the footnotes to the texts under discussion in NJB and RNAB.

[135]A footnote on Matt 5:32 in the TOB focuses on translation rather than on practice. Matthew's text allows for divorce in the case of *porneia,* for which there are three possible translations: 1) unchastity [leaving the precise forms of unchastity unspecified]; 2) adultery; 3) illicit union [the option chosen for the TOB translation]. Marcel Dumais likewise discusses the possible translations, but considers pre-marital sex (that is, the sexual union of a woman to a man other than her future husband) rather than (the generic) unchastity as one of the possibilities. Cf. M. Dumais, "Couple et sexualité," p. 53.

[136]Interesting, in this regard, is the fact that each of the four latest commentaries on Matthew by German Roman-Catholic authors interpret *porneia* as adultery. See above, note 107, with references to commentaries by Luz (1985), Schnackenburg (1985, 1988), Sand (1986), and Gnilka (1986, 1988).

[137]Unlikely, but not impossible. It would appear that Matthew, whose community included some relatively affluent members, accommodated the first beatitude to fit the needs of his community. Luke's "poor," that is the materially and financially impoverished, have become Matthew's "poor in spirit." Cf. Matt 5:2 and Luke 6:20 (cf. v. 24).

[138]Cf. H.-T. Wrege, *Die Überlieferungsgeschichte,* p. 68; Alexander Sand, "Die Unzuchtsklausel," pp. 127–129.

[139]See above, p. 188.

[140]See above, p. 188.

[141]In Matt 18:23 and 25:19, we have, however, the technical formula *"sunairô logon*-to settle accounts."

[142]There are many phrases that recur in Matthew's gospel in refrain-like fashion. Among those which have already been cited in the present study are "you have heard that it was said" and "let anyone with ears listen!" But there are many others, for example, "the kingdom of heaven is like."

[143]For an analysis of the community's attempt to define itself within this context, see especially J. A. Overman, *Matthew's Gospel and Formative Judaism.*

[144]Many exegetes, as has been already noted, maintain that, according to Matthew's rendition of the conflict with the Pharisees (Matt 19:3-9), the Matthean Jesus did, in fact, side with the Shammaites. They esteem that the formulation of the Pharisees' question in verse 3 is a test in which Jesus is asked to choose between the Hillelites and the Shammaites, and that he eventually sides with the Shammaites. D. A. Carson, however, opines that "on any understanding of what Jesus says . . ., he agrees with neither Shammai nor Hillel." Cf. D. A. Carson, "Matthew," p. 411.

[145]According to the Mishnah, "the essential formula in the bill of divorce is, 'Lo, thou art free to marry any man' " (*m. Giṭ.* 9:3). Even though the marriage

contracts from Elephantine do not explicitly mention a certificate of divorce, the divorce provisions of these contracts also speak of a divorced woman's freedom to marry. Cf. R. Yaron, *Aramaic Papyri*, p. 64. These provisions are comparable to those found in the Code of Hammurabi and various Assyrian laws. Cf. ANET pp. 172, 183.

[146]Note that in both Matt 19:3-9 and Matt 5:31-32 (cf. v. 20) Matthew presents Jesus' teaching on divorce as a contrast to the Pharisees behavioral norm in this regard. David Hill notes that in some Pharisaic circles, the frequency of divorce was an open scandal. Cf. David Hill, *The Gospel of Matthew*. NCB (London: Oliphants, 1972) p. 280.

[147]See above, pp. 207-208.

[148]I use this term in contradistinction to "Jewish-Christian." The latter makes reference to Christians with a Jewish heritage, both ethnic and religious, but whose distinctiveness from Judaism is manifest. "Christian-Jewish" makes reference to Jews who acknowledged Jesus as Messiah, that is, Christians of Jewish heritage prior to the separation between church and synagogue.

[149]Cf. *m. Sota* 5:1, "she is forbidden to the husband." See K. Berger, *Die Gesetzesauslegung*, p. 567; D. Hill, *Matthew*, p. 281; U. Luz, *Matthew*, p. 275; R. Schnackenburg, *Matthäusevangelium*, 1, p. 57. Luz cites not only *m. Sota* 5:1 but also *b. Git.* 90b and Wis 18:22 in evidence. Comp. Matt 1:19. It is also possible that a man who had not fathered a child within ten years of marriage also believed that he was duty-bound to divorce his wife and, in that case, to marry another.

[150]Cf. A. Sand, *Matthäus*, pp. 116, 390. Note that *y. Qidd.* 1:1, commentating on Gen 2:24, articulates the views of some ten rabbis to the effect that God granted the right to divorce only to Israel. Within Christianity, *Herm. Man.* 4. 1. 5-6 required a husband to divorce an adulterous wife, but did not allow him to remarry.

[151]See the brief discussion by Angelo P. O'Hagan in "Divorce—Marriage in tension with this Age," *SBibFrLA* 22 (1972) 95-108, esp. pp. 99-102.

[152]Cf. Matt 13:52.

[153]Cf. Josephus, *Antiquities*, IV, 8, 24; Matt 19:3.

[154]Pace Isaksson who states that "we have been unable to find in the rabbinic literature any example of the word *zenût* being used to denote adultery" (*Marriage and Ministry*, p. 134, n 1), Lövestam demonstrates that the verb with its derivatives is frequently used to connote adultery and cites *t. Sota* 6a, 6b, 10a; *t. Qidd.* 66a; *t. Yebam.* 11b, 38b, 56b; *Num. Rab.* 9:6, 25a; 9:9, 26a; *t. Ketub.* 44b, 46a, 81a, 101a; *t. Šabb.* 88b; *t. Sanh.* 50b; *Sipra* 21:9 (94c) and *Sipre Deut* 22:1 (118a) as examples. Cf. E. Lövestam, "Divorce and Remarriage," p. 58.

NOTES—CHAPTER 7

¹On the criterion of dual exclusion, see my *Introduction,* pp. 181–182. For a more extended presentation of these criteria, with bibliographic references, see Edward Schillebeeckx, *Jesus: An Experiment in Christology* (New York: Cross-road, 1979) pp. 88–98. For a nuanced reflection on the criteria, see Ben F. Meyer, *The Aims of Jesus* (London: SCM, 1979) pp. 86–87 and J. P. Meier, *A Marginal Jew,* pp.167–195.

²Cf. R. H. Fuller, "The Decalogue," p. 250, who writes: "The multiple attestation of this tradition and its consistency with Jesus' characteristic radicalism argues for its authenticity."

³Cf. E. P. Sanders and M. Davies, *Studying,* p. 328.

⁴Ibid.

⁵That is, as attested by Matt 5:31-32; Luke 16:18; 1 Cor 7:10-11.

⁶That is, Matt 19:3-12 and Mark 10:2-12.

⁷Ibid. [His emphasis].

⁸Cf. J. Jeremias, *The Proclamation of Jesus,* p. 225. See also Berndt Schaller, "Ehescheidung und Wiederheirat," pp. 226–246; David R. Catchpole, "The Synoptic Divorce Material as a Traditio-Historical Problem," *BJRL* 57 (1974) 92–127; R. Trevijano Etcheverría, "Matrimonio y divorcio en Mc 10, 2-12 y par.," *Burgense* 18 (1977) 113–151, p. 123; E. Schweizer, *Matthew,* pp. 123–124; J. Gnilka, *Matthäusevangelium,* 1, pp. 165, 170; etc.

There are, of course, specific configurations within this general approach. Catchpole, for example, begins with 1) Mark 10:9 as the simplest of all the forms of the saying; 2) 1 Cor 7:10b, 11b as the next most simple form; 3) the rulings of Mark 10:11-12 (including v. 12, see, p. 111) on which 4) Matt 19:9 is dependent; 5) Luke 16:18; of which 6) Matt 5:32 is secondary. Schweizer identifies seven stages in the development of the tradition: 1) the apodictic logion of Mark 10:9; 2) its reformulation as a legal dictum (Mark 10:11); 3) its extension to women (Mark 10:12; 1 Cor 7:10-11); 4) an exception for mixed marriages (1 Cor 7:12-16); 5) the prohibition against remarriage (Mark 10:11-12; 6) the possibility of dissolution of a mixed marriage; and 7) the Matthean exception.

⁹Cf. H. Baltensweiler, *Die Ehe,* pp. 60–64; H.-T. Wrege, *Die Überlieferungsgeshichte,* p. 67 (at least for Luke 16:18a); A. Stock, "Matthean Divorce Texts," p. 24; P. Hoffmann, "Jesu Stellungnahme," p. 113; J. A. Fitzmyer, (*Luke X-XXIV*), p. 1120.

¹⁰G. Lohfink, "Jesus und die Ehescheidung," p. 208.

¹¹Cf. U. Luz, *Matthew,* p. 280.

¹²Cf. A. Isaksson, *Marriage and Ministry,* pp. 72–104, 102.

¹³Cf. Mark 10:12.

¹⁴Cf. Y. Zakovitch, "Woman's Rights," p. 33 and Gerhard Delling, "Das Logion Markus 10, 11 und seine Abwandlungen im Neuen Testament," in *Stu-*

dien zum Neuen Testament und zum hellenistischen Judentum. Gesammelte Aufsätze 1950–1968 (Göttingen: Vandenhoeck und Ruprecht, 1970), pp. 226–235, esp. pp. 228–229. Apparently Zakovitch would claim that Mark's two-part statement (Mark 10:11-12) represents the older tradition, but he does not explicitly so state. Most New Testament scholars, on the other hand, think that Mark 10:12 is a Markan adaptation of the tradition. Cf., for example, W. Stenger, "Zur Rekonstruktion eines Jesusworts," p. 106.

[15]According to Stenger, the "another" of Matt 19:9 no longer refers to the divorcée (as in Matt 5:32, Luke 16:18 and Q). Cf. W. Stenger, "Zur Rekonstruction eines Jesusworts," p. 109.

[16]See Stenger's schema, "Zur Rekonstruction eines Jesusworts," p. 118.

[17]With regard to the discussion about which of the various New Testament versions of the Jesuanic logion is the most primitive, Ulrich Luz candidly states that the candidacy of Mark 10:11 is the most improbable. Cf. U. Luz, *Matthew,* p. 279.

[18]Harvey correctly notes that Jesus did not intend to utter a rule or a law, but that the logion on divorce "was almost immediately appropriated as a rule for the Christian community." Cf. A. E. Harvey, *Strenuous Commands,* pp. 85, 83.

[19]My colleague, Jan Lambrecht, Walter Schmithals and Wolfgang Schenk are among a relatively small number of contemporary authors who hold that Mark made use of Q. Their theory has been vigorously combatted by Frans Neirynck in "Recent Developments in the Study of Q," in Jöel Delobel, *Logia: Les paroles de Jésus—The Sayings of Jesus.* BETL, 59 (Louvain: University Press, 1982) pp. 29-75, esp. pp. 41-53. Among these authors, only Schmithals has specifically addressed the issue of the dependence of Mark 10:11 on Q in print. Cf. W. Schmithals, *Das Evangelium nach Markus. Kapitel 9, 2-16, 20.* Ökumenischer Taschenbuchkommentar zum Neuen Testament, 2/2 (Gütersloh: Mohn— Würzburg: Echter, 1979) pp. 441-442. Schmithals' hypothesis is that the Q-saying was "Whoever divorces his wife and marries another commits adultery; whoever marries a divorcée commits adultery."

The critical question is whether Mark was familiar with documentary Q or whether he was aware of traditional sayings of Jesus, which were eventually collated, perhaps with some editorial modification, in documentary Q. I believe that the latter hypothesis is more likely.

[20]Cf. R. A. Edwards, *A Theology of Q.*

[21]Cf. Luke 24:19.

[22]Cf. John 1:45; 6:14; Matt 21:11; Luke 24:19; Acts 3:22.

[23]Cf. John F. O'Grady, *The Four Gospels and the Jesus Tradition* (New York— Mahwah: Paulist, 1989) p. 19.

[24]Cf. Matt 14:3-12; Mark 6:17-29; Luke 3:19-20.

[25]"Herodias took upon her to confound the laws of our country, and divorce herself from her husband, while he was alive, and was married to Herod, her husband's brother by the father's side" (*Antiquities of the Jews* XVIII, 6, 4).

[26]See, especially, Matthew who places the same call to repentence on the lips of John the Baptist (Matt 3:2) and Jesus (Matt 4:17).

²⁷There are, in fact, some authors who view such criticism as an historical situation behind the Pharisees' provocative question in Mark 10:2, especially since Mark presents the Pharisees as being in collusion with the Herodians in a plot to kill Jesus (cf. Mark 3:6). See, for example, W. L. Lane, *Commentary on the Gospel of Mark.* NICNT (Grand Rapids, MI: Eerdmans, 1974), p. 374, and R. W. Herron, "Mark's Jesus," pp. 276-277.

I have already presented my reasons for suggesting that the conflict story of Mark 10:2-9 is a Markan literary creation and so would not want to draw the plot against Jesus (Mark 3:6), the prophetic criticism of Antipas (Mark 6:18), and the Pharisees' question (Mark 10:2) into a tight relationship. However, the prophetic criticism of Antipas suggests an historical setting in which Jesus, the prophet, might have uttered a criticism of divorce.

²⁸See above, pp. 179-183. My argument at that point was developed on literary rather than on historical grounds.

²⁹Cf. Mark 10:2; Matt 14:4; 19:3.

³⁰Admittedly it took generations for the distinctive contours of the church to emerge, particularly with regard to its mixed nature (Jew and Gentile), its historicity (as a result of the so-called delay of the Parousia), and its distinctiveness from Judaism (as a result of the separation from the synagogue, to which the First and Fourth Gospels give ample witness), but these are issues which cannot be properly treated within the present study.

³¹Cf. Matt 13:1-9; Luke 8:4-8.

³²Cf. Matt 13:18-23; Luke 8:11-15.

³³Note the motif of eschatological reversal in the corresponding woe (Luke 6:24).

³⁴From a different vantage point, Heinrich Baltensweiler has also argued that Jesus' utterances in this regard were re-interpreted by the early church. In Baltensweiler's opinion, Jesus himself demonstrated a fair amount of freedom in contrast to the sexual rigorism of his day, but the later church took a more narrow position. In its theological reflection it also linked the marriage between Christians to the Christ event itself. See H. Baltensweiler, "Ehe und Partnerschaft—biblisch gesehen," *Kirchenblatt für die reformierte Schweiz* 137 (1981) 150-151.

³⁵Cf. my *Studies,* pp. 304, 324.

³⁶See Yarbrough's *Not Like Gentiles.*

³⁷Cf. Lev 18:2-3, 24-25, 27-28.

³⁸See, for example, the discussion of James D. G. Dunn, "Jesus and Ritual Purity: A Study of the Tradition History of Mk 7, 15," in *À cause de l'Évangile. Études sur les Synoptiques et les Actes* offertes au P. Jacques Dupont, O.S.B. à l'occasion de son 70e anniversaire. LD, 123 (Paris: Cerf, 1985) pp. 251-276.

³⁹Cf. my "House Churches," pp. 43-44.

⁴⁰Cf. B. Cohen, "Concerning Divorce."

⁴¹Cf. B. Brooten, "Frauen;" "Zur Debatte."

⁴²The extension of the prohibition to women has the allure of casuistry which, in my judgment, precludes the application of the saying to women as part of the earliest formulation of the Jesuanic logion.

⁴³One might presumably argue, however, that it is the whole process, i.e., divorce with remarriage, which is considered adulterous.

⁴⁴It is quite possible that the Markan "against her" (*ep'autên*, Mark 10:11) is a redactional attempt to stipulate that divorce itself is comparable to adultery.

⁴⁵See above, p. 217.

⁴⁶Cf. Matt 19:9. See also Luke 16:18, with regard to which a number of authors have suggested that "and marries another" is an addition to the Q-tradition, perhaps under the influence of Luke's reading of Mark. See above, p. 182, and p. 309, note 165.

⁴⁷The version of the saying in Mark 10:11-12 then becomes similar to that of Luke 16:18. Mark 10:12, however, states that a woman who divorces her husband and remarries commits adultery, whereas Luke 16:18b says that it is the man who marries the divorced woman who commits adultery.

⁴⁸On the importance of "one flesh" in early Christian tradition, cf. B. Kaye, "One Flesh" and Marriage," *Colloquium* 22 (1990) 46-57 and Stephen Francis Miletic, *'One Flesh': Eph. 5.22-24, 5.31. Marriage and the New Creation.* AnBib, 115 (Rome: Pontifical Biblical Institute, 1988).

⁴⁹Cf. John 13:35.

⁵⁰There is also the problematic case of the wife who had not borne children. Under Talmudic Law, divorce followed by the husband's marriage to another woman was the norm. Under the Law, a man who divorced his wife because of childlessness would marry another who, presumably, would bear him a child and thereby enable him to fulfill the command of Gen 1:28.

⁵¹The setting which Mark 10:10 provides for the logion of 11-12 is another clear example of the early church's wrestling with the significance of the saying.

⁵²Cf. *Herm, Man.* IV, 29. See the pertinent commentary by Henri Crouzel, "La indisolubilidad," pp. 72-74.

Select Bibliography

Abrahams, Israel. *Studies in Pharisaism and the Gospels*, 1. Cambridge: University Press, 1917.

Adinolfi, Mario. "Il Celibato di Gesù," *BeO* 13 (1971) 145-158.

Adinolfi, Mario. "Il matrimonio nella libertà dell'etica escatologica di 1 Cor. 7," *Anton* 51 (1976) 133-169.

Adinolfi, Mario. "Il ripudio secondo Mal 2, 14-16," *BeO* 12 (1970) 247-256.

Adinolfi, Mario. "Motivi parenetici del matrimonio e del celibato in 1 Cor. 7," *RivB* 26 (1978) 71-91.

Aland, Kurt. *Did the Early Church Baptize Infants?* The Library of History and Doctrine. London: SCM, 1963.

Albertz, Martin. *Die synoptischen Streitgespräche. Ein Beitrag zur Formgeschichte des Urchristentums.* Berlin: Trowitzsch, 1921.

Albright, W. F. and C. S. Mann, *Matthew: Introduction, Translation, and Notes.* AB, 26. Garden City: Doubleday, 1971.

Allo, E.-B. *Saint Paul: première épître aux Corinthiens.* EBib. 2nd. ed.: Paris, Lacoffre, 1956.

Alonso Díaz, Jose. "La indisolubilidad del matrimonio o el divorcio hoy visto por escrituristas y téologos," *Studium Ovetense* 3 (1975) 203-226.

Alt, Albrecht. "The Origins of Israelite Law," in *Essays on Old Testament History and Religion.* Garden City: Doubleday, 1967, pp. 79-103.

Alter, Robert and Frank Kermode, eds. *The Literary Guide to the Bible*. Cambridge: Harvard University Press, 1987.

Ambrozic, Aloysius M. "Indissolubility of Marriage in the New Testament: Law or Ideal?" *Studia Canonica* 6 (1972) 269–288.

Amusin, J. D. *Kumranskaja obš ina*. Moscow: Izdatel'stvo 'Nauka', 1983.

Arendzen, John P. "Ante-Nicene Interpretations of the Sayings on Divorce," *JTS* 20 (1919) 230–241.

Atkinson, David. *To Have and to Hold: The Marriage Covenant and the Discipline of Divorce*. Grand Rapids: Eerdmans, 1979.

Baarda, T., A. F. J. Klijn, and W. C. van Unnik. *Miscellanea neotestamentica*. NovTSup, 48. Leiden: Brill, 1978.

Baasland, Ernst. "Die *perî*-Formel und die Argumentation (ssituation) des Paulus," *Studia Theologica* 42 (1988) 69–87.

Baillet, M., et al. *Les "petites grottes" de Qumran: Planches*. DJD, 3. Oxford: Clarendon, 1962.

Baillet M., J. T. Milik and R. de Vaux, eds., *Les "petites grottes" de Qumran*. DJD, 3. Oxford: Clarendon, 1962.

Balch, David L. "1 Cor 7:32–35 and Stoic Debates about Marriage, Anxiety, and Distraction," *JBL* 102 (1983) 429–439.

Balch, David L. "Backgrounds of I Cor. vii: Sayings of the Lord in Q; Moses as an Ascetic *theos anêr* in II Cor. iii," *NTS* 18 (1972) 351–364.

Balducelli, Roger. "The Decision for Celibacy," *TS* 36 (1975) 219–242.

Baltensweiler, Heinrich. "Die Ehebruchklauseln bei Matthäus," *TZ* 15 (1959) 340–356.

Baltensweiler, Heinrich. *Die Ehe im Neuen Testament: Exegetische Untersuchungen über Ehe, Ehelosigkeit und Ehescheidung*. ATANT, 52. Zurich: Zwingli, 1967.

Baltensweiler, Heinrich. "Ehe und Partnerschaft—biblisch gesehen," *Kirchenblatt für die reformierte Schweiz* 137 (1981) 150–151.

Balz, Horst. "*hagios*, etc.," *EDNT*, 1, 16–20.

Bammel, Ernst. "Markus 10:11f. und das jüdische Eherecht," *ZNW* 61 (1970) 95–101.

Banks, Robert. *Jesus and the Law in the Synoptic Tradition*. SNTSMS, 28. Cambridge: University Press, 1975.

Barberena, Tomas Garcia. *El vínculo matrimonial. ¿Divorcio o indisolubilidad?* BAC, 395. Madrid: La editorial catolica, 1978.

Bard, Terry R. "Julius Kaplan, Hyman Klein, and the Saboraic Element," in J. Neusner, ed., *The Formation of the Babylonian Talmud,* pp. 61–74.

Barni, L. "Il recente dibattito sul 'logion' degli eunuchi (Mt 19, 10-12)," *StudPat* 34 (1987) 129–151.

Barrett, C. K. *A Commentary on the First Letter to the Corinthians.* HNTC. New York: Harper & Row, 1968.

Barth, Gerhard. "Matthew's Understanding of the Law," in G. Bornkamm, et al., *Tradition and Interpretation in Matthew,* pp. 58–164.

Barthélemy, Dominique and J. T. Milik, eds. *Qumran Cave I.* DJD, 1. Oxford: Clarendon, 1955.

Bauer, Johannes B. "Bemerkungen zu den matthäischen Unzuchtsklauseln (Mt 5, 32; 19, 9)," in J. Zmijewski and E. Nellessen, eds., *Begegnung mit dem Wort,* pp. 23–33.

Bauer, Johannes B. "De coniugali foedere quid edixerit Matthaeus?" (Mt 5, 31 s; 19, 3-9)," *VD* 44 (1966) 74–78.

Bauer, Walter. "Matth. 19, 12 und die alten Schriften," in *Neutestamentliche Studien Georg Heinrici zu seinem 70. Geburtstag dargebracht von Fachgenossen, Freunden und Schülern.* UNT, 6. Leipzig: Hinrichs, 1914, pp. 235–244.

Baumert, Norbert. "Brautwerbung—das einheitliche Thema von 1 Thess 4, 3-8," in R. F. Collins, ed., *The Thessalonian Correspondence,* pp. 316–339.

Baumert, Norbert. *Ehelosigkeit und Ehe im Herrn: Eine Neuinterpretation von 1 Kor 7.* FB, 47. Würzburg: Echter, 1984.

Baumgarten, Joseph M. *Studies in Qumran Law.* SJLA, 24. Leiden: Brill, 1977.

Beasley-Murray, G. R. *Baptism in the New Testament.* London: Macmillan, 1963.

Behm, Johannes. "*sklêrokardia,*" *TDNT,* 3, 613–614.

Bellinzoni, Arthur J. *The Sayings of Jesus in the Writings of Justin Martyr.* NovTSup, 17. Leiden: Brill, 1967.

Benoit, Pierre and Boismard, Marie-Emile. *Synopse des Quatre Evangiles en français.* Paris: Cerf, 1980.

Berger, Klaus. *Die Gesetzesauslegung Jesu: Ihr historischer Hintergrund im Judentum und im Alten Testament,* 1: *Markus und Parallelen.* WMANT, 40 (Neukirchen-Vluyn: Neukirchener Verlag, 1972) VIII: "*Ehescheidung und Ehebruch,*" pp. 508–575.

Berger, Klaus. "Hartherzigkeit und Gottes Gesetz. Die Vorgeschichte des antijüdischen Vorwurfs in Mc 10:5," *ZNW* 61 (1970) 1–47.

Best, Ernest. "1 Corinthians 7:14 and Children in the Church," *IBS* 4 (1990) 158–166.

Betz, Hans Dieter. *Galatians: A Commentary on Paul's Letter to the Church in Galatia.* Hermeneia. Philadelphia: Fortress, 1979.

Beyer, Klaus. *Semitische Syntax im Neuen Testament.* SUNT, 1. Göttingen: Vandenhoeck und Ruprecht, 1962.

Black, Matthew and Georg Fohrer, eds. *In Memoriam Paul Kahle.* BZAW, 103. Berlin: Topelmann, 1968.

Blackman, Philip. *Mishnayoth, 3: Order Nashim.* London: Mishna, 1953.

Blank, Josef, et al. *Die Frau im Urchristentum.* QD, 95. Freiburg-Basel-Vienna: Herder, 1983.

Blau, Ludwig. *Die jüdische Ehescheidung und der jüdische Scheidungsbrief. Eine historische Untersuchung,* 1, 2. *Jahresbericht der Landes-Rabbinerschule in Budapest für das Schuljahr 1910–1911.* Budapest, 1911, 1912. Republished: Westmead, Gregg, 1970.

Blenkinsopp, Joseph. "Deuteronomy," NJBC, 94–109.

Blinzler, Josef, *"Eisin eunouchoi:* Zur Auslegung von Mt 19 12," *ZNW* 48 (1957) 254–270; revised, and with an additional bibliographic note, as " 'Zur Ehe unfähig . . .' "—Auslegung von Mt 19, 12," in J. Blinzler, *Aus der Welt und Umwelt des Neuen Testaments. Gesammelte Aufsätze,* 1 (Stuttgart: Katholisches Bibelwerk, 1969) pp. 20–40.

Blinzler, Josef. "Justinus Apol. I, 15, 4 und Matthäus 19, 11-12," in A. Descamps and A. de Halleux, eds., *Melanges bibliques en hommage au R. P. Béda Rigaux* (Gembloux: Duculot, 1970) 45–55.

Blinzler, Josef. "Die Strafe für Ehebruch in Bibel und Halacha. Zur Auslegung von Joh. VIII. 5," *NTS* 4 (1957–1958) 32–47.

Blinzler, Josef. "Zur Auslegung von I Kor 7, 14," in J. Blinzler, O. Kuss, and F. Mussner, eds., *Neutestamentliche Aufsätze. Festschrift für Prof. Josef Schmid zum 70. Geburtstag.* Regensburg: Pustet, 1963, pp. 23–41; reprinted, with an additional bibliographic note, as "Die 'Heiligkeit' der Kinder in der alten Kirche—Zur Auslegung von 1 Kor 7, 14," in *Aus der Welt und Umwelt des Neuen Testaments. Gesammelte Aufsätze,* 1. Stuttgart: Katholisches Bibelwerk, 1969, pp. 158–184.

Blomberg, Craig L. "Marriage, Divorce, Remarriage and Celibacy," *Trinity Journal* 11 (1990) 161–196.

x

Blum, William. *Forms of Marriage: Monogamy Reconsidered.* Spearhead, 106–108. Eldorat: AMECEA Publications, 1989.

Bockmuehl, M. N. A. "Matthew 5.32; 19.9 in the Light of Pre-rabbinic Halakah," *NTS* 35 (1989) 291–295.

Bonsirven, Joseph. *Le divorce dans le Nouveau Testament.* Paris: Desclée, 1948.

Boring, Eugene. "How May We Identify Oracles of Christian Prophets in the Synoptic Tradition? Mark 3:28-29 as a Test Case," *JBL* 91 (1972) 501–521.

Bornkamm, Gerhard, Gerhard Barth, and H. J. Held, *Tradition and Interpretation in Matthew.* NTL. London: SCM, 1963.

Bourgeault, Guy. "Fidelité conjugale et divorce. Essai de théologie biblique," *ScEs* 24 (1972) 155–175.

Bouwman, Gijs. *"epitrepô,"* *EDNT*, 2, 43–44.

Bouwman, Gijs. "Paulus en het celibaat," *Bijdragen* 37 (1976) 379–390.

Branick, Vincent. *House Church in the Writings of Paul.* Zacchaeus Studies: New Testament. Wilmington: Glazier, 1989.

Bratcher, Robert G. *A Translator's Guide to the Gospel of Matthew.* Helps for Translators. London-New York: United Bible Societies, 1981.

Bratcher, Robert G. and Eugene A. Nida. *A Translator's Handbook on the Gospel of Mark.* Helps for Translators, 2. Leiden: Brill, 1961.

Braun, Herbert. *Spätjüdisch-häretischer und frühchristlicher Radikalismus,* 2. BHT, 24. Tübingen: Mohr, 1957.

Brayer, Menachem M. "The Role of Jewish Law Pertaining to the Jewish Family, Jewish Marriage and Divorce," in J. Freid, ed., *Jews and Divorce,* pp. 1–43.

Brooke, George J., ed. *Temple Scroll Studies.* JSOTSup, 7. Sheffield: JSOT, 1989.

Brooks, Stephenson H. *Matthew's Community: The Evidence of His Special Sayings Material.* JSNTSup, 16. Sheffield: JSOT, 1987.

Brooten, Bernadette, "Konnten Frauen im alten Judentum die Scheidung betreiben? Überlegungen zu Mk 10, 11-12 und 1 Kor 7, 10-11," *EvT* 42 (1982) 65–80.

Brooten, Bernadette, "Zur Debatte über das Scheidungsrecht der jüdischen Frau," *EvT* 43 (1983) 466–478.

Brown, Raymond E. *The Birth of the Messiah: A Commentary on the Infancy Narratives in Matthew and Luke.* Garden City: Doubleday, 1977.

Bruce, F. F. *1 & 2 Corinthians*. NCB, London: Oliphants, 1971.

Bruce, F. F. *New Testament History*. Garden City: Doubleday, 1969.

Brunec, Michael. "Tertio de clausulis divortii Mt 5, 32 et 19, 9," *VD* 27 (1949) 3-16.

Bultmann, Rudolf. *"aphiêmi, ktl,"* *TDNT,* 1, pp. 509-512.

Bultmann, Rudolf. *The History of the Synoptic Tradition*. Oxford: Basil Blackwell, 1963.

Burggraeve, Roger. "The Radicalness of the Gospel and the Necessity for a Reflective Ethics of Peace: In Search of the Specificity of Ethical Pronouncements in the New Testament," in R. Burggraeve and Marc Vervenne, eds., *Swords into Plowshares: Theological Reflections on Peace*. LTPM, 8. Louvain: Peeters—Grand Rapids: Eerdmans, 1991.

Burkill, T. A. "Two into One: The Notion of Carnal Union in Mark 10:8; 1 Cor. 6:16; Eph. 5:31," *ZNW* 62 (1971) 115-120.

Burkitt, F. C. "The Hebrew Papyrus of the Ten Commandments," *JQR* 15 (1903) 392-408.

Byron, Brian. "1 Cor 7:10-15: A Basis for Future Catholic Discipline on Marriage and Divorce?" TS 34 (1973) 429-445.

Byron, Brian. "The Brother or Sister Is Not Bound: Another Look at the New Testament Teaching on the Indissolubility of Marriage," *New Blackfriars* 52 (1971) 514-521.

Byron, Brian. "General Theology of Marriage in the New Testament and 1 Cor. 7:15," *AusCR* 49 (1972) 1-10.

Cambier, J.-M. "Doctrine paulinienne du mariage chrétien. Etude critique de 1 Co 7 et Ep 5, 21-33 et essai de leur traduction actuelle," *EglTh* 10 (1979) 13-59.

Caron, Gerard. "Did Jesus Allow Divorce? (Mt. 5:31-32). A Preaching Problem," *AFER* 24 (1982) 309-316.

Carras, George P. "Jewish Ethics and Gentile Converts: Remarks on 1 Thes 4,3-8," in R. F. Collins, ed., *The Thessalonian Correspondence,* pp. 306-315.

Carson, D. A. "Matthew," in *The Expositor's Bible Commentary,* 8. Regency Reference Library. Grand Rapids: Zondervan, 1984, pp. 1-599.

Catchpole, David R. "The Synoptic Divorce Material as a Traditio-Historical Problem," *BJRL* 57 (1974) 92-127.

Catlidge, D. R. "1 Corinthians 7 as a Foundation for a Christian Sex Ethic," *JR* 55 (1975) 220-234.

Cazelles, Henri, "Mariage dans le N.T., I: la doctrine paulinienne," *DBSup,* 5, 928-931.

Cazelles, Henri, ed. *La vie de la Parole: De l'Ancien au Nouveau Testament. Etudes d'exégèse et d'hermeneutique bibliques offertes à Pierre Grelot.* Paris: Desclée, 1987.

Christiaens, Marc. "Pastoraal van de echtscheiding volgens Matteüs. Vragen rond de 'ontuchtclausule' " *TvT* 23 (1983) 3-23.

Clancy, J. B. "Liberating the Chained: Jesus' Attitude Toward Divorce," *Daughters of Sarah* 15 (1989) 10-13.

Clarke, W. K. Lowther. "The Excepting Clause in St Matthew," *Theology* 15 (1927) 161-162.

Clarke, W. K. Lowther. *New Testament Problems.* New York: Macmillan, 1929.

Cohen, Boaz. "Concerning Divorce in Jewish and Roman Law," *Proceedings of the American Academy for Jewish Research* 21 (1952) 3-34.

Coiner, H. G. "Those 'Divorce and Remarriage' Passages (Matt. 5:32; 19:9; 1 Cor. 7:10-16), With Brief Reference to the Mark and Luke Passages," *CTM* 39 (1968) 367-384.

Collins, Raymond F. *Christian Morality: Biblical Foundations.* Notre Dame: Notre Dame University, 1986.

Collins, Raymond F. "House Churches in Early Christianity," *Tripod* 55 (1990) 38-44.

Collins, Raymond F. *Introduction to the New Testament.* Garden City: Doubleday, 1983.

Collins, Raymond F. *Letters That Paul Did Not Write: The Epistle to the Hebrews and the Pauline Pseudepigrapha.* GNS, 28. Wilmington: Glazier, 1988.

Collins, Raymond F. *Studies on the First Letter to the Thessalonians.* BETL, 66. Louvain: University Press, 1984.

Collins, Raymond F. *These Things Have Been Written: Studies on the Fourth Gospel.* LTPM, 2. Louvain: Peeters—Grand Rapids: Eerdmans, 1990.

Collins, Raymond F., ed., *The Thessalonian Correspondence,* BETL, 87. Louvain: University Press, 1990.

Condon, Kevin. "Apropos of the Divorce Sayings," *IBS* 2 (1980) 40-51.

Conrad, Edgar W. and Edward G. Newing, eds., *Perspectives on Language and Text: Essays and Poems in Honor of Francis I. Andersen's Sixtieth Birthday.* Winona Lake, Ind.: Eisenbrauns, 1987.

Considine, Thomas P. "Except it be for Fornication," *AusCR* 33 (1956) 214–223.

Considine, Thomas P. "The Pauline Privilege (Further examination of 1 Cor. vii, 12-7)," *AusCR* 40 (1963) 107–119.

Conzelmann, Hans. *A Commentary on the First Epistle to the Corinthians*. Hermeneia. Philadelphia: Fortress, 1975.

Corbett, Percy Elwood. *The Roman Law of Marriage*. 2nd. ed.: Aalen, Scientia, 1979.

Coté, Pierre-René. "Les eunuques pour le Royaume (Mt 19,12)," *EglT* 17 (1986) 321–334.

Countryman, L. William. *Dirt, Greed & Sex: Sexual Ethics in the New Testament and their Implications for Today*. London: SCM, 1989.

Craigie, Peter C. *The Book of Deuteronomy*. NICOT. Grand Rapids: Eerdmans, 1976.

Creed, J. M. *The Gospel According to St. Luke: The Greek Text with Introduction, Notes and Indices*. London: Macmillan, 1930.

Crouzel, Henri. *L'église primitive face au divorce du premier au cinquième siècle*. Théologie historique, 13. Paris: Beauchesne, 1971.

Crouzel, Henri. "La indisolubilidad del matrimonio en los padres de la iglesia," in T. G. Barberena, ed., *El vínculo matrimonial,* pp. 61–116.

Crouzel, Henri. "Quelques remarques conçernant le texte patristique de Mt 19, 9," *BLE* 82 (1981) 83–92.

Crouzel, Henri. "Le texte patristique de Matthieu v. 32 et xix. 9," *NTS* 19 (1972) 98–119.

Cullmann, Oscar. *Le baptême des enfants et la doctrine biblique du baptême*. Cahiers théologiques de l'actualité protestante, 19/20. Neuchatel-Paris: Delachaux & Niestlé, 1948.

Cullmann, Oscar. *Baptism in the New Testament*. SBT, 1. Chicago: Regnery, 1950.

Daly, Robert J., ed. *Christian Biblical Ethics. From Biblical Revelation to Contemporary Christian Praxis: Method and Content*. New York—Ramsey, N.J.: Paulist, 1984.

Danby, Herbert. *The Mishnah Translated from the Hebrew with Introduction and Brief Explanatory Notes*. Oxford: Clarendon, 1933.

D'Angelo, Mary Rose. "Remarriage and the Divorce Sayings Attributed to Jesus," in W. P. Roberts, ed., *Divorce and Remarriage,* pp. 78–106.

da Silva, A. P. "Ainda uma teoria sobre Mt 5, 32 e 19, 9? (No atual debate sobre o divórcio)," *RCB* 11 (1974) 112–119.

Daniel, Constantin. "Esséniens et eunuques (Matthieu 19.10-12)," *RevQ* 6 (1968) 353–390.

Danieli, E. "Eccetto in caso di fornicazione" (Mt. 5, 32; 19, 9)," *PalCler* 48 (1969) 1297–1300.

Danker, Frederick W. "Hardness of Heart: A Study in Biblical Thematic," *CTM* 44 (1973) 89–100.

Daube, David. *The New Testament and Rabbinic Judaism.* London: Athione, 1956.

Daube, David. "Pauline Contributions to a Pluralistic Culture: Recreation and Beyond," in D. G. Miller and D. Y. Hadidian, eds., *Jesus and Man's Hope*, 2, pp. 223–245.

David, Jakob and Franz Schmalz, eds. *Wie unauflösich ist die Ehe? Eine Dokumentation.* Aschaffenburg: Pattloch, 1969.

Davies, Philip R. *The Damascus Covenant: An Interpretation of the "Damascus Document."* JSOTSup, 25. Sheffield: JSOT, 1983.

Davies, W. D. and Dale C. Allison. *A Critical and Exegetical Commentary on the Gospel According to Matthew*, 1. ICC. Edinburgh: T. & T. Clark, 1988.

Davies, W. D. *The Setting of the Sermon on the Mount.* Cambridge: University Press, 1966.

Dawes, Gregory W. " 'But if you can gain your freedom' (1 Corinthians 7:17-24)," *CBQ* 52 (1990) 681–697.

De La Serna, Eduardo. "¿Divorcio en Mateo?" *RevistB* 51 (1989) 91–110.

Delling, Gerhard. "Das Logion Markus 10, 11 und seine Abwandlungen im Neuen Testament," *NovT* 2 (1958) 92–115; reprinted in *Studien zum Neuen Testament*, pp. 226–235.

Delling, Gerhard. "Nun aber sind sie heilig," in *Gott und die Götter. Festgabe für Erich Fasser zum 60. Geburtstag.* Berlin: Evangelische Verlagsanstalt, 1958, pp. 84–93; reprinted in *Studien zum Neuen Testament*, pp. 257–269.

Delling, Gerhard. "Lexikalisches zu *teknon*," in . . . *und fragten nach Jesus: Beiträge aus Theologie, Kirche und Geschichte. Festschrift für Erich Barnikol zum 70. Geburtstag.* Berlin: Evangelische Verlagsanstalt, 1964, pp. 35–44; reprinted in *Studien zum Neuen Testament*, pp. 270–280.

Delling, Gerhard. *Studien zum Neuen Testament und zum hellenistischen Judentum. Gesammelte Aufsätze 1950-1968.* Göttingen: Vandenhoeck & Ruprecht, 1970.

Delling, Gerhard. "Zur Exegese von I. Kor. 7, 14," in *Studien zum Neuen Testament,* pp. 281-287.

Delobel, Jöel, ed. *Etudes de critique textuelle du Nouveau Testament.* BETL, 78. Louvain: University Press, 1987.

Delobel, Jöel, ed., *Logia: Les paroles de Jésus—The Sayings of Jesus.* BETL, 59. Louvain: University Press, 1982.

Delorme, J. "Le mariage, les enfants et les disciples de Jésus. Mc 10, 2-16," *AsSeign* 58 (1974) 42-51.

de Merode de Croy, Marie. "The Role of Woman in the Old Testament," *Concilium* 16 (1980) 71-80.

Deming, Will. "Mark 9.42-10.12, Matthew 5.27-32, and *B. Nid.* 13b: A First-Century Discussion of Male Sexuality," *NTS* 36 (1990) 130-141.

Derrett, J. Duncan M. "The Teaching of Jesus on Marriage and Divorce," in *Law in the New Testament.* London: Darton, Longman & Todd, 1970, pp. 363-388.

Descamps, A.-L. "Les textes évangéliques sur le mariage," *RTL* 9 (1978) 258-286; 11 (1980) 5-50; reprinted in *Jésus et l'église. Etudes d'exégèse et de théologie.* BETL, 77 (Louvain: University Press, 1987) pp. 510-583; translated as "The New Testament Doctrine on Marriage," in R. Malone and J. R. Connery, eds., *Contemporary Perspectives on Christian Marriage,* pp. 217-273, 347-363.

Dexinger, Ferdinand. "Der Dekalog im Judentum," *BLit* 59 (1986) 86-95.

Dibelius, Martin. *From Tradition to Gospel.* New York: Scribner's, n.d.

Diderichsen, Borge Krag. *Den markianske skilsmisserperikope: Dens genesis og historiske placering.* Aarhuus: Gyldendal, 1962.

Diekhans, Mariano. "Mt 19, 9 (5, 32)" *REB* 28 (1968) 425-427.

Díez Macho, Alejandro. "Cristo instituyo el matrimonio indisoluble," *Sef* 37 (1977) 261-291.

Díez Macho, Alejandro. *Indisolubilidad del matrimonio y divorcio en la biblia. La sexualidad en la biblia.* Madrid: Fe catolica, 1978.

Dinter, P. E. "Disabled for the Kingdom: Celibacy, Scripture & Tradition," *Commonweal* 117 (1990) 570-577.

Dodd, C. H. *The Parables of the Kingdom.* London: Nisbet, 1935.

Donahue, J. R. "Divorce: New Testament Perspectives," *Month* 154 (1981) 113-120.

Doyle, Thomas P., ed. *Marriage Studies, 3: Reflections in Canon Law and Theology.* Washington: Canon Law Society of America, 1985.

Draisma, Sipke, ed. *Intertextuality in Biblical Writings: Essays in honour of Bas van Iersel.* Kampen: Kok, 1989.

Driver, S. R. *A Critical and Exegetical Commentary on Deuteronomy.* ICC. Edinburgh: T. & T. Clark, 1895.

du Plessis, I. J. "The Ethics of Marriage according to Matt. 5:27-32," *Neot* 1 (1967) 28-34.

Dubarle, A.-M. "Mariage et divorce dans l'Évangile," *OrSyr* 9 (1964) 61-74.

Dubarle, A.-M. "Les textes évangéliques sur le mariage et le divorce," in H. Cazelles, ed., *La vie de la Parole,* pp. 333-344.

Dulau, P. "The Pauline Privilege is it promulgated in the first Epistle to the Corinthians?" *CBQ* 13 (1951) 146-152.

Dumais, Marcel. "Couple et sexualité selon le Nouveau Testament," *EglT* 8 (1977) 47-72.

Dungan, David L. *The Sayings of Jesus in the Churches of Paul: The Use of the Synoptic Tradition in the Regulation of Early Church Life.* Oxford: Blackwell—Philadelphia: Fortress, 1971.

Dunn, James D. G. "Jesus and Ritual Purity: A Study of the Tradition History of Mk 7, 15," in *À cause de l'Évangile. Études sur les Synoptiques et les Actes offertes au P. Jacques Dupont, O.S.B., à l'occasion de son 70e anniversaire.* LD, 123. Paris: Cerf, 1985.

Duplacy, Jean. "Notes sur les variantes et le texte original de Matthieu 19, 9," in J. Delobel, ed., *Études de critique textuelle,* pp. 387-412.

Dupont, Jacques. *Les béatitudes,* 3. EBib. Paris: Gabalda, 1973.

Dupont, Jacques, ed. *Jésus aux origines de la christologie.* BETL, 40. New expanded edition: Louvain, University Press, 1989.

Dupont, Jacques. *Mariage et divorce dans l'évangile: Matthieu 19, 3-12 et parallèles.* Bruges: Desclée de Brouwer, 1959.

Durrwell, F. X. "Indissoluble et destructible mariage," *Revue de droit canonique* 36 (1986) 214-242.

Easton, B. S. *The Gospel according to St. Luke: A Critical and Exegetical Commentary.* Edinburgh: Clark, 1926.

Easton, B. S. "New Testament Ethical Lists," *JBL* 51 (1932) 1-12.

Edgar, Thomas R. "Divorce & Remarriage for Adultery or Desertion," in H. Wayne House, ed., *Divorce and Remarriage,* pp. 155-169.

Edgar, W. "Le divorce et le remariage," *RevRef* 36 (1985) 185-202.

Edwards, Richard A. *A Theology of Q: Eschatology, Prophecy, and Wisdom.* Philadelphia: Fortress, 1976.

Ellingworth, P. "Text and Context in Mark 10:2, 10," *JSNT* 5 (1979) 63–66.

Elliott, J. K., "Paul's Teaching on Marriage in I Corinthians: Some Problems Considered," *NTS* 19 (1972–73) 219–225.

Ellis, W. G., "A Scriptural Viewpoint on Divorce," *ThEd* 38 (1988) 33–40.

Epstein, Louis. *The Jewish Marriage Contract.* New York: Jewish Theological Seminary of America, 1927; reprinted, New York: Arno, 1973.

Epstein, Louis M. *Sex Laws and Customs in Judaism.* New York: KTAV, 1967.

Erdmann, Walter. *Die Ehe im alten Griechenland.* Munich: Beck, 1934.

Evans, C. F. *Saint Luke.* TPINTC. London: SCM—Philadelphia: Trinity Press International, 1990.

Ewald, George R. *Jesus and Divorce: A Biblical Guide for Ministry to Divorced Persons.* Waterloo, Ont.—Scottdale, Penn.: Herald, 1991.

Farla, Piet. "The two shall become one flesh:" Gen. 1.27 amd 2.24 in the New Testament Marriage Texts," in S. Draisma, ed., *Intertextuality in Biblical Writings,* pp. 67–82.

Fascher, Erich. *Der erste Brief des Paulus an die Korinther.* THKNT, 7/1. Berlin: Evangelische Verlagsanstalt, 1975.

Fee, Gordon D. "1 Corinthians 7:1 in the *NIV,*" *JETS* 23 (1980) 293–302.

Fee, Gordon D. *The First Epistle to the Corinthians.* NICNT. Grand Rapids: Eerdmans, 1987.

Feuillet, André. "L'indissolubilité du mariage et le monde féminin d'après la doctrine évangélique et quelques autres données bibliques parallèles," *ScrTh* 17 (1985) 415–461.

Filson, Floyd V. "Broken Patterns in the Gospel of Matthew," *JBL* 75 (1956) 227–231.

Firmage, Edwin B., Bernard G. Weiss and John W. Welch, eds., *Religion and Law: Biblical-Judaic and Islamic Perspectives.* Winona Lake, Ind.: Eisenbrauns, 1990.

Fischer, James A. "1 Cor. 7:8-24—Marriage and Divorce," *BR* 23 (1978) 26–36; reprinted in R. J. Daly, ed., *Christian Biblical Ethics,* pp. 245–255.

Fitzer, Gottfried. *"Porneia,"* *EWNT,* 3, 328–333.

Fitzmyer, Joseph A. "Divorce among First-Century Palestinian Jews," in *H. L. Ginsberg Volume.* ErIsr, 14 (Jerusalem: Israel Exploration Society, 1978) pp. 103*-110*, 193.

Fitzmyer, Joseph A. *The Gospel According to Luke,* AB, 28, 28A. Garden City: Doubleday, 1981, 1985.

Fitzmyer, Joseph A. *Luke the Theologian: Aspects of His Teaching.* New York-Mahwah: Paulist, 1989.

Fitzmyer, Joseph A., "The Matthean Divorce Texts and Some New Palestinian Evidence," *TS* 37 (1976) 197–226; reprinted in *To Advance the Gospel: New Testament Essays.* New York: Crossroad, 1981, pp. 79–111.

Fitzmyer, Joseph A. "Paul," *NJBC,* 1329–1337.

Fitzmyer, Joseph A. "Pauline Theology," *NJBC,* 1382–1416.

Fjärstedt, Biörn. "Fråga och svar i Matt. 19, 3-12," *SEA* 33 (1968) 118–140.

Fleming, Thomas V. "Christ and Divorce," *TS* 24 (1963) 106–120.

Foerster, Werner. *"Eirênê,"* TDNT, 2, 400–420.

Ford, Josephine Massyngberde. " 'Hast Thou Tithed Thy Meal?' and 'Is Thy Child Kosher?' " (1 Cor. x. 27 ff and 1 Cor. vii, 14), *JTS* 17 (1966) 71–79.

Ford, Josephine Massyngberde. *A Trilogy on Wisdom and Celibacy.* Notre Dame: Notre Dame University Press, 1967.

Forster, Edward Morgan. *Aspects of the Novel.* Reprinted: New York, Penguin, 1962.

Freid, Jacob, ed., *Jews and Divorce.* New York: KTAV, 1968.

Friedman, Mordechai A. "Divorce upon the Wife's Demand as Reflected in Manuscripts from the Cairo Genizah," *The Jewish Law Annual* 4 (1981) 103–126.

Fuller, Reginald. "The Decalogue in the New Testament," *Int* 43 (1989) 243–255.

Furnish, Victor P. *The Moral Teaching of Paul.* 2nd. rev. ed.: Nashville: Abingdon, 1985.

Furnish, Victor P. *Theology and Ethics in Paul.* Nashville, New York: Abingdon, 1968.

Furnish, Victor Paul. "Der 'Wille Gottes' in paulinischer Sicht," in D. A. Koch, et al., *Jesu Rede von Gott,* pp. 208–221.

Galot, Jean. "La motivation évangélique du célibat," *Greg* 53 (1972) 731–758.

Gamba, G. G. "La 'eunuchia' per il Regno dei Cieli. Annotazioni in margine a Matteo 19, 10–12," *Salesianum* 42 (1980) 243–287.

Garland, David E. "A Biblical View of Divorce," *RevExp* 84 (1987) 419–432.

Garland, David E. "The Christian's Posture Toward Marriage and Celibacy: 1 Corinthians 7," *RevExp* 80 (1983) 351–362.

Gaster, Theodor H. *The Dead Sea Scriptures in English Translation with Introduction and Notes.* 3rd. ed.: Garden City, Doubleday, 1976.

Geiger, Ruthild. "Die Stellung der geschiedenen Frau in der Umwelt des Neuen Testaments," in J. Blank, et al., *Die Frau im Urchristentum,* pp. 134–157.

Geldard, Mark. "Jesus' Teaching on Divorce: Thoughts on the Meaning of *porneia* in Matthew 5:32 and 19:9," *Churchman* 92 (1978) 134–143.

Gerhardsson, Birger. *Memory and Manuscript: Oral Tradition and Written Transmission in Rabbinic Judaism and Early Christianity.* ASNU, 22. Lund: Gleerup, 1961.

Gerstenberger, Erhard S. and Wolfgang Schrage. *Frau und Mann.* Kohlhammer Taschenbücher: Biblische Konfrontationen, 1013. Stuttgart: Kohlhammer, 1980.

Giavini, G. "I Cor. 7: nuove ricerche. Matrimoni misti e 'privilegio paolino,'" *ScuolCatt* 108 (1980) 255–263.

Giavini, G. "Nuove e vecchie vie per la lettura delle clausole di Matteo sul divorzio," *ScuolCatt* 99 (1971) 83–93.

Giblin, C. H. "1 Corinthians 7—a Negative Theology of Marriage and Celibacy?" *TBT* 41 (1969) 2839–2855.

Gnilka, Joachim. *Das Evangelium nach Markus (Mk 8, 27-16, 20).* EKKNT 2/2. Zurich: Benziger—Neukirchen-Vluyn: Neukirchener Verlag, 1979.

Gnilka, Joachim. *Das Matthäusevangelium.* HTKNT 1/1, 2. Freiburg-Basel-Vienna: Herder, 1986, 1988.

Goehring, James E., et al. *Gospel Origins & Christian Beginnings: In Honor of James M. Robinson.* Sonoma, CA: Polebridge, 1990.

Goldberg, Nathan. "The Jewish Attitude Toward Divorce," in J. Freid, ed., *Jews and Divorce,* pp. 44–90.

Goldenberg, Robert. "B. M. Lewin and the Saboraic Element," in J. Neusner, ed., *The Formation of the Babylonian Talmud,* pp. 51–60.

Gooch, P. W. "Authority and Justification in Theological Ethics: A Study in 1 Corinthians 7," *Journal of Religious Ethics* 11 (1983) 62–74.

Goulder, Michael D. *Luke—A New Paradigm,* 2. JSNTSup, 20. Sheffield: JSOT, 1989.

Goulder, Michael D. *Midrash and Lection in Matthew.* London: SPCK, 1974.

Green, Barbara. "Jesus' Teaching on Divorce in the Gospel of Mark," *JSNT* 38 (1990) 67–75.

Greenfield, G. "Paul and the Eschatological Marriage," *SWJT* 26 (1983) 32–48.

Greeven, Heinrich. "Ehe nach dem Neuen Testament," *NTS* 15 (1969) 365–388; also published in G. Krems and R. Mumm, eds., *Theologie der Ehe.* Regensburg: Pustct, 1969, pp. 37–79.

Grundmann, Walter. *Das Evangelium nach Matthäus.* THKNT, 1. Berlin: Evangelische Verlagsanstalt, 1968.

Guelich, Robert A. "The Antitheses of Matthew v. 21–48: Traditional and/or Redactional," *NTS* 22 (1975–1976) 444–457.

Guelich, Robert A. *The Sermon on the Mount: A Foundation for Understanding.* Waco: Word, 1982.

Gundry, R. H. *The Use of the Old Testament in Matthew's Gospel with Special Reference to the Messianic Hope.* NTSup, 18. Leiden: Brill, 1967.

Guthrie, Donald. *New Testament Introduction.* 4th. rev. ed.: Downers Grove, Ill.: Intervarsity, 1990.

Haacker, Klaus. "Ehescheidung und Wiederverheiratung im Neuen Testament," *TQ* 151 (1971) 28–38.

Haenchen, Ernst. *The Acts of the Apostles: A Commentary.* Oxford: Basil Blackwell, 1971.

Häring, Bernard. *No Way Out? Pastoral Care of the Divorced and Remarried.* London: St. Paul Publications, 1989.

Harrington, Daniel J. *The Gospel of Matthew.* Sacra Pagina, 1. Collegeville: The Liturgical Press, 1991.

Harrington, Wilfrid J. "Jesus' Attitude Towards Divorce," *ITQ* 37 (1970) 199–209.

Harrington, Wilfrid J. "The New Testament and Divorce," *ITQ* 39 (1972) 178–187.

Harrison, A. R. W. *The Law of Athens: The Family and Property.* Oxford: Clarendon, 1968.

Hartin, Patrick J. *James and the Q Sayings of Jesus.* JSOTSup, 47. Sheffield: JSOT, 1991.

Hartin, Patrick J. "James and the Q Sermon on the Mount/Plain," in David J. Lull, ed., *Society of Biblical Literature 1989 Seminar Papers.* Atlanta: Scholars, 1989, pp. 440–456.

Harvey, A. E. *Strenuous Commands: The Ethic of Jesus.* London: SCM.—Philadelphia: Trinity International, 1990.

Hasler, Victor. *"eirênê, ktl.," EDNT,* 1, 394–397.

Hauck, Friedrich and Siegfried Schulz. *"Porneia, ktl.," TDNT,* 6, 579–595.

Haudebert, P. "Abrogation ou accomplissement de la loi mosäique? (Luc 16, 16-18)," *Impacts* 4 (1984) 15–26.

Havener, Ivan. *Q: The Sayings of Jesus.* GNS, 19. Wilmington: Glazier, 1987.

Hemelsoet, Ben. "Créé à l'image de Dieu: la question du divorce dans Marc X," in T. Baarda, et al., *Miscellanea neotestamentica,* pp. 49–57.

Herron, Robert W., Jr. "Mark's Jesus on Divorce: Mark 10:1-12 Reconsidered," *JETS* 25 (1982) 273–281.

Heth, William Alexander. "Another Look at the Erasmian View of Divorce and Remarriage," *JETS* 25 (1982) 263–272.

Heth, William Alexander. "Divorce, but No Remarriage," in H. W. House, ed., *Divorce and Remarriage,* pp. 73–129.

Heth, William Alexander and Gordon J. Wenham. *Jesus and Divorce: Towards an Evangelical Understanding of New Testament Teaching.* London: Hodder & Stoughton, 1984.

Heth, William Alexander. *Matthew's "Eunuch Saying" (19:12) and Its Relationship to Paul's Teaching on Singleness in 1 Corinthians 7.* Dallas Theological Seminary doctoral dissertation, 1986 (Ann Arbor: U. of Michigan, 1987).

Heth, William Alexander. "The Meaning of Divorce in Matthew 19:3-9," *Churchman* 98 (1984) 136–152.

Heth, William Alexander. "Unmarried 'for the Sake of the Kingdom' (Matthew 19:12) in the Early Church," *GTJ* 8 (1987) 55–88.

Heylen, Victor., ed. *Mislukt huwelijk en echtscheiding: Een multidisciplinaire verkenning.* Sociologische Verkenningen, 2. Louvain: University Press, 1972.

Hill, David. *The Gospel of Matthew.* NCB. London: Oliphants, 1972.

Hobbs, T. R. "Jeremiah 3, 1-5 and Deuteronomy 24,1-4," *ZAW* 86 (1974) 23-29.

Hoffmann, Paul. "Jesu Stellungnahme zur Ehescheidung und ihre Auswirkungen im Urchristentum," in P. Hoffmann and Volker Eid, *Jesus von Nazareth und eine christliche Moral.* QD, 66. Freiburg-Basel-Vienna: Herder, 1975, pp. 109-131.

Hoffmann, Paul. *Studien zur Theologie der Logienquelle.* NTAbh, NF, 8. Münster: Aschendorff, 1972.

Holmes, Michael W. "The Text of the Matthean Divorce Passages: A Comment on the Appeal to Harmonization in Textual Decisions," *JBL* 109 (1990) 651-664.

Holwerda, D. E. "Jesus on Divorce: An Assessment of a New Proposal," *CTJ* 22 (1987) 114-120.

Hoose, B. "Imitating Jesus and Allowing Divorce," *Priests & People* 1 (1987) 210-212.

Horsley, Richard A. *Sociology and the Jesus Movement.* New York: Crossroad, 1989.

House, H. Wayne, ed. *Divorce and Remarriage: Four Christian Views.* Downers Grove, Ill.: Intervarsity, 1990.

Huizing, Peter J., M. J. M. Hageman, et al., *Wat God verbonden heeft . . . : Beschouwingen over Huwelijk, Echtscheiding en Kerkrecht.* Nijmegen: Baarn, 1991.

Hultgren, Arland J. *Jesus and His Adversaries: The Form and Function of the Conflict Stories in the Synoptic Tradition.* Minneapolis: Augsburg, 1979.

Hurd, J. C, Jr. *The Origin of 1 Corinthians.* London: SPCK, 1965.

Hutter, Manfred. "Das Ehebruch-Verbot im altorientalischen und alttestamentlichen Zusammenhang," *BLit* 59 (1986) 96-104.

Isaksson, Abel. *Marriage and Ministry in the New Temple: A Study with Special Reference to Mt 19.3-12 and 1 Cor. 11.3-16.* Lund: Gleerup, 1965.

Jeremias, Joachim. *Infant Baptism in the First Four Centuries.* The Library of History and Doctrine. London: SCM, 1960.

Jeremias, Joachim. *Jerusalem in the Time of Jesus: An Investigation into Economic and Social Conditions during the New Testament Period.* London: SCM, 1969.

Jeremias, Joachim. "Die missionarische Aufgabe in der Mischehe (1.Kor. 7, 16)," in *Neutestamentliche Studien für Rudolf Bultmann zum siebzigsten Geburtstag.* BZNW, 21 (Berlin: Töpelmann, 1954) pp. 255–260; reprinted in *Abba: Studien zur neutestamentlichen Theologie und Zeitgeschichte.* Göttingen: Vandenhoeck und Ruprecht, 1966, pp. 292–298.

Jeremias, Joachim. *New Testament Theology,* 1: *The Proclamation of Jesus.* NTL. London: SCM, 1971.

Jeremias, Joachim. *The Origins of Infant Baptism: A Further Study in Reply to Kurt Aland.* SHT, 1. Naperville, Ill.: Allenson, 1963.

Jeremias, Joachim. *The Parables of Jesus.* Rev. ed.: London, SCM, 1963.

Jewett, Robert. *A Chronology of Paul's Life.* Philadelphia: Fortress, 1979.

Johnson, Luke Timothy. *The Gospel of Luke.* Sacra Pagina, 3. Collegeville: The Liturgical Press, 1991.

Johnson, Sherman E. "The Gospel According to Matthew," *IB,* 7, p. 482.

Jones, F. Stanley. *"Freiheit" in den Briefen des Apostels Paulus: Eine historische, exegetische und religionsgeschichtliche Studie.* GTA, 34. Göttingen: Vandenhoeck & Ruprecht, 1987.

Kähler, Else. *Die Frau in den paulinischen Briefen: unter Berücksichtigung des Begriffes der Unterordnung.* Zurich: Gotthelf, 1960.

Kamlah, Erhard. *Die Form der katalogischen Paränese im Neuen Testament.* WUNT, 7. Tübingen: Mohr, 1964.

Kapera, Zdzislaw J. "A Review of East European Studies on the Temple Scroll," in G. J. Brooke, ed., *Temple Scroll Studies,* pp. 275–286.

Karpiński, R. "Nierozerwalność małżeństwa w Nowym Testameńcie. Mt 5, 32 i 19, 9," *RuchBLit* 18 (1965) 77–88.

Käsemann, Ernst. "Sentences of Holy Law in the New Testament," in *New Testament Questions of Today.* NTL. Philadelphia: Fortress—London: SCM, 1969, pp. 66–81.

Kaser, Max. *Das römische Privatrecht.* 2nd. ed.: Munich, Beck, 1971; *Roman Private Law.* 3rd. ed.: Pretoria, University of South Africa, 1980.

Katz, Peter. "Mark 10, 11 Once Again," *BT* 11 (1960) 152.

Kaye, B. " 'One Flesh' and Marriage," *Colloquium* 22 (1990) 46–57.

Kennedy, George A. *New Testament Interpretation Through Rhetorical Criticism.* Chapel Hill, NC—London: University of North Carolina Press, 1984.

Kerber, Walter, ed. *Sittliche Normen: zum Problem ihrer allgemeinen und unwandelbaren Geltung.* Düsseldorf: Patmos, 1982.

Kermode, Frank. "Matthew" in R. Alter and F. Kermode, eds., *The Literary Guide to the Bible.* Cambridge: Harvard University, 1987, pp. 307–401.

Ketter, Peter. " 'Nicht alle fassen dieses Wort.' Bemerkungen zu Mt 19, 10-12," *Pastor bonus* 49 (1938-39) 311-323.

Kilgallen, John J. "To What are the Matthean Exception-Texts (5, 32 and 19, 9) an Exception?" *Bib* 61 (1980) 102-105.

Kilpatrick, George D. *The Origins of the Gospel According to St. Matthew.* Oxford: Clarendon, 1946.

Kingsbury, Jack Dean. *Matthew.* Proclamation Commentaries. Philadelphia: Fortress, 1977.

Kingsbury, Jack Dean. *Matthew as Story.* 2nd. rev. ed.: Philadelphia: Fortress, 1988.

Kirchschläger, Walter. *Ehe und Ehescheidung im Neuen Testament. Überlegungen und Anfragen zur Praxis der Kirche.* Vienna: Herold, 1987.

Kirchschläger, Walter. "Ehe und Ehescheidung—Rückfragen an Bibel und Kirche," *Diakonia* 19 (1988) 305-316.

Kissinger, Warren S. *The Sermon on the Mount: A History of Interpretation and Bibliography.* ATLA Bibliography Series, 3. Meteuchen, N.J.: Scarecrow, 1975.

Kloppenborg, John S. *The Formation of Q: Trajectories in Ancient Wisdom Collections.* Studies in Antiquity & Christianity. Philadelphia: Fortress, 1987.

Kloppenborg, John S. *Q Parallels: Synopsis, Critical Notes, and Concordance.* Foundations and Facets: New Testament. Sonoma, Calif.: Polebridge, 1988.

Koch, Dietrich-Alex, et al. *Jesu Rede von Gott und ihre Nachgeschichte im frühen Christentum: Beiträge zur Verkündigung Jesus und zum Kerygma der Kirche. Festschrift für Willi Marxsen zum 70. Geburtstag.* Gütersloh: Mohr, 1989.

Kodell, Jerome. "The Celibacy Logion in Matthew 19:12," *BTB* 8 (1978) 19-23.

Koester, Helmut. "1 Thessalonians—Experiment in Christian Writing," in *Continuity and Discontinuity in Church History: Essays Presented to George Huntston Williams on the Occasion of his 65th Birthday*. Studies in the History of Christian Thought, 19. Leiden: Brill, 1979, pp. 33–44.

Koester, Helmut. *Introduction to the New Testament, 2: History and Literature of Early Christianity*. Philadelphia: Fortress, 1982.

Krämer, Helmut. "Eine Anmerkung zum Verständnis von Mt 15, 6a," *Wort und Dienst* 16 (1981) 67–70.

Kravetz, Julius. "Divorce in the Jewish Tradition," in J. Freid, ed., *Jews and Divorce*, pp. 149–157.

Krems, Gerhard and Reinhard Mumm, eds. *Theologie der Ehe*. Regensburg: Pustet, 1969.

Kretzer, Armin. "Die Frage: Ehe auf Dauer und ihre mögliche Trennung nach Mt 19, 3-12, in H. Merklein and J. Lange, eds., *Biblische Randbemerkungen*, pp. 218–230.

Kruse, H. "Eheverzicht im Neuen Testament und in der Frühkirche," *FKT* 1 (1985) 94–116.

Kubo, Sakae, "I Corinthians vii. 16: Optimistic or Pessimistic?" *NTS* 24 (1978) 539–544.

Kunkel, W. "Matrimonium," *PW*, 14:2, 2259–2286.

Lambrecht, Jan. "Jesus and the Law: An Investigation of Mk 7, 1-23," in J. Dupont, ed., *Jésus aux origines de la christologie*, pp. 358–415, 428–429.

Lambrecht, Jan. "Q-Influence on Mark 8, 34-9, 1," in J. Delobel, ed., *Logia*, pp. 277–304.

Lambrecht, Jan. *The Sermon on the Mount: Proclamation & Exhortation*. GNS, 14. Wilmington: Glazier, 1985.

Lane, William L. *Commentary on the Gospel of Mark*. NICNT. Grand Rapids: Eerdmans, 1974.

Laney, J. Carl. "Deuteronomy 24:1-4 and the Issue of Divorce," *BSac* 149 (1992) 3–15.

Laney, J. Carl. "No Divorce & No Remarriage," in H. W. House, ed., *Divorce and Remarriage: Four Christian Views*, pp. 15–54.

Laney, J. Carl. "Paul and the Permanence of Marriage in 1 Corinthians 7," *JETS* 25 (1982) 283–294.

Lattke, Michael. "Holiness and Sanctification in the New Testament," in E. W. Conrad and E. G. Newing, eds., *Perspectives on Lan-*

guage and Text: Essays and Poems in Honor of Francis I. Andersen's Sixtieth Birthday. Winona Lake, Ind.: Eisenbrauns, 1987, pp. 351-357.

Lehmann, Manfred R. "Gen 2, 24 as the Basis for Divorce in Halakhah and New Testament," *ZAW* 72 (1960) 263-267.

Leroy, Herbert. *"aphiêmi,* etc.," *EDNT,* 1, 181-183.

Lévi-Strauss, Claude. *The Elementary Structures of Kinship.* Rev. ed.: Boston, Beacon, 1969.

Levy, Ernst. *Der Hergang der römischen Ehescheidung.* Weimar: Böhlaus, 1925.

Lietzmann, Hans. *An die Korinther 1-2.* HNT, 9. 14th. ed.: Tübingen, Mohr, 1949.

Lightfoot, J. B. *Notes on Epistles of St. Paul from Unpublished Commentaries.* London: Macmillan, 1895.

Lindars, Barnabas. *New Testament Apologetic: The Doctrinal Significance of Old Testament Quotations.* London: SCM, 1961.

Lipinski, Eduard. "The Wife's Right to Divorce in the Light of an Ancient Near-Eastern Tradition," *The Jewish Law Annual* 4 (1981) 9-27.

Lohfink, Gerhard. "Jesus und die Ehescheidung. Zur Gattung und Sprachintention von Mt 5,32," in H. Merklein and J. Lange, eds., *Biblische Randbemerkungen,* pp. 207-217.

Lohfink, Gerhard. *Wem gilt die Bergpredigt? Beiträge zu einer christlichen Ethik.* Freiburg: Herder, 1988.

Lohmeyer, Ernst. *Das Evangelium des Matthäus.* KEK 1/2. 11th. ed.: Göttingen: Vandenhoeck und Ruprecht, 1951.

Lohse, Eduard. "Ich aber sage euch," in E. Lohse, ed., *Der Ruf Jesu und die Antwort der Gemeinde,* pp. 189-203; reprinted in *Die Einheit des Neuen Testaments. Exegetische Studien zur Theologie des Neuen Testaments.* Göttingen: Vandenhoeck und Ruprecht, 1973, pp. 73-87.

Lohse, Eduard. *Der Ruf Jesu und die Antwort der Gemeinde: exegetische Untersuchungen Joachim Jeremias zum 70. Geburtstag von seinen Schülern.* Göttingen: Vandenhoeck und Ruprecht, 1970.

Lohse, Eduard. *Theological Ethics of the New Testament.* Minneapolis: Fortress, 1991.

Louw, Johannes P. and Eugene A. Nida. *Greek-English Lexicon of the New Testament Based on Semantic Domains,* 1: *Introduction & Domains.* 2nd. ed.: New York, United Bible Societies, 1989.

Lövestam, Evald. *Äktenskapet i Nya testamentet.* Lund: Gleerup, 1950.

Lövestam, Evald. "*Apoluein* en gammalpalestinensisk skilsmässoterm," *SEA* 27 (1962) 132–152.

Lövestam, Evald. "Divorce and Remarriage in the New Testament," *Jewish Law Annual* 4 (1981) 47–65.

Lövestam, Evald. "De synoptiska Jesus-orden om skilsmässa och omgifte: referensramar och implikationer," *SEA* 43 (1978) 65–73.

Luck, William F. *Divorce and Remarriage: Recovering the Biblical View.* San Francisco: Harper & Row, 1987.

Lüdemann, Gerd. *Paul, Apostle to the Gentiles: Studies in Chronology.* Philadelphia: Fortress, 1984.

Lührmann, Dieter. "The Gospel of Mark and the Sayings Collection Q," *JBL* 108 (1989) 51–71.

Luz, Ulrich. *Matthew 1-7: A Commentary.* Minneapolis: Augsburg, 1989.

MacDonald, Dennis Ronald. *There Is No Male and Female.* HDR, 20. Philadelphia: Fortress, 1987.

MacDonald, Margaret Y. "Early Christian Women Married to Unbelievers," *SR* (1990) 221–234.

MacDonald, Margaret Y. "Women Holy in Body and Spirit: The Social Setting of 1 Corinthians 7," *NTS* 36 (1990) 161–181.

Mackin, Theodore. "Ephesians 5:21-33 and Radical Indissolubility," in T. P. Doyle, ed., *Marriage Studies,* 3, pp. 1–45.

MacRae, George W. "New Testament Perspectives on Marriage and Divorce," in L. G. Wrenn, ed., *Divorce and Remarriage,* pp. 1–15; reprinted in J. J. Young, ed., *Ministering to the Divorced Catholic,* pp. 37–50 and G. W. MacRae, *Studies in the New Testament and Gnosticism.* GNS, 26. Wilmington: Glazier, 1988, pp. 115–129.

Mahoney, Aidan. "A New Look at the Divorce Clauses in Mt 5, 32 and 19, 9," *CBQ* 30 (1968) 29–38.

Maier, Johann. *The Temple Scroll: An Introduction, Translation & Commentary.* JSOTSup, 34. Sheffield: University of Sheffield, 1985.

Malan, François Stephanus. *Paulus se annwysings in 1 Korintiërs 7 ten Opsigte van die Huwelik en die ongehude Staat.* D.D. thesis, University of Pretoria, 1980.

Malbon, Elizabeth Struthers. *Narrative Space and Mythic Meaning in Mark.* San Francisco: Harper & Row, 1986.

Malone, Richard and John R. Connery, eds., *Contemporary Perspectives on Christian Marriage: Propositions and Papers from the*

International Theological Commission. Chicago: Loyola University, 1984.

Mann, C. S. *Mark: A New Translation with Text and Commentary*. AB, 27. Garden City: Doubleday, 1986.

Manson, T. W. "The Old Testament in the Teaching of Jesus," *BJRL* 34 (1951–1952) 312–322.

Manson, T. W. *The Sayings of Jesus*. London: SCM, 1949.

Manson, T. W. *The Teaching of Jesus: Studies of Its Form and Content*. 2nd. ed.: Cambridge: Harvard University Press, 1955.

Margot, J.-C. "L'indissolubilité du mariage selon le Nouveau Testament," *RTP* 17 (1967) 391–403.

Marín, Francisco. "Un recurso obligado a la tradición presinóptica," *EstBib* 36 (1977) 205–216.

Marrow, Stanley B. "Marriage and Divorce in the New Testament," *ATR* 70 (1988) 3–15.

Marshall, I. H. *The Gospel of Luke: A Commentary on the Greek Text*. NICNT. Grand Rapids: Eerdmans, 1978.

Martin, Bruce L. "Matthew on Christ and the Law," *TS* 44 (1983) 53–70.

Martin, Ralph P. "St. Matthew's Gospel in Recent Study," *ExpTim* 80 (1969) 132–136.

Martin, Ralph P. *The Spirit and the Congregation: Studies in 1 Corinthians 12–15*. Grand Rapids: Eerdmans, 1984.

Marucci, Corrado. "Clausole Matteane e critica testuale: In merito alla teori di H. Crouzel sul testo originale di Mt 19, 9," *RivB* 38 (1990) 301–325.

Marucci, Corrado. *Parole di Gesù sul divorzio: ricerche scritturistiche previa ad un ripensamento teologico, canonistico e pastorale della dottrina cattolica dell'indissolubilità del matrimonio*. Aloisiana, 16. Naples: Morcelliana, 1982.

Marxsen, Willi. *Mark the Evangelist: Studies on the Redaction History of the Gospel*. Nashville: Abingdon, 1969.

Massaux, Edouard. *L'influence de l'Évangile de saint Matthieu sur la littérature chrétienne avant saint Irenée*. BETL, 75. Louvain: University Press, 1986.

Mateos, Juan and Fernando Camacho. *El Evangelio de Mateo: Lectura comentada*. Madrid: Cristiandad, 1981.

Matura, Thaddée. "Le célibat dans le Nouveau Testament d'après l'exégèse récente," *NRT* 97 (1975) 481–500, 593–604; "Celibacy in the New Testament," *TD* 24 (1976) 39–45.

Mayes, A. D. H. *Deuteronomy*. NCB. Grand Rapids: Eerdmans, 1979.

McCaughey, J. D. "Marriage and Divorce: A Response to Dr. Powers' Comments," *Colloquium* 5 (1972) 42-43.

McCaughey, J. D. "Marriage and Divorce: Some Reflections on the Relevant Passages in the New Testament," *Colloquium* 4 (1972) 24-39.

McKeating, Henry. "Sanctions Against Adultery in Ancient Israelite Society," *JSOT* 11 (1979) 57-72.

McKenzie, John L. "Looking at What Jesus Said: A Bill of Divorce," *Commonweal* (May 23, 1980) 301-305.

Meeks, Wayne A. *The First Urban Christians: The Social World of the Apostle Paul*. New Haven-London: Yale University, 1983.

Megivern, James J. *Bible Interpretation*. Official Catholic Teaching. Wilmington, N.C.: McGrath, 1978.

Meier, John P. *A Marginal Jew: Rethinking the Historical Jesus,* 1. ABRL. Garden City: Doubleday, 1991.

Meier, John P. *Law and History in Matthew's Gospel*. AnBib, 71. Rome: Pontifical Biblical Institute, 1976.

Meier, John P. *The Vision of Matthew: Christ, Church and Morality in the First Gospel*. Theological Inquiries. New York—Ramsey—Toronto: Paulist, 1978.

Merendino, Rosario Pius. *Das deuteronomische Gesetz: Eine literarkritische, gattungs- und überlieferungsgeschichtliche Untersuchung zu Dt 12-26*. BBB, 31. Bonn: Hanstein, 1969.

Merk, Augustin. *Novum Testamentum Graece et Latine*. 8th. ed.: Rome, Pontifical Biblical Institute, 1957.

Merklein, Helmut. " 'Es ist gut für den Menschen, eine Frau nicht anzufassen.' Paulus und die Sexualität nach 1 Kor 7," in J. Blank, et al., *Die Frau im Urchristentum*, pp. 225-253.

Merklein, Helmut and Joachim Lange, eds., *Biblische Randbemerkungen: Schülerfestschrift für Rudolf Schnackenburg zum 60. Geburtstag*. 2nd. ed.: Würzburg, Echter, 1974.

Metzger, Bruce M. *A Textual Commentary on the Greek New Testament: A Companion Volume to the United Bible Societies' Greek New Testament*. London-New York: United Bible Societies, 1971.

Meyer, Ben F. *The Aims of Jesus*. London: SCM, 1979.

Michaelis, Wilhelm. *"opthalmos," TDNT,* 5, 376.

Mielziner, Moses. *Introduction to the Talmud*. 4th. ed.: New York, Bloch, 1968.

Miletic, Stephen Francis. *"One Flesh": Eph. 5.22-24, 5.31. Marriage and the New Creation.* AnBib, 115. Rome: Pontifical Biblical Institute, 1988.

Miller, Donald G. and Dikran Y. Hadidian, eds., *Jesus and Man's Hope,* 2. Pittsburgh: Theological Seminary, 1971.

Minestroni, I. "Matrimonio, celibato e passaggio a seconde nozze," *Ric-BRel* 8 (1973) 61–94.

Moffatt, James. *The First Epistle of Paul to the Corinthians.* MNTC. London: Hodder and Stoughton, 1943.

Moingt, Joseph. "Le divorce 'pour motif d'impudicité' (Matthieu 5, 32; 19, 9)," *RSR* 56 (1968) 337–384; translated as "Ehescheidung 'auf Grund von Unzucht,' (Matth 5, 32/19, 9)," in J. David and F. Schmalz, eds., *Wie unauflöslich ist die Ehe?,* pp. 178–222.

Moiser, Jeremy. "A Reassessment of Paul's View of Marriage with Reference to 1 Cor 7.," *JSNT* 18 (1983) 103–122.

Molldrem, Mark J. "A Hermeneutic of Pastoral Care and the Law/Gospel Paradigm Applied to the Divorce Texts of Scripture," *Int* 45 (1991) 43–54.

Moloney, Francis J. "Matthew 19, 3-12 and Celibacy: A Redaction and Form Critical Study," *JSNT* 2 (1979) 42-60; in Italian, in A. M. Triacca, ed., *Verginità Consecrata.* Rome: LAS, 1979.

Montague, George T. *Companion God: A Cross-Cultural Commentary on the Gospel of Matthew.* New York—Mahwah: Paulist, 1989.

Moore, George F. *Judaism in the First Centuries of the Christian Era: The Age of the Tannaim,* 2. Cambridge: Harvard University Press, 1927.

Morgenthaler, Robert. *Statistik des neutestamentlichen Wortschatzes.* Zurich: Gotthelf, 1958.

Mueller, James R. "The Temple Scroll and the Gospel Divorce Texts," *RevQ* 38 (1980) 247–256.

Murphy-O'Connor, Jerome. "The Divorced Woman in 1 Cor 7:10-11," *JBL* 100 (1981) 601–606.

Murphy-O'Connor, Jerome. "An Essene Missionary Document? CD II, 14-VI, 1," *RB* 77 (1970) 201–229.

Murphy-O'Connor, Jerome. "The First Letter to the Corinthians," *NJBC,* 798–815.

Murphy-O'Connor, Jerome. "Works without Faith in I Cor., Vii, 14," *RB* 84 (1977) 349–361.

Murray, Gregory. "What Defiles a Man?" DR 106 (1988) 297–298.

Nautin, Pierre. "Divorce et remariage dans la tradition de l'église latine," *RSR* 62 (1974) 7–54.

Neckebrouck, Valeer. "Paulus' houding tegenover het huwelijk in I Kor 7 volgens de hedendaagse exegese," *Bijdragen* (1963) 171–191.

Neirynck, Frans. *Duality in Mark: Contributions to the Study of the Markan Redaction.* BETL, 31. Rev. ed.: Louvain, University Press, 1988.

Neirynck, Frans. "Het evangelisch Echtscheidingsverbod," *Collationes Brugenses et Gandavenses* 4 (1958) 25–46.

Neirynck, Frans. "De Jezuswoorden over Echtscheiding," in V. Heylen, ed., *Mislukt huwelijk en echtscheiding,* pp. 127–141; reprinted, with additional note, in *Evangelica: Gospel Studies—Études d'évangile.* BETL, 60. Louvain: University Press, 1982, pp. 821–834.

Neirynck, Frans. "Huwelijk en Echtscheiding in het Evangelie," *Collationes Brugenses et Gandavenses* 6 (1960) 123–130.

Neirynck, Frans and Frans Van Segbroeck. *New Testament Vocabulary: A Companion Volume to the Concordance.* BETL, 65. Louvain: University Press, 1984.

Neirynck, Frans. "Paul and the Sayings of Jesus," in A. Vanhoye, ed., *L'Apôtre Paul: Personnalité, style et conception du ministère.* BETL, 73. Louvain: University Press, 1986, pp. 265–321.

Neirynck, Frans. *Q-Synopsis: The Double Tradition Passages in Greek,* Studiorum Novi Testamenti Auxilia, 13. Louvain: University Press, 1988.

Neirynck, Frans. "Recent Developments in the Study of Q," in J. Delobel, *Logia,* pp. 29–75; reprinted in F. Neirynck, *Evangelica, II.* BETL, 99 (Louvain: University Press, 1991), pp. 409–464.

Neirynck, Frans. "Synoptic Problem," *NJBC,* 587–595.

Nembach, Ulrich. "Ehescheidung nach alttestamentlichem und jüdischem Recht," *TZ* 26 (1970) 161–171.

Nepper-Christensen, Poul. "Utugtsklausulen og Josef i Matthaeusevangeliet," *SEA* 34 (1969) 122–146.

Neusner, Jacob, ed., *The Formation of the Babylonian Talmud: Studies in the Achievements of Late Nineteenth and Twentieth Century Historical and Literary-critical Research.* SPB, 17. Leiden: Brill, 1970.

Neusner, Jacob. *The Memorized Torah: The Mnemonic System of the Mishnah.* BJS, 96. Chico, Calif.: Scholars, 1985.

Newman, Barclay M. and Philip C. Stine, *A Translator's Handbook on the Gospel of Matthew.* Helps for Translators. London-New York-Stuttgart: United Bible Societies, 1988.

Nicoláu, Miguel. "Virginidad y continencia en la Sagrada Escritura," *Manresa* 47 (1975) 19-40.

Niederwimmer, Kurt. *Askese und Mysterium: über Ehe, Ehescheidung und Eheverzicht in den Anfängen des christlichen Glaubens.* FRLANT, 113. Göttingen: Vandenhoeck und Ruprecht, 1975, pp. 13-24.

Noth, Martin. *Leviticus: A Commentary.* OTL. London: SCM, 1965.

O'Grady. John F. *The Four Gospels and the Jesus Tradition.* New York—Mahwah: Paulist, 1989.

O'Hagan, Angelo P. "Divorce—Marriage in tension with this Age," *SBibFrLA* 22 (1972) 95-108.

O'Neill, J. C. "1 Corinthians 7, 14 and Infant Baptism, in A. Vanhoye, ed., *L'apôtre Paul,* pp. 357-361.

O'Rourke, John J. "The Scriptural Background of can. 1120," *The Jurist* 15 (1955) 132-137.

O'Shea, William J. "Marriage and Divorce: The Biblical Evidence," *AusCR* 47 (1970) 89-109.

Oepke, Albrecht. "Urchristentum und Kindertaufe," *ZNW* (1930) 81-111.

Olsen, V. Norskov. *The New Testament Logia on Divorce: A Study of their Interpretation from Erasmus to Milton.* GBE, 10. Tübingen: Mohr, 1971.

Omanson, Roger L. "Acknowledging Paul's Quotations," *BT* 43 (1992) 201-213.

Omanson, Roger L. "Some Comments about Style and Meaning: 1 Corinthians 9.15 and 7.10," *BT* 34 (1983) 135-139.

Orge, Manuel. "El propósito temático de 1 Corintios 7: Un discernimiento sobre la puesta en práctice del ideal de la continencia sexual y el celibato," *Claretianum* 27 (1987) 5-125, 28 (1988) 5-114; 31 (1991) 125-152.

Orr, William F. and James Arthur Walther. *I Corinthians: A New Translation. Introduction with a Study of the Life of Paul, Notes, and Commentary.* AB, 32. Garden City: Doubleday, 1976.

Osburn, Carroll D. "The Present Indicative in Matthew 19:9," *ResQ* 24 (1981) 193–203.

Osiek, Carolyn. "Christian Prophecy: Once Upon a Time?" *CurTM* 17 (1990) 290–297.

Ott, Anton. *Die Auslegung der neutestamentlichen Texte über die Ehescheidung.* NTAbh, 3. Münster: Aschendorff, 1911.

Ott, Anton. *Die Ehescheidung im Matthäusevangelium.* Würzburg: Rita, 1939.

Otwell, John H. *And Sarah Laughed: The Status of Women in the Old Testament.* Philadelphia: Westminster, 1977.

Overman, J. Andrew. *Matthew's Gospel and Formative Judaism: The Social World of the Matthean Community.* Minneapolis: Fortress, 1990.

Patrick, Dale. *Old Testament Law.* Atlanta: John Knox, 1985.

Peabody, David Barrett. *Mark as Composer.* New Gospel Studies, 1. Macon: Mercer University Press, 1987.

Pesch, Rudolf. *Freie Treue: Die Christen und die Ehescheidung.* Freiburg: Herder, 1971.

Pesch, Rudolf. *Das Markusevangelium,* HTKNT 2/2. Freiburg: Herder, 1984.

Pesch, Rudolf. "Die neutestamentliche Weisung für die Ehe," *BibLeb* 9 (1968) 208–221.

Pesch, Rudolf. " 'Paulinische Kasuistik'. Zum Verständnis von 1 Kor 7, 10–11," in J. A. Verdes and E. J. A. Hernandez, eds., *Homenaje a Juan Prado,* pp. 433–442.

Peters, Adrian. "St. Paul and Marriage: A Study of 1 Corinthians Chapter Seven," *AFER* 6 (1964) 214–224.

Phipps, Willliam E. "Is Paul's Attitude towards Sexual Relations Contained in 1 Cor. 7.1?" *NTS* 28 (1982) 125–131.

Piatelli, Daniela. "The Marriage Contract and Bill of Divorce in Ancient Hebrew Law," *The Jewish Law Annual* 4 (1981) 66–78.

Polag, Athanasius. *Fragmenta Q: Textheft zur Logienquelle.* Neukirchen-Vluyn: Neukircher, 1979.

Porten, Bezalel. *Archives from Elephantine: The Life of an Ancient Jewish Military Colony.* Berkeley and Los Angeles: University of California, 1968.

Porter, Stanley E. and Paul Buchanan. "On the Logical Structure of Matt 19:9," *JETS* 34 (1991) 335–339.

Powers, B. W. "Marriage and Divorce: The Dispute of Jesus with the Pharisees, and its Inception," *Colloquium* 5 (1972) 34–41.

Pryke, E. J. *Redactional Style in the Marcan Gospel: A Study of Syntax and Vocabulary as Guides to Redaction in Mark.* SNTSMS, 33. Cambridge: University Press, 1978.

Przybyła, A. E. "List rozwodowy w prawie Mojżesza," *Zycie i Myśl* 26 (1976) 54–63.

Puigdollers, Rodolfo. "Notas para una interpretación de 1 Cor 7," *RCT* 3 (1978) 245–260.

Quesnell, Quentin. "Made Themselves Eunuchs for the Kingdom of Heaven," *CBQ* 30 (1968) 335–358.

Rabin, Chaim. *The Zadokite Documents.* Oxford: Clarendon, 1954.

Rabinowitz, Abraham Hirsch, "Commandments, the 613," *EncJud,* 5, 760–783.

Ramaroson, L. "Une nouvelle interpretation de la 'clausule' de Mt 19, 9," *ScEs* 23 (1971) 247–251.

Reisser, H. "*Porneuô,*" in Lothar Coenen, Erich Beyreuther, Hans Bietenhard, eds., *Theologisches Begriffslexikon zum Neuen Testament,* 2/2. Wuppertal: Brockhaus, 1971, pp. 1506–1509.

Rhoads, David and Donald Michie. *Mark as Story.* Philadelphia: Fortress, 1982.

Richardson, P. " 'I Say, not the Lord': Personal Opinion, Apostolic Authority and the Development of Early Christian Halakah," *TynBul* 31 (1980) 65–86.

Riesner, Rainer. *Jesus als Lehrer. Eine Untersuchung zum Ursprung der Evangelien-Überlieferung.* WUNT, 2, 7. 2nd. ed.: Tübingen, Mohr, 1984.

Rigaux, Béda. "Réflexions sur l'historicité de Jésus dans le message paulinien," in *Studiorum paulinorum congressus internationalis catholicus 1961,* 2. AnBib, 18. Rome: Pontifical Biblical Institute, 1963, pp. 265–274.

Riley, Harold. *The Making of Mark: An Exploration.* Macon, GA: Mercer University Press, 1989.

Robbins, Vernon K. *Jesus the Teacher: A Socio-rhetorical Interpretation of Mark.* Philadelphia: Fortress, 1984.

Roberts, R. L., "The Meaning of *chorizo* and *douloo* in 1 Cor 7:10-17," *ResQ* 3 (1965) 179–184.

Roberts, William P., ed., *Divorce and Remarriage: Religious and Psychological Perspectives.* Kansas City, Mo.: Sheed & Ward, 1990.

Robertson, Archibald and Alfred Plummer. *A Critical and Exegetical Commentary on the First Epistle of St Paul to the Corinthians.* ICC. 2nd. ed.: Edinburgh, Clark, 1967.

Rodenbusch, E. "Die Komposition von Lukas 16," *ZNW* 4 (1903) 243–254.

Rordorf, Willy. "Marriage in the New Testament and the Early Church," *JEH* 20 (1969) 193–210.

Ryan, S. "Survey of Periodicals. Indissolubility of Marriage," *Furrow* 24 (1973) 150–159.

Ryrie, Charles C. "Biblical Teaching on Divorce and Remarriage," *GTJ* 3 (1982) 177–192.

Sabatowich, Jerome. "Christian Divorce and Remarriage," *BT* 25 (1987) 253–255.

Sabourin, Leopold: "The Divorce Clauses (Mt 5:32; 19:9)," *BTB* 2 (1972) 80–86.

Sand, Alexander. *Das Evangelium nach Matthäus.* RNT. Regensburg: Pustet, 1986.

Sand, Alexander. *Reich Gottes und Eheverzicht im Evangelium nach Matthäus.* SBS, 109 (Stuttgart: Katholisches Bibelwerk, 1983).

Sand, Alexander. "Die Unzuchtsklausel in Mt 5, 31.32 und 19, 3-9," *MTZ* 20 (1969) 118–129.

Sanders, E. P. *Jesus and Judaism.* London: SCM, 1985.

Sanders, E. P. and Margaret Davies. *Studying the Synoptic Gospels.* London: SCM—Philadelphia: Trinity Press International, 1989.

Sanders, E. P. "When Is a Law a Law?" in Edwin B. Firmage, Bernard G. Weiss and John W. Welch, eds., Religion and Law: Biblical Judaic and Islamic Perspectives. Winona Lake, Ind.: Eisenbrauns, 1990, pp. 139–158.

Sandmel, Samuel. "Jewish and Christian Marriage: Some Observations," *HeyJ* 11 (1970) 237–250.

Schaller, Berndt. " 'Commits adultery with her', not 'against her', Mk 10:11," *ExpTim* 83 (1972) 107–108.

Schaller, Berndt. "Die Sprüche über Ehescheidung und Wiederheirat in der synoptischen Überlieferung," in E. Lohse, ed., *Der Ruf Jesu und die Antwort der Gemeinde,* pp. 226–246.

Schechter, Solomon. *Fragments of a Zadokite Work.* Documents of Jewish Sectaries, 1. Cambridge: University Press, 1910.

Schenk, Wolfgang. *Synopse zur Redenquelle der Evangelien: Q-Synopse und Rekonstruktion in deutscher Übersetzung mit kurzen Erläuterungen.* Düsseldorf: Patmos, 1981.

Schereschewsky, Ben-Zion. "Divorce," *EncJud,* 6, 122–135.

Schereschewsky, Ben-Zion. "Marriages, Prohibited," *EncJud,* 11, 1051–1054.

Schillebeeckx, Edward. *Jesus: An Experiment in Christology.* New York: Crossroad, 1979.

Schmid, Josef. *Das Evangelium nach Matthäus.* RNT, 1. 3rd. ed.: Regensburg, Pustet, 1956.

Schmithals, Walter. *Das Evangelium nach Markus. Kapitel 9, 2-16, 20.* Ökumenischer Taschenbuchkommentar zum Neuen Testament, 2/2. Gütersloh: Mohn—Würzburg: Echter, 1979.

Schmithals, Walter. *Gnosticism in Corinth: An Investigation of the Letters to the Corinthians.* Nashville: Abingdon, 1971.

Schnackenburg, Rudolf. "Die Ehe nach dem Neuen Testament," in *Schriften zum Neuen Testament: Exegese in Fortschritt und Wandel.* Munich: Kösel, 1971, pp. 414–434.

Schnackenburg, Rudolf. *Matthäusevangelium.* Die Neue Echter Bibel 1/1, 2. Würzburg: Echter, 1985, 1987.

Schnackenburg, Rudolf. *The Moral Teaching of the New Testament.* London: Burns & Oates, 1965.

Schneider, Gerhard. "Jesu Wort über die Ehescheidung in der Überlieferung des Neuen Testaments," *TTZ* 80 (1971) 65–87; reprinted in *Jesusüberlieferung und Christologie. Neutestamentliche Aufsätze 1970–1990.* NovTSup, 67. Leiden: Brill, 1992, pp. 187–209.

Schneider, Heinrich. "Der Dekalog in den Phylakterien von Qumran," *BZ* 3 (1959) 18–31.

Schniewind, Julius. *Das Evangelium nach Matthäus.* NTD, 2. 5th. ed.: Göttingen, Vandenhoeck und Ruprecht, 1950.

Schottroff, Luise, et al. *Essays on the Love Commandment.* Philadelphia: Fortress, 1978.

Schürmann, Heinz. "Neutestamentliche Marginalien zur Frage nach der Institutionalität, Unauflösbarkeit und Sakramentalität der Ehe," in *Kirche und Bibel.* Paderborn: Schöningh, 1979, pp. 409–430.

Schürmann, Heinz. *Traditionsgeschichtliche Untersuchungen zu den synoptischen Evangelien.* Kommentare und Beiträge zum Alten und Neuen Testament. Düsseldorf: Patmos, 1968.

Schürmann, Heinz. "Die Verbindlichkeit konkreter sittlicher Normen nach dem Neuen Testament, bedacht am Beispiel des Ehescheidungsverbotes und im Lichte des Liebesgebotes," in W. Kerber, ed., *Sittliche Normen,* pp. 107–123.

Schüssler Fiorenza, Elisabeth. *In Memory of Her: A Feminist Theological Reconstruction of Christian Origins.* New York: Crossroad, 1983.

Schüssler Fiorenza, Elisabeth. "Women in the Pre-Pauline and Pauline Churches," *USQR* 33 (1978) 153–166.

Schütz, John Howard. *Paul and the Anatomy of Apostolic Authority.* SNTSMS, 26. Cambridge: University Press, 1975.

Schulz, Siegfried. *Q: Die Spruchquelle der Evangelisten.* Zurich: Theologischer Verlag, 1972.

Schweizer, Eduard. *The Good News According to Luke.* Atlanta: John Knox, 1984.

Schweizer, Eduard. *The Good News According to Mark.* Atlanta: John Knox, 1970.

Schweizer, Eduard. *The Good News According to Matthew.* Atlanta: John Knox, 1975.

Schweizer, Eduard. "Scheidungsrecht der jüdischen Frau? Weibliche Jünger Jesu?" *EvT* 42 (1982) 294–300.

Segalla, Giuseppe. "Il testo piú antico sul celibato: Mt 19, 11-12," *StudPat* 17 (1970) 121–137.

Sélis, Claude. "La répudiation dans le Nouveau Testament," *Lumière et Vie* 206 (1992) 39–49.

Seim, Turid Karlsen "Seksualitet og ekteskap, skilsmisse og gjengifte i 1. Kor. 7" *NorTT* 81 (1980) 1–20.

Shaner, Donald W. *A Christian View of Divorce According to the Teaching of the New Testament.* Leiden: Brill, 1964.

Sickenberger, Joseph. "Die Unzuchtsklausel im Matthäusevangelium," *TQ* 123 (1942) 189–206.

Sigal, Phillip. *The Halakah of Jesus of Nazareth according to the Gospel of Matthew.* Ph.D. thesis, University of Pittsburgh, 1979.

Smith, Morton. *Jesus the Magician.* New York: Harper and Row, 1978.

Soares Prabhu, George M. *The Formula Quotations in the Infancy Narrative of Matthew: An Enquiry into the Tradition History of Mt 1-2.* AnBib, 63. Rome: Biblical Institute, 1976.

Soulen, Richard N. "Marriage and Divorce: A Problem in New Testament Interpretation," *Int* 23 (1969) 439-450.

Stanton, Graham N. "The Origin and Purpose of Matthew's Gospel: Matthaean Scholarship from 1945 to 1980," *ANRW* II/25, 3, 1889-1951.

Stein, Robert H. "Is It Harmful for a Man to Divorce His Wife?" *JETS* 22 (1979) 115-121.

Stein, Robert H. *The Method and Message of Jesus' Teachings.* Philadelphia: Westminster, 1978.

Stendahl, Krister. *The Bible and the Role of Women.* Philadelphia: Fortress, 1966.

Stendahl, Krister. *The School of St. Matthew and its Use of the Old Testament.* ASNU, 20. Uppsala: Almqvist & Wiksells, 1954.

Stenger, Werner. "Zur Rekonstruktion eines Jesusworts anhand der synoptischen Ehescheidungslogien (Mt 5, 32; 19, 9; Lk 16, 18; Mk 10, 11f.)," *Kairos* 26 (1984) 194-205; reprinted in *Strukturale Beobachtungen zum Neuen Testament.* NTTS, 12. Leiden: Brill, 1990, pp. 104-118.

Steurenagel, Carl. *Das Deuteronomium.* HAT. Göttingen: Vandenhoeck und Ruprecht, 1898.

Stock, Augustine. "Matthean Divorce Texts," *BTB* 8 (1978) 24-33.

Stott, J. R. W. "The Biblical Teaching on Divorce," *Churchman* 85 (1971) 165-174.

Stramare, Tarcisio. "Clausole di Matteo e indissolubilitéa del matrimonio," *BeO* 17 (1975) 65-74.

Stramare, Tarcisio. "Matteo divorzista?" *Divinitas* 15 (1971) 213-235.

Strecker, Georg. "Die Antithesen der Bergpredigt," *ZNW* 69 (1978) 36-72.

Strecker, Georg. *Der Weg der Gerechtigkeit: Untersuchung zur Theologie des Matthäus.* FRLANT, 82. 3rd. ed.: Göttingen, Vandenhoeck und Ruprecht, 1971.

Strobel, August. *Der erste Brief an die Korinther.* Zürcher Bibelkommentare: NT 6/1. Zurich: Theologischer Verlag, 1989.

Suggs, M. Jack. "The Antitheses as Redactional Products," in Luise Schottroff, et al., *Essays on the Love Commandment.* Philadelphia: Fortress, 1978, pp. 93-107.

Swidler, Leonard. *Biblical Affirmations of Women.* Philadelphia: Westminster, 1979.

Taylor, Charles. *Sayings of the Jewish Fathers.* 2nd. ed.: Cambridge, University Press, 1897.

Taylor, Richard J. "Divorce in Matthew 5:32; 19:9: Theological Research and Pastoral Care," *ClR* 55 (1970) 792–800.

Taylor, Vincent. *Behind the Third Gospel: A Study of the Proto-Luke Hypothesis.* Oxford: Clarendon, 1926.

Taylor, Vincent. *The Gospel According to St. Mark.* 2nd. ed.: London, Macmillan, 1966.

Taylor, Vincent. "The Original Order of Q" in *New Testament Essays.* London: Epworth, 1970, 95–118.

Taylor, Vincent. "The Order of Q" in *New Testament Essays.* London: Epworth, 1970, pp. 90–94.

Teeple, Howard M. "The Oral Tradition that Never Existed," *JBL* 89 (1970) 56–68.

Theissen, Gerd. *The Social Setting of Pauline Christianity: Essays on Corinth.* Studies of the New Testament and Its World. Philadelphia: Fortress, 1982.

Thomas, J. "Tout est grâce. Lecture de Matthieu 19, 1-12," *Christus* 29 (1982) 338–344.

Thompson, T. L. "Catholic View on Divorce," *JES* 6 (1969) 53–67.

Tolbert, Mary Ann. *Sowing the Gospel: Mark's World in Literary-Historical Perspective.* Minneapolis: Fortress, 1989.

Tomson, Peter J. *Paul and the Jewish Law: Halakha in the Letters of the Apostle to the Gentiles.* CRINT, 3/1: *Jewish Traditions in Early Christian Literature.* Assen: Van Gorcum, 1990.

Trevijano Etcheverría, Ramón. "Matrimonio y divorcio en la sagrada escritura," in T. G. Barberena, ed., *El vínculo matrimonial,* pp. 3–59.

Trevijano Etcheverría, Ramón. "Matrimonio y divorcio en Mc 10, 2-12 y par.," *Burgense* 18 (1977) 113–151.

Trilling, Wolfgang. *Das wahre Israel. Studien zur Theologie des Matthäus-Evangeliums.* 3rd. ed.: Munich, Kösel, 1964.

Trilling, Wolfgang. "Zum Thema: Ehe und Ehescheidung im Neuen Testament," *TGl* 74 (1984) 390–406.

Tuckett, Christopher M. "1 Corinthians and Q," *JBL* 102 (1983) 607–619.

Turner, Nigel. *A Grammar of New Testament Greek.* Vol. 3: *Syntax.* Edinburgh: Clark, 1963.

Turner, Nigel. "The Translation of *Moixatai ep' Autên* in Mark 10:11," *BT* 7 (1956) 151-152.

Ulonska, Herbert. Christen und Heiden: Die paulinische Paränese in 1 Thess 4, 3-8," *TZ* 43 (1987) 210-218.

Vallauri, Emiliano. "Le clausole matteane sul divorzio. Tendenze esegetiche recenti," *Laurentianum* 17 (1976) 82-112.

van Eupen, Th. A. G., ed. *(On)ontbindbaarheid van het Huwelijk.* Annalen van het Thijmgenootschap, 58/1. Hilversum: Brand, 1970.

van Gansewinkel, Albert. "Ehescheidung und Wiederheirat in neutestamentlicher und moraltheologischer Sicht," *TGl* 76 (1986) 193-211.

van Gansewinkel, Albert. "Ursprüngliche oder grundsäztliche Unauflösbarkeit der Ehe," *Diakonia* 3 (1972) 88-93.

Vanhoye, Albert, ed. *L'apôtre Paul Personnalité, style et conception du ministère.* BETL, 73. Louvain: University Press, 1986.

van Iersel, Bas. *Reading Mark.* Edinburgh: T. & T. Clark, 1989.

van Tilborg, Sjef. "Mattheüs 19, 3-12 en het onontbindbare huwelijk," in Th. A. G. van Eupen, ed., *(On)ontbindbaarheid van het Huwelijk,* pp. 23-34.

Vargas-Machuca, Antonio. "Los casos de 'divorcio' admitidos por S. Mateo (5, 32 y 19, 9). Consecuencias para la teología actual," *EstEcl* 50 (1975) 5-54.

Vargas-Machuca, Antonio. "Divorcio e indisolubilidad del matrimonio en la Sagrada Escritura," *EstBib* 39 (1981) 19-61.

Vattioni, Francesco. "A propos de Marc 10, 6," *ScEs* 20 (1968) 433-436.

Vawter, Bruce. "Divorce and the New Testament," *CBQ* 39 (1977) 528-542; reprinted in *The Path of Wisdom: Biblical Investigations.* Background Books, 3. Wilmington: Glazier, 1986, pp. 238-256.

Vawter, Bruce. "The Divorce Clauses in Mt 5, 32 and 19, 9," *CBQ* 16 (1954) 155-167.

Venetz, H.-J. "Die Ehe unter dem Anspruch der Bergpredigt. Neue Kommentare zum Matthaüsevangelium," *Orientierung* 52 (1988) 229-233.

Verdes, J. Alvarez and E. J. Alonso Hernandez, eds., *Homenaje a Juan Prado: Miscelanea de estudios biblicos y hebraicos.* Madrid: CSIC, 1975.

Vermes, Geza. "The Decalogue and the Minim," in M. Black and G. Fohrer, eds., *In Memoriam Paul Kahle,* pp. 232-240.

364 *Select Bibliography*

Vermes, Geza. "Sectarian Matrimonial Halakhah in the Damascus Rule," *JJS* 25 (1974) 197-202.

Vidigal, J. R. "O Direito Matrimonial na Bíblia," *RCB* 1 (1977) 395-408.

Vijver, Enrique, "El uso de la Biblia en cuestiones éticas; El caso del divorcio," *Cuadernos de Teología* 8 (1987) 17-33.

Viviano, Benedict T. "The Gospel According to Matthew," *NJBC,* 630-674.

Vokes, F. E. "The Ten Commandments in the New Testament and First Century Judaism," in *Studia Evangelica,* 5 (= TU 103; Berlin: Akademie, 1968) pp. 146-154.

Volkmann, Hans. *Zur Rechtsprechung im Principat des Augustus. Historische Beiträge.* Munich: Beck, 1935.

Von Dehsen, Christian D. *Sexual Relationships and the Church: An Exegetical Study of 1 Corinthians 5-7.* Ph.D. thesis, Union Theological Seminary, New York City. Ann Arbor: UMI, 1987.

von Rad, Gerhard. "*Shalôm,*" in "*eirênê,*" TDNT, 2, 400-422.

Walther, Georg. "Übergreifende Heiligkeit und Kindertaufe im Neuen Testament," *EvT* 25 (1965) 668-674.

Wambacq, B. N. "Matthieu 5, 31-32. Possibilité de divorce ou obligation de rompre une union illégitime," *NRT* 104 (1982) 34-49.

Wansbrough, Henry. "Divorce in the New Testament," *Ampleforth Journal* 83 (1978) 57-63.

Ward, M. R. "Once Married Always Married?—A Biblical Review and Synthesis," *Churchman* 87 (1973) 190-197.

Weber, Robertus. *Biblia Sacra iuxta vulgatam versionem,* 2. Stuttgart: Württembergische Bibelanstalt, 1969.

Wedderburn, A. J. M. "Keeping Up With Recent Studies, 8: Some Recent Pauline Chronologies," *ExpTim* 92 (1980) 103-108.

Weder, Hans. "Perspektive der Frauen?" *EvT* 43 (1983) 175-178.

Weiss, Johannes. *Der erste Korintherbrief.* KEK, 5. 9th. ed.: Göttingen, Vandenhoeck und Ruprecht, 1910.

Wenham, Gordon J. "Gospel Definitions of Adultery and Women's Rights," *ExpTim* 95 (1984) 330-332.

Wenham, Gordon J. "Matthew and Divorce: An Old Crux Revisited," *JSNT* 22 (1984) 95-107.

Wenham, Gordon J. "May Divorced Christians Remarry?" *Churchman* 95 (1981) 150-161.

Wenham, Gordon J. "Restoration of Marriage Reconsidered," *JJS* 30 (1979) 36–40.

Wenham, Gordon J. "The Syntax of Matthew 19.9," *JSNT* 28 (1986) 17–23.

Wenham, J. W. *The Elements of New Testament Greek.* Cambridge: University Press, 1965.

West, A. "Sex and Salvation: A Christian Feminist Study of 1. Corinthians 6.12–7.39," *Modern Churchman,* 29 (1987) 17–24.

Wevers, J. W. *Septuaginta: Vetus Testamentum Graecum auctoritate Academiae Scientiarum Gottingensis editum,* 1: *Genesis.* Göttingen: Vandenhoeck & Ruprecht, 1974.

Wibbing, Siegfried. *Die Tugend- und Lasterkataloge im Neuen Testament und ihre Traditionsgeschichte unter besonderer Berücksichtigung der Qumran-Texte.* BZNW, 25. Berlin: Töpelmann, 1959.

Wiebe, Phillip H. "Jesus' Divorce Exception," *JETS* 32 (1989) 327–333.

Wiebe, Phillip H. "The New Testament on Divorce and Remarriage: Some Logical Implications," *JETS* 24 (1981) 131–138.

Wijngards, J. N. M. "Do Jesus' Words on Divorce (Lk. 16:18) Admit of No Exception?" *Jeevadhara* 6 (1975) 399–411.

Wili, H.-U. "Das Privilegium Paulinum (1Kor 7, 15f)—Pauli eigen Lebenserinnerung? (Rechtshistorische Anmerkungen zu einer neueren Hypothese)," *BZ* 22 (1978) 100–108.

Wilkins, Michael J. *The Concept of Disciple in Matthew's Gospel: As Reflected in the Use of the Term Mathêtês.* NovTSup, 59. Leiden: Brill, 1988.

Williams, James G. "Paraenesis, Excess, and Ethics: Matthew's Rhetoric in the Sermon on the Mount," *Semeia* 50 (1990) 163–187.

Wilson, Stephen G. *Luke and the Law.* SNTSMS, 50. Cambridge: University Press, 1983.

Winer, Georg B. *A Treatise on the Grammar of New Testament Greek Regarded as a Sure Basis for New Testament Exegesis.* Edinburgh: Clark, 1882.

Winter, Paul. "Sadoqite Fragments IV 20, 21 and the Exegesis of Genesis 1 27 in Late Judaism," *ZAW* 68 (1956) 71–84.

Wire, Antoinette Clark. *The Corinthian Women Prophets: A Reconstruction through Paul's Rhetoric.* Minneapolis: Fortress, 1990.

Wire, Antoinette Clark Wire. "Prophecy and Women Prophets in Corinth," in James E. Goehring, et al., *Gospel Origins & Christian Beginnings,* pp. 134–150.

Witherington, Ben. "Matthew 5.32 and 19.9—Exception or Exceptional Situation?" *NTS* 31 (1985) 571–576.

Wolff, Hans Julius. *Beiträge zur Rechtsgeschichte Altgriechenlands und des hellenistisch-römischen Ägyptens.* Weimar: Böhlaus, 1961.

Wrege, Hans-Theo. *Die Überlieferungsgeschichte der Bergpredigt.* WUNT, 9. Tübingen: Mohr, 1968.

Wrenn, Lawrence G., ed., *Divorce and Remarriage in the Catholic Church.* New York: Newman, 1973.

Yadin, Yigael. "L'attitude essénienne envers la polygamie et le divorce," *RB* 79 (1972) 98–100.

Yadin, Yigael. *Megillat ha-Migda.* Jerusalem: The Israel Exploration Society and the Shrine of the Book, 1977. ET: *The Temple Scroll.* Jerusalem: The Israel Exploration Society and the Shrine of the Book, 1983.

Yadin, Yigael. *The Temple Scroll: The Hidden Law of the Dead Sea Sect.* London: Weidenfeld and Nicolson, 1985.

Yamauchi, Edwin M. "Cultural Aspects of Marriage in the Ancient World," *BSac* 135 (1978) 241–252.

Yarbrough, O. Larry. *Not Like the Gentiles: Marriage Rules in the Letters of Paul.* SBLDS, 80. Atlanta: Scholars, 1984.

Yaron, Reuven. *Introduction to the Law of the Aramaic Papyri.* Oxford: Clarendon, 1961.

Yaron, Reuven. "The Restoration of a Marriage," *JJS* 17 (1966) 1–11.

Young, James J., ed., *Ministering to the Divorced Catholic.* New York: Paulist, 1979.

Young, James J. "New Testament Perspectives on Divorce Ministry," *Pastoral Psychology* 33 (1985) 205–216.

Zakovitch, Yair. "The Woman's Rights in the Biblical Law of Divorce," *The Jewish Law Annual* 4 (1981) 28–46.

Załęski, Josef. "1 Kor 7, 12a w świetle patrystycznej i współczesnej egzegezy," *STV* 16 (1978) 17–30.

Załęski, Josef. "Elementy egzegezy patrystyznej we współczesnych interpretacjach tekstu Mt 5, 32 czy 19, 9," *ColTh* 47 (1977) 43–63.

Załęski, Josef. "Nierozerwalność małżeństwa według 1 Kor 7, 10-11," *STV* 26 (1988) 137-146.

Załęski, Josef. "Problem 'wyjątku' w 1 Kor 7, 15-16," *ColTh* 53 (1983) 43-63.

Zerwick, Max and Mary Grosvenor. *A Grammatical Analysis of the Greek New Testament,* 2. Rome: Biblical Institute, 1979.

Zerwick, Maximilian. "De matrimonio et divortio in Evangelio," *VD* 4 (1960) 193-212.

Zimmermann, Heinrich. Neutestamentliche Methodenlehre: Darstellung der historisch-kritischen Methode. 7th. ed., reworked by Klaus Kleisch: Stuttgart, Katholisches Bibelwerk, 1982.

Zmijewski, Josef and Ernst Nellessen, eds., *Begegnung mit dem Wort. Festschrift für Heinrich Zimmermann.* BBB, 53. Bonn: Hannstein, 1980.

Zmijewski, Josef. "Neutestamentliche Weisungen für Ehe und Familie," *SNTU* 9 (1984) 31-78.

Index of Scripture References

370   *Index of Scripture References*

21:7	268		95, 96, 100,	**Proverbs**	
21:14	264		110, 111, 112,	8:23	275
22:13	264, 268		113, 114, 115,	17:10	283
24:5-9	302		137–140, 141,	25:21-22	240
24:20	152		145, 152, 154,		

Numbers

15:37-51	300
30:10	264, 268
35:16	305
35:17	305
35:18	305
35:20-21	304

Deuteronomy

5:17	152
5:18	100, 143, 152
5:20	298
6:4-9	300
6:4	300
7:3	246
10:16	275, 283
11:13-21	300
12-26	311, 352
17:14	84
17:17	84, 85, 266, 268
19:21	152
22:13-21	311
22:13-18	190
22:18-19	193
22:19	268
22:22	190, 311
22:23-27	311
22:28-29	190, 193, 311
22:29	268
23:1	84, 286
23:14	188, 190, 310
24:1-22	95
24:1-4	95, 167, 189–194, 201, 208, 210, 229, 245, 264, 268, 275, 283, 300, 303, 311, 312, 316, 321, 345, 348
24:1	64, 74, 78, 90,

continued:
158, 162, 166, 169, 171, 184, 188, 199, 206, 210, 211, 212, 213, 230, 264, 275, 278, 283, 301, 309, 311, 312, 321

24:3	264
24:4	264
25:5-10	290
24:5	311
25:5-10	311
27:22	84

Judges

19:2	304

Ruth

1:20-21	304

2 Samuel

12:22	

1 Kings

3:16-27	304
14:24	270

2 Chronicles

30:8	283

Nehemiah

13:25	246

Psalms

31:1	238
32:1	256
94:6	304
94:8	283

Qoheleth

3:11	275

Isaiah

1:15	303
1:23	304
9:1	272
10:2	304
14:4-21	305
24:17	83, 194
29:13	141, 162
47:3	315
50:1	191, 311, 314
52:4	253
54:4	304
56:3-5	287
56:4	290
63:17	283

Jeremiah

2:20	310
3:1-5	275, 345
3:1	311
3:7-10	191, 314
3:8	264, 274, 311
4:4	275, 283

Ezekiel

3:7	283
16:41	310
20:25	283

Daniel

16:63	190

Hosea

2:4	191, 311
6:6	16

Micah

1:7	310

Index of Names